Social Exclusion and the Criminal Justice System

This book presents the results of the latest in a long-running research project using the RIMES instrument, developed by scholars in Spain. Here, RIMES is used to measure the extent of social exclusion resulting from the penal system in comparative perspective. The volume shows the results of the application of the instrument in seven criminal justice systems: Germany, Italy, Spain, Poland, England and Wales, California and New York.

Divided into two parts, the first provides a general overview of the RIMES instrument, including a discussion of the theoretical model and the methodology. The second part focuses on the results of the application of RIMES in the seven jurisdictions. The comparative results are organised according to the nine dimensions included in the RIMES instrument: control of public spaces; legal safeguards; sentencing and sanctions systems; harshest penalties; prison rules; preventive intervention; legal and social status of offenders and ex-offenders; police and criminal records; and youth criminal justice. The last chapter summarises the comparative results and ranks them in terms of the findings on social exclusion.

The book will be of interest to academics, researchers and policy-makers working in the areas of Comparative Criminal Justice, Criminology, Criminal Law and Policy.

Elisa García-España, University of Malaga, Spain.

Anabel Cerezo, University of Malaga, Spain.

New Advances in Crime and Social Harm

Series Editors: David Nelken and Claire Hamilton

This series seeks to publish original cutting-edge contributions to the fields of criminology, criminal justice and penology. Volumes include discussions of Foucault and 'governmentality'; critical criminology; victims and criminal justice; corporate crime; comparative criminology and women's prisons.

All titles in the series:

Law, Drugs, and the Politics of Childhood
From Protection to Punishment
Simon Flacks

The Politics of Punishment
A Comparative Study of Imprisonment and Political Culture
Louise Brangan

Remorse and Criminal Justice
Multi-Disciplinary Perspectives
Edited by Steven Tudor, Richard Weisman, Michael Proeve and Kate Rossmanith

Crimmigration under International Protection
Constructing Criminal Law as Governmentality
Rottem Rosenberg-Rubins

Privacy, Technology, and the Criminal Process
Edited by Andrew Roberts, Joe Purshouse and Jason Bosland

Social Exclusion and the Criminal Justice System
A Comparative Analysis
Edited by Elisa García-España and Anabel Cerezo

For more information about this series, please visit: www.routledge.com/New-Advances-in-Crime-and-Social-Harm/book-series/AICSERIES

Social Exclusion and the Criminal Justice System

A Comparative Analysis

Edited by Elisa García-España and Anabel Cerezo

Routledge
Taylor & Francis Group
LONDON AND NEW YORK

First published 2024
by Routledge
4 Park Square, Milton Park, Abingdon, Oxon OX14 4RN

and by Routledge
605 Third Avenue, New York, NY 10158

Routledge is an imprint of the Taylor & Francis Group, an informa business

British Library Cataloguing-in-Publication Data
A catalogue record for this book is available from the British Library

ISBN: 978-1-032-62312-2 (hbk)
ISBN: 978-1-032-66175-9 (pbk)
ISBN: 978-1-032-66176-6 (ebk)

DOI: 10.4324/9781032661766

Typeset in Galliard
by Apex CoVantage, LLC

Contents

Figures

Contributors

Aguilar-Jurado, Juan Antonio

PhD student at the University of Malaga (Spain)

Juan Antonio Aguilar-Jurado has a master's degree in criminal law and criminal policy. He has worked at the Institute of Criminology and in the area of criminal law at the mentioned university. He has published papers and book chapters about public attitudes towards crime, immigration and criminal policy.

Arenas-García, Lorea

Lecturer in criminology at the University of Extremadura (Spain)

Lorea Arenas-García has several master's degrees in crime and social intervention with minors, criminal law and criminal policy, applied sociology and advanced statistical methods. Her main areas of research are electronic monitoring, green criminology and gender violence.

Becerra-Muñoz, José

Associate professor in criminal law at the University of Malaga (Spain)

José Becerra-Muñoz is researcher in the Institute of Criminology at the University of Malaga. His research interests are related to criminal policy and criminal law-making. He coordinates the Criminal Law-Making Policy Working Group of the European Society of Criminology.

Casado-Patricio, Elena

Postdoctoral researcher in criminology at the University of Malaga (Spain)

Elena Casado-Patricio is graduate holds a PhD in legal and social sciences. Her main lines of research are procedural justice, juvenile justice and immigration; especially unaccompanied foreign minors in street situations.

Cerezo, Anabel

Full professor in criminal law and criminology at the University of Malaga (Spain)

Anabel Cerezo is currently the Director of Institute of Criminology at the University of Malaga. Her areas of research span the subjects of victimology, prisons, domestic violence, cybercrime and criminal policy. She has authored and co-authored several books and journals and published well over 50 papers in conference proceedings.

Contreras-Román, María

Postdoctoral fellow in criminology at the Center for the Study and Prevention of Crime (CRIMINA) at the University of Elche (Spain)

Maria Contreras-Román is PhD in social and legal sciences. Her main fields of research include sentencing, community penalties, desistance of crime, collateral sanctions, immigration and effectiveness of the penal justice system.

Corral-Maraver, Noelia

Assistant professor in criminal law at National University of Distance Education (UNED), Madrid (Spain)

Noelia Corral-Maraver main research interests are criminal policy, EU criminal law, terrorism and imprisonment sentences. She has several pre- and post-doctoral scholarships and research contracts and has carried out research stays in prestigious international institutions. She also has numerous high-quality publications.

Díez-Ripollés, José Luis

Emeritus professor in criminal law at the University of Malaga (Spain)

José Luis Díez-Ripollés is founder and former head of the Andalusian Institute of Criminology (1990–2017), at the University of Malaga. Author of books and articles on criminal justice policy, criminal law, criminal law making and criminology. Co-founder of the think tank, Grupo de estudios de política criminal (1989). Awarded with the Rafael Salillas Prize to prestigious criminologists and doctor honoris causa from various universities, among other accolades. Vicepresident of the Intenational Penal and Penitentiary Foundation (IPPF).

García-España, Elisa

Full professor in criminal law and criminology at the University of Malaga (Spain)

Elisa García-España is the director of the Observatory of Criminal Control System Toward Immigrants (OCSPI) since 2014. She conducts research into the ways in which the criminal control system responds to immigrants. She is co-founder of the Spanish Society of Criminology.

Güerri, Cristina

Tenure track professor in criminology at Universitat Pompeu Fabra in Barcelona (Spain)

Cristina Güerri holds a PhD in law. Her research has mainly focused on prisons and imprisonment, where she has worked on topics like quality of prison life, prison officers, imprisoned migrants, body searches or complaints and requests.

Izco-Rincón, María
Assistant professor in criminology at the University of Malaga (Spain)
María Izco-Rincón has a PhD in legal and social sciences at the University of Malaga. Her main lines of research are female crime desistance, criminal policy and security policies from a gender perspective. She is member of the Board of Directors of the Spanish Society of Criminological Research (SEIC).

Pérez-Jiménez, Fátima
Associate professor in criminal law at the University of Malaga (Spain)
Fátima Pérez-Jiménez is PhD in law at the University of Málaga. She is also an expert in criminology. One of her main lines of research is in the field of juvenile delinquency and justice. She is currently initiating a new line of research in the evaluation of the effectiveness of the chain of control and punishment of environmental damages and crimes.

Prado-Manrique, Bertha Verónica
PhD fellow researcher at the University of Malaga (Spain)
Bertha Verónica Prado-Manrique has a law degree from the Pontifical Catholic University of Peru, a master's degree in criminal law and criminal policy from the University of Malaga.

Rando-Casermeiro, Pablo
Lecturer in criminal law and criminology at the University of Seville (Spain)
Pablo Rando-Casermeiro's main line of research is the social exclusion caused by penal systems in various Western countries, with special attention to its effects on migrants and groups on the margins.

Introduction

Anabel Cerezo

Comparative criminal policy is currently one of the most promising and ambitious areas of research in criminal law and criminology. The research team led by Professor Díez-Ripollés has been studying comparative criminal policy for some time through various research projects. In 2006, the Ministry of Education and Science funded the first of these, the research project entitled "Citizen security as an inspiring criterion for criminal intervention" (SEJ2006–07242/JURI), whose principal investigator was Professor Díez-Ripollés. This was followed by four more, the first two being "Securitarian criminal policy: indicators, biases, instruments and international diffusion" (DER2009–0888) and "The evolution of Western criminal policy in a world of progressive social exclusion" (DER2012–32070), in both the principal investigator was Professor Díez-Ripollés. The third project was "The measurement of social exclusion caused by the criminal policy of developed Western countries" (DER2015–64846-P), whose principal investigators were professors Díez-Ripollés and García-España and, finally, "Social Exclusion as a Criterion for Comparative Criminal Policy: The Application of RIMES Instrument (AP-RIMES)" (PGC2018–096073-B-100), with professors García-España and Cerezo as principal investigators. Sixteen years later, the research team continues enjoying the trust and support from the Spanish government, this time through the Ministry of Science and Innovation, to continue carrying out comparative criminal policy research. We have just been awarded the project entitled "New application of RIMES instrument: Criminal political comparison according to the criterion of social exclusion (AP-RIMES+) (PID2021–127973OB-I00), whose principal investigators are professors Anabel Cerezo and Pablo Rando-Casermeiro.

To contextualise this book, *Social Exclusion and the Criminal Justice System: A Comparative Analysis*, we need to review the research trajectory of the team through the different projects that we have mentioned. The main objectives of the project "Citizen security as an inspiring criterion for criminal intervention" (2006–2009) were, first, to evaluate the performance of the criminal political model of citizen security in the prevention of traditional crime. And, second, to check its effectiveness in the prevention and prosecution of new forms of crime in technologically advanced societies.

DOI: 10.4324/9781032661766-1

The second project "Securitarian criminal policy: indicators, biases, instruments and international dissemination" (2010–2012), focused its objectives i) on studying the determining factors in the strengthening of punitive rigorism in Spain; ii) on examining how new types of economic crime evade the rigorist model; and iii) on seeking an instrument with the potential to compare international criminal policy.

Based on the results of these previous projects, Díez-Ripollés developed a theoretical model with which to compare the criminal policy of developed Western countries according to the inclusive/exclusive nature of their criminal justice systems. This led to the project "The evolution of Western criminal policy in a world of progressive social exclusion" (2013–2015), which had four main objectives: i) to identify the common factors among the countries of the developed Western world that could explain the evolution of their criminal policy towards homogenisation in terms of social exclusion, characterised by greater punitive rigorism; ii) to operationalise a set of indicators, based on punitive rules and practices, that would be able to capture national differences in criminal intervention based on the socially exclusionary effects on those affected by criminal law; iii) to identify good criminal political practices in Western countries with socially inclusive criminal intervention models; and iv) to broaden the empirical knowledge of the criminal or criminal political reality of Spain and the Ibero-American countries.

Later, the project "The measurement of social exclusion generated by the criminal policy of developed Western countries (RIMES)" (2016–2018) aimed to design an instrument to measure the social exclusion generated by the criminal policy of developed Western countries. The goal was to provide the international community with an effective tool for comparing the various national penal systems. Based on the results of its application, national criminal policies could be designed to be less socially exclusive. The result was the RIMES instrument, a validated tool for measuring social exclusion composed by 39 items – 25 punitive rules and 14 punitive practices. This pilot application of this instrument was done in Spain.

Finally, the aim of the "Social exclusion as a criterion for political-criminal comparison: Application of the RIMES instrument (AP-RIMES)" Project (2019–2021) was the application of RIMES, previously verified in Spain, in five countries: four of the largest European countries (Germany, England and Wales, Italy and Poland) and the two states in the US with the largest populations, California and New York.

This book presents the results of this latest AP-RIMES project. These results have allowed us to draw up a continuum from the lowest to the highest level of social exclusion caused by the penal system. On this continuum, we have subsequently placed the criminal justice systems of the six jurisdictions analysed.

All members of the research team participated in the book. It is structured in 15 chapters, divided in two parts. The first one gives a general overview to

RIMES instrument. In the first chapter, Becerra-Muñoz explains whether it is possible to evaluate criminal policy and its usefulness. In the following chapter, Díez-Ripollés presents his theoretical model based on the social inclusion/exclusion dimension as a criterion for comparative criminal policy and illustrates the need for adequate instruments to compare criminal policies, respectively. In the third chapter, Díez-Ripollés presents the RIMES instrument as a proposal for the comparative analysis of national criminal policy and explains the reasons why he considers the RIMES instrument to be effective in reducing crime. In the fourth chapter, Arenas-García illustrates methodological issues concerning the construction, validation and application of the RIMES instrument. To end this part, García-España explains the pilot application of RIMES in Spain.

The second part of this book focus on the results of the application of RIMES in seven Western jurisdictions. The reader will find the comparative results of the criminal justice systems analysed, organised according to the nine dimensions included in the RIMES instrument: i) control of public spaces (Rando Casermeiro); ii) legal safeguards (Prado-Manrique); iii) sentencing and sanctions systems (Izco-Rincón); iv) harshest penalties (Corral-Maraver); v) prison rules (Arenas-García); vi) preventive intervention (Casado-Patricio and Güerri); vii) legal and social status of offenders and ex-offenders (Contreras-Román), viii) police and criminal records (Aguilar-Jurado); and ix) youth criminal justice (Pérez-Jiménez).

The last chapter presents the balance of RIMES application. It was written by the two main researchers of this project, García-España and Cerezo. This chapter includes a detailed explanation of the position of the criminal justice systems analysed in the continuum from less to more social exclusion. It also summarises the main findings of RIMES application in Western jurisdictions. Finally, it provides interesting insights for comparative criminal policy.

Before concluding this introduction, we would like to thank the different universities and international research centres who helped the research team during the RIMES application:

The Department of Criminology of University of Cambridge (UK). Its collaboration facilitated the collection of normative and empirical data to implement the RIMES instrument in England and Wales. It also allowed to discuss the implications of the information collected.

John Jay College of Criminal Justice (United States). The contact with researchers of this centre allowed us to obtain relevant empirical information to apply RIMES instrument in New York and California. These researchers also helped us to contact with other research institutions such as the Vera Institute of Justice (United States).

California State University – San Bernardino (United States). We contacted researchers from the Department of Criminal Justice to present and discuss the legislation and accurate statistical data to implement RIMES in California.

The University of Tuebingen (Germany). We consulted with researchers from the Endowed Professorship of Crime Prevention and Risk Management to discuss the legislation and statistical data needed to answer the items of RIMES in Germany.

Jagiellonian University in Krakow and the Department of Criminal Law at the University of Warsaw (Poland). We contacted researchers from the Department of Criminology to discuss the resolution of the RIMES items in Poland. Its collaboration allowed us to contact with officials of the Polish penitentiary system.

The University of Verona (Italy). Specifically, we would like to thank the researchers from the Criminal Law Department, with whom we were able to discuss the resolution of RIMES items in Italy. In addition, their collaboration allowed to contact with officials from the Italian Ombudsman's Office to answer specific items in the Italian case.

Finally, we consider the results of the application of the RIMES instrument to be an important contribution to international comparative criminal policy studies. The application of this instrument fills a gap in empirical research on the socially exclusionary effects caused by the punitive rules and practices in force in Western criminal justice systems on the priority groups of criminal intervention: suspected, prosecuted, convicted and ex-convicted persons. We trust that, as the RIMES instrument is applied in more countries, we will enrich international criminal political comparisons. As well as to influence, with good and accredited reasons, the design of less exclusionary criminal policies.

Part I

A general overview to RIMES instrument

1 A roadmap for comparative criminal policy research[1]

José Becerra-Muñoz

1 Introduction

Despite the fact that we live in a globalised world where communication and information flow in real time worldwide, the evolution and dissemination of knowledge is uneven, depending on the academic discipline and the geographic region at hand. While some disciplines move forward at a very similar pace – like robotics, biology, astronomy or civil engineering – there are other areas of knowledge where there is no such level of mutual alignment across different regions, and criminal policy is one of them.

There are factors that do not contribute to this internationally coordinated progress. In the first place, criminal policy has a strong link to the cultural, social and legal context, which is different in each place and requires a specific analytic effort to be taken into account. This extra effort is not necessary in disciplines that study phenomena that occur identically anywhere in the world.

Secondly, language also plays an essential role and does so in two different ways. On the one hand, and in connection with the above, knowing the language spoken in different places is essential if you want to access the information needed for research, particularly when you intend to work with primary data. Along with this, but on a different level, is the issue of what we could call the language in which scientific research in each field is reported. While in most disciplines deemed global English has become the language of communication, in criminal policy the debate in national or language communities is much more prominent. This does not mean that there is no international discussion on criminal justice policy, but the mentioned communities generate a scientific production to be interpreted internally and is richer than the international one (in the same way that there are local studies in botany or geology, for example, but global knowledge of the discipline is predominant).

1 This is a translated, expanded and updated version of the book chapter Becerra Muñoz, J. "La utilidad de la política criminal comparada" [The utility of comparative criminal policy] in *La exclusión social generada por el sistema penal. Su medición internacional por RIMES*. Cerezo Domínguez, Ana Isabel; García España, Elisa (coords.). Tirant lo Blanch. 2023. Pp. 21–45. ISBN 978-84-1147-609--6.

DOI: 10.4324/9781032661766-3

It is therefore, basically, an intra-community scientific production discipline which, for the most part, operates apart from other linguistic regions and is influenced by an Anglo-Saxon perspective, the only one among Western countries that has the capacity to strongly cross borders.

Thirdly, even when comparing criminal policy with other social sciences, such as anthropology, criminology or sociology (that share a large number of features and sometimes overlap with criminal policy) we can see there is also a basis of internationally recognised and validated theoretical frameworks and methodologies. Why, then, has criminal policy not adopted a model similar to that of those social sciences and still maintains a regionalist or nationally-rooted profile?

While this is not the place to answer this question in absolute terms, one possible explanation for this is the strong influence that the academic tradition of the legal world – particularly criminal law – has had on the study of criminal policy. This branch of law uses a methodology that goes beyond national borders (the legal theory of crime, the theory of legal sources, rational methods of interpretation of regulations, etc.), but only homogenised (and only to a certain extent) among those legal models based on civil law, therefore, within the scope of continental Europe.

Besides, the object of study in legal approaches is so connected to national legislation that it is frequently confined to the borders of the analyst's country. More or less systematic comparisons with related legal systems do happen (in Spain this happens especially with the German and Italian systems and to a lesser extent with the Portuguese system), but there is no global legal debate strongly influencing compared criminal policy as it happens at national level.

This situation, with a scientific production based on single-case studies and on objects of study with strong national roots, generates a scientific community that is extremely fragmented. This type of scientific production, without global pretensions, does not prepare its results for an international debate – neither methodologically nor conceptually – but rather works from an internal perspective and expects for an imaginary interested reader to reflect on it in comparative terms.

Conversely, the issues of criminal policy are universal and strongly interconnected internationally: power and politics, social conflicts, the media and international organisations. Therefore, its study requires equally transnational tools and concepts, as well as scientifically standardised criteria that go beyond the disciplines that form it.

The framework provided by comparative studies can be particularly helpful in the further development of a criminal policy with global aspirations. In those studies, the effort does not fall on the reader but on the researcher, who must fit his or her research into a scientific model where vocabulary, method and concepts are shared, and where he or she must become familiar with the state of the art of the issue at hand at international level.

The following paper aims to bring together in one place some of the basic standards that should be the common ground to keep on building a comparative criminal policy. It will particularly focus on methodological aspects. This is important to build an initial debate on the minimum quality of scientific works (which usually translates into admission criteria for journals and publishers) and to be able to hold, after and apart from this paper, material debates on the basis of the results.

These standards intend to merge proposals for comparative studies in social sciences as well as in law since both areas of knowledge meet in criminal policy and are an essential part of it.

2 Comparative research

It seems reasonable to say that comparison is something essential to scientific research in general terms. Research usually compares objects of study, their characteristics or both, whatever method is used. This statement, made at the time by Harold D. Lasswell in his article "The Future of the Comparative Method" (1968, p. 3) has led several authors to argue that, in reality, there is no comparative method since the scientific method is itself a comparative method.

While it is true that scientific research is comparison, this is a broad and general notion of the term that can be further specified. This is certainly the meaning commonly used in social and legal sciences when they refer to a "comparative method" (Ragin, 2014, p. 1).

In this second sense, authors such as the political scientist Lijphart unambiguously defend that the comparative method is really a method and not only an approach reflecting the interests of the researcher (1971, p. 682). The author places the comparative method as one of the four basic methods to demonstrate general empirical propositions, along with the experimental, statistical and case-study methods (1971, p. 682). The fact that the United Nations, the World Bank and many NGOs use comparative research, both for their reports and for political decision-making (Karstedt, 2018, p. 5), supports this view of the comparative method, which would be characterised as follows.

First, comparison is a cross-cutting factor in the research that launches it and must be implemented in a systematic and critical way (Laiz Castro and Roman, 2003, p. 84); second, the starting point is a theoretical framework that gives meaning and guides the comparison; third, the central objective of the work is the comparison itself; fourth, all the methodological decisions and technical instruments that are used are suitable for it (Piovani and Krawczyk, 2017, p. 826); and fifth, such comparisons are made by establishing empirical relationships between variables.[2]

2 The measurement of variables would not be comparative method but rather an essential basis for its implementation (Lijphart, 1971, p. 684), a clarification also found in the legal world when dealing with "foreign law studies", useful to gather information but not strictly comparative law analysis (del Barrio-Fernández, 2017, p. 118)

This approach has created a subfield called "comparative studies" or "comparative research". Although its boundaries as a sub-discipline are not peaceful (Ragin, 2014, p. 3; del Barrio-Fernández, 2017, p. 96, 125 et seq.), the term "comparative" is usually found together with scientific field labels. This is the case with "comparative law", "comparative politics", "comparative education", "comparative criminology", etc.

Discussions about the autonomy of this approach have forced its defenders to debate thoroughly about it and elaborate arguments on its characteristics. These efforts are much more visible in social sciences, where the link with the scientific method has forced comparatists to study in depth what is genuine and different in the research that is compared.

Without pretending to resolve this long debate here, we will agree for the purposes of this paper, together with Lijphart, that comparative research refers to the "how" but not to the "what" (1971, p. 682). It is, therefore, a certain transversal methodological approach that, in each field of knowledge, is applied to different subjects, undertaking the necessary adaptations for it. This is the reason why it is common for writings on the subject to discuss both methodological and material aspects, the former being of interest for comparative research in general, and the latter for the discipline or topic in question.

There is a substantial difference on this between social and legal studies. Despite a long tradition of comparative law studies (Morán, 2002, p. 503), there has not been an in-depth debate on the method of such research, especially in the field of public and constitutional law (Claes and de Visser, 2012, p. 145; López Garrido et al., 2017, p. 37). Del Barrio-Fernández states that "there is hardly a reasonable consensus as to the elements that are essential to the comparative method or even whether it exists" and that it is an "infra-theorised" issue (2017, pp. 95 and 99). It is also unusual to expressly define the object of study (del Barrio, 2017, p. 58) or justify the methodology used in works of this nature. In legal sciences it has been standard practice to refer to methodology in a more superficial way (or not at all) (Morán, 2002, p. 522), with expressions such as "focus on similarities and differences", "make a systematic comparison", "explicitly compare", "perform a critical analysis", etc. (del Barrio-Fernández, 2017, p. 106). Adams and Bomhoff would agree with such view, arguing that "comparative work does not make its methodological choices sufficiently clear" (2012, p. 1).

A good example of this are Valcke's reflections on comparative law methodology. In her detailed description of the decision-making process carried out in her comparative research on contract law in France and England, she exposes a mixture of intuition and logic in her methodological choices (Valcke, 2012). Although this does not necessarily mean that it is a useless or incorrect investigation, the scarcely standardised vocabulary and criteria offers a craftsman-like work, which is very difficult to replicate and limits the chances of an objective evaluation of her approach, methods and results.

The extensive literature on social research methods allows for almost any imaginable scientific approach and there is still room for specificities when needed. It would be wise for legal comparative research to benefit from the existing methodological framework and, in fact, it would probably come to enrich it (with a similar view, from compared constitutional law: Meuwese and Versteeg, 2012).

But, to what extent are comparative studies carried out in the different academic disciplines? One way to find out is to perform a search for the term "comparative"[3] in the titles of journals and editorial collections included in the *Scopus source list*. The result is informative:

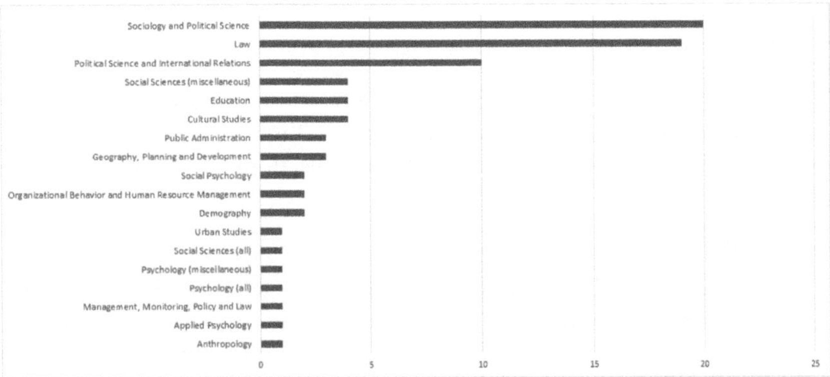

Figure 1.1 Sub-subjects according to the number of journals in them that contain the word "comparative" in their title

Source: Own elaboration based on information from *Scopus*

The graph above (Figure 1.1) shows the sub-subjects with which each journal identifies itself (the presence of editorial collections is rather anecdotal). Bearing in mind that each journal can be connected to more than one sub-subject and that we have focused only in those related to social and legal sciences, it is interesting to see that the most frequent connection for comparative studies journals is with "sociology and political science", followed by "law" and, at some distance, by "political science and international relations".

This information supports the statements made by Avendaño, in the sense that political science has been the social science that has promoted the greatest number of studies of this nature (2014, p. 334). This is also why Karstedt uses the example of political science to argue about the potential of comparative criminology (2018, p. 6). This data also shows the potential of comparative studies for criminal policy, a discipline whose three fundamental pillars are sociology, political science and law.

Finally, it is also necessary to discuss from the beginning of this work what would be covered by the *object of study* of comparative approaches, as there is

3 The search was conducted in English with the term "*comparative*". The word *"compared"* did not produce any results.

a range of options that can create some confusion. By adapting Landman and Luengo's classification, we can say that in social and legal sciences the object of study has two levels: the first is the territorial level, so that international organisations, countries, regions, cities, neighborhoods, etc. can be compared; and the second level is the actual artifact that will be compared at a given level: phenomena, players, institutions, rules and processes or a combination of them (2014, p. 41). In this paper we will focus on comparisons that are made at country level, whatever the phenomena, players, rules or processes.

3 Characteristics of comparative research

Once the "what is" of comparative research has been discussed, other aspects of it will be addressed, such as "what it is for" or "how it is done". To do so we will rely on Bennett's structure with some modifications (2009, pp. 172–173).

3.1 Usefulness

It is reasonable that the globalised world in which we currently live requires global knowledge. To that end, comparative studies can provide with information and contextualisation to the different national realities (Aláez-Corral et al., 2018, p. 33 et seq.). Interestingly enough, knowledge of diverse national realities produces a mirror effect, thanks to which one's own reality can be evaluated as a step prior to its transformation (Díez-Ripollés, 2020, pp. 105–106; Claes and de Visser, 2012, p. 145).

In general, comparative legal studies have been used as "a source of inspiration in domestic law reform" and in fields like legal philosophy the comparison of legal systems has provided with arguments to debate on theories about the nature of law (Valcke, 2012, p. 22; also Claes and de Visser, 2012, p. 145).

In the case of criminal policy specifically, they are particularly useful to deepen the coordination of national policies when managing transnational criminal phenomena, such as drug trafficking or terrorism (Bennett, 2009, pp. 173–176). In fact, in the context of international organisations, such as the European Union or the United Nations, diagnoses derived from comparative studies can be an important argument both to legitimise coordinated political agendas (as highlighted by Piovani and Krawczyk from the sphere of comparative research in education (2017, p. 827), Valcke from contract law (2012, p. 22–23) or Claes and de Visser from European constitutional law (2012, p. 145), and to strengthen international jurisdictions (as argued by Vichinkeski-Teixeira from a comparative constitutional law angle (2020, pp. 316–317)).

Outside the legal perspective, this type of studies also allows building an inventory of "good practices" which, while not guaranteeing the successful transplanting of initiatives from one system to another, does make it possible to analyse experiences which, with the appropriate adaptations, can be useful in different places. The other side of this coin is to avoid problems, for example, in the implementation of a certain policy, through the study of what happened in other countries where adverse effects occurred.

From a more general view, comparative studies offer the possibility of turning to other territories to study variables that in local contexts offer a very narrow range, thereby preventing the establishment of significant relationships between variables. This is something that can happen, for example, with variables that in certain places offer very homogeneous results, such as those related to racial, cultural, economic or linguistic diversity. On the other hand, from the perspective of theoretical developments, these investigations allow further progress to be made in the verification of theories that were ultimately created in the light of observations made at a given place and time (Bennett, 2009, pp. 173–176).

3.2 Extent and method

These two dimensions are inevitably related, so we will study them together.

The first of these, "extent", refers to the number of countries analysed, which allows for a distinction to be made between studies with a greater or lesser number of countries. We speak of an intensive strategy when few cases are studied in great depth and an extensive strategy when many cases are studied in a more superficial way.

On the other hand, the "method" refers to the empirical method used: either quantitative or qualitative.

Studies of a comparative nature can be placed at any point within an area where extent and method are combined, as can be seen in the grey area of the following Table 1.1:

Table 1.1 Combination of number of countries and methods

		Method	
		Quantitative	*Qualitative*
		Mixed methods	
Number of countries	Many	A	B
	Few	C	D

Source: Own elaboration

3.2.1 Experimental and statistical methods

In the first of the possible situations, A, we usually speak of multiple or n-large comparisons, regarding the number of countries (more than 30) (Avendaño, 2014, p. 349) and "variable-oriented" in terms of method, because a macro vision is adopted to analyse the relationship between the variables under study. Here we can find works that use the experimental method. This allows the control of variables to the extent that, through the study of two identical groups and introducing a change in only one of them, the effects produced exclusively by such change can be detected. The experimental method is very rarely used in social sciences in general, due to the practical difficulties for its implementation, as well as the ethical problems it can raise (Barberet et al., 2019, p. 116 et seq.). Some authors, such as Laiz and Román, go so far as to claim that experimentation in comparative politics is impossible (2003, p. 5).

We also find the statistical method, which uses mathematical tests to draw conclusions about a number of already measured variables. With this method, the search for patterns and correlations between subsamples of data is essential, but it is a less robust method than the experimental one as it gives up randomness in the sample selection. This is very common in the social sciences, as the universe to be investigated is often not even known by researchers (Della Porta, 2013, p. 226) (for example, a study on the security perception of illegal immigrants in a city, which is usually a hidden population). This situation may be compensated with larger samples that allow the analysis of subsamples and thus achieve statistically significant results.

These methods offer greater certainty in the relationships identified between variables and the possibility of detecting anomalous cases (Landman and Luengo, 2014, p. 81), although they also pose difficulties for further investigation and usually require giving up a large number of variables in order to select only those that offer commensurable information (Avendaño, 2014, p. 336).

Besides, in this sense it is important to bear in mind that the use of quantitative methodologies involves a complex process to transform a certain theoretical concept into elements that can be measured. To do this, the concept is first broken down into a number of dimensions through which all its facets are described. Next, the different dimensions are operationalised into significant, valid and reliable indicators and, finally, these indicators are broken down into variables that make up the observation units and to which a certain score can be assigned, which will be subsequently treated with statistical techniques.

These scores can be coded so that they translate into simple dichotomous measures (for example, social exclusion/non-social exclusion) or categories can also be established, so that countries can be assigned to one of several groups (totally exclusionary, somewhat exclusionary, little exclusionary, not exclusionary). Finally, interval scales can also be created (for example, from 1–10) to reflect the extent to which the measured concept is present (Landman and Luengo, 2014, pp. 82–83).

As regards case B of our scheme, this is a very unlikely combination since, when trying to compare a large number of countries, there are usually not enough resources for an in-depth study of each country.

3.2.2 The case method

The situation is different when we have a small sample of countries (between two and eight, according to Avendaño, 2014, p. 336). This type of studies is usually based on a qualitative methodology (case D), although it is not unthinkable to use a quantitative methodology if the number of countries, although small, allows for it (case C). In the usual case, i.e., the qualitative work, we normally talk about case studies, where an object of study is chosen for an in-depth analysis of its characteristics and the mechanisms that make it work, for which this methodology techniques are used, such as observation, document analysis, life stories, etc. (Lijphart, 1971, p. 683 et seq.; Piovani and Krawczyk, 2017, p. 828; Alonso Pujiula, 2019, p. 34). In this situation, the cases under study are usually deliberately selected within the universe of possible cases, they are more intensive than extensive works and focus on the differences among countries rather than on the relationships among variables. This is the so-called "comparable-cases strategy", "focused comparison" or, also, "case-oriented comparison" (Landman and Luengo, 2014, pp. 54, 96).

From a qualitative perspective, countries – that is, cases – are analysed as a combination of characteristics, as a whole. As Ragin argues, "configurations" are compared in a holistic approach different from the usual analytical attitude in quantitative methodologies (2014, p. 3). For his part, Della Porta claims that these studies are suitable to form concepts, for a detailed description or to design theories, and are even particularly useful to discover social mechanisms. This author also argues that the existence of many data points can lead, not only to the building of theories, but also to their verification through the non-probabilistic disapproval of hypotheses (2013, pp. 225 and 226).

3.2.3 Combination of several methods

Finally, we should take into account that, although the distinction made so far is very useful, as well as the combination of methods and the number of countries, the reality of research is sometimes much more fluid and difficult to classify in one of the alternatives described in Table 1.1.

This scheme works particularly well in studies that use only one research technique or a single paradigm (either qualitative or quantitative). However, there are more ambitious proposals that connect various methodological approaches in a coordinated manner, thus increasing the complexity of approaches, and providing with more holistic results and, in the same way, making it difficult to classify them according to the parameters we have just seen. This is the case, on the one hand, of mixed methods and, on the other, of triangulation.

Without this being the place to elaborate too much on it, we will say that mixed methods defend the approach to the object of study through a combination of qualitative and quantitative methodologies (Vichinkeski-Teixeira refers to it from the field of comparative constitutional law, without calling it this way; 2020, p. 323.). This third pragmatic way is based on reducing the inherent limitations of any research method by using a diversity of them (Barberet et al., 2019, p. 250) and also the possibility of using the specific potential of each of them in those situations where it is most appropriate.

This combination of methods in the same investigation can be done in different ways. Several research techniques can be planned to complete the study sequentially, such as, for example, when in-depth interviews (qualitative) stand as a basis for the design of a questionnaire (quantitative). Or several research techniques can be implemented simultaneously or successively to achieve a much richer interpretation of the results. An example of the latter would be to organise focus groups and a questionnaire, and to interpret the results from both techniques cumulatively.

Although they are not the same, this connects with triangulation, a broader concept than that of mixed methods since there may be a triangulation of methods, theories, data or even researchers (Barberet et al., 2019, p. 253). The philosophy behind triangulation focuses specifically on reaching the same point using different paths, which allows to enrich the information and analyses but, above all, allows to verify the reliability and validity of the data obtained in each situation.

Only when the triangulation of methods is used and qualitative as well as quantitative methods are in place (a triangulation can use several qualitative methods) there will be a mixed methods triangulation.

Ultimately, methodological options are multiple and can be adapted to the various possible scenarios. It will be the researcher's task, and to his or her credit, to be able to find the optimal design taking into account the limitations that are always present. We will elaborate more on this in the following sections.

3.2.4 Can single-case studies be compared?

We cannot end this section without mentioning one of the usual discussions related to extent: the number of cases. More specifically whether it is possible to refer to a "comparative method" in cases where the object of study is a single case. Landman and Luengo argue that if a single-country research intends to make inferences through "some form of comparison" and use concepts applicable to more countries, this will be comparative research (2014, p. 51). This is a plausible argument if, for example, we are thinking of increasing the number of observations by analysing several historical moments of a single country. Apart from cases as clear as this, admitting that we speak of comparative research when facing the study of a single case is counterintuitive and encourages the argument (incorrect, in our opinion) that all research is comparative and that, therefore, this approach does not have autonomy.

In this sense, forcing the argument can be counterproductive and the benefits are unclear. Research about a single country has the capacity to take knowledge forward by generating theories (Laiz Castro and Roman, 2003, p. 86) and is perfectly acceptable in the context of single-case studies.

3.3 The design

The "design" dimension allows us to speak of what distinguishes the comparative approach from the rest, and therefore, of a methodological construction specific to this field of work.

The strategies commonly used in comparative studies are the so-called "design of systems of maximum similarity" (or DSMS) and "design of systems of maximum difference" (or DSMD) (Laiz Castro and Roman, 2003, p. 87).

In comparisons between countries carried out from sociology or political science, it is common for the design of comparative research to look for very similar cases in order to reduce the impact of control variables. This is usual in the so-called "area studies" which focus on specific geographical regions that share a common ground, be it cultural, linguistic, religious, etc. When choosing countries that belong to the same geographical area and share historical, cultural or economic aspects, for example, it can be more easily assumed that variations in the dependent variable occur as a consequence of the impact of independent variables and not of those that are deemed parameterised (Della Porta, 2013, p. 229). This is why, for example, comparisons of the prison population in the European Union and the United States, as the one carried out in 2012 (see Becerra Muñoz, 2012), make sense despite the fact that the United States prison population rate is closer to countries like El Salvador, Turkmenistan, Rwanda, Cuba or Thailand.[4] The United States and EU countries are all characterised as "Western countries" because they share features that allow for such type of comparisons.

This is what Rodríguez-Devesa refers to, from criminal law studies, when arguing that comparing legal systems is comparing solutions to problems and, for this to be possible, they must be identical or, at least, homogeneous problems. The author defends the design of systems of maximum similarity – even probably without knowing it – and explains the need to take into account a series of factors: an adequate level of institutional development (in the case of criminal policy, regarding police forces, courts and other technical professionals needed for the proper functioning of formal social control institutions); the existence of a similar legal-technical level among the countries being compared; a reasonable intensity in the prosecution of crimes; and a economic system solid enough to be able to articulate an adequate criminal policy (1979, p. 6 et seq.).

Despite this, no matter how many common features a number of countries may have, the interference from context-related variables can never be safely excluded, so researchers always have to assume that observations never clearly reflect the effect of independent variables.

Along with this design focused on identifying similar cases, there is also the possibility of using the opposite technique: the selection of very different cases (DSMD), where the approach is usually different (Barberet et al., 2019, p. 259). While similar cases allow systemic aspects to be analysed, the design with very different cases usually descends to a lower level of analysis where individual behaviour is studied. In this way, if the existence of a relationship

4 See the rate per 100,000 inhabitants according to the World Prison Brief. www.prisonstudies.org/. Consulted on 19/05/2021.

between variables is demonstrated in very different cases, it can be assumed that such a relationship is not connected to the context, the place and the specific historic moment in which it has been studied (Della Porta, 2013, p. 230). This type of design is common to explain a specific event that has taken place – such as a revolution, a coup d'état or a striking economic recovery. Countries that show such situations are selected and the independent variables that are considered explanatory of it are analysed (which may involve a selection bias that we will discuss further on) (Landman and Luengo, 2014, p. 102).

Although comparative research usually opts for a DSMS or a DSMD, it is also possible to combine them in the same study (Landman and Luengo, 2014, p. 102). This allows for a third approach to be considered, such as the "*indirect design of differences or joint strategy of similarities and differences*". This type of design consists of several stages and aims to discover the differences among several cases or countries. In the first stage, to identify the conditions explaining the existence of a phenomenon, cases that are different and in which this phenomenon is observed are compared with cases also different where it does not occur. The second stage compares cases that are similar but generate phenomena that are not the one studied and are taken as a control of what was analysed in the first stage (Laiz Castro and Roman, 2003, p. 88).

The distinction between similar and different case designs can also be used to modify the objectives of the investigations. Similar case designs are used to extend the validity of an explanatory hypothesis developed in one country to others in its environment, while different case designs seek to discover generalisable results.

Finally, as regards the qualification of each country as different or similar to another, some classifications take into account general factors, but this is a process that must be carried out and justified on a case-by-case basis, according to the objectives and methodology of each study. Parrado-Díez and Olmeda-Gómez provide an example of general classification for the study of public administrations. The authors identify four major Western administrative traditions: Napoleonic, Anglo-American, Germanic and Scandinavian (2013, pp. 33 et seq.).

3.4 Time

Comparative studies can be cross-sectional, that is, carried out exclusively at a certain time, or longitudinal, in which the "time" variable is introduced into the study through identical measurements at several historical moments.

In the latter case, the number of countries may remain the same, but not the number of observations, which would growth allowing analysis of time series data without losing the depth of a detailed study of few countries. In addition to time series studies, combinations of countries and certain recurring events – such as terrorist attacks, regulatory reforms or other relevant events – can also be conducted. This combination of countries and events taking place at different points in time generates a matrix of data that can be studied using statistical methods without, again, giving up the deep study of a limited number of countries (Landman and Luengo, 2014, p. 106).

In comparative studies, it is common to refer to all this as "synchronic" comparison, when a comparison of several countries is made at the same time, and 'diachronic' comparison, when different moments in time are analysed (Laiz Castro and Roman, 2003, pp. 89 et seq.).

4 Criteria for the selection of cases: a question of balance

As a result of what we have seen in the previous section, we could say that, when taking research decisions on the various aspects mentioned, it is essential to evaluate them all together and reach the best possible balance. Large samples allow to carry out statistical analyses, hence Lijphart recommends to always increase the sample as much as possible, both geographically and temporarily (i.e., by adding the longitudinal analysis to the cross-sectional one), because any enlargement of the sample increases the possibilities of controlling the variables involved (1971, p. 686). But this argument applies, logically, as long as we can obtain information of sufficient quality and that our goal is to extrapolate those results.

But if instead of that we intend to make a detailed description of complex phenomena, we will have to take into account Della Porta's precautions when warning of the risk assumed by expanding the number of countries subject to comparison or the time range covered by it. As these are complex realities on which "hard" data are rare, the interference of variables beyond the control of the researcher is a real risk that may generate biased assumptions due to misconceptions about the reality of a certain country (2013, p. 225). In these cases, and contrary to what happens with standard quantitative studies, the increase of the sample size under study can have counterproductive effects and must be carefully assessed by the research team in the light of the theoretical framework used.

It is therefore a question of striking the right balance at the time of making the scientific decision. It should not be forgotten that the variable-oriented study of many countries requires statistical and computer skills, while, if the study is case-oriented, the knowledge of languages and the ability to do extensive fieldwork will be essential (Landman and Luengo, 2014, p. 99).

For example, the original approach of the comparative analysis carried out in 2013 (Becerra Muñoz, 2013) was to study the legislative systems of several European countries, together with the United States and Japan, and to do it with a qualitative approach through documentary analysis. After the first findings about Japan, historical, cultural and political differences arose between this country and the rest (even despite the similarities in the structure of the legislative power itself). It was decided at an early stage of the research to discard its study. Ignorance of the characteristics of a country like Japan for a Spanish researcher without any prior connection to this country could prevent a correct interpretation of the results.

In this sense, Landman and Luengo mention a direct proportional relationship between the number of countries and the level of abstraction of the research to be carried out. The higher the level of abstraction, the greater the number of countries that can be included (as long as we deal with concepts that are applicable in different contexts), while a small sample of countries will enable the researcher to analyse concepts with a greater degree of specificity and detail (2014, p. 50). Back to the example of the comparative study on the legislative power, since the work was performed with a small number of Western countries (Germany, Spain, France, Italy, the United States and the United Kingdom) a certain degree of detail was possible in the analysis of the legislative processes for criminal law-making, the role of parliamentary committees, the characteristics of parliamentary support services, etc. And this was possible due to the fact that all the countries studied were democracies with rules regarding the separation of powers, a more or less perfect bicameral parliamentary system and a formally regulated parliamentary procedure.

Taking into account the precautions explained so far, selecting the countries that will be subject to comparative analysis is not a simple task nor is there a list of criteria directly applicable to all the investigations.

Despite this, we can enumerate a number of criteria that help to reflect on the characteristics of the candidate countries in a systematic way, something that will often require to seek information about such countries, depending on the case. Thus, following the compilation made by Della Porta (2013, p. 227 et seq.), to be included in a compared study a country should be:

1. *Appropriate* to the kind of theoretical problem posed by the researcher;
2. *Important* for the phenomenon being studied;
3. *Empirically invariable* as regards its classification criterion; for instance, if it is a candidate because of its position in the Human Development Index it must have a stable position in it;
4. *Transparent*, i.e., capable of showing the degree of availability of data that will be needed;
5. *Comparable*, there must be some similarities in a number of relevant dimensions (or differences, depending on the design);
6. *Independent or autonomous*, since strong dependencies among countries may involve that, in reality, the same phenomenon is being studied several times;
7. *Representative*, that is, capable of reflecting the properties of the entire population;
8. With sufficient *extent or range* in the values recorded on relevant variables.

In spite of such a list of criteria, deciding which unit or case to include in the study is not easy and requires compromise solutions, as it is impossible to satisfy all criteria simultaneously. In general, besides the above, it is important that the decision-making process for these studies is based on standardised procedures, which aims to ensure that the studies are repeatable (Della Porta, 2013, p. 228).

Lijphart's argument is relevant at this point, warning of the need to study a reasonable number of variables about each case. The author argues that, otherwise, we can pursue an exhaustiveness that is actually illusory, given the impossibility of studying all the variables that define a given case. His recommendation in this regard is to focus on the "key variables" and to admit the limitations of the comparative method as part of its nature (1971, p. 690).

5 Threats to comparisons

As in all scientific studies, comparative analyses are subject to a number of threats. These are problems that do not necessarily invalidate the results but need to be addressed carefully so as not to jeopardise the research.

As Laiz Castro and Roman argue, the fact that these are comparative studies restricts the range of possibilities for observation and analysis even more than is common in other types of research; to which must be added, in general, the problems with the information to be worked with (2003, p. 5). Other authors highlight the problems arising from language, cultural, sociological and political differences that particularly affect comparative studies, an argument that is very common among legal scholars (Rodríguez Devesa, 1979, p. 8 et seq.; Morán, 2002, p. 523; del Barrio-Fernández, 2017, p. 113).

Landman and Luengo describe the impact of the "usual suspects" in social research, such as selection bias, spurious relationships between variables, fallacies such as the ecological fallacy or equivalence problems of theoretical concepts in different countries (2014, p. 56 et seq.; also Valcke, 2012, p. 31).

In general, these are threats to be taken into account in any research work, but they can have a particular impact in comparative studies due to their specific nature. Knowledge of these threats is essential, both at the planning stage of the work and in the interpretation of results, and must be combined with the use of techniques to counteract their effects.

6 Conclusions

Comparative studies are in a position (they already do) to offer results of great interest for criminal policy and, if this discipline is to increase its international relevance, both theoretical and applied, one promising avenue is to develop a conceptually and methodologically sound comparative criminal policy.

As we have seen, it is not peaceful to decide whether or not there is an autonomous subdiscipline of comparative studies. In spite of this, in both social and legal sciences, it is possible to turn to other realities not only for information that enriches the analysis, but also to provide with a solvent and systematised comparison that allows us to offer theoretical developments and quality empirical analyses. Despite the mentioned scant attention to methodological aspects in comparative legal studies, most authors who do deal with them warn that the comparison must be scientific if it is to maintain its rigour (del Barrio-Fernández, 2017, p. 99).

In this work we have had the opportunity to see that comparison is a complex task, which should not be approached intuitively and which requires the use of a number of tools, a correct assessment of the specific needs of this form of research and to find a difficult balance between what is optimal and what is possible.

We have presented here only the tip of the iceberg of the conceptual building blocks that comparative criminal policy has to deal with, in the hope that it will serve as a basic guide for further progress in the investigation of criminal phenomena, and the response to them.

It is not unreasonable to think that comparative criminal policy in the one that holds at least part of the secret to the utility and relevance of criminal policy studies for public decision-makers and, ultimately, for citizens.

References

Adams, M., & Bomhoff, J. (2012). Comparing law: Practice and theory. In M. Adams & J. Bomhoff (Eds.), *Practice and theory in comparative law* (pp. 1–22). Cambridge University Press.

Aláez Corral, B., Balaguer Callejón, F., Leopoldo Canosa Usera, R., García Morales, M. J., García Roca, F. J., and Pérez Tremps, P. (2018). Encuesta: El método comparado en Derecho constitucional. *Teoría y realidad constitucional*, *41*, 15–56. https://doi.org/10.5944/trc.41.2018.22124

Alonso Pujiula, S. (2019). *La política de drogas en España y Países Bajos. Un análisis comparado desde la perspectiva neo-institucionalista* [Doctoral dissertation, Universidad Complutense de Madrid].

Avendaño, O. (2014). Lo viejo y lo nuevo de la comparación en Ciencia Política. In E. Valenzuela (Ed.), *Manual de Ciencia Política: herramientas para la comprensión de la disciplina*. RIL Editores.

Barberet, R., Bartolomé, R., & Fernández Molina, E. (2019). *Metodología de investigación en criminología* (1st ed.). Tirant lo Blanch.

Becerra Muñoz, J. (2012). Las prisiones españolas vistas desde Europa. Un análisis comparado. *Revista de derecho penal y criminología* (3ª época, n. 7, 25 pp, pp. 381–406).

Becerra Muñoz, J. (2013). *La toma de decisiones en política criminal: bases para un análisis multidisciplinar*. Tirant lo Blanch.

Bennett, R. R. (2009). Comparative criminological and criminal justice research and the data that drive them. *International Journal of Comparative and Applied Criminal Justice*, *33*(2), 171–192.

Claes, M., & de Visser, M. (2012). Reflections on comparative method in European constitutional law. In M. Adams & J. Bomhoff (Eds.), *Practice and theory in comparative law* (pp. 143–169). Cambridge University Press.

del Barrio-Fernández, N. (2017). *El derecho comparado como disciplina científica para abordar la diversidad jurídica de un mundo global* [Doctoral dissertation, Universidad Europea de Madrid].

Della Porta, D. (2013). Análisis comparativo: la investigación basada en casos frente a la investigación basada en variables. In M. Keating & D. Della Porta (Eds.), *Enfoques y metodologías de las ciencias sociales: una perspectiva pluralista* (pp. 211–237). Ediciones Akal.

Díez-Ripollés, J. L. (2020). La utilidad política criminal del instrumento RIMES. In A. I. Cerezo Domínguez (Ed.), *La política criminal y la exclusión social* (pp. 103–120). Tirant lo blanch.

Karstedt, S. (2018). 'Is big picture criminology policy relevant? Comparative criminology, evidence-based policy and the scale of our discipline', European Criminology Award Acceptance Speech. *Criminology in Europe, 17*(3), 4–9.

Laiz Castro, C., & Roman, P. (2003). *Política comparada.* McGraw Hill.

Landman, T., & Luengo, C. (2014). *Política comparada Una introducción a su objeto y métodos de investigación.* Alianza Editorial.

Lasswell, H. D. (1968). The future of the comparative method. *Comparative Politics, 1*(1), 3–18.

Lijphart, A. (1971). Comparative politics and the comparative method. *The American Political Science Review, 65*(3), 682–693.

López Garrido, D., Massó Garrote, M. F., Pegoraro, L., & Bastarreche Bengoa, T. (2017). *Derecho constitucional comparado.* Tirant lo Blanch.

Meuwese, A., & Versteeg, M. (2012). Quantitative methods for comparative constitutional law. In M. Adams & J. Bomhoff (Eds.), *Practice and theory in comparative law* (pp. 230–257). Cambridge University Press.

Morán, G. M. (2002). El derecho comparado como disciplina jurídica: la importancia de la investigación y la docencia del Derecho Comparado y la utilidad del método comparado en el ámbito jurídico. *Anuario da Facultade de Dereito da Universidade da Coruña, 6*, 501–529.

Parrado Díez, S., & Olmeda Gómez, J. A. (2013). *Gobiernos y administraciones públicas en perspectiva comparada.* Tirant lo Blanch.

Piovani, J. I., and Krawczyk, N. (2017). Comparative studies: Historical, epistemological and methodological notes. *Educação e Realidade, 42*(3), 821–839.

Ragin, C. C. (2014). *The comparative method: Moving beyond qualitative and quantitative strategies.* University of California Press.

Rodríguez Devesa, J. M. (1979). El Derecho comparado como método de política criminal. *Anuario de derecho penal y ciencias penales, 32*(1), 5–14.

Valcke, C. (2012). Reflections on comparative law methodology – getting inside contract law. In M. Adams & J. Bomhoff (Eds.), *Practice and theory in comparative law* (pp. 22–48). Cambridge University Press.

Vichinkeski Teixeira, A. (2020). El método en derecho constitucional comparado: contribuciones críticas para una metodología constitucional comparativa. *Opinión Jurídica, 19*(39), 311–329.

2 Social inclusion and comparative criminal justice policy[1]

José Luis Díez-Ripollés

1 Introduction

a. Recent years have witnessed an increase in the focus upon comparative criminal justice policy studies by criminology and criminal law scholars. Not wholly removed from this is the fact that in industrialised countries, criminal policy has become one of the most controversial public policy issues due to many factors. Social agents and pressure groups with very different origins and interests have become actively involved in national criminal policy reforms, thus giving rise to significant changes in crime control systems.

The attention given to this phenomenon has paved the way for the documentation of a wide range of national strategies regarding crime prevention and crime reduction which, on occasion, have yielded varying results. In fact, it has become common to observe academic analyses which are able to classify industrialised countries into descriptive categories arising from different traditions and criminal policy practices (Cavadino and Dignan, 2006; Tonry, 2007a; Lappi-Seppälä, 2008).

Garland's influential book, *The Culture of Control* (2001: viii–ix, 7), however, provided a suggestive hypothesis which was destined to shape the debate over comparative criminal justice policy. The author analyzed the socio-political factors that were linked to late modern society and how these made possible the consolidation of a new model of criminal policy in the United States and the United Kingdom, characterised as it was by the toughening of their criminal justice systems. At the outset of his study, however, Garland intimated that industrialised Western countries could be undergoing similar social changes as those that had led, or would eventually lead, to a more rigorous criminal policy. The implicit idea was that national punitive strategies

1 This chapter is a slightly modified version of the original English paper published in 2013 in the *Journal of Scandinavian Studies in Criminology and Crime Prevention,* Vol. 14 n° 1, pp. 62–78. It has been considered advisable to keep the original version because of its influence on the subsequent configuration of RIMES instrument.

DOI: 10.4324/9781032661766-4

would eventually converge into more homogeneous policies and practices in line with the Anglo-Saxon model.

Garland's interpretation was, in fact, highly suggestive. Consequently, empirical and theoretical studies, which took this hypothesis into account when analyzing what was occurring in various different countries, proliferated (Pratt et al., 2005; Tonry, 2007). Yet soon, contrasting positions were adopted in which it was considered that such an analytical framework was incorrect and which instead, intended to demonstrate that in the developed West, different criminal policy models and trends coexisted, and were sometimes even opposing in nature, thus contradicting what Garland had suggested (Nelken, 2005, 2010; Tonry, 2007a; Roché, 2007; Lappi-Seppälä, 2008).

Notwithstanding the differing starting points, nor the intensity with which each national system has evolved, the assumption of a generalised trend in the Western world towards harsher criminal policies has become entrenched. That said, this does not preclude that due to differences in the pace of change the degree of divergence between the United States and Western Europe may have increased in recent years, or that certain regions in Eastern Europe or Latin America may have developed in a more independent manner from the rest (Zielinska, 2005; Díez-Ripollés and García Pérez, 2008; Kerezsi and Lévay, 2008).

b. It has also been pointed out that crime reduction and prevention strategies are going through a phase of intense politicisation (Garland, 2001: 13–14, 168–173), on the basis of which, the following three phenomena should be noted.

First, criminal policy no longer reflects ideological differences; albeit to a greater or lesser extent these shape the design of other public policies. Politicians alike have discovered the enormous political pull that a tough-on-crime/criminals approach provides when drawing in votes, thus practically blurring the difference between the left and right-wing approach towards crime control (Tham, 2001; Díez-Ripollés, 2004). Only traces remain of old distinctive traits, such as a strong left-wing resistance to stigmatise offenders, or the occasional reluctance of the right towards excessive punitive interventions regarding the invasion of the personal sphere (Tham, 2001; Balvig, 2004; Levy, 2007).

Secondly, and as opposed to what one is expected to believe, when establishing criminal policy, strictly partisan considerations prevail against authentic social demands or social reality, in need of being addressed.

Daily mainstream media content therefore depends, to a large extent, upon information released by official or institutional sources. As such, these sources may focus media attention on the issues that they deem important. Likewise, the popular demand for harsher punitive action is usually based upon a diffused concern regarding crime management which has been encouraged by the overwhelming presence of crime news in the media, something which neither corresponds to the low levels of personal fear of crime nor the moderate punitive attitudes of the society in respect of specific criminal behaviours (Beckett, 1997; Roberts and Hough, 2002; Tonry, 2004; Cavadino and Dignan, 2006).

The link between the intensity of crime control and the current crime rates in any given country is also called into questioned. For instance, the rates of imprisonment appear to be more the result of criminal policy decisions than the reflection of crime levels (von Hofer, 2003; Beckett and Sasson, 2004; Lappi-Seppälä, 2008; Larrauri Pijoan, 2009),[2] and this also appears to be the case in relation to the volume of police forces and their practices (Greenberg et al., 1985; Scheingold, 1991; Hinds, 2005). This lack of a direct correlation corroborates the fact that in the shaping of criminal policy, ethical or ideological judgments weigh more heavily against utilitarian or efficacy-related considerations (Scheingold, 1991; von Hofer, 2004; Bondeson, 2005), and yet it also serves to reminds us that crime is prevented by the social fabric of a nation and not by criminal law alone, in keeping with the theory of social control (Young, 2003; Tonry, 2004).

Thirdly, criminal policy practices abroad or international obligations are steadily gaining more influence over the manner in which crime prevention and crime reduction is dealt with at national level. The most prestigious models at international level, especially those implemented in the United States, have penetrated national criminal policy decision centres on a widespread scale; this is a positive interaction, and justifies the studies of comparative criminal policy, although occasionally it may alter, by means of notable argument, initiatives that are closely related to national realities or resources (Wacquant, 2000; Brodeur, 2007; Pratt, 2008b). International or regional obligations in criminal law progress in number and demand, and they have certified only too well their capacity to transform national policies; their influence must be assessed, by and large, in a positive manner as well, although their development process and standardised trend may frequently spark off justified tensions and resistance in certain regions, i.e., Nordic and Latin American countries (Lahti, 2000; Kyvsgaard, 2004; Lappi-Seppälä, 2006).

2 Punitive moderation as an objective

For the reasons already discussed above, current comparative criminal policy has a strong tendency to contrast different national systems in terms of their harsh or more lenient punitive approach. This dimension has become the point of reference for many studies and currently dominates the comparative debate.

2 The question is energetically debated at the moment. There are reluctant positions, or even openly contrary ones, to the alleged lack of correlation between the rates of crime and the rates of imprisonment (Young, 2003; Roché, 2007; Nelken, 2010).

This analytic framework has an unquestionably ideological background. It assumes that national criminal justice systems, notwithstanding their inescapably distressing nature, should make it their utmost priority to guarantee that those who come into conflict with criminal law enforcement will suffer as little as possible, as a consequence of their suspicious or criminal conduct. In short, it urges a reduction in the suffering of those subjected to criminal control (Nelken, 2005; Cavadino and Dignan, 2006; Tonry, 2007). This objective is so important that it justifies that comparative criminal policy studies are guided by the aim of determining the degree to which different national systems choose punitive moderation and how such criteria steer comparisons among different countries.

However, drawing up analytical frameworks of comparative criminal policy on the degree of punitive moderation achieved by different national systems entails a number of significant theoretical and methodological shortcomings. From a theoretical point of view, the objective of punitive moderation places itself in an exceedingly poor context. In fact, one could consider it a humanitarian approach to criminal policy that is content with guaranteeing that the whole criminal justice system, regardless of the accepted model or desired results, does not arrive at unacceptable levels of severity. Hence, it is said that it is an analytical proposal which is only critically capacitated in respect of policies that lead to an increase in criminal reactions but not against those which maintain or diminish such reactions (Brodeur, 2007; Webster and Doob, 2007).

This does not mean that punitive moderation is a trivial attribute or goal. On the contrary, and as we shall see, it is necessarily weaved into a broader and more complex analytic proposal of which it constitutes an essential element. Actually, assigning punitive moderation a prominent role simply correlates to the adoption of procedural justice as a criminal policy model, in this case, emphasising the intensity and expansion of criminal reactions. Yet, the author maintains that procedural justice, without prejudice to the essential role legal safeguards have to play in any criminal justice system, does not fulfill all the necessary criteria to become a crime control strategy, in other words, a criminal policy model (Zaffaroni, 2007).

Legal guarantees erect themselves as a convincing and indispensable bulwark for the preservation of civil liberties and citizens' fundamental rights when exercising *ius puniendi*. Moreover, their influence on the conceptual framework of criminal responsibility and its determining role in criminal procedure, on the sanctions system and its implementation, should be borne in mind and respected by policymakers as part of any given criminal-policy strategies. However, procedural justice lacks the necessary content to support a public policy of criminal scope: this requires a strategy of social intervention which, integrated into the set of public policies, develops specific and measurable objectives aimed at preventing crime within acceptable social parameters. Procedural justice stops at the identification and strengthening of these legal safeguards, values and concepts common to any criminal policy in agreement with a rule-of-law-based criminal law, and gives no indication as to which political-criminal alternative, among those compatible with such principles, one should select.

From a methodological point of view, the objective of punitive moderation uses exceedingly limited indicators. In fact, the most prominent indicator it uses is the incarceration rate per 100,000. This indicator has indeed many virtues: it is easily accessible from various reliable sources; it provides long-standing data sets ranging over extended time periods; it focuses on the most severe punishment that a criminal law system may impose except for the death penalty; and it is usually a sanction which adequately reflects the outcome of penal policies and practices of particular criminal justice systems (Cavadino and Dignan, 2006; Tonry, 2007).

However, criminological and crime-policy literature has repeatedly revealed its limitations: above all, for unduly focusing the evaluation of the punitive strength of a criminal justice system on the use of imprisonment and thus, marginalising other indicators with a strong capacity to express the punitiveness of a system, such as the number of criminal proceedings and sentences, the average length of penalties, the intensity and frequency of alternative sanctions to prison and the rules on accumulation of penalties, amongst others.

In addition to this, as the relative use of prison in different national systems shall be measured, the almost exclusive use of the incarceration rate per 100,000 leaves out other relevant indicators, such as the average length of imposed prison sentences, the number of admissions to prison, and the effective average stay in prison or confinements outside the penal system (Nelken, 2005; Tonry, 2007; Tamarit Sumalla, 2007).[3] Moreover, one should not forget certain practices that may distort the figures, such as the use of waiting lists for admission into prison or the use of general pardons (Balvig, 2004; Levy, 2007; Nelken, 2009). This aside, the preceding methodological critique does not question the undoubted significance that the rate of incarceration and its associated indicators have upon the characterisation of relevant aspects of a criminal justice system. What needs to be argued are the over simplistic unilateral visions that seek to evaluate an entire criminal justice system or, in other words, its punitiveness, based solely on data concerning the rate of incarceration. This should not impede, however, that in more complex analyses of comparative criminal justice this indicator is afforded a significant role (see below).

3 Social exclusion as an objective

a. Another way of conducting a comparative criminal policy analysis is studying the capacity of the corresponding national crime control systems to minimise the social exclusion of those who enter into conflict with criminal

3 As of yet, there has been consistent lines of argument on the remarkable ability that the incarceration rate has to effectively subsume all those other indicators regarding the use of prison (Webster and Doob, 2007: 305–309; Lappi-Seppälä, 2008: 322–332).

law. This implies that crime control systems can be assessed by the performance they offer in terms of the acquisition, recovery, consolidation or, at least, non-worsening of an acceptable level of social inclusion for suspects and offenders. The social inclusion/exclusion dimension reflects two opposing approaches to the objective of preventing crime in people who are prone to enter into conflict with criminal law.

The social-inclusive approach intends to ensure that the suspect or offender, after having been in direct contact with the crime control system, find themselves in the same or better individual and social conditions to voluntarily conduct their lives in accordance to the law. The social-exclusive approach, instead, intends to ensure that the suspect or offender, after having been exposed to the crime control system, find themselves in individual and social conditions that make it more difficult for them to break the law or to avoid being caught (Cavadino and Dignan, 2006). Naturally, and as occurred with the high/low punitive dimension, these are not two incompatible perspectives, but somehow a continuum between two extremes within which we may find all sorts of combinations and emphases.

Our analytical proposal is based on the fundamental hypothesis that the maintenance of a certain level of social inclusion for suspects, felons and ex-felons is one of the most effective strategies for crime prevention; and on the correlative hypothesis that an increase in the levels of social exclusion for suspects, felons and ex-felons by the criminal control system fosters greater levels of crime in the mid and long term.

Both hypotheses are dependent on a definitive demonstration (Beckett and Western, 2001; Karstedt, 2006; Downes and Hansen, 2006; Savage et al., 2008). The approach of doing a comparative criminal policy analysis focusing on the social inclusion/exclusion dimension could contribute decisively to their verification. In fact, in order to proceed in the empirical verification of both hypotheses, we need a detailed description on the extent to which national criminal justice systems are socially inclusive or exclusive. Thus, it is necessary to develop and validate indicators that are capable of identifying the characteristic features of this dimension and of proving any advances towards one direction or the other. Only then will it be possible to carry out research on the possible correlations between the level of inclusion/exclusion of a crime control system and its achievements in relation to crime prevention.

b. In the author's opinion, an adequate contextualisation of the debate on the levels of social inclusion/exclusion of contemporary intervention against crime leads us back to the field of public policy, within which criminal policy is included. More specifically, it drives us towards the programmatic confrontation between two models of society which, in terms of current political economy, are represented by welfarism and neoliberalism. The criminal policy objective of social inclusion thus fits the objective of building a welfare state and society, which includes as one of its pillars special attention towards the socially underprivileged, among which many of the people who are prone to enter into conflict with criminal law may be found (Young, 1998; Wacquant, 2000; Garland, 2001; Cavadino and Dignan, 2006; Downes and Hansen, 2006).

Whatever the nuances, the implementation of criminal policies based on welfarist principles has suffered strong attacks in recent years. The root causes of its problems lie in the expansive capacity shown by a neoliberal political economy, which has led countries like the United States to no longer pursue a welfare state and which has caused significant cutbacks in some of its fundamental components in Central and Northern European democracies, even if this coincided historically with the 'temporary' adoption of this model by Southern and Eastern European democracies (Garland, 2001; Beckett and Sasson, 2004; Downes and Hansen, 2006).

Consequently, political agents have eliminated or drastically reduced any proposal that meant a step towards more inclusive societies from their programmes. What is especially surprising is the restraint experienced by Nordic social democracies, and its contrast with previous long-term policies (Tham, 2001; Balvig, 2004; Nuotio, 2007); or the criminalisation of public policies by means of applying techniques that are specific to the crime control system, inevitably afflictive and stigmatising, to areas that were foreign to these techniques up until recently, such as the family, education, and work; one author has talked about governing through crime, referring to a type of governance in which criminal law is the model through which many social problems are approached (Simon, 2007).

c. Questioning of the social welfare model and reluctance to adopt inclusive public policies have contributed to the abandonment or removal of the social inclusion/exclusion dimension when analyzing criminal policy.

However, within the doctrine there is a significant sector that supports the objective of a socially inclusive criminal policy based on welfarism, or, if anything, the methodological usefulness of the social inclusion/exclusion dimension to evaluate specific national crime control systems (Young, 2003; Beckett and Sasson, 2004; Wacquant, 2000; Garland, 2001; Downes and Hansen, 2006; Lévay, 2007; Kerezsi and Lévay, 2008; Lappi-Seppälä, 2008). It is nevertheless surprising how little has been done so far to develop specific methodological tools in order to obtain the maximum cognitive potential from the social inclusion/exclusion dimension. As has already been pointed out, models of analysis, with their corresponding indicators, are required in order to measure this dimension in different countries in a standardised way.

d. Before turning to the proposal for typological analysis set out in this chapter, it is worth recalling that using social inclusion as a point of reference in criminal policy comparison implies the adoption of an analytical approach which substantially differs from the one adopted by punitiveness.[4] In other words, social inclusion/exclusion and low/high punitiveness are not two parallel dimensions. In fact, on some occasions the interests behind social inclusion may even lead to imposing greater preventive control measures or increased afflictive reactions against crime than those adopted by virtue of the interests behind social exclusion.[5]

In any case, the usual tendency is that social inclusion and punitive moderation are closely related. What we have tried to highlight in this section is that the social inclusion/exclusion dimension contributes to the understanding of criminal policy through an approach that is both richer and of greater complexity.

4 A proposal for typological analysis

a. In this section, the chapter aims to develop an instrument of analysis that will enable us to determine where different national crime control systems lie in a continuum between two conceptually opposing extremes: one occupied by the most socially inclusive crime control systems, and the other, where we find the most socially exclusive crime control systems.

The inclusive or exclusive social effects the author is interested in studying will not be those produced by a certain crime control system on the nation's entire population. It goes far beyond our purposes to determine the contributions of different criminal policies in relation to the levels of social inclusion in all aspects of society. Our objective is limited to the people that are a priority for crime prevention and prosecution bodies, that is, those who are, have been or are prone to be directly subject to criminal control in their condition as an ex-convict, a convict or someone having been prosecuted for or suspected of criminal offences.

To determine the extent to which the different criminal justice systems respond to either of the two models, it is necessary to identify punitive regulations

4 It also differs from the approach which focuses on the social reintegration of the offender. Although we will not go into this point in depth, it is worth noting that the criminal policy purpose behind social inclusion is aimed at aspects that go beyond treatment and social reintegration activities for convicted offenders. In this sense, it intends to pay attention to relevant regulations and practices in the field of primary and secondary prevention. In any case, the compatibility of the reintegration approach with the social inclusion objective we propose is evident.

5 On the compatibility between the persistence of a social reintegration model and an increasingly rigorous approach: In Canada, Moore and Hannah-Moffat, 2005. In Belgium, Cartuyvels, 2005.

and practices that consistently reflect more socially inclusive or exclusive effects on the people previously referred to. These regulations and practices must be turned into indicators that will enable a comparison between countries to be made. These indicators must have an internal structure that allow us either to establish scores along a scale from highly social inclusive effects to highly social exclusive effects, or to draw conclusions on the inclusive or exclusive effects from the presence or absence of certain regulations or practices.

Moreover, since it is the author's intention to identify the different crime control systems within a continuum between two extremes defined by the two most contrasting crime control systems in terms of the socially inclusive or exclusive effects they produce, and since there is no intention to use theoretical but authentic models, the indicators chosen must have some additional qualities. In the first place, they must refer to punitive regulations and practices that are widespread in the Western developed world, either because they are applied to a certain extent in each country, or because their potential implementation is a current issue in contemporary debate on criminal policy. Secondly, the empirical values of these indicators must reflect a variance such that they can show clear contrasts between national systems, which would consequently mean that they make use of these regulations or practices (from which these indicators have been developed) in a very different way.

This way, it is possible to point out the two models of criminal policy currently applied in Western societies that are the most distinct in terms of their socially inclusive or exclusive effects, hence placing them at the two extremes of the social inclusion/exclusion spectrum.

In order to achieve the final objective, that is, to verify the meaning of these indicators in the different national systems and to place each of the studied countries at a specific point in the continuum, there is still one point missing. It is necessary to weigh up the different indicators so as to give them, and the values obtained within them, a specific relative significance that will mean the obtained results may be quantified in a uniform scale, and thus transferred to the corresponding position within the social inclusion/exclusion dimension.

b. Having presented the main ideas of our analytical model, two hypotheses will now be presented whose verification would pave the way for a full use of the model.

The first hypothesis states that a list of nine major areas of penal intervention, or pools, are especially adequate to reveal relevant inclusionary/exclusionary effects that, as a whole, offer a comprehensive picture of the corresponding criminal justice system, as well as they are able to compare different national crime control systems according to these effects.

These nine pools are:

1 Public space control
2 Legal and due process safeguards

3 Sentencing and sanction systems
4 Harshest penalties
5 Prison rules
6 Preventive intervention
7 Legal and social status of felons and ex-felons
8 Police and criminal records
9 Youth criminal justice

Other potential pools have been discarded for different reasons.

These major areas of penal intervention may also be disaggregated into 25 sub-areas or bundles. These bundles, grouped accordingly into the nine pools, are the following:

1 Public space control: gated communities, video-surveillance, private space exclusion policies
2 Legal and due process safeguards: undermining of due process safeguards, hindering of judicial reviews
3 Sentencing and sanctions systems: judicial discretion, aggravated provisions for recidivists, extensive use of prison, intermediate sanctions, electronic monitoring
4 Harshest penalties: death penalty, life prison sentence, long-term prison sentences
5 Prison rules: living conditions in prison, prisoners' rights, release on parole
6 Preventive intervention: indefinite preventive detention, pre-trial detention
7 Legal and social status of felons and ex-felons: disenfranchisement, deprivation of further political rights, accessibility to social resources
8 Police and criminal records: expansion and accessibility of records, public lists of ex-offenders
9 Youth criminal justice: age thresholds, differentiated treatment from adults

Alike to the pools, other potential bundles have been discarded for different reasons.

Therefore, all the indicators (rules or practices) to be part of the instrument must be incorporated into one of these pools and bundles. They will be the independent variables to be considered in our model of analysis, even though they are grouped for descriptive reasons into the aforementioned nine pools and 25 bundles. It would not be necessary to control a vast number of variables, but just a limited but sufficient number for the weighed calculation of the social inclusion/exclusion scale as a whole and by pools.[6]

6 A more detailed explanation of the content of each of the pools and bundles would be advisable, but due to limited space, this cannot be done in this paper. In a future work that will focus on the selected indicators for every pool and bundle, we will be able to explain them more thoroughly. As an example, within 'aggravated provisions for recidivists', one end would be compulsory life sentence for repeated recidivists and re-offenders, irrespective of the gravity

c. The second hypothesis states the two most contrasting criminal policy models in terms of their social inclusion/exclusion effects on the groups under study are, on the one hand, in the early 21st century in the Western industrialised world, the United States of America –its federal system and the system being applied in most of its states– and, on the other hand, the Nordic European countries – Denmark, Finland, Norway and Sweden.

The United States' crime control system would constitute the most socially exclusive criminal policy model for suspects and offenders and, consequently, would be at the head of a significant number of other developed countries, especially in the Anglo-Saxon world (Young, 2003; Wacquant, 2000; Beckett and Sasson, 2004; Nelken, 2009).

At the other end of the scale, the Nordic European countries would embody the most socially inclusive criminal policy models for suspects and offenders. They would clearly head up the list, followed by other European and some American countries (Lappi-Seppälä, 2007; Pratt, 2008a, 2008b; Nelken, 2009).

If the author's hypothesis is correct, using the indicators mentioned in the previous section should give the result that the two aforementioned crime control systems, despite slight internal differences, lie at opposite ends of the social inclusion/exclusion spectrum.

This hypothesis which, as with the majority in social science, is based on a particular, subjective perception is widely accepted among criminal policy experts; in these circles, the idea that there is a clear opposition between neoliberal and social democratic criminal policy models is widespread, with continental Europe occupying an intermediate position. In this context, the United States and the Nordic countries would thus most accurately represent the corresponding opposing models (Cavadino and Dignan, 2006; Lappi-Seppälä, 2007; Downes and Hansen, 2006).

---

of their last offence, while the other end would be recidivism as discretionary aggravating circumstance; within 'indefinite preventive detention', one end would be the existence of a corresponding provision for dangerous persons after serving a sentence, and the other end would be no indefinite preventive detention provision; within 'disenfranchisement', one end would be disenfranchisement of felons and ex-felons on a permanent basis, while the other end would be no disenfranchisement for felons and ex-felons; within 'expansion and accessibility of records', one end would be criminal records as commodity, ready to be sold to private companies for further commercial distribution, and the other end would be non-accessibility of criminal records except to judges and restricted public officials; within 'long-term prison sentences' -apart from 'life sentence'- one end would be an average over 10 per cent of prisoners serving prison sentences over 20 years, the other end would be no prisoner serving more than 20 years of imprisonment. The intention is to select no more than three or four rules or practices for every pool.

5 Methodological explanation

Once the evaluative approach has been laid out, which should be established in order to conduct criminal policy comparisons, and the typological analysis enabling its potential advantages has also been carried out, the author will then confront possible objections against this proposal in the remainder of this chapter.

The first set of objections has to do precisely with the selection of those *wide-baseline evaluative frames*, turned into dependent variables, which supposedly enable different countries to be classified in terms of powerfully evocative yet unrealistic images. It is claimed that criteria such as punitiveness, the least possible intervention, social inclusion, the balance between safety and freedom or other criteria used to arrange the variety of crime control models at the national level, often only reflect the preconceived attitudes and disturbing analytical self-restraints of the analyst (Nelken, 2010), forming prejudices which, in a vain attempt to find a running thread aimed at simplifying the complex reality before our eyes, adapt to the obtained results so that they can fit onto a predetermined analysis scheme, as if it were a Procrustean couch.

In fact, any attempt to compare strategies of crime control according to one single evaluative pattern is full of risks. Moreover, the desire to draw uniform and overall conclusions can easily lead us to fall into a trap which can only be painstakingly circumvented. That said, all comparative analyses are subjected to this methodological context. They require categorising criteria that goes beyond the peculiarities of the various units that need interpretation. In such matters, when identifying and evaluating the different components of each crime control system, one can only adopt a critical and cautious attitude. In these conditions, I believe that the chosen criterion of social inclusion/social exclusion has, as described above, an unquestionable theoretical-political and social-scientific legitimacy. This is not, of course, a denial of its strong integration within an identifiable criminal policy program.

The second set of objections relates to *the success in selecting the pools and bundles* from which the independent variables are taken.

The selected pools and bundles are largely related to the effects produced by criminal prosecution, although some of them are associated with crime prevention activities. On closer examination, it is possible to confirm that more than half of the areas and subareas of penal intervention concentrate on sanctions and their enforcement while the rest refer to criminal law and procedure, and police interventions in that order. This indicates that even when focusing the attention on especially underprivileged groups, the chapter does not intend to cover the entire spectrum of crime control interventions, either preventive or prosecutorial.[7]

7 In other words, we can affirm that there is an overrepresentation of indicators linked to tertiary criminalisation, followed by secondary and primary criminalisation. This diverse representation of the various stages of criminalisation is closely related to its differential capacity to influence the social inclusion/exclusion criterion, as we advance in the criminalisation process, not to mention other arguments.

In any case, it should be highlighted that the selection of these areas and sub-areas, as opposed to others, was performed according to a careful analysis of the literature. It is, indeed, easy to find references to those variables in different studies of comparative criminal policy (Beckett and Sasson, 2004; Cavadino and Dignan, 2006; Lévay, 2007; Tonry, 2007; Tamarit Sumalla, 2007; Pratt, 2008a, 2008b; Lappi-Seppälä, 2008). They are not, however, usually structured in such a systematic way, probably because studies tend to handle a smaller number of penal control fields, and because such studies are not linked to the determination of inclusive or exclusive social effects. Moreover, these studies use another set of variables not included here for various reasons.

Either which way, it should be borne in mind that the proposed pools and bundles and their disaggregated indicators need an empirical validation of their capabilities in order to identify socially inclusive or exclusive effects of the corresponding crime control system, as well as for establishing differences among various national systems of crime control.

The third set of objections refers to the *two criminal justice policy models* which have been hypothetically chosen as *antagonistic*, that is, those existing in the United States of America, on the one hand, and those existing in Nordic countries, on the other. This hypothesis, as mentioned above, is welcomed in criminal-policy think-tanks but it must answer a number of methodological criticisms which shall be addressed here.

The selection of the two antagonistic models may be decisively conditioned by factors other than the real contrast between the two groups of national systems. No one in the Western world could miss the special visibility of the United States' criminal rules and practices derived from its political dominance. On the other hand, the European Nordic countries have for decades accumulated a prestige for stable, equalitarian, and socially and economically successful societies that have encouraged an ideal image that tends to move uncritically across any of their public policies. It could, therefore, be the case that the general connotations of the two groups of countries selected may overshadow other national models that are more entitled to be located in the extreme ends of the continuum of social inclusion/social exclusion dimension (Nelken, 2010).

In this regard, the author would like to emphasise that the scope of the proposed research refers only to criminal policies of western industrialised countries. This significantly narrows the group of countries upon which the analytic framework based on the social inclusion/exclusion dimension shall be developed, notwithstanding later extensions to other geographic regions or socioeconomic areas. Within that frame, the political importance and influence that a country may have is in fact a good reason for selecting it provided that its model does of course correspond to those extreme characteristics; faced with two countries with similar traits, that which has major influence upon the rest of the countries of our scope shall undoubtedly be held in preference.

A further objection is that in order to make the differences between the two antagonistic models more significant, a good number of similarities must concur between them at the time of comparison. This demands, first and foremost, an in-depth knowledge of the two systems of crime control to be compared and, secondly, paying special attention not to prioritise the differences against the similarities (Nelken, 2010).

The two national models belonging to the same political, social and economic area, that is, the Western, capitalist and democratic developed world, enables us to anticipate that we are looking at systems with abundant common traits, which are, in addition, well known by the analysts involved. Added to this is the specific fact that both groups of countries have shared the same crime control ideology rehabilitation for several decades of the second half of the 20th century to a degree of proximity with no comparison in other western countries, except for some that are Anglo-Saxon. Interestingly, from 1980s, a progressive divergence among them has been taking place, thus providing us with tools of the utmost importance for comparative analysis (Lappi-Seppälä, 2007).

Without a doubt, both conflicting national models, constituted as they are, in the case of the United States by the federal and the states systems, and in the case of Nordic countries by those of Denmark, Finland, Norway and Sweden, are homogenous. The significant existing differences in criminal policy across the various states of the United States are well known; they can even be categorised geographically (Hinds, 2005; Zimring, 2005). Several studies have also pointed out the differences among Nordic countries, which, for example, highlight more inclusive traits in the criminal justice systems of Norway and Finland as opposed to those of Denmark and Sweden, or stress the dissimilarities in attitudes towards crime between Sweden and Denmark (Bondeson, 2005; Lappi-Seppälä, 2006).

It would be naive to deny the above-mentioned disparities. However, an external observer would not have serious difficulties in perceiving the remarkable similarities in criminal policy among the states of the US or within Nordic countries. Their internal connections are much closer than those related to other national systems. In the same way, the striking contrast between the two groups of criminal justice systems is hardly questionable from a more in-depth treatment of their respective characteristics. Moreover, the aim is to conduct a general depiction of the two groups of national systems by selecting those rules and practices which could accurately reflect the different performance of their criminal law enforcement systems in accordance with the hypothesis outlined. Certainly, the author does not intend to run a detailed description of the different models compared, let alone the specific systems of criminal justice integrated in each model.

When working with real and non-theoretical models, however, this frame of analysis is subject to revision at any given moment. Minor changes occurring in any of the antagonistic models can significantly affect the studied dimension and, in the worst scenario, we would be obliged to replace the national model subject to comparison.

In any event, it is not expected that a substantial criminal policy change of the selected models shall be witnessed in the near future, thus pushing us to adjust their position at opposing ends of the social inclusion/exclusion continuum. Undoubtedly, an alternative to meet this contingency would be to work with theoretical models. The author maintains, however, that this option does not hold any weight: the greater robustness and ease of construction of theoretical antagonistic models would be overshadowed by the loss of discursive power which is granted when dealing with real models. In the unlikely event of finding that either of the two antagonistic models is no longer tenable, it would seem appropriate to maintain its configuration prior to its transformation. As such, we would always be considering a model that has been real until very recently.

Another phenomenon that cannot be ruled out is that of a gradual approximation between the two antagonistic models. This would undermine the explanatory power of a method based on a continuous dimension between two opposing models. This may actually be already happening to some extent (Cavadino and Dignan, 2006). Particularly motivated for financial reasons, an increasing number of crime policy reforms are being announced in several states of the US, and these may have a significant influence upon the configuration of their criminal justice systems: these would affect sensitive sectors, such as the use of proportionality in sentencing, judicial discretion, enforcement of prison penalties, intermediate sanctions or drug policy (Steen and Bandy, 2007). Limited growth of law-and-order measures in Nordic countries is also noticeable which, without jeopardising the welfarist approach, questions the persistence of a markedly criminal policy (Tham, 2001; von Hofer, 2004; Balvig, 2004; Pratt, 2008b).

However, without losing sight of ongoing transformations, the announced changes or those that are under way, have an uncertain future before them. And, in any case, we have a long way to go before the sharp contrast that now occurs between the two opposing models is substantially blurred.

6 Conclusions

Comparative criminal justice is emerging as one of the most promising areas for criminal policy research, due to the increasing interrelationship of criminal policy decisions adopted by different countries. Progress in this direction demands, however, a scrupulous approach to different national criminal policies.

One should bear in mind that conducting a thorough analysis of the traits of each national policy to be compared is practically impossible as no comparative analyses require such a thorough approach. Thus, it becomes fundamentally essential to identify the evaluative framework of any given criminal policy, as this could help us determine the dependent variable that could, in turn, enable the analytical process and provide us with a reliable context for the interpretation of our findings.

This study has successfully proven that punitive moderation does not fulfill the necessary conditions to become the pattern, either for interpretation of criminal policy, or, consequently, for comparative criminal policy analyses. As such, the author maintains that the goal of social inclusion for those who are the most directly affected by the criminal justice system offers a more comprehensive and far-reaching evaluative view of the reality of the various criminal justice systems at national level, thus allowing for far more illustrative comparisons.

By adopting this analytical guideline, the chapter has identified a set of areas and sub-areas of penal intervention, which have been converted into pools and bundles, from which a limited number of punitive rules and practices can be drawn as independent variables or indicators. They include different prosecutorial and, to a lesser degree, crime prevention activities. The author maintains that these elements will allow each and every criminal justice system across western industrialised countries to be evaluated in terms of their performance in achieving the objective mentioned above. Moreover, and because it is the aim of the chapter to obtain comparable results, it is assumed that those elements that are present in varying degrees in all western industrialised countries, are adjustable and have a strong discriminatory capacity.

On a separate note, the chapter also proposes that comparative tasks are unfolded through the location of different national criminal justice systems, from the scores obtained in the different indicators, within a continuous social inclusion/exclusion dimension. At the opposing ends of this dimension, one would not find two refined theoretical models, but rather two, real and antagonistic criminal policy models in the western industrialised world. The chapter's second hypothesis, which shall be expanded upon in a different study,[8] is therefore to place the criminal policy model of the United States, including its federal system and the system of the majority of its states, on the end of social exclusion, while at the other end, that of social inclusion, under which the Nordic European countries – Denmark, Finland, Norway and Sweden – would be placed. The crime control systems of the other countries in the region would be distributed across either end of the dimension.

Without neglecting methodological difficulties that a project like this has to confront, the chapter has attempted to demonstrate in the latter half that such difficulties are not insurmountable. As such, an analytic tool has been established around two fundamental hypotheses that can be used in comparative criminal justice policy and which very likely will enable us to identify punitive rules and practices with the best performance in terms of the social inclusion of those who come in contact with criminal law, in addition to identifying the national systems which more successfully achieve that goal.

References

Balvig, F. (2004). When Law and Order Returned to Denmark. *Journal of Scandinavian Studies in Criminology and Crime Prevention*, 5(2), 167–187. https://doi.org/10.1080/14043850410010711

Beckett, K. (1997). *Making Crime Pay. Law and Orden in Contemporary American Politics.* Oxford University Press.

8 See other chapters of this volume. Additionally, Díez-Ripollés 2014, 2016.

Beckett, K., and Western, B. (2001). Governing Social Marginality. Welfare, Incarceration, and the Transformation of State Policy, in Garland, D. (ed.) *Mass Imprisonment. Social Causes and Consequences.* Sage Publications.
Beckett, K., and Sasson, T. (2004). *The Politics of Injustice. Crime and Punishment in America.* Sage Publications.
Bondeson, U. (2005). Levels of Punitiveness in Scandinavia: Descriptions and Explanation, in Pratt, J., Brown, D., Brown, M., Hallsworth, S., and Morrison, W. (eds.) *The New Punitiveness: Trends, Theories and Perspectives.* Willan Publishing.
Brodeur, J.-P. (2007). Comparative Penology in Perspective, in Tonry, M. (ed.) *Crime, Punishment and Politics in Comparative Perspective. Crime and Justice, 36.* University of Chicago Press.
Cartuyvels, Y. (2005). Las amenazas a la seguridad ciudadana y la respuesta político-criminal: una perspectiva belga, in Díez-Ripollés, J.L., Prieto del Pino, A.M., and Soto Navarro, S. (eds.) *La política legislativa penal en Occidente. Una perspectiva comparada.* Tirant lo Blanch.
Cavadino, M., and Dignan, J. (2006). *Penal Systems. A Comparative Approach.* Sage Publications.
Díez-Ripollés, J.L. (2004). El nuevo modelo penal de la seguridad ciudadana. *Revista Electrónica de Ciencia Penal y Criminología*, 6, 1–34. http://crimi-net.ugr.es/recpc/06/recpc06-03.pdf
Díez-Ripollés, J.L. (2014). El control de espacios públicos como técnica de exclusión social. Algunos contrastes regionales. *Revista española de investigación criminológica (REIC).* 4 nº 12. www.criminologia.net
Díez-Ripollés, J.L. (2016). Collateral Sanctions for Offenders and Ex-Offenders. Contrasts between the United States of America and Nordic European Countries. *European Criminal Law Review*, 6, 234–264.
Díez-Ripollés, J.L., and García Pérez, O. (eds.) (2008). *La política legislativa penal iberoamericana en el cambio de siglo. Una perspectiva comparada.* Edisofer/B de F.
Downes, D., and Hansen, K. (2006). Welfare and Punishment in Comparative Perspective, in Amstrong, S., and McAra, L. (eds.) *Perspectives on Punishment.* Oxford University Press.
Garland, D. (2001). *The Culture of Control. Crime and Social Order in Contemporary Society.* University of Chicago Press.
Greenberg, D., Kessler, R., and Loftin, C. (1985). Social Inequality and Crime Control. *The Journal of Criminal Law and Criminology*, 76(3), 684–704.
Hinds, L. (2005). Crime Control in Western Countries, in Pratt, J., Brown, D., Brown, M., Hallsworth, S., and Morrison, W. (eds.) *The New Punitiveness: Trends, Theories and Perspectives.* Willan Publishing.
Karstedt, S. (2006). Democracy, Values and Violence. *Annals of the American Academy of Political Social Science*, 605, 50–81.
Kerezsi, K., and Lévay, M. (2008). Criminology, Crime and Criminal Justice in Hungary. *European Journal of Criminology*, 5(2), 239–260. https://doi. org/10.1177/1477370807087646
Kyvsgaard, B. (2004). Youth Justice in Denmark, in Tonry, M., and Doob, A. (eds.) *Crime and Justice.* n. 31. University of Chicago Press.
Lahti, R. (2000). Towards a Rational and Humane Criminal Policy. Trends in Scandinavian Penal Thinking. *Journal of Scandinavian Studies in Criminology and Crime Prevention*, 1(2), 141–155. https://doi. org/10.1080/14043850030076135

Lappi-Seppälä, T. (2006). Finland: A Model of Tolerance, in Goldson, B., and Muncie, J. (eds.) *Comparative Youth Justice* (pp. 177–195). Sage Publications.
Lappi-Seppälä, T. (2007). Penal Policy in Scandinavia. *Crime and Justice*, 36(1), 217–295. https://doi.org/10.1086/592812
Lappi-Seppälä, T. (2008). Trust, Welfare, and Political Culture: Explaining Differences in National Penal Policies. *Crime and Justice*, 37(1), 313–387. https://doi.org/10.1086/525028
Larrauri Pijoan, E. (2009). La economía política del castigo. *Revista electrónica de ciencia penal y criminología*, 11, 1–22.
Lévay, M. (2007). 'Social Exclusion': A Thriving Concept in Contemporary Criminology; Social Exclusion and Crime in Central and Eastern Europe, in Aromaa, K. (ed.) *Penal Policy, Justice Reform and Social Exclusion*. HEUNI.
Levy, R. (2007). Pardons and Amnesties as Policy Instruments in Contemporary France. *Crime and Justice*, 36(1), 551–590. https://doi. org/10.1086/592811
Moore, D., and Hannah-Moffat, K. (2005). The Liberal Veil: Revisiting Canadian Penalty, in Pratt, J., Brown, D., Brown, M., Hallsworth, S., and Morrison, W. (eds.) *The New Punitiveness: Trends, Theories and Perspectives*. Willan Publishing.
Nelken, D. (2005). When Is a Society Non-Punitive? The Italian Case, in Pratt, J., Brown, D., Brown, M., Hallsworth, S., and Morrison, W. (eds.) *The New Punitiveness: Trends, Theories and Perspectives*. Willan Publishing.
Nelken, D. (2009). Comparative Criminal Justice: Beyond Ethnocentrism and Relativism. *European Journal of Criminology*, 6(4), 291–311. https://doi.org/10.1177/1477370809104684
Nelken, D. (2010). *Comparative Criminal Justice*. Sage Publications.
Nuotio, K. (2007). The Rationale of the Nordic Policy Compared with the European Approach, in Nuotio, K. (ed.) *Festchrift in honour of Raimo Lahti. Forum iuris*. University of Helsinki.
Pratt, J., Brown, D., Brown, M., Hallsworth, S., and Morrison, W. (eds.) (2005). *The New Punitiveness: Trends, Theories and Perspectives*. Willan Publishing.
Pratt, J. (2008a). Scandinavian Exceptionalism in an Era of Penal Excess. Part I. *British Journal of Criminology*, 48(3), 119–137. https://doi.org/10.1093/bjc/azm072
Pratt, J. (2008b). Scandinavian Exceptionalism in an Era of Penal Excess. Part. II. *British Journal of Criminology*, 48(3), 275–292. https://doi. org/10.1093/bjc/azm073
Roberts, J., and Hough, M. (2002). *Changing Attitudes to Punishment*. Willan Publishing.
Roché, S. (2007). Criminal Justice Policy in France: Illusions of Severity. *Crime and Justice*, 36(1), 471–550. https://doi.org/10.1086/592813
Savage, J., Bennett, R., and Danner, M. (2008). Economic Assistance and Crime: A Cross-national Investigation. *European Journal of Criminology*, 5(2), 217–238. https://doi.org/10.1177/1477370807087645
Scheingold, S. (1991). *The Politics of Street Crime. Criminal Process and Cultural Obsession*. Temple University Press.
Simon, J. (2007). *Governing Through Crime. How the War on Crime Transformed American Democracy and Created a Culture of Fear*. Oxford University Press.
Steen, S., and Bandy, R. (2007). When the Policy Becomes the Problem. Criminal Justice in the New Millenium. *Punishment and Society*, 9(1), 5–26. https://doi.org/10.1177/1462474507070548

Tamarit Sumalla, J. (2007). Sistema de sanciones y política criminal. Un estudio de derecho comparado europeo. *Revista electrónica de ciencia penal y criminología*, 9, 1–40.

Tham, H. (2001). Law and Order as a Leftist Project? The Case of Sweden. *Punishment and Society*, 3(3), 409–426. https://doi. org/10.1177/14624745010030030O4

Tonry, M. (2004). *Thinking About Crime. Sense and Sensibility in American Penal Culture*. Oxford University Press.

Tonry, M. (ed.) (2007b). *Crime, Punishment and Politics in Comparative Perspective. Crime and Justice 36*. University of Chicago Press.

Tonry, M. (2007a). Determinants of Penal Policies. *Crime and Justice*, 36(1), 1–48. https://doi.org/10.1086/518582

von Hofer, H. (2003). Prison Population as Political Constructs: The Case of Finland, Holland and Sweden. *Journal of Scandinavian Studies in Criminology and Crime Prevention*, 4(1), 21–38. https://doi. org/10.1080/14043850310009921

von Hofer, H. (2004). Crime and Reactions to Crime in Scandinavia. *Journal of Scandinavian Studies in Criminology and Crime Prevention*, 5(2), 148–166.

Wacquant, L. (2000). *Las cárceles de la miseria*. Alianza Editorial.

Webster, C.M., and Doob, A. (2007). Punitive Trends and Stable Imprisonment Rates in Canada. *Crime and Justice*, 36(1), 297–369. https://doi.org/10.1086/592807

Young, J. (1998). From Inclusive to Exclusive Society, in Ruggiero, V., South, N., and Taylor, I. (eds.) *The New European Criminology. Crime and Social Order in Europe*. Routledge.

Young, J. (2003). *La sociedad excluyente. Exclusión social, delito y diferencia en la modernidad tardía*. Marcial Pons.

Zaffaroni, R. (2007). *El enemigo en el derecho penal*. Ediciones Coyoacán.

Zielinska, E. (2005). El impulso de la legislación penal en Polonia: quién y qué hay detrás, in Díez-Ripollés, J.L., Prieto del Pino, A.M., and Soto Navarro, S. (Coords). *La política legislativa penal en Occidente. Una perspectiva comparada*. Tirant lo Blanch.

Zimring, F. (2005). Política criminal y legislación penal en la experiencia estadounidense reciente, in Ripollés, J.L., Prieto del Pino, A.M., and Soto Navarro, S. (Coords). *La política legislativa penal en Occidente. Una perspectiva comparada*. Tirant lo Blanch.

3 RIMES

An instrument to compare national criminal justice policies from the social exclusion dimension

José Luis Díez-Ripollés

1 Introduction

The current comparative criminal justice policy shows a strong tendency to compare different national crime control systems according to their higher or lower level of punitiveness. This analytical approach is based on an undisputed premise: Every crime control system should have as one of its primary goals to ensure that those entering into conflict with criminal law would suffer a moderate affliction because of their offending or suspicious behaviour (Hinds, 2005; Cavadino & Dignan, 2006; Downes & Hansen, 2006; Tonry, 2007; Lappi-Seppälä, 2008; Larrauri Pijoan, 2009).

However, using the level of punitiveness achieved by the respective crime control systems as guiding principle for the comparative analyses of criminal justice policy has a number of theoretical and methodological shortcomings.

Among the former, it should be noted that the goal of punitive moderation places itself in a scant ideological context. It represents a humanitarian approach to criminal policy, which would be recognised to the extent that it guaranteed that the severity of criminal sanctions do not exceed a certain limit, regardless of whether the set of criminal policy goals pursued and the criminal justice model adopted to achieve them are correct.

Among the methodological shortcomings, it is highlighted that – even if such approach is accepted – it uses exceedingly limited indicators of punitive moderation: In fact, almost all comparisons are built, basically, around the incarceration rate per 100,000 inhabitants. Indeed, this indicator has many virtues: It is easily accessible from various reliable sources, it focuses on one of the most severe sanctions that a criminal law system may impose and it provides a good example of the set of punitive policies and practices of a particular criminal justice system. Nevertheless, the fact of focusing the evaluation of the punitiveness of a criminal justice system on the use of imprisonment marginalises other indicators with a strong capacity for expression, such as, for example, the number of criminal proceedings that end in conviction or the average length of imposed sentences. Moreover, the intensity in the use of imprisonment also depends on, for instance, the number of admissions to prison, the average stay in prison or the confinements outside the penal system (Balvig,

DOI: 10.4324/9781032661766-5

2004; Brodeur, 2007; Webster & Doob, 2007; Roché, 2007; Snacken, 2007; Zaffaroni, 2007; Pratt, 2008; Nelken, 2010; Díez-Ripollés, 2011, 2013).

The proposal described in this article advocates for an international criminal policy comparison based on a more enriched and comprehensive approach, using an organised diversity of indicators. This does not mean that the goal of punitive moderation, or the indicator measuring it, should be discarded.

2 Theoretical model

The theoretical model adopted to design this research is based on the one presented by Díez-Ripollés (2011, 2013) and chooses as comparison element the level to which the different crime control systems minimise the social exclusion of those coming into conflict with the criminal law.

The aforementioned theoretical model does not refer to the effects of the crime control system on the overall population. It confines itself to those individuals and groups who are priority targets of criminal prevention and prosecution bodies, namely those who have been, are or are likely to be subjected to crime control as suspects, defendants, offenders or ex-offenders.

The search for either social exclusion or social inclusion of those individuals prone to enter into conflict with criminal law reflects two contrasting approaches to the criminal policy goal of preventing crime. The socially exclusionary approach is essentially aimed at achieving the incapacitation of the groups referred to, which implies ensuring that suspects, defendants, offenders or ex-offenders – after their contact with penal institutions – find themselves in individual and social conditions where it will be more difficult for them to break the law or to avoid being discovered. Conversely, the social inclusive approach seeks, above all, the social reintegration of those groups, so that suspects, defendants, offenders or ex-offenders – after their contact with penal institutions – find themselves in the same or better individual and social conditions in order to voluntarily lead a law-abiding life.

Consequently, the different national crime control systems would have to be evaluated according to the greater or lesser adherence of their penal intervention models to either of the two approaches. Our research intends, more modestly, to measure the longer or shorter distance of the diverse crime control systems with respect to a strict socially exclusionary approach.

Two assumptions underlie this analytic model: First, generating or strengthening the social exclusion of the mentioned groups by the criminal prosecution bodies leads to more crime in the mid- and long-term. Second, achieving a significant level of social inclusion of those groups reduces crime in the mid- and long-term. Both assumptions are pending empirical demonstration and this research does not consider them as hypothesis to be verified. The intention is to design and, subsequently, implement, an instrument for international comparison (the RIMES instrument) that affords to classify national crime control systems in accordance with their socially exclusionary effects, in line with that theoretical model described. It would provide the basis to prove in the future the correctness, or not, of the assumptions above.

This instrument, which would turn operational the theoretical model, must consist of a set of indicators allowing for the measuring of the level to which the different national criminal justice systems produce socially exclusionary effects on the referred groups. Such indicators must have the following features:

They must refer to actual punitive rules and practices, that is, those that are effectively applied in Western developed countries. For that matter, a punitive rule is understood as a legal standard usually, although not always, included in the criminal law system, setting forth certain consequences against certain behaviours or situations related to crime control. A punitive practice means the way in which different social agencies effectively react against behaviours or situations related to crime control, in accordance or not with the provisions laid down by the law. The fact that the contents of certain chosen rules and practices may overlap would have to be taken into consideration when configuring the instrument.

In order to design the instrument, the primary criterion to select the punitive rules and practices was their solid capability to measure significant socially exclusionary effects on the groups of the study. In no case it is intended to identify punitive rules and practices measuring the production of relevant social inclusion effects on the mentioned groups.

The chosen set of indicators would reflect in a comprehensive manner the reality of the criminal policy model in their respective countries, as concerns their socially exclusionary effects on the groups under study. In this regard, the theoretical model of Díez-Ripollés (2011, 2013) identifies nine major areas of penal intervention especially adequate to reveal relevant exclusionary effects that, as a whole, offer a comprehensive picture of the corresponding criminal justice system. The nine areas or pools are control of public spaces, legal safeguards, sentencing and sanction systems, harshest penalties, prison rules, preventive intervention, legal and social status of offenders and ex-offenders, police and criminal records and youth criminal justice. These nine pools of punitive rules and practices may be divided into a total of 25 subgroups or bundles.[1] Therefore, all the indicators to be part of the instrument must be incorporated into one of these pools and bundles.

1 Which are the following: Control of public spaces (gated communities, video-surveillance, restriction of access to public spaces). Legal safeguards (undermining of due process safeguards, hindering or restriction of legal remedies). Sentencing and sanction systems (judicial discretion, aggravated provisions for recidivists, extensive use of prison, community sanctions, electronic monitoring). Harshest penalties (death penalty, life imprisonment, long-term prison sentences). Prison rules (living conditions in prison, respect for prisoners' rights, release on parole). Preventive intervention (pre-trial detention, indefinite preventive detention). Legal and social status of offenders and ex- offenders (disenfranchisement, deprivation of further civil rights, accessibility to social resources). Police and criminal records (extension and accessibility of records, community notifications). Youth criminal justice (age thresholds, treatment differentiated from adults).

The indicators eventually chosen should have discriminating capacity, for example, they should show relevant variations among the different criminal justice systems in the Western developed countries.

The instrument would be built on the agreement existing among leading experts from different Western developed countries that the punitive rules and practices selected produce significant social exclusion on any of the following groups: suspects, defendants, offenders and ex-offenders. The intention was not to verify empirically that such punitive rules or practices effectively generate social exclusion. Such verification was replaced here by its validation through a broad consensus of experts.

Once the RIMES instrument is ready, it would be implemented in Western developed countries. When results from a significant number of countries were available, comparisons among the diverse national criminal policy models in force would be carried out from a highly significant dimension: the social exclusion they generate in groups especially affected by criminal intervention. Among other actions, the countries would be placed on a scale measuring their scoring from the set of the instrument's indicators or the indicators grouped by pools. The data obtained would be useful to know and explain contemporary criminal policies, as well as to take informed criminal policy decisions.

3 Objectives

The aim of this research project was to make operational the above-mentioned theoretical model through the design, development and implementation of an instrument capable of measuring, in comparative terms, the social exclusion generated on suspects, defendants, offenders and ex-offenders by the current crime control systems of Western developed countries.

The research had the following specific objectives:

1 To identify a set of punitive rules and practices that generate social exclusion, which are also suitable to be part of the instrument for comparative measurement.
2 To validate the rules and practices based on the previous selection, using a qualitative and quantitative method of content validation by inter-judge agreement that implies the collaboration of numerous international experts. Such validation process should probably reduce the number of surviving punitive rules and practices, from which, on the basis of additional operational criteria, should be selected those that would be configured as indicators in the final RIMES instrument for comparative measurement.

4 Development of the RIMES instrument for comparative measurement

The development and validation of the RIMES instrument has been performed following a qualitative methodological strategy through the Delphi method (Cruz Ramírez, 2009) and the technique of content validation by judgment of experts (Escobar-Pérez & Cuervo-Martínez, 2008; Cabero Almenara & Barroso Osuna, 2013). This methodology was chosen because it was deemed the most suitable to reach a consensus on the content and the validity of the instrument by way of a systematic, formal and thorough process. This is the recommended approach when there is not enough information available to take decisions (Reguant-Álvarez & Torrado-Fonseca, 2016).

For the previous selection of punitive rules and practices, most members of the Criminal Law Department and the Institute of Criminology from the University of Málaga made up the group of experts. The Delphi method was applied to them in order to check their level of expertise in the topics to be addressed. The results were satisfactory since the majority of the group included a sufficient number of persons with a PhD who were deemed experts in more than one pool. This allowed covering the whole range of knowledge required.

In achieving the proper RIMES instrument, the judgment of experts was applied for its validation. 97 international experts from 18 different countries participated in the process.

The procedures carried out to select items, to choose the experts and to validate the instrument are described below.

4.1 First phase: initial formulation of the instrument

Between March and December 2013, a research team – made up by 19 experts in criminal policy, penal law or criminology belonging to the University of Malaga – performed the works to identify a set of punitive rules and practices that they considered produce greater effects of social exclusion on the target groups described according to the theoretical model of Díez-Ripollés.

The team members were distributed in the nine thematic pools according to their fields of expertise and with the aim of striking a balance between more and less experienced members. Two or three persons were in charge of each pool, with some experts participating in more than one. A coordination team was responsible for answering any possible methodological queries and for the management of the process.

Among the instructions given were those referring to the features that the items to be identified must have, which were already listed in the theoretical framework. The following characteristics must also be added:

- a The punitive rules and practices had always to be formulated in a positive way, in other words, expressing their socially exclusionary potential, and only a dichotomous reply ("yes" or "no") had to be admitted.
- b An acceptable balance between rules and practices had to be sought.
- c An effort had to be made for identifying rules and practices able to be distributed in similar numbers among the different pools of the theoretical model inspiring the research.
- d At the time of selecting the punitive rules and practices, data on compared criminal justice policy must be taken into consideration.

e The Spanish or English language could be used in the initial working documents. However, it should be noted that the instrument to be validated later must be written in English, and the only valid version had to be the English one.

Each of the nine research groups would only submit to the whole research team those rules and practices that reached consensus within the group.

Throughout this period, the members of each group held many meetings and frequently consulted the coordinating team. Gradually, as the work of each group was finished, 18 meetings were held with the whole research team where a critical review was carried out regarding the rules and practices proposed by each group, and those that were approved through the assent of the entire team were finally selected. The result of such work was the identification of 278 punitive rules and practices, distributed among the nine pools.

As of that first selection, the members of the coordinating team then performed a detailed analysis of such rules and practices, in order to verify content overlapping, either total or partial, among the rules and practices of the same pool or located in several pools. This resulted in a first reduction in the number of items (rules and practices) of the instrument being developed, up to 250 items in total.

Subsequently, in February 2014, the four members of the coordinating team agreed to examine each item against three criteria consistent with the theoretical and methodological premises that must be at the foundation of the instrument. The three criteria were the following: Completeness, which expressed the special relevance of the information supplied. Extension, ensuring that the information did not deal with matters that was exceedingly particular or specific. Ease of access, whereby the information was expected to be relatively simple to obtain.

Each item was given a score of 1 or 0 for each criterion, according to whether it was deemed fulfilled or not. Once the scorings of all the team's members had been accumulated, each item was reviewed, and a decision was taken to exclude all those that did not exceed 4 points in the whole set of criteria. The result was 221 items that complied with such requirements.

Then, between March and April 2014, a decision was taken to submit the set of items that passed that first review pursuant to the three mentioned criteria to a new revision by the same coordinating team. In this case, besides proposing a stricter application of the criteria already used, two new ones were added: Discrimination capacity, so that the item allowed differentiation among the countries under study; and clarity, that is, that the item could be easily understood.

The scoring for each criterion and its accumulation were carried out like the previous review. Once the results had been obtained, the coordinating team takes the following decisions: To keep all those items with an accumulated scoring of 3 or 4 in each five criteria. To exclude those items that obtained an accumulated scoring of 0 or 1 in the completeness or discrimination criteria. To evaluate those items with accumulated scores that did not fit into any of the previous situations. To apply the extension criterion, taking as reference the pools where the different items were included, that is, to prevent a pool from having too many items referring to the same issue. To ensure that there was an acceptable proportion between rules and practices within each pool.

After the application of these criteria, the result obtained was 126 items in total (see the site: https://rimesproject.files.wordpress.com/2018/11/formulacic3b3n-inicial-del-instrumento-rimes.pdf) distributed in a homogeneous manner among the nine pools, out of which 79 were punitive rules and 47 punitive practices.

It should be noted that throughout the two reviews carried out by the coordinating team, occasional improvements were introduced in the formulation of items that had been accepted and other items leading to partial overlapping were rejected.

4.2 *Second phase: validation of the instrument*

In this second phase, the plan was to validate the instrument obtained up to that point using the content validity method through the judgment of experts. Since the goal was to establish an instrument for comparative measurement applicable to Western industrialised countries, its validation required the collaboration of many experts from the Western developed part of the world, and therefore a major part of the effort had been devoted to the selection of this elite group.

4.2.1 *Final version of the instrument to be validated, selection of experts and creation of the validation questionnaires*

Between the end of 2014 and the beginning of 2015 several important tasks were carried out, in order to prepare the validation process.

A After establishing the items to be submitted to validation by the experts, the English version of such items was formulated. It was already partially done in previous phases, but it needed a final version. Once the first English version of the 126 items had been drafted, it was sent for review to an English-speaking jurist/criminologist. Several communications were exchanged with her, especially to ensure that there were no negative formulations of the items and that the most appropriate technical terms had been selected to describe the different items. Then, at the end of 2015, the final English version was ready.

B Tasks were undertaken for the selection of those experts that must validate the instrument, getting into contact with them and obtaining their acceptance.

Previously, the criteria for the selection of experts had to be determined. After an intense debate among the members of the coordinating team, and with the advice of the methodologists, the criteria finally established were the following:

a The experts must carry out their professional career in Western developed countries and, through all of them the following five geographical areas should be encompassed: Northern Europe, Central Europe, Eastern Europe, Southern Europe and English-speaking countries in and out of Europe.
b The experts must be involved in the fields of criminal justice policy, penal law or criminology, and had an accredited and significant experience in the academic or professional activities referring to the prevention or prosecution of crimes. Their experience must span a period of over 10 years. The academic experts must have a doctorate (PhD).
c A moderate balance must be ensured between academics and professionals, men and women, and different ideological orientations.
d The country of origin of said experts should be distributed among the geographical areas mentioned, so that no country was over-represented as regards the others. Nevertheless, countries with a smaller population should contribute with fewer experts.
e The goal was to obtain around 100 experts coming from 20 different countries.

With those criteria, a first identification was conducted for a group of academics and professionals who were international references in their respective countries for the above-mentioned fields. Efforts were made to find two experts per country, although it was assumed that for small countries one could be enough. Given the relevance of the targeted persons, in most cases they were already known beforehand by members of the research team. In a few cases, consultations were carried out from bibliographic sources, contributions to conferences, memberships in certain organisations and other judgment elements. In all cases, the focus was on people with a long academic or professional background, and therefore their experience far exceeded 20 years. The aim was to get a balanced selection, based on the already-mentioned requirements.

Then, the coordinating team contacted those persons, informed them of the on-going research project, asked them if they wished to participate and explained to them that they would be required to provide three contributions, if they accepted. The first was to complete a brief questionnaire with some personal data. The second consisted of giving three names of colleagues in their own country who, in their opinion, had the required academic or professional experience to take part in the project. The third was to participate in the second validation phase of the questionnaire, which would refer to those items having passed the first validation phase. Not all the experts initially contacted accepted to participate, although quite a significant number of them did. So the coordinating team got in touch with other experts in their respective countries who complied with the aforementioned conditions. Finally, after having contacted 58 experts from 20 countries, 28 experts from 18 countries accepted to participate (see Table 3.1). The coordinating team got in touch with all of them again so that they would complete the first two contributions that were required.

As the selection of this group of experts progressed and the coordinating team asked them to provide the first two contributions, the names of the three experts they proposed from their own country by using the 'snowball' technique, were collected. The coordinating team examined these new experts to verify that they met, individually or as a whole, the criteria set for all experts. The majority of first experts supplied the three asked names, but they sometimes offered less or none at all. Besides, in some cases, those experts whose names had been supplied did not meet the required profile or, even if they did, they had to give way to others with a profile that allowed the team to complete the group needed, adapted to the goals. Finally, a certain number of experts from this second group declined to participate in the project after the letter had already been sent with the information on the nature of the project and the contribution they were required to supply in the first validation phase of the research project. And a few of them, in spite of having accepted to participate, in the end did not. In all these cases, the coordinating team either contacted the first experts again asking them to provide new names, or else it proceeded to search them through similar means to those used with the first experts selected. As far as possible, an effort was made to keep the ratio of three new experts from the same country from where the experts initially selected came from, which was not always achieved. Ultimately, although the coordinating team started with 84 accepting experts in this second group, it could only effectively count on 71 new experts from the same 18 countries (see Table 3.1) of the experts first selected.

In short, the selection of experts materialised in the effective participation of 97 experts from 18 countries in the validation of the questionnaire, as shown in Table 3.1. The method followed for the validation of the RIMES instrument makes advisable to mention the experts participating in the process, in order to ascertain their prominence, relevance and diversity within the fields of criminal policy, criminal law and criminology.

Table 3.1 Experts selected in both groups, by country

Country	*1st Experts' Group*	*2nd Experts' Group*
Germany	Frieder Dünkel Rita Haverkamp	Ineke Pruin Christine Morgenstern Harald Arnold Tillmann Bartsch
Belgium	Stephan Parmentier Sonja Snacken	Tom Daems Jenneke Christiaens Els Dumortier Sofie De Kimpe

(*Continued*)

Table 3.1 (Continued)

Country	*1st Experts' Group*	*2nd Experts' Group*
Canada	Anthony Doob	Cheryl Webster
		Howard Bebbington
		Jane B. Sprott
Denmark	Anette Storgaard	Signe Herving
		Ditte Nyggard
		Louise Hansen
United States	Emilio Viano	Clairissa Breen
	James Jacobs	Alison Mikkor
		Katharine Tinto
		Elisabeth Nevins
		Lila Kazemian
Spain	Elena Larrauri	Ester Blay Gil
		Lorena Antón García
		Josep Cid Moliné
		Juan José Medina Ariza
	José Luis de la Cuesta	Ana Isabel Perez Machio
		Isabel Germán Mancebo
		Xabier Arana Berastegi
Finland	Tapio Lappi-Seppälä	Mikko Aaltonen
		Janne Kivivuori
		Henrik Linderborg
France	Laurence Dumoulin	Jacques DeMaillard
		Sebastian Roché
The Netherlands	John Vervaele	Michiel Lutchtman
	René Van Swaaningen	Jolande uit Biejerse
		Marijke Malsch
		John Blad
Hungary	Miklós Levay	Zoltan Fleck
		Eszter Sárik
		Szilveszter Póczik
United Kingdom	Nicole Padfield	Jane Dominey
	Gillian McIvor	Wendy Fitzgibbon
		Joel Miller
		Niall Hamilton-Smith
		Paul Quinton
Ireland	Michael Reilly	Eimear Spain
		Mary Rogan
		Claire Hamilton
Italy	Lorenzo Picotti	Roberto Flor
	Fabio Quassoli	Ivan Salvadori
		Roberto Cornelli
		Alvise Sbraccia
		Andrea Molteni
New Zealand	Warren Young	John Pratt
		Yvette Tinsley
Poland	Beata Gruszczynska	Pawel Ostaszewski
	Krzysztof Krajewsky	Bárbara Błońska
		Grzegorz Bogdan
		Krzysztof Wilamowski
		Witold Klaus

Country	*1st Experts' Group*	*2nd Experts' Group*
Portugal	Candido Da Agra Augusto Silva Dias	Diogo Da Costa Jorge Quintas José Leal Inês Ferreira Leite Ana Sofia Xavier Marques
Romania	Florin Streteanu	Daniel Nitu Sergiu Bogdan Raluca Morosanu
Switzerland	Marcelo Aebi Nicolás Queloz	Giang Ly Isenring Manon Jendly Anne-Claude Scheidegger Frédéric Gisler Raphael Brossard

Source: Own elaboration

C In February 2015, the coordinating team approved the design of the questionnaire through which the validation of the 126 items initially selected, and its implementation process, would be carried out, in the following terms:

a The questionnaire of items should be validated after going through two turns of examinations by the experts. The 84 experts recruited in the second phase of experts' selection mentioned above participated at the first turn. The 28 experts initially recruited took part at the second turn.

b At the first turn, the experts had to validate the 126 items submitted to them and resulting from the identification, selection and review processes conducted by the research team. Each expert would handle one third of the items included in the initial questionnaire. This led to the division of the questionnaire into three blocks of 42 items. The experts must complete questionnaire 1 (including items 1 to 42 of the entire questionnaire), 2 (items 43 to 84) or 3 (items 85 to 126) at random, assigning them successively one of the three, depending on the time of confirming their participation in the validation process.

c The partial questionnaires to be completed at the first turn had the following elements: A first part with a brief explanation of the basic concepts of what must be measured, with examples, and the instructions for an adequate reply to the questions made about the items of the questionnaire attached. These questions were two: The first referred to the clarity of the corresponding item, for instance, if the semantic content was well understood. The second would be on the suitability of the punitive rule or practice mentioned in the item to generate social exclusion in the groups under study. Each of the two questions raised for each item must be given a score of 1 to 5 in a Likert scale, where 1 was the lowest value for clarity or suitability and 5 was the highest value for those dimensions. The second part should contain the list of items, which should permit answering both questions of each of them in the same line. The third part consisted of a form to be completed by the expert, including a number of personal and professional questions similar to those already posed to the first group of experts when they accepted to participate.

The questionnaires must be completed online using the Qualtrics program. This is an innovative research platform for complex decision-making, of simple design and execution. To this end, an e-mail with the appropriate link to the platform was sent to each expert.

d At the second turn, those items having passed the validation criteria of the first turn should be submitted for validation to the first group of experts. In this case, if its size estimated was confirmed, the whole questionnaire resulting therefrom should be divided into two parts, assigning one-half or the other half of the questionnaire to the experts, based on criteria to be determined later on. In other words, 14 experts should complete each part of the questionnaire. If the number of items having passed the first turn was lower than 40, the entire questionnaire resulting therefrom would be applied to each participant in this group of experts.

e The questionnaires to be completed at the second turn should include the following elements: The first part, similar to the questionnaires at the first turn, except for an additional information related to the nine pools where all the items of the instrument to be validated were distributed. This was because the questions to be replied were no longer two, but three. To the two questions already contained in the questionnaires of the first turn, a third one was added, inquiring on the appropriateness of including the corresponding item in a specific pool. A score of 1 to 5 on a Likert scale must be given to all three questions, in the same way as the previous turn. The second part of the questionnaire would contain the list of items, with three lines each to answer to the three questions. The third part of the questionnaire of the first turn should not be included, since such information was obtained previously, as already said.

The questionnaires were sent to the experts, and they must be completed in the same way as the previous turn.

4.2.2 Validation of the questionnaire by experts: first turn

The periods initially given to complete questionnaires 1, 2 and 3 of the first turn ranged between one and two months. Nevertheless, practice showed that those periods were too optimistic, since the completion and collection of these questionnaires extended throughout a period of 15 months, up to May 2016. To the delay in replying by a significant group of those experts – which compelled to send, in the worst case, up to three reminders – was added the fact that other experts, despite having accepted, finally did not reply and it was necessary to find new experts from the appropriate countries, apart from other incidents. Finally, questionnaire 1 was completed by 26 experts from

18 countries, questionnaire 2 by 23 experts from 17 countries and questionnaire 3 by 22 experts from 16 countries. In other words, a response rate of 84.52 per cent out of the total number of questionnaires sent; two questionnaires 1, five questionnaires 2 and six questionnaires 3 remained uncompleted.

Once the research team had the answers to the questionnaires, they were analyzed through an inter-judge reliability statistical test consisting of Aiken's V coefficient for validation (Aiken, 1980). Based on this coefficient, all those items with a coefficient lower than 0.70 were deemed not validated, in principle. This resulted in 62 items validated as regards clarity and 81 for suitability, out of 126 items submitted to validation (see Tables 3.2 and 3.3).

Table 3.2 Aiken's V Coefficient results according to suitability

Aiken's V Coefficient intervals	*N*
0.80 and higher	42
0.75–0.79	19
0.70–0.74	20
Not validated	45
TOTAL	81

Source: Own elaboration

Table 3.3 Clarity scores of 81 validated items

With problems in clarity	*Aiken's V Coefficient intervals*	*n*
No problems	0,70 and higher	62
Some problems	0,60–0,69	13
With problems	0,50–0,59	6

Source: Own elaboration

Considering these results, the research team implemented the following decisions, with the aim of improving the operability of the instrument being developed:

a To use as reference point for the configuration of the second turn questionnaire those items having obtained Aiken's coefficients not lower than 0.70 for suitability and clarity.
b To allow the inclusion at the second turn questionnaire of some items that, having obtained a coefficient between 0.55 and 0.69 for clarity, had in any case an Aiken's coefficient not lower than 0.70 for suitability, and were necessary to satisfy the other criteria immediately infra mentioned (letter c).

   If they were finally included at the second turn questionnaire of validation, an additional effort would be made in their wording for improved clarity.

c To reduce, with respect to the second turn, the number of items in the questionnaire. To that end, all the items with the above-mentioned qualities would be reviewed according to the following three criteria:

   i Redundancy of the item, in other words, the fact of addressing an issue – even if there was no overlapping of content – that was similar to other within the same pool.
   ii Search of a certain proportion among items that constitute either rule or prac-tice within each pool and in the questionnaire in general.
   iii Keeping a number of items per pool that is similar enough.
   iv Scoring for clarity.

The result of all that work was a questionnaire with 65 items at the second turn, distributed among nine pools, each one of them comprising between 5 and 11 items, which amounted to a total of 44 rules and 21 practices.

4.2.3 Validation of the questionnaire by experts: second turn

Once the structure and extension of the questionnaire to be submitted for validation to the experts at the second turn was known, between September and October 2016, the research team adopted the following additional decisions regarding methodology:

a The questionnaire should be divided into two: Questionnaire 1 would have 33 items, and questionnaire 2, 32 items. Items were distributed at random between the two partial questionnaires that must be completed.
b The experts at this second turn were divided into two subgroups, so that one would answer questionnaire 1 and the other, questionnaire 2. Such division of experts was decided not to be carried out at random, since it was intended to have an equivalent group heterogeneity, based on the personal features already obtained from each one of these experts.

Both questionnaires were sent at the end of October 2016. At the close of that year the collection of the questionnaires sent was concluded, with a high response rate (92.85 per cent), since 26 out of the 28 questionnaires sent were completed: 13 of questionnaire 1 and 13 of questionnaire 2.[2]

After applying Aiken's V validation coefficient to the items of both questionnaires, for clarity coefficients higher than 0.60 were obtained in all the items, while for suitability coefficients equal or higher than 0.70 were obtained in 55 of the 65 items, and for appropriateness coefficients equal or higher than 0.70 were obtained in 63 out of the 65 items (see Table 3.4).

2 One of the pending questionnaires was not received due to death of the expert, and the other one owing to lack of time connected with an appointment for a relevant academic management office.

Table 3.4 Aiken's V coefficient results

Aiken's V coefficient intervals	*Clarity*	*Suitability*	*Pool appropriateness*
0.80 and higher	45	35	56
0.75–0.79	12	13	5
0.70–0.74	1	7	2
0.69 and lower	7	10	1
Not validated	0	0	1
TOTAL	65	65	64

Source: Own elaboration

After discarding all those items with values lower than 0.70 in Aiken's V coefficient for suitability and appropriateness, the result was a questionnaire made up by 55 items. Out of those, for clarity only three items obtained an Aiken's coefficient between 0.63 and 0.69, the remainder got a coefficient equal or higher than 0.70.

4.3 Final configuration of the RIMES instrument

At the beginning of 2017, the research team was pleased to realise that, after the two validation turns, it had achieved to have the experts validate a significant number of items: 55 out of the 126 at the beginning the inter-judge validation process. Yet, the number of validated items was excessive for the instrument implementation to be feasible. It was therefore decided that the whole team would carry out a new review of those 55 items by applying the following criteria:

a To seek that a number of items of around 35 make up the final instrument, not exceeding the limit of 40 items in any case.
b To preserve as far as possible those items that obtained the highest scores in Aiken's coefficient for suitability.
c To ensure that those items finally selected have high scores for clarity.
d To value the ease of access for obtaining information that provide the item's content.
e To review again the redundancy of each item.
f To continue trying to achieve a certain balance between rules and practices within each pool and the instrument in general.
g. To ensure that no pool has a number of items – between rules and practices – lower than three.
h. There should be no big difference among pools as regards the number of items.

After several meetings of the entire research team, where a detailed procedure was adopted for verification of all these requisites, in February 2017 a final agreement was reached regarding the RIMES instrument that consisted of

39 items, including 26 rules and 13 practices, and a number of items ranging between 4 and 5 within each pool (see Table 3.5).

Table 3.5 Scores of definitive selected items

Aiken's V coefficient intervals	*Clarity*	*Suitability*	*Pool appropriateness*
0.80 and higher	31	30	38
0.75–0.79	7	8	1
0.70–0.74	1	1	0
0.63–0.69	0	0	0
Not validated	0	0	0
TOTAL	39	39	39

Source: Own elaboration

The list of those items finally selected, with the scoring for clarity, suitability and appropriateness obtained by each one at the second turn of the validation is as follows (see Table 3.6):

Table 3.6 Validation according to Aiken's V coefficient

R or P	*Pools*	*List of indicators*	*Clarity*	*Suitability*	*Pool appropriateness*
R	7	93. Nationals sentenced to imprisonment for any criminal offence are not eligible for welfare benefits for a certain period after having served their sentences.	0.92	0.96	0.96
R	7	92. Those sentenced to up to 3 years of imprisonment for any criminal offence are not eligible for public housing for a certain period after having served their sentences.	0.96	0.96	0.98
R	3	36. Default imprisonment is the sole alternative to non-payment of a fine.	0.94	0.94	0.94
P	8	107. The media regularly disclose the full names, current addresses or pictures of ex-felons.	0.98	0.94	0.94
R	9	117. Youth justice provides custodial sanctions of over 10 years.	0.90	0.94	0.94

R or P	*Pools*	*List of indicators*	*Clarity*	*Suitability*	*Pool appropriateness*
R	7	86. Those sentenced to up 3 years of imprisonment for any criminal offence may be deprived of the right to vote for over 4 years after serving their sentences.	0.88	0.92	0.92
R	7	88. Legally resident foreigners may be deported if they receive a custodial sentence up to one year or a non-custodial sentence.	0.85	0.92	0.88
R	8	101. The criminal records of any citizen are legally accessible through internet.	1	0.92	0.98
P	8	110. Most companies with over 100 employees require a clean criminal record for recruitment.	0.87	0.90	0.94
P	9	126. Alien minors are deported because of an offence.	0.85	0.90	0.90
R	7	91. Those sentenced to up to 3 years of imprisonment are prohibited from doing certain jobs not connected with their offences or with law enforcement for a period of more than 5 years after their sentence has been completed.	0.71	0.88	0.87
R	1	1. Any person may be arrested for repeated street begging.	0.94	0.88	0.96
R	1	3. At its discretion, the police may enforce restrictions on specific individuals to access some public spaces (parks, squares, streets . . .).	0.85	0.88	0.92
R	4	43. Life imprisonment without release is legally available.	0.87	0.87	0.98
P	4	52. In over 80% of life sentences those serving time are from an ethnic minority background or were living in poverty.	0.87	0.87	0.85
R	9	120. Minors' criminal records keep legal effects after reaching the age of majority	0.87	0.87	0.88

(*Continued*)

Table 3.6 (Continued)

R or P	*Pools*	*List of indicators*	*Clarity*	*Suitability*	*Pool appropriateness*
P	1	11. Discriminatory street police interventions (stop and search, arrests, frisks/body searches . . .) targeting specific groups occur regularly.	0.88	0.85	0.92
R	6	79. The maximum statutory term for pretrial detention exceeds 3 years.	0.90	0.85	0.85
R	9	113. Youth justice applies to children who are 12 years old or younger.	0,85	0.85	0.90
R	3	33. In the case of prison sentences, neither probation as an alternative to sentencing nor suspended sentences are envisaged in the law.	0.77	0.83	0.96
P	3	38. At least three quarters of the inmates are serving their sentences in closed prisons.	0.88	0.83	0.92
R	4	42. Death penalty is legally available.	1.00	0.83	0.94
R	1	2. An individual may be arrested for loitering.	0.79	0.83	0.92
R	8	100. Anyone may request information about other people's criminal records without needing to argue grounds established by law.	0.81	0.83	0.94
R	2	21. The criminal justice system lacks indigent defense services.	0.83	0.81	0.92
P	4	50. Those sentenced to life imprisonment regularly serve more than 25 years.	0.96	0.81	0.88
R	5	55. The system lacks a specific prison regime for young adults.	0.96	0.81	0.90
P	5	68. Family and intimate visits take place at intervals of over one month.	0.98	0.81	0.92
R	3	35. The law lacks provisions for penalties other than prison (community service, fines, house arrest) in case of less serious felonies.	0.83	0.81	0.92
R	5	62. The law lacks statutory provisions regulating inmates' legal assistance for penitentiary matters.	0.79	0.81	0.88

R or P	*Pools*	*List of indicators*	*Clarity*	*Suitability*	*Pool appropriateness*
P	9	121. Custodial sanction is one of three most common sanctions applied to minors.	0.83	0.79	0.90
R	5	64. The law requires payment of fees by the inmate before claiming judicial review of penitentiary decisions.	0.77	0.79	0.88
R	6	74. Preventive detention may last for an unlimited period of time.	0.83	0.79	0.94
P	6	82. Over 30% of the prison population is in pre-trial detention.	0.96	0.77	0.85
R	2	22. Payment of court fees is legally required from the defendant in order to get access to appellate review	0.79	0.77	0.87
P	2	25. A significant number of mentally ill inmates serve their sentences in regular correctional facilities.	0.85	0.77	0.75
P	3	37. The incarceration rate is higher than 120 inmates per 100,000 inhabitants.	0.87	0.77	0.85
P	6	81. The average length of preventive detention exceeds 5 years.	0.77	0.77	0.87
R	2	24. The regular term for police detention established by the law exceeds 5 days.	0.79	0.73	0.90

Source: Own elaboration

The final instrument, structured by pools, is formulated hereinafter (see Table 3.7):

Table 3.7 Final instrument, by pools

Pools	*Rules*	*Practices*
1. Control of public spaces	1. Any person may be arrested for repeated street begging 2. An individual may be arrested for loitering 3. At its discretion, the police may enforce restrictions on specific individuals to access some public spaces (parks, squares, streets)	11. Discriminatory street police interventions (stop and search, arrests, frisks/body searches) targeting specific groups occur regularly

(*Continued*)

Table 3.7 (Continued)

Pools	*Rules*	*Practices*
2. Legal safeguards	21. The criminal justice system lacks indigent defense services 22. Payment of court fees is legally required from the defendant in order to get access to appellate review 24. The regular term for police detention established by the law exceeds five days	25. A significant number of mentally ill inmates serve their sentences in regular correctional facilities
3. Sentencing and sanctions systems	33. In the case of prison sentences, neither probation as an alternative to sentencing nor suspended sentences are envisaged in the law 35. The law lacks provisions for penalties other than prison (community service, fines, house arrest) in case of less serious felonies 36. Default imprisonment is the sole alternative to non-payment of a fine	37. The incarceration rate is higher than 120 inmates per 100,000 inhabitants 38. At least three quarters of the inmates are serving their sentences in closed prisons
4. Harshest penalties	42. Death penalty is legally available	50. Those sentenced to life imprisonment regularly serve more than 25 years
	43. Life imprisonment without release is legally available	52. In over 80% of life sentences those serving time are from an ethnic minority background or were living in poverty[3]
5. Prison rules	55. The system lacks a specific prison regime for young adults 62. The law lacks statutory provisions regulating inmates' legal assistance for penitentiary matters 64. The law requires payment of fees by the inmate before claiming judicial review of penitentiary decisions	68. Family and intimate visits take place at intervals of over one month
6. Preventive intervention	74. Preventive detention may last for an unlimited period of time	81. The average length of preventive detention exceeds five years
	79. The maximum statutory term for pretrial detention exceeds three years	82. Over 30% of the prison population is in pre-trial detention

3 This item was later replaced by another validated item, item 46. See explanation about the decision in Chapter 5.

Pools	*Rules*	*Practices*
7. Legal and social status of offenders and ex-offenders	86. Those sentenced to up three years of imprisonment for any criminal offence may be deprived of the right to vote for over four years after serving their sentences 88. Legally resident foreigners may be deported if they receive a custodial sentence up to one year or a non-custodial sentence 91. Those sentenced to up to three years of imprisonment are prohibited from doing certain jobs not connected with their offences or with law enforcement for a period of more than five years after their sentence has been completed 92. Those sentenced to up to three years of imprisonment for any criminal offence are not eligible for public housing for a certain period after having served their sentences 93. Nationals sentenced to imprisonment for any criminal offence are not eligible for welfare benefits for a certain period after having served their sentences	
8. Police and criminal records	100. Anyone may request information about other people's criminal records without needing to argue grounds established by law 101. The criminal records of any citizen are legally accessible through internet	107. The media regularly disclose the full names, current addresses or pictures of ex-felons 110. Most companies with over 100 employees require a clean criminal record for recruitment[4]
9. Youth criminal justice	113. Youth justice applies to children who are 12 years old or younger	121. Custodial sanction is one of three most common sanctions applied to minors
	117. Youth justice provides custodial sanctions of over 10 years 120. Minors' criminal records keep legal effects after reaching the age of majority	126. Alien minors are deported because of an offence

4 This item was later replaced by another validated item, item 99. See explanation about such decision in Chapter 5.

Once available the RIMES instrument, the research team started its application in Spain, as a pilot project, before proceeding to its application to additional countries. This first application experience and its results will be explained in another chapter.

6 Conclusions

This research started on the assumption that the criminal policy knowledge needs rigorous methodological instruments that may enable it to evaluate and propose correct and efficacious crime control policies.

For this purpose, it was necessary to choose a criterion for the analysis of contemporary criminal policy with the capacity of showing significant, comprehensive and consistent results. Contrary to the usual criminal policy reflection nowadays, this research has chosen the dimension of the social exclusion that crime control may generate on groups particularly affected by punitive intervention.

Selecting a promising analytical criterion is not enough, but it must become operative, so that it may develop all its potentials, both explanatory and critical. The RIMES tool for the comparison of national criminal justice policies from the perspective of the social exclusion they produce on particularly sensitive groups, the creation of which is explained in this article, constitutes the achievement of such goal.

Said instrument, which measures the presence in a certain national crime control system of punitive rules and practices that are socially exclusionary, has been validated in a methodologically rigorous manner, through a double inter-judge valuation where about 100 experts from 18 countries in the Western developed world have participated.

Its implementation in a large number of Western developed countries would allow to compare their respective national criminal justice policies based on a particularly significant dimension concerning the performance of its crime control systems. Therefore, it will be possible to draw a continuum within a scale among national criminal policies that are more or less socially exclusionary, identifying the level to which the exclusionary intervention techniques are expanding in the Western developed world, and grouping those results in nine relevant fields of criminal intervention.

Ultimately, it would provide information of great relevance in order to promote and design criminal justice policies that are less socially exclusionary for those groups most affected by criminal intervention.

References

Aiken, L. (1980). Content Validity and Reliability of Single Items or Questionnaires. *Educational and Psychological Measurement*, 40, 955–959.

Balvig, F. (2004). When Law and Order Returned to Denmark. *Journal of Scandinavian Studies in Criminology and Crime Prevention*, 5(2), 167–187. https://doi.org/10.1080/14043850410010711

Brodeur, J.-P. (2007). Comparative Penology in Perspective, in Tonry, M. (ed.) *Crime, Punishment and Politics in Comparative Perspective. Crime and Justice, 36.* University of Chicago Press.

Cabero Almenara, J., and Barroso Osuna, J. (2013). La utilización del juicio experto para la evaluación de TIC: El coeficiente de competencia experta. *Bordón*, 65(2), 1–14.

Cavadino, M., and Dignan, J. (2006). *Penal Systems. A Comparative Approach.* Sage Publications.

Cruz Ramírez, M. (2009). *El método Delphi en las investigaciones educacionales.* Editorial Academia.

Díez-Ripollés, J. L. (2011). La dimensión inclusión/exclusión social como guía de la política criminal comparada. *Revista Electrónica de Ciencia Penal y Criminología*, 13, 12. http://criminet.ugr.es/recpc/13/recpc13-12.pdf

Díez-Ripollés, J. L. (2013). Social Inclusion and Comparative Criminal Justice Policy. *Journal of Scandinavian Studies in Criminology and Crime Prevention*, 14, 62–78.

Downes, D., and Hansen, K. (2006). Welfare and Punishment in Comparative Perspective, in Amstrong, S., and McAra, L. (eds.) *Perspectives on Punishment. The Contours of Control.* Oxford University Press.

Escobar-Pérez, J., and Cuervo-Martínez, A. (2008). Validez de contenido y juicio de expertos: Una aproximación a su utilización. *Avances en medición*, 6, 27–37.

Hinds, L. (2005). Crime Control in Western Countries, in Pratt, J., Brown, D., Brown, M., Hallsworth, S., and Morrison, W. (eds.) *The New Punitiveness: Trends, Theories and Perspectives.* Willan Publishing.

Lappi-Seppälä, T. (2008). Trust, Welfare, and Political Culture: Explaining Differences in National Penal Policies. *Crime and Justice*, 37(1), 313–387. https://doi.org/10.1086/525028

Larrauri Pijoan, E. (2009). La economía política del castigo. *Revista electrónica de ciencia penal y criminología*, 11, 1–22.

Nelken, D. (2010). *Comparative Criminal Justice.* Sage Publications.

Pratt, J. (2008). Scandinavian Exceptionalism in an Era of Penal Excess. Part I. *British Journal of Criminology*, 48(3), 119–137. https://doi.org/10.1093/bjc/azm072

Reguant-Álvarez, M., and Torrado-Fonseca, M. (2016). El método Delphi. *REIRE, Revista d'Innovació i Recerca en Educació*, 9(1), 87–102.

Roché, S. (2007). Criminal Justice Policy in France: Illusions of Severity, in Tonry, M. (ed.) Crime, Punishment and Politics in Comparative Perspective. *Crime and Justice*, 36(1), 471–550. https://doi.org/10.1086/592813

Snacken, S. (2007). Penal Policy and Practice in Belgium, in Tonry, M. (ed.) Crime, Punishment and Politics in Comparative Perspective. *Crime and Justice*, 36(1), 127–215. https://doi.org/10.1086/592805

Tonry, M. (2007). Determinants of Penal Policies, in Tonry, M. (ed.) Crime, Punishment and Politics in Comparative Perspective. *Crime and Justice*, 36(1), 1–48. https://doi.org/10.1086/518582

Webster, C. M., and Doob, A. (2007). Punitive Trends and Stable Imprisonment Rates in Canada, in Tonry, M. (ed.) Crime, Punishment and Politics in Comparative Perspective. *Crime and Justice*, 36(1), 297–369. https://doi.org/10.1086/592807

Zaffaroni, R. (2007). *El enemigo en el derecho penal.* Ediciones Coyoacán.

4 Constructing, validation and application of the RIMES instrument

Methodological issues[1]

Lorea Arenas-García

1 Introduction

The comparison of different crime control systems is a complex task. Comparative criminal justice policy has traditionally focused its analysis on the level of punitiveness exerted by each national crime system, presupposing certain humanitarian limits in the enforcement of penalties and using exceedingly limited indicators of punitive moderation. As pointed out by Díez-Ripollés & García-España (2019, p. 2), the traditional approach is impaired since nearly all comparisons are basically built around the incarceration rate per 100,000 inhabitants. Such circumstance marginalises other indicators with a strong capacity for expression, such as, for example, the number of criminal proceedings that end in conviction or the average length of imposed sentences.

As a consequence, an international criminal justice policy comparison should begin with a more enriched and comprehensive approach, using – to this end – a broad set of indicators (Díez-Ripollés & García-España, 2019, p. 2). The methodology that operationalises generic or abstract concepts in empirical and observable indicators in order to establish measurement instruments is used in many fields of knowledge, with different purposes. For example, in sociology scales that verify public opinion on certain phenomena are quite common; in psychology, the creation of tests to evaluate personality and behaviour features is widely used; and those tests are also used in natural sciences, as many indicators have been formulated in relation to them. Said instruments are, in turn, applied to different sociodemographic contexts in order to carry out international comparisons. Proof of that would be the Social Progress Index (SPI) or the database of the World Health Organization (WHO).

In the criminal justice policy arena, there are several secondary data sources enabling comparison among countries by using basic indicators, such as the incarceration rate, the overcrowding rate, the number of alternative measures

1 This chapter is an adaptation and update of the work: Arenas-García, L. (2021). Constructing and validating an instrument for comparing national criminal justice policies. *Revista Criminalidad*, *63*(3), 107–125. This article was published under the terms of a Creative Commons Attribution 4.0 license and we are allowed to reproduce it here.

DOI: 10.4324/9781032661766-6

to imprisonment, etc. Notable among those is the World Prison Brief (at global level) and the "SPACE" annual statistical reports from the Council of Europe (at European level). Such information has been traditionally used to identify criminal justice policy trends among countries in rigorist terms, even though there is no instrument to verify those trends empirically; thus, the importance of establishing a set of valid and reliable indicators to enable generalisation. In order to address this need, Díez-Ripollés and his team have developed several research projects that are pioneers in the creation, and subsequent validation of an instrument for international comparison that affords to classify national crime control systems according to their socially exclusionary effects.

This paper describes the methodology adopted in these projects based on a specific theoretical framework (see Chapter 3), addressing the following aspects: the justification of the method adopted for each research objective (create, validate and apply a measurement instrument); its execution phases; the appropriateness of the statistical tests used; as well as the limitations faced. All the information presented here has been extracted from the Executive Report, a document that summarises the development of the different phases of execution of the RIMES Project from March 2013 to July 2017, and also from the RIMES Minutes and AP-RIMES Minutes.

2 Creation of the instrument

The socially exclusionary theoretical approach is a theoretical definition that lacks the necessary accuracy to measure the phenomena which it refers to. It is a construct or abstract idea that cannot be directly observed, the function of which is essentially synthetic. In other words, to determine if a country is closer to or farther away from the socially exclusionary approach, it is necessary to operationalise its content translating it into empiric variables or measurable indicators. In this context, implementing the method of creation of indicators is justified by three essential reasons: the aim is to verify a particular theoretical model; there are no similar measurement instruments which prevents the possibility of building the instrument based on others; and it does not preclude the integration of indicators traditionally used in the sphere of comparative criminal justice policy. The methodology of creating indicators requires them to be valid and reliable (Casas, 1989; González Blasco, 1994; Lazarsfeld, 1985; Messick, 1989; Prieto & Delgado, 2010; Rey del Castillo, 2004; Sierra-Bravo, 2008).

Messick (1989), whose theory on the validity of tests has had a deep influence in literature, defined "validity" as follows:

> The validity is a global evaluative judgment of the degree to which empirical data and theoretical logic support the conception and convenience of the inferences and actions carried out based on scores produced by tests or others measuring instruments.
>
> (p. 19)

Other authors describe it as "the gap between the concept and those indicators chosen for its representation" (Estévez-García & Pérez-García, 2007, p. 55) or "the justification that the items to measure criterion are a representative sample of the content to be evaluated" (Prieto & Delgado, 2010, p. 70). In turn, to measure validity it is essential to use a tripartite structure of criterion, content and construct (Hernández-Sampieri et al., 2006).

Criterion validity is reached upon comparison of data obtained with others that have been previously used to measure the same concept. And this is only possible by taking indicators already validated in previous research, as would be the already mentioned incarceration rate by 100,000 inhabitants. Content validity has been traditionally defined by Nunnally (1973) and Mehrens & Lehmann (1982) as "the degree to which the items making up the sample represent the content subject that is being measured" (Escurra, 1988, p. 105). In other words, it examines whether the measurement includes the variety of meanings which such concept may adopt, whether they are relevant for the main theoretical construct, and it is therefore important to draw up a list with the largest possible number of indicators so they can later on be discarded. As regards validity of the construct, it refers to the theoretical or abstract ideas which are at the basis of research and from which operational definitions arise. If the latter properly reflect the theoretical meaning of a concept, the construct's validity will be greater. In our case, the construct is the theoretical definition of social exclusion arising from a larger theoretical framework.

Likewise, the creation of indicators methodology requires them to be reliable, that is, to be able to obtain consistent results in successive measurements of the same phenomenon. In this sense, reliability refers to "the consistency of the measurement, the possibility to replicate the results obtained with an instrument if it is applied in different occasions" (Estévez-García & Pérez-García, 2007, p. 55).

As regards the procedure of variables operationalisation, it was developed by Lazarsfeld (1985) who differentiates four successive steps (see Figure 4.1 below).

Such procedure was adapted and implemented throughout the whole the research by the research team. The first two steps were developed around the concept that had been theoretically substantiated by Díez-Ripollés in previous research. The author had already provided a theoretical notion defining the main features of exclusion and its pools. On the basis of this theoretical tour, and in order to comply with the procedure of operationalising the variables, a group of researchers specialised in penal law, criminology and criminal justice policy was set up (phase 1) so that they may assess the theoretical concept of the project (phase 2: steps 1 and 2), by carrying out its operationalisation through the creation of indicators classified in different dimensions of the exclusion (phase 3: step 3), in order to end with a rigorous selection of them (phase 4: step 4).

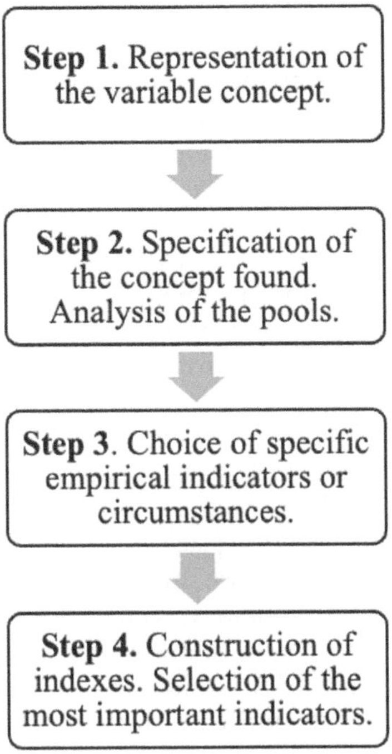

Figure 4.1 Procedure of operationalisation of variables

2.1 Setting up a group of researchers (phase 1)

The fact of having an expert judgment offers great advantages to establish knowledge. An expert is:

> An individual, group of individuals or bodies that can offer maximum competence, conclusive assessments regarding a given problem; make real and objective forecasts on the effect, applicability, feasibility and relevance which the proposed solution may have in practice; and provide recommendations on what may be done to improve it.
>
> (Crespo, 2007, p. 7)

Experts provide a greater level of deepening in the matter; their answers are detailed and their contents have a high theoretical quality (Cabero Almenara & Barroso Osuna, 2013, pp. 1–2). That is way their relevance for creating indicators is justified. In this first phase, there were 20 researchers assigned to the research project and it was assumed that they were experts in the matter. In order to determine such aspect with objective criteria, the Delphi method was partially applied (Cruz, 2009, pp. 19–60). This method has been quite frequently used in the last few years for individual self-assessment, so as to know their expertise competence (Blasco et al., 2010; García & Fernández, 2008; López, 2008; Oñate, 2001).

Said method gives validity to the methodological process by confirming the expert level of the research group as regards each dimension or pool, by allowing to establish criteria for the inclusion or exclusion of experts. It specifically assesses five different argument sources, namely: knowledge of the problem's current status, understanding the problem, capacity to analyze the problem, experience in theoretical research development and experience in empirical research development. In order to implement the Delphi protocol, a brief three-page questionnaire was drawn up and sent on line to each team member, so as to know their individual and professional characteristics, as well as their competence or expertise level in each theoretical dimension or pool, that is, the expert had to score in a 1-to-5 Likert scale if their level of expertise was very low (1), low (2), medium (3), high (4) or very high (5).

As regards the statistical testing used, some statistical descriptions of the group were carried out in the first place (frequency, averages, minimum and maximum range) so as to develop, later on, the mathematical procedure described in the Delphi methodology, which allows to accept or refuse the researcher, according to his/her own evaluation, thanks to the calculation of coefficient K or expert knowledge coefficient.

The first descriptive results showed that, for the most part, researchers had medium and high scores. As seen in the table below, they were classified in four categories and ranges according to the average score obtained in the pools: very low (1–1.50), low (1.51–2.50), medium (2.51–3.50), high (3.51–4.50) and very high (>4.50). Only researcher no. 14 was classified within the "very high" score category by achieving the largest average, over 4.50 (4.71 points), while also being the expert with the highest number of publications. The second group includes 5 researchers within the "high" category, made up by those numbered 2, 10, 12, 20 and 5. Their averages were between ranges 3.51 and 4.50. We then find a third group, which is larger and includes 12 researchers in the "medium" category, with an average between 2.51 and 3.50 points. And a last group of two researchers (numbered 1 and 19) with "low" level and averages between 1.51 and 2.50 points. It was similarly determined that pool number 5 had the highest score, with 355 points: the highest score which a pool could obtain was 500 points (if all judges granted 5 points). It was also the pool with the highest score as regards the following argument sources: "knowledge of the problem's current status", "understanding the problem" and "capacity to analyze the problem". This was followed by pool 3 (340 points), 4 (337 points) and 2 (334). Finally, it was found that researchers had more experience in developing theoretical research in pools 2 and 3, and more empirical experience in pools 3 and 5.

As regards determination of coefficient K or expert level, it was carried out by calculating the subtotal addition of the knowledge level coefficient on the subject under study (kc) and the average of argument sources (Ka), in other

Table 4.1 Group statistical descriptions according to maximum scoring in the pool, average, range and category

Researchers (N°)	*High score*	*Total pool average*	*Ranges*	*Categories*
14	212	4.71	> 4.50	Very high
2	189	4.20	3.51–4.50	High
10	173	3.84	3.51–4.50	High
12	173	3.84	3.51–4.50	High
20	162	3.60	3.51–4.50	High
5	160	3.56	3.51–4.50	High
4	148	3.29	2.51–3.50	Medium
13	144	3.20	2.51–3.50	Medium
17	142	3.16	2.51–3.50	Medium
11	138	3.07	2.51–3.50	Medium
3	136	3.02	2.51–3.50	Medium
8	133	2.96	2.51–3.50	Medium
9	132	2.93	2.51–3.50	Medium
6	127	2.82	2.51–3.50	Medium
7	125	2.78	2.51–3.50	Medium
18	124	2.76	2.51–3.50	Medium
15	119	2.64	2.51–3.50	Medium
16	117	2.60	2.51–3.50	Medium
1	107	2.38	1.51–2.50	Low
19	105	2.33	1.51–2.50	Low

Source: Own elaboration

words, K=1/2 (Kc + Ka). The coefficient has a minimum value of 0 and a maximum of 1, considering as high level of competence when the coefficient is equal to or higher than 0.75. It is noted that in Table 4.2 there is a minimum of four researchers with a high level of competence (K=0.75 or >) in each pool and a maximum of 11. Sorting the number of researchers with a high level of competence from lowest to highest, it is noted that: the first pool includes four researchers; the sixth pool includes five; the eighth, six; in pools second and third there are seven; in the ninth pool there are eight researchers; in the fourth, 10 and in the fifth, 11.

Finally, coefficient K was calculated at group level, and it was determined that it stood at 0.55 points, an average score which revealed that the team did not consider itself an expert in all the issues to be covered by the questionnaire and that, even if there were some individuals deemed experts in more fields and others in fewer fields, the team as a whole did not achieve a high level of competence, possibly due to the presence of researchers at early training stages. In spite of it, this aspect was not necessarily taken as negative or restricting, since it allowed for the adoption of future methodological decisions, as was the fact of ensuring the presence of researchers with a high level of competence in the nine working groups created ad hoc – one in each pool – in the subsequent creation of indicators.

Table 4.2 Coefficient K per researcher and pool

K	*P1*	*P2*	*P3*	*P4*	*P5*	*P6*	*P7*	*P8*	*P9*
R1	0.77	0.3	0.3	0.53	0.53	0.52	0.49	0.53	0.52
R2	0.71	0.54	0.96	0.96	0.96	0.96	0.96	0.88	0.85
R3	0.4	0.91	0.94	0.87	0.69	0.52	0.74	0.4	0.52
R4	0.72	0.91	0.72	0.87	0.94	0.69	0.56	0.4	0.72
R5	0.85	1	0.83	0.78	0.83	0.83	0.83	0.92	0.45
R6	0.67	0.43	0.64	0.51	0.74	0.39	0.72	0.24	0.78
R7	0.52	0.76	0.74	0.74	0.76	0.52	0.52	0.52	0.52
R8	0.71	0.74	0.56	0.74	0.76	0.37	0.76	0.56	0.54
R9	0.69	0.91	0.71	0.87	0.56	0.37	0.56	0.37	0.73
R10	0.64	0.64	0.64	0.64	0.82	0.64	0.76	0.98	1
R11	0.71	0.73	0.72	0.73	0.72	0.54	0.7	0.6	0.67
R12	0.81	0.71	0.96	0.83	0.96	0.76	0.76	0.84	0.8
R13	0.72	0.72	0.72	0.87	0.72	0.94	0.56	0.4	0.72
R14	1	0.98	0.98	0.98	0.98	0.96	1	0.9	0.96
R15	0.67	0.37	0.6	0.53	0.76	0.35	0.53	0.72	0.7
R16	0.52	0.76	0.49	0.74	0.59	0.38	0.69	0.56	0.4
R17	0.56	0.73	0.8	0.69	0.58	0.56	0.56	0.54	1
R18	0.49	0.69	0.76	0.35	0.78	0.47	0.35	0.78	0.76
R19	0.35	0.52	0.71	0.92	0.52	0.35	0.54	0.35	0.49
R20	0.58	0.74	0.58	0.76	0.98	0.73	0.89	0.58	0.98

Source: Own elaboration

2.2 *Theoretical assessment of the concept (phase 2)*

Another essential aspect of the instrument creation process was verifying if all members of the research team had properly understood the theoretical concept around which all the indicators would be established or operationalised. Although it was a concept that had already been theoretically substantiated by the author (Díez-Ripollés, 2011, 2013), the team was asked if it was precise and clear, by means of an e-mail message that was individually and collectively answered by the research team members. 65 per cent of the researchers (13 out of 20) replied by asking something else, 6 individually and 7 collectively; the remaining 35 per cent did not raise any objection to the proposed concept. In spite of being deemed a concise and clear definition, it led to doubts regarding: whether it was a too optimistic definition, since it aimed to prevent the subject from committing a crime or to avoid being discovered; if this was the case, if such goals were achieved, anybody would accept a socially exclusionary control system; vague in relation to the "materially" concept; exceedingly normative; and confusing as to whether the exclusionary character comes from adopting measures that make reintegration of the subject into society difficult or impossible, or else by the mere imposition of a criminal penalty. It was concluded that the exclusionary character was caused by adopting measures that hindered the reintegration of the subject into society, thus forcing those in conflict with penal law to follow the path of crime, since they do not have the possibility to be reintegrated into society. This is way the criminal sanction is identified with the simple exclusion from society. Later on, all doubts – after being systematised –were discussed and clarified in a group meeting, until consensus was reached.

2.3 Operationalisation of the concept broken down into pools (phase 3)

Once the theoretical doubts had been cleared, the concept was operationalised so that it could be measured in the nine exclusion pools that have already been mentioned. Each one of them would include a significant number of indicators in order to cover all aspects of the dimension, either as real punitive rules or practices, i.e., that are effectively applied or the implementation of which is considered in the Western developed countries. An indicator formulated as a rule represents a legal standard which usually, though not always, is included in the criminal law and establishes certain consequences for certain behaviours or situations related with crime control, like, for example: the enshrinement of death penalty in the Criminal Code. For its part, punitive practices measure the way in which the different social agencies effectively react to behaviours or situations related with crime control, whether or not in agreement with the provisions established by the law. For example: applying the death penalty to individuals belonging to certain ethnic minorities to a much greater extent than to others groups.

In order to facilitate the creation of indicators, the coordinating group divided the research group into nine working subgroups of two or three individuals, according to the specialisation and expertise proved at each dimension, and established the methodological criteria to build those indicators so that they may truly represent the exclusion concept; in other words, to be valid. And these were: (1) the diverse rules or practices chosen for each pool should be drafted to admit only dichotomous replies (of "Yes" or "No"); (2) an effort should be made to include a good number of rules and practices –so that later on the best could be chosen-, they should be as expressive as possible and without there being any overlapping among them; (3) the indicators should be drafted in the same sense, that is, with the "yes" reply meaning exclusion, and the "no", inclusion; (4) an effort should be made to include both rules and practices in each pool; (5) and they had to be drafted in English.

Likewise, the coordinating team established a schedule of successive working meetings for groups and subgroups. The former, a total of 18, underwent a critical review of the rules and practices proposed for each pool by each subgroup, and the go-ahead to those finally selected was given through the assent of the whole team. General meetings were established as a time for reflection, in order to reinterpret – from different perspectives – each one of the items that were being built. Such work resulted in the identification of 278 punitive rules and practices distributed among the nine groups.

2.4 *Selection of indicators (phase 4)*

Taking into account the large volume of resulting indicators, it was agreed they would be reduced in order to obtain a handy and manageable instrument. It was decided that the way to carry this out would be through the implementation of three selection criteria of the indicator, which would assess its: completeness, which expresses the special relevance of the information supplied or its importance; extension, ensuring that the information does not deal with aspects that are exceedingly particular or specific; and ease of access, whereby the information is expected to be relatively simple to obtain.

This task was only carried out by the four members of the coordinating team individually. They filled in a questionnaire that was designed for such purpose, by scoring 1 when the criterion was fulfilled, and 0 when it could not be deemed fulfilled. Each indicator could obtain a maximum score of 12 points, if all team members gave 1 point to each one of the three criteria referred to.

Once the first questionnaire had been sent and, in view of the results, it was decided to discard those indicators with 4 points or less, thus reducing the instrument to 221 indicators. Then another round was carried out, which improved the selection criteria by introducing two new ones: the item's capacity to discriminate among countries and the clarity of the wording, i.e., that the indicator be easily understood.

Once the results from this round were obtained, those items with scores of 4 and 3 points were selected, and items with 1 or 0 points in completeness or in discrimination were removed, since the team considered that these two criteria were essential. Thanks to this procedure, the instrument was reduced to 202 items. Subsequently and for a period of one month, the coordinating team reviewed all the pools in successive group meetings, starting with those with a larger number of indicators. The goal was to perform a detailed review of the extension of those items with accumulated scoring that had not been excluded in the previously described situations, but that could be removed or recast since they dealt with topics that were too specific or repeated. Such task was carried out while at the same time seeking a balance in the distribution of rules and practices. As shown in the figure below, once the selection process was finished, 76 items were discarded, many of them from pools 1, 5, 6 and 7, thus obtaining an instrument of 126 items made up of 79 rules (63 per cent) and 47 practices (37 per cent).

It should be noted that throughout the whole 'cleaning' process, the number of rules was always higher than the number of practices, even though the progressive reduction of both kept a certain proportion. As regards the final distribution of rules and practices in each pool (see Table 4.3), as was to be expected, for most of the dimensions, the rules were higher -in percentage terms- than the practices, particularly in pools 2 and 7, where the gap was greater, as opposed to pools 6 and 8, whose distribution was 50/50.

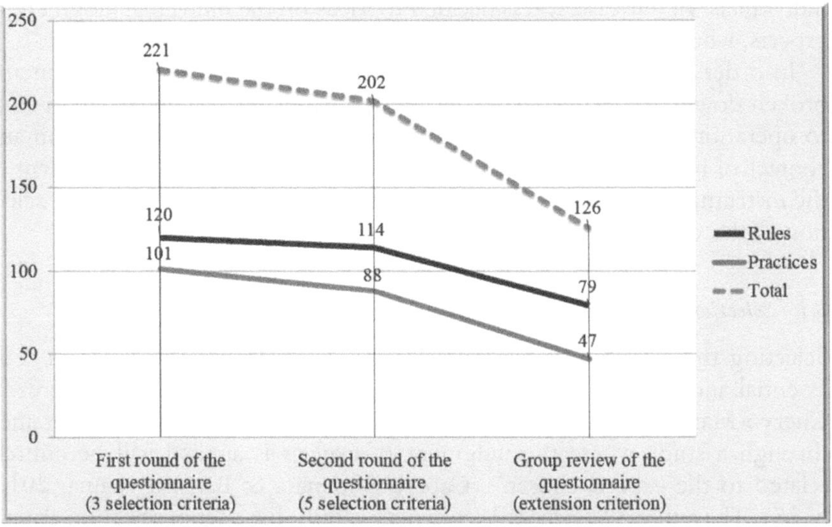

Figure 4.2 Number of rules and practices according to selection procedures and criteria

Table 4.3 Number of rules and practices selected per pool

Pools	*Rules*	*%*	*Practices*	*%*	*Total*	*%*
Pool 1	8	66.67	4	33.33	12	100
Pool 2	11	73.33	4	26.67	15	100
Pool 3	9	64.29	5	35.71	14	100
Pool 4	7	53.85	6	46.15	13	100
Pool 5	13	68.42	6	31.58	19	100
Pool 6	6	50.00	6	50.00	12	100
Pool 7	9	75.00	3	25.00	12	100
Pool 8	7	50.00	7	50.00	14	100
Pool 9	9	60.00	6	40.00	15	100
Total	79	63	47	37	126	100

Source: Own elaboration

3 Validation of the instrument

Once the instrument was established with 126 indicators, the validation process of its content was engaged through the judgment of international experts. Prior to this, it was translated into English and then reviewed by a Spanish-speaking British woman who specialised in law and criminology.

Content validity is a methodology widely used to know if the indicators of a measurement instrument are relevant and representative of the baseline theoretical construct (Ding & Hershberger, 2002). Such validation is usually carried out through the judgment of experts, in other words, via the assessment carried out by very qualified and reputed scientific and professional individuals. In our case, it was decided to focus on the individual judgment of experts, where each expert validated the instrument's items individually.

In order to carry out said task, a rigorous procedure was undertaken and broken down into four stages. This allowed to arrange the information so as to operationalise and achieve efficiency in the process, namely: selection and contact of international experts (stage 1), design and online management of the instrument (stage 2), statistical analysis of results (stage 3) and final selection of the strongest indicators (stage 4).

3.1 Selection and contact of international experts (stage 1)

Selecting the experts that will take part in the instrument's validation is an essential and critical aspect of the methodological process (Escobar-Pérez & Cuervo-Martínez, 2008, pp. 28–29), since "the quality of the results obtained through a study where the judgment of experts is applied will be entirely related to the experts chosen" (Cabero Almenara & Barroso Osuna, 2013, p. 28). The authors Skjong & Wentworth (2000) list a set of selection criteria that should be taken into account: the academic and practical background, their reputation within the community, their motivation and availability to participate, as well as their impartiality. At the same time, the methodological requirements proper to targeted qualitative sampling added another two criteria: to achieve a theoretical saturation thanks to the creation of prototype expert categories; and geographical representativeness, since the instrument was designed for its implementation in the Western developed countries.

Taking into account such methodological requirements, the goal was to choose experts in 20 countries from Central Europe, Eastern Europe, Northern Europe, Southern Europe and English-speaking countries in and out of Europe. Finally, the participation of 18 of them was achieved (except in Austria and Sweden), namely: Belgium, Canada, Denmark, Finland, France, Germany, Hungary, Ireland, Italy, the Netherlands, New Zealand, Poland, Portugal, Romania, Spain, Switzerland, England and United States.

Efforts were also made to ensure that: experts where academics and professionals who held a doctorate (PhD)[2] and had extensive knowledge and experience (over 10 years) in the field of crime prevention or prosecution; to have a balance – as far as possible – between academics and professionals, gender and political orientation; and to have diversity according to the pool's specialisation.

Methodological debate on the adequate number of experts for validation through the judgment of experts is very varied. Some authors suggest a range of 2 to 20 experts (Gable & Wolf, 1993; Grant & Davis, 1997), while others

2 Initially, the requisite of having a PhD was established for both groups (academic and professional individuals). However, during the selection process it was decided that the professional group would not be required to comply said condition, in order to increase the possibilities of finding people with a highly practical profile.

suggest a lower amount of around 10 (Hyrkas et al., 2003). In our case we decided to increase considerably the number of experts, so as to facilitate management of a very wide-ranging instrument, achieve the saturation of experts' prototype and obtain an adequate geographical representation.

The targeted sampling was carried out smoothly since they were individuals with a great reputation in the academic and/or professional field, whose experience largely exceeded 20 years. The coordinating team contacted those experts who met the requirements and asked them to take part in the project. This was carried out via an e-mail with an attached circular letter including the necessary information with regard to their performance within the research. If they accepted to participate, such letter described two key actions that were required of them: to supply the name of three experts that were motivated and available for the validation of the questionnaire; and the commitment of the former to validate a questionnaire, once the group of experts formed by the provided names had done it. In this way, the first group of experts facilitated the location and selection of the second group of experts, by using a non-probabilistic and targeted snowball sampling, since it was necessary to identify potential experts who, in the case of non-academic professionals, where more difficult to find. In other words, the sampling worked as a chain based on the help that the first group of experts provided to the coordinating team in order to identify and locate the required profiles.

As the experts of the first group accepted to participate, a brief online questionnaire was sent to them in order to collect diverse personal and professional information, so as to verify that they effectively met the selection criteria. Thanks to this method 58 experts were located, out of which 28 accepted to participate. As regards the individual and professional features of the group, it was found that: 71 per cent of them were men, a percentage which is consistent with the usual distribution of the senior academic population; they were, on average, 58 years old and had a standard deviation of 7.4 years, since at the time of fulfilling the questionnaire the youngest was 42 and the oldest, 71; they were mainly of Spanish, German, Swiss, Polish, British, US, Italian, Portuguese, Belgian and Dutch origin (all of them with a percentage of 7.1); with a progressive political orientation (92.3 per cent); teachers (85.7 per cent) who had developed –or were developing- their work in the academic field (71 per cent); with the expert who had the widest professional experience in such field encompassing 21.4 years (vs. 19.2 of the one in the professional field); whose research was of empirical and theoretical nature, and was therefore a predominantly mixed profile (75 per cent); they were experts in more than one pool (90 per cent of cases), and specifically, 60.7 per cent was an expert in three or less, while 39.2 per cent, in six or less and 3.5 per cent in more than six; and the greatest specialisation focused on pools 9 and 4 (13.9 per cent and 11.9 per cent, respectively).

The first group supplied a number of experts somewhat lower than the 84 that were expected. After the refusal of some of them to collaborate, we had 59 experts to form the second group. In order to comply with the pre-established quota, the coordinating team sought – usually through the internet – experts with the required profile. Thanks to this technique, 12 new individuals were added to the previous 59, thus obtaining a participation of 84.5 per cent, or 71 experts. As regards the individual and professional features of the second group, it was found that: the distribution of experts per gender was very balanced (51 per cent women and 49 per cent men); the youngest was 33 years and the oldest 65, with an average of 44 years and a standard deviation of 8.4 years; the questionnaire was fulfilled by experts from 18 countries; 79 per cent of the experts were considered to be progressive; they used to be teachers (71.8 per cent); that had developed – or were developing – their work in the academic field (50.7 per cent), followed by those who had a mixed (40.8 per cent) and professional (8.5 per cent) profile; with more work experience in the academic field than in the professional one (an average of 14 years vs. 10 years); whose research was predominantly mixed or theoretical-practical (63.4 per cent). They were specialists in more than one pool: particularly, 81.4 per cent was specialised in three pools or less; and 18.5 per cent of them in six pools or less, especially of pools 3 and 6 (22.9 per cent and 12.8 per cent, respectively).

Once the personal and professional characteristics of the selected groups had been analyzed, the information was incorporated into the prototypical categories predefined by the team. This is what literature calls the expert's 'biogram' profile (Cabero Almenara & Barroso Osuna, 2013, p. 28) and its prior setting-up reduces the possibility of introducing methodological biases in the instrument's validation, since an indicator may be validated, at the same time, by two experts with completely different profiles, thus achieving a greater reliability and saturation of the sample.

With this is mind, 18 categories were set up, as shown in Figure 4.3, and divided into two axes of political orientation: conservative or progressive. Within each of them, several things were considered: the expert's academic, professional or mixed character; his/her experience in theoretical or empirical research, or both; his/her specialisation as regards the pool and his/her gender. The criteria for including the expert in the categories established ad hoc were implemented by taking into account if the case met the condition or not. The field of specialisation and the gender were not included in the formula and were accessory in the counting. It was, nevertheless, taken into account subsequently to balance the sample, allowing for an adequate distribution thereof.

In the first group, category 11 – corresponding to a progressive academic profile, with experience in theoretical and empirical research – was the most represented one, with 50 per cent of the cases, followed by category 14 (25 per cent) and category 12 (14.2 per cent). Only one expert was included in categories 1, 3 and 18 (3.6 per cent respectively), and there was no representation for the remainder. Again, in the second group, category 11 was the most frequent (28.2 per cent), followed by category 14 (21.1 per cent), 12 (8.5 per cent) and categories 15 and 5 (7 per cent). Presence was somewhat reduced

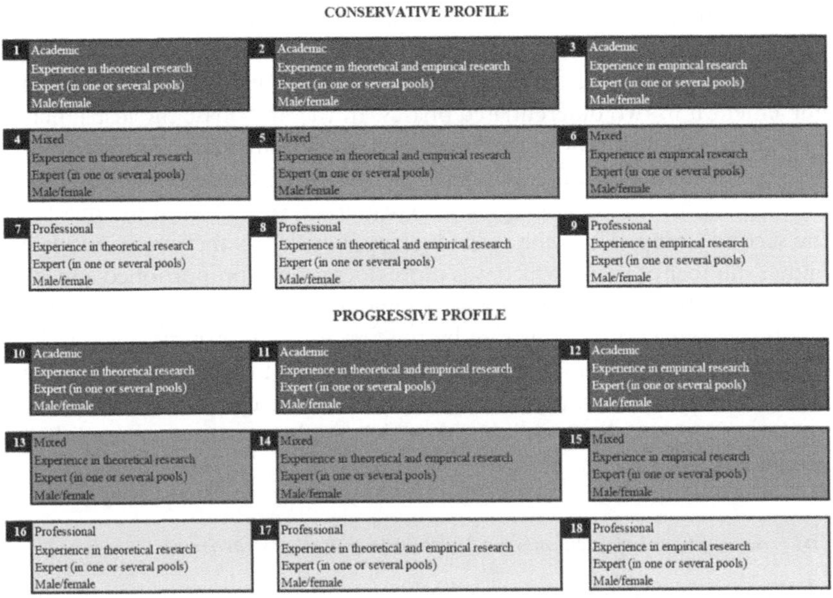

Figure 4.3 Selection and inclusion of experts in prototypical categories

in categories 3 and 13 (5.6 per cent and 4.2 per cent, respectively), followed by categories 10 and 17 (2.8 per cent) and, very occasionally (1.4 per cent), in categories 1, 2, 6, 8 and 18. Some experts (5.6 per cent) could not be classified in any category, since their political orientation or the type of research they performed were unknown.

3.2 *Design and online management of the instrument (stage 2)*

Content validation was carried out in compliance with a series of methodological criteria, both in the design or planning of its content and in the way it is managed. As regards the instrument's design, determination of the number of questions, their order and drafting, they were implemented by taking into account the following guidelines (Sierra-Bravo, 2008, pp. 316–317): to include a pre-established number of questions to prevent it from being exceedingly long (i); that such questions were arranged in a logical and visually attractive way (ii); and with very specific procedural instructions (iii); and the items of which would be set out at random (iv).

(i) Including a reduced number of items

An exceedingly long instrument can be tiresome and monotonous at the time of filling it out (Sierra-Bravo, 2008, p. 317). This will reduce the respondent's motivation and will have a negative influence in the response rate. In general terms, no more than half an hour should be needed to complete it (Fowler, 1993, p. 103). In order to find a solution for this situation, and taking into account the size of the baseline instrument (126 items), it was decided to implement it in two differentiated phases. In the first phase the instrument of 126 items – broken down into three parts of 42 items – was exclusively delivered to the second group, i. e., three questionnaire models were designed to be delivered to the three subgroups of experts resulting from the division of the second group. Thus, the second group, which was the largest, validated a higher number of items, which was more operational, proportioned and statistically consistent. In the second validation phase, the number of indicators that had to be validated – in this case by the first group of experts – was reduced to 65, which was still a large number of indicators to be validated by a single expert. For this reason, two questionnaires were designed: one with 33 items and another one with 32, and they were delivered to two subgroups of the first group, with 14 experts each.

(ii) Arrangement of questions in a logical and visually attractive way

The questionnaires were structured in three parts. The first one had two initial sheets containing the objective of the research, its theoretical concept and pools, as well as the instructions to fill them in. The second part included the total number of indicators to be validated. Each item had to be answered before proceeding to the next page. Capital letters and colors were used to highlight certain key words, while the headings of each set of items were repeated every so often in order to remind the scoring criteria. In the third part there was a brief questionnaire with personal and professional questions (applied only to the second group of experts), followed by an open field for comments and a final message of appreciation (last page). Personal information was required after validation of the items, for two reasons: some questions could be embarrassing or difficult to answer (like, for example, age and political orientation) and this could even condition the emotional state of the respondent before starting. Besides, it was a relief or escape after the concentration required in the main central part of the questionnaire.

(iii) Specific instructions for the procedure

The purpose of the research and the theoretical concept were explained with two illustrative examples. In the sheet with the pools and instructions of the procedure there was an indication on how to score the clarity, relevance and appropriateness of the items. In other words, this was intended to ensure compliance of the methodological process which suggests "to elaborate on both the pools and the indicators being measured by each item of the test" (Escobar-Pérez & Cuervo-Martínez, 2008, p. 30).

As may be seen in the figure hereinbelow, experts from the second group had to rate in a double Likert scale (from 1 to 5) the clarity and relevance of

	CLARITY					ITEM RELEVANCE WITH THE EXCLUSION DIMENSION				
	1	2	3	4	5	1	2	3	4	5
11. Discriminatory street police interventions (stop and search, arrests, frisks/body searches...) targeting specific groups occur regularly.	○	○	○	○	○	○	○	○	○	○
12. More than 50% of cities with population over 25,000 have fixed CCTV cameras in public places.	○	○	○	○	○	○	○	○	○	○
13. Police arrests under legal criteria which are not strictly defined are permitted.	○	○	○	○	○	○	○	○	○	○
14. Police arrests for minor offences not punished with custodial penalties are allowed.	○	○	○	○	○	○	○	○	○	○
15. Reversal of the burden of proof is legally envisaged for a significant number of offences.	○	○	○	○	○	○	○	○	○	○

Figure 4.4 Questionnaire model of the second group

1. At least 30% of all pre-trial detainees are finally acquitted or their cases are dismissed.

	1	2	3	4	5
CLARITY	○	○	○	○	○
Item RELEVANCE for measuring social exclusion	○	○	○	○	○
Item APPROPRIATENESS for being included in the pool "Preventive intervention"	○	○	○	○	○

Figure 4.5 Questionnaire model of the first group

each item. In such scale, designed on the basis of the Dunn protocol (1999 et al.), 1 meant poor clarity or relevance of the indicator to explain or measure social exclusion, while 5 was the maximum score.The questionnaire model of the first group was very similar to that of the second group (see figure below), except for the inclusion of a third criterion: the appropriateness of the item to the predefined pools. Nevertheless, unlike the second group, these experts received, together with the questionnaire, an additional e-mail with a circular letter explaining the progress of the project and the next steps to be taken.

(iv) Randomness of questions

The random arrangement of questions in the questionnaire prevents the "halo" or "contagion" effect – which happens when questions whose answers may influence one another are placed together – from occurring (Sierra-Bravo, 2008, pp. 317–318). Upon remittance of the questionnaire to the second group, the classification of experts in one subgroup or another one was determined by the order of arrival of his/her name, thus ensuring randomness of experts in each questionnaire. However, questions were not distributed at random in each instrument, but they were rather distributed by pools, successively. This aspect was improved when the questionnaire was passed onto the first group: efforts were made not only to try that personal and professional variables of the expert in each subgroup were as balanced as possible to achieve maximum extra-group homogeneity and intra-group heterogeneity, but items of the partial questionnaires were also distributed at random.

In relation to the way in which the questionnaire was managed, it was decided to implement it online or by e-mail for both groups of experts. All questionnaire models were created and sent through the Qualtrics platform, since it provides a professional and specialised service for this type of methodology. The questionnaire sent by e-mail offered many advantages (López-Roldan & Fachelli, 2015, p. 15), and it was the most adequate method for our research, namely: it is quick, inexpensive, allows simultaneous access to far places (a particularly useful aspect, given the geographical representation of the sample), avoids any influence from the interviewer's action, enables to carry out a comprehensive follow-up of the questionnaire's fulfilment status (open, on-going or finalised), measures the minutes spent in completing it, allows to send reminders, facilitates systematisation of the information received, thanks to its exportation to different databases and self-generates statistical reports.

Likewise, the Qualtrics platform, as opposed to other existing, less specialised programs, had its own e-mail server that sent electronic mails by using the e-mail addresses of the main researchers, even if they had been drawn up and supervised by other members of the coordinating team. This feature favored constant communication before, during and after completing the questionnaire. Besides, this avoided distractions in the communication channel, because it was always the same interlocutors (the main researchers) who sent and signed the messages, being closest to the expert and representing the greatest authority. Another advantage was that those cases refused as spam were minimal, since the e-mail addresses were "trustworthy" or recognised by the e-mail server of the experts.

Thanks to this method, there was a high response rate in each phase: 84.5 per cent for experts of the second group (37 per cent in part 1; 32 per cent in part 2 and 31 per cent in part 3) and 92.8 per cent for those of the first group (in both parts of the questionnaire). The first group was the only one that carried out this task within the established period (two months), as opposed to the second group, that greatly exceeded it (they took some 15 months). As regards the time needed to complete the questionnaire, both groups took, on average, 20 to 30 minutes. Once this task was finished, a participation certificate – together with a present – were sent to them by post and by electronic means.

3.3 Statistical analysis of results (stage 3)

After each round of the questionnaire, analyses were carried out from both a quantitative (scores) and a qualitative (comments of the experts) perspective. From a quantitative point of view, special attention was given to the results that started to be drawn from the tests, since they were closely related to the content validity or, in other words, optimal statistical results ensured the items' validity and reliability (Escobar-Pérez & Cuervo-Martínez, 2008, p. 30). To this end, several tests were carried out by using basic statistical parameters (mean, mode, median, standard deviation, minimum and maximum ranges) and inter-judge reliability tests in both groups, particularly Aiken's V validation coefficient (Aiken, 1980, 1985).

There are several ways to assess content validity through an agreement among judges. However, Aiken's V coefficient is the most adequate for its determination, as opposed to other similar ones that are commonly used, as the Index of Agreement (IA) and the Binomial Test (BT). Its simplicity of calculation (Merino-Soto & Livia-Segovia, 2009, p. 169), its capacity to obtain values that can be compared according to the size of the sample of judges (Cordón, 2015, pp. 2–8), and the possibility to assess its statistical significance (Escurra, 1988, p. 107) represent its main advantages.

Aiken's V is regarded as:

> The ratio of a data obtained from the maximum addition in the difference of possible values. It may be calculated over the assessments of a group of judges with relation to an item or as the assessments of a judge with respect to 1.
>
> (Escurra, 1988, p. 107)

Its size includes a range of 0.00 up to 1.00 (Merino-Soto & Livia-Segovia, 2009, p. 169). In this way, obtaining a 1 – which is the greatest possible magnitude – shows a perfect agreement among the evaluated judges and a smallest variability in their answers and, conversely, a low coefficient – lower than 0.50 – means a lack of agreement among the judges. Formerly, the Aiken's V coefficient obtained was compared with a table of values (Cordón, 2015, p. 4). Nevertheless, years later, Penfield & Miller (2004) introduced in the equation confidence intervals to determine the probability of occurrence of an event, taking into account the confidence level chosen by the researcher (Cordón, 2015, p. 4). According to Merino-Soto and Livia-Segovia "as the size of the sample increases, the range of the interval shall be smaller and, therefore, calculating coefficient V will be more accurate" (2009, p. 171). In our case, the confidence interval was very adequate (0.95), the cut-off validation coefficient was high (items with Aiken's V = 0 and/or > 0.70) and the sample size, very large, as compared to the one generally used for this methodology. All these aspects improved the test's accuracy.

By applying this statistical method to the second group of experts, 81 indicators – out of 126 – with an Aiken's V higher than 0.70 were validated in the relevance criterion. This criterion was deemed predominant vs. the one of clarity, because those items that were unclear could be reformulated with a more precise drafting in the second round of the questionnaire to the first group of experts. Out of the 81 validated items, 20 were validated with an Aiken's V in the 0.70–0.74 interval, 19 in the medium 0.75–0.79 interval and, nearly half of them (42), with an Aiken's V equal to or higher than 0.80. It should be noted that 62 of the 81 validated items for relevance were also validated as regards clarity and, particularly, 62 of them obtained 0.70 and over, 13 of them, 0.60–0.69, and 6 of them, 0.50–0.59. All in all, the results brought to light the high validity and reliability of the proposed indicators upon obtaining 64 per cent of the total (81 of 126) with a coefficient greater than 0.70 in relevance.

A qualitative review was conducted on the comments made by experts in the mentioned open field that was included in the questionnaire. In the first place, those comments that were just congratulations on the work performed were discarded (two comments) and the remainder (22 comments) focused on the following topics: confusion regarding the baseline theoretical definition, lack of clarity issues in the drafting of the item and its measurement, and difficulties to understand the task required of the expert. As regards the first topic, it was considered that some indicators could lead to exclusion, but also to inclusion. As for the second, the comments were that: some questions were long and difficult to understand; the negative wording used ("there is a lack of", "there is no", etc.) made the items less clear; certain terms could be vague in different countries and their translation did not have the exact same ring for the English-speaking individual; some items seemed to measure two aspects in the same item, that is, they appeared to be double-barreled questions, which could affect their adequate measurement, as well as the fact of using certain percentages instead of others. Finally, in some cases it was not properly understood whether the expert's opinion on the items was required or if answers should reflect the reality of their country.

In view of the comments, we noticed that the lack of clarity both in the wording of some indicators -due to their translation or complexity-, and the explanation of the research objective and the procedure to be followed by the expert, was the main problem detected. In order to solve it, three essential tasks were carried out: to reduce the volume of validated indicators by reinforcing the eligible selection criteria, to re-write those items that were unclear but could be included in the following phase and to send a circular letter with a detailed description, and a reminder, of the research objectives and its progress. The first two tasks were implemented with the participation of the whole research group that, in successive meetings, established the following selection criteria: to maintain those items with 0.70 or higher scoring in clarity; to consider -as the case may be- those items with 0.70 or higher in relevance and over 0.54 in clarity; to remove items that were similar to others, i. e., that measure very similar aspects; to maintain a similar number of indicators in each pool; and to find a balance between rules and practices and among the pools themselves. Thanks to this process, the questionnaire was reduced from 81 to 65 items, that were distributed in nine pools (with 5 to 11 items in each of them), 12 of which were rewritten to improve their clarity in group sessions of the research team. In short, a selection had been made of those items that were the most valid to be delivered to the first group of experts.

3.4 *Final selection of indicators: the final instrument (stage 4)*

Once the questionnaire was completed by the first group of experts, we noted that validity as regards clarity increased in comparison with the previous round. As shown in the table hereinunder, in this occasion there was no indicator below 0.63, and therefore those items that had been rewritten no longer posed comprehension problems. Besides, the number of indicators between intervals 0.75–0.79, and 0.80 and higher, increased considerably: they went from 41 items in the first round (25+16) to 57 (45+12). These results showed that the method used to clarify the most problematic items had produced good results. On the other hand, we noted a loss of validity in the relevance criterion, since 8 of the 65 items that had previously obtained a coefficient equal to or higher than 0.70 where now classified in the 0.63–0.69 interval. In other words, such items had obtained a larger consensus in the second group than in the first one. As regards appropriateness to the pool, there was only one item – with a coefficient of 0.35 – that was not validated.

However, the 65 indicators obtained out of the final validation were still a very high number to achieve the management and dissemination of the instrument. Besides, eight of them no longer passed the 0.70 cut-off limit. It was therefore decided to establish new methodological criteria, very similar to the

Table 4.4 Scoring of the 65-item-instrument according to the group and to criteria of clarity, relevance and appropriateness to the pool

Aiken's V intervals	*Clarity (first group)*	*Clarity (second group)*	*Relevance (first group)*	*Relevance (second group)*	*Appropriateness to the pool (second group)*
0.80 and higher	25	45	41	35	56
0.75–0.79	16	12	14	13	5
0.70–0.74	12	1	10	7	2
0.63–0.69	7	7	0	8	1
Not validated	5	0	0	0	1
TOTAL	**65**	**65**	**65**	**65**	**64**

Source: Own elaboration

ones set in the previous reduction of the instrument but, in this occasion, with two additional criteria: to obtain a number of items of around 35 but, in any case, they would not exceed 40; and to ensure a minimum of three items by pool (between rules and practices).

In order to carry out the screening, the research team analyzed the first two items of each pool with the highest score in Aiken's V as regards relevance, since predictably a greater agreement would be reached on them, while validity increased again regarding the item's relevance, upon exclusion of those below 0.70. In the second round, the team reviewed the third item with highest scores and, in the third round, the remainder. With this procedure a final instrument of 39 items was achieved (see Díez-Ripollés & García-España, 2019, pp. 19–24), 26 of which were rules and 13 were practices. All of them had coefficients that were equal to or higher than 0.70 in the three criteria and, in many cases, they exceeded 0.80 in clarity (31 items), relevance (30 items) and appropriateness to the pool (38 items). In summary, efforts were made to ensure that, by implementing a methodological procedure similar to the one adopted during the whole project to reduce the number of items, the final amount would consist of the most robust indicators to measure social exclusion. The success of this methodological procedure was mostly due to the high number of items that were validated in both phases, given that such high level of baseline validation provided flexibility to the research team at the time of choosing among them, as well as establishing selection criteria that were ever more varied and demanding.

4 The application of the instrument

Once the instrument was developed and validated, it was applied in five European countries (Germany, Spain, Italy, England and Poland) and two North American states (New York and California). Although the following chapters will deal exhaustively with the results obtained in each territory and those methodological issues arising as a result of its implementation, this section briefly describes the general process followed. The first step was to carry out a pilot project in Spain. The objective was to check whether the method designed for the collection and analysis of information was valid and reliable and, therefore, reproducible in the rest of the countries. The pilot consisted on the design and use of protocols with standardised fields designed ad hoc to collect data from different sources (primary and secondary) that would allow verifying in dichotomous terms the existence – or not – of each indicator, as well as identifying possible biases associated with the methodological criteria already used and referred to above. To this end, the team of researchers was divided into pairs that, independently, worked on the same indicators of the questionnaire and then checked – in group meetings – if they had achieved the same results and if the collection method developed was reliable.

After completion of the pilot, the instrument was implemented internationally in the above-mentioned countries. The same collection protocol was used as in the pilot, although on this occasion each pair of researchers was assigned a country to which to administer the questionnaire. This decision was based on: the greater workload that the research team had to assume, since each couple had to answer all the items of the questionnaire; the difficulty of collecting data in countries with different criminal political contexts, in particular certain legal concepts; lack of knowledge or difficult access to sources of information (especially primary sources); and the language difference. However, many of these difficulties – and others of a methodological nature that arose in practice – were discussed and addressed by the research team in numerous group meetings until the completion of the questionnaires of all countries. Once the protocols were finalised, they were sent to international experts from each sample country to review whether both the methodological steps adopted to collect the information, and the response given to the item, were correct.

The most important methodological difficulty, which could not be corrected by the team after repeated attempts, was to respond to item 52 ("In more than 80 per cent of cases, life imprisonment is imposed on ethnic or racial minorities, or the poor"). Considering that once the indicator was applied, it did not achieve good results in terms of access to the required data, it was replaced by rule 46 ("A minimum of more than 20 years is required to be eligible for a review of life imprisonment") complying with the methodological selection criteria mentioned in section 2.4. This was possible thanks to the high number of items validated with an Aiken V higher than 0.70 in suitability (46 had 0.77) in almost all the baskets of the questionnaire and that could be exchanged for similar ones if those selected to make up the final instrument presented problems in their application. That is, the difficulty of access to the data modified the originally validated instrument by one item, motivating that all countries had to fill out a new protocol for this indicator and that item 52 has been omitted in the next chapters.

As for the statistical procedure developed to estimate the position of each country or state on a numerical exclusion scale from 0 to 10, or from 0 to 100 (in which 0 is less exclusion and 10/100 is a lot of exclusion) was based on the sum of the weights, that is, on the coefficients obtained in Aiken V for suitability of each indicator, handling different estimation parameters. These are: the maximum points to be obtained in case of having all the affirmative answers or total sum of yeses, the points that do not add up because the item has been answered negatively, and those that were left uncounted for not having responded to the indicator, that is, the lost data. The figure below shows the calculation template used by the research team. As can be seen, in the left column appears the list of items specifying whether they are rules or practices, as well as their weight or V of Aiken in suitability.

The fourth column indicated by the arrow was the only one that the researcher had to modify to transcribe the results obtained in the protocols. If the answer had been a yes, a 1 should be imputed, if it was negative a 0, and if the data was not known, an X. To the right of the column to be filled in by the researcher was the "sum of weights" (in the fifth column). In this, marking 1

	FINAL INSTRUMENT (39 ITEMS)	AIKEN'S V SUITABILITY	TO BE FILLED IN BY THE RESEARCHER	SUM OF WEIGHTS	On a scale of 10	On a scale of 100	MARGINS OF ERROR OPTION 1	On a scale of 10	On a scale of 100
		WEIGHT					27.87	8.46	84.63
				26.03	7.91	79.05	1.84		
R	93. Nationals sentenced to imprisonment for any criminal offence are not eligible for welfare benefits for a certain period after having served their sentences.	0.96	X	0.96			0.96		
R	92. Those sentenced to up to 3 years of imprisonment for any criminal offence are not eligible for public housing for a certain period after having served their sentences.	0.96	1	0.96			0.00		
P	107. The media regularly disclose the full names, current addresses or pictures of ex-felons.	0.94	1	0.94			0.00		
R	36. Default imprisonment is the sole alternative to non-payment of a fine.	0.94	0	0.00			0.00		
R	117. Youth justice provides custodial sanctions of over 10 years.	0.94	1	0.94			0.00		
R	86. Those sentenced to up 3 years of imprisonment for any criminal offence may be deprived of the right to vote for over 4 years after serving their sentences.	0.92	1	0.92			0.00		
R	101. The criminal records of any citizen are legally accessible through internet.	0.92	1	0.92			0.00		
R	88. Legally resident foreigners may be deported if they receive a custodial sentence up to one year or a non custodial sentence.	0.92	1	0.92			0.00		
P	99. Private employers which are not related to private security companies or to those working with children or vulnerable adults are entitled to request information about criminal records to potential employees.	0.88	0	0.00			0.00		
P	126. Alien minors are deported because of an offence.	0.90	1	0.90			0.00		
R	91. Those sentenced to up to 3 years of imprisonment are prohibited from doing certain jobs not connected with their offences or with law enforcement for a period of more than 5 years their sentence has been completed.	0.88	1	0.88			0.00		
R	1. Any person may be arrested for repeated street begging.	0.88	1	0.88			0.00		
R	3. At its discretion, the police may enforce restrictions on specific individuals to access some public spaces (parks, squares, streets...).	0.88	X	0.00			0.88		
R	43. Life imprisonment without release is legally available.	0.87	1	0.87			0.00		
R	120. Minors' criminal records keep legal effects after reaching the age of majority.	0.87	1	0.87			0.00		
P	11. Discriminatory street police interventions (stop and search, arrests, frisks/body searches...) targeting specific groups occur regularly.	0.85	1	0.85			0.00		

Figure 4.6 RIMES final instrument calculation template

added the integer coefficient while if 0 had been entered 0 was added. The X, or "I don't know", also added 0. The total sum was shown in the top box of the fifth column. Thus, a country that scored 26.03 points out of a possible maximum of 32.93 (the sum of all the items in the questionnaire) allowed us to place it in a position of 7.91 on a scale of 10 and 79.05 per cent out of 100 percent.

However, there were two items (marked with X) for which we did not find the required data and it was necessary to establish margins of error. Here it is necessary to clarify that we are not facing a probabilistic sampling in which these margins are applied on the known finite population because we hardly have cases. Therefore, multiple imputation and regression tests were not used, but a statistical method adjusted to the result of a questionnaire playing for it with margins of variation. For example, if we have marked two items with an X whose weights are 0.88 and 0.96 and, on the other hand, the sum of known items is 25.90, we know that a maximum of 1.84 exclusion could be added to 25.90. That is, 25.90 is what we already have of exclusion, but it is likely to reach 27.74 points (25.90 + 1.84), which would place the country in a position of 8.40 on a scale of 10, and 84% exclusion over 100.

The template allows you to compare at a glance the difference in points and percentages between the "real scales" and the estimated ones with the margins of error. In this example there is a margin of error of 5.56 per cent between the two (84–78.4 = 5.56 per cent), or in other words, that country could be 5.56 per cent more exclusionary than it is. We set the percentage of variation that we consider reasonable at 5 per cent because it is the most common in probability sampling, which implied not stopping answering more than two items.

5 Methodological limitations

The great complexity and scale of the project did not lack methodological limitations -understood as difficulties or aspects that could have been improved-throughout the process of creation and validation of the instrument. This section summarises the most important ones (see Tables 4.5 and 4.6) and a set of recommendations are proposed to be implemented in the future, in order to establish this type of instruments.

At the creation phase of the instrument, the group of researchers that had been set up showed an intermediate level of expertise, since some of its members did not consider themselves as experts, either because they were in the early stages of academic and research training, or because they had not previously handled certain topics. Even though this circumstance was not restrictive, given that the pools were subsequently balanced with researchers of different levels, the replacement of two low-level members within the team of 20 experts would have increased the group's coefficient K. Thus, the Delphi method would have been applied in a more comprehensive way, since one of its goals is the refusal by part of the coordinating team of those potential experts with worse self-assessments, and to that end, to establish cut-off points for inclusion and to apply, usually, the Ebel method (Cruz, 2009, pp. 21–23).

As regards the consultation carried out to evaluate the clarity of the initial construct, the baseline was a theoretical concept already used by Díez-Ripollés in several publications and recognised in the academic field. In any case, it was decided to ask team members if they understood it properly and if they thought it was adequate to define social exclusion. However, the request was sent by the coordinating team to the remainder of the group by e-mail, and this facilitated that – in spite of having asked just the opposite – many researchers replied to such e-mail in a collective way, thus influencing one another and

Table 4.5 Limitations faced regarding the creation of the instrument

Creation phases	*Limitations*	*Recommendations*
Phase 1. Setting up a group of researchers.	Partial development of the Delphi method. Not removing 2 low-level experts.	a) Full implementation of the Delphi method; and b) successive repetition of coefficient K's test.
Phase 2. Consultation on the construct's clarity.	Contagion of opinions on the concept among the research group's members.	c) To combine scales of individual opinion (1 to 5) with an open field.
Phase 3. Operationalisation in pools.	The research team did not discuss or validate the pools.	d) To validate the pools with less clear (1 to 5) and an open field.
Phase 4. Selection of indicators	None.	None.

Source: Own elaboration

creating opinion subgroups. Besides, in that request it was not specified that the aspects of the concept to be assessed were two: its clarity (whether it was understood or not) and its relevance to define social exclusion. Even though the group sessions that took place after collecting the e-mails helped reach a consensus on the theoretical concept, they omitted the first step of individual reflection by means of a measurement scale for the objective quantification of the clarity and relevance of the concept. In the same way, no discussion or validation of the pools was carried out by the research team, which could have been performed with the procedure mentioned above, that is, by using scales.

In the instrument validation phase, the second and third stage also had limitations. It is well known that two of the main limitations of the questionnaire method by e-mail are low rate of answers and slowness (López-Roldan & Fachelli, 2015, p. 15). The first one did not take place since it was an intentional sampling, i. e., among the parts (primary researcher and expert/s) there was a mutual professional recognition, which granted enough motivation to carry out the task. Besides, although some members of the second group were strangers for the coordinating team, the knowledge of the field of study and the large number of international experts participating in it was sufficient reinforcement of the commitment to the research. As regards the timeframe of the instrument delivery, there was a gap of one year between the period established for questionnaire filling by the second group and its effective completion. Maybe the established deadlines were too optimistic, considering the large number of experts involved and the virtual nature of the reminder, much less effective than a personal one. Actually, this fact did not impact the quality of the research, it just delayed it. It was assumed that generating more reliable final statistical results was conditional upon obtaining a high rate of answers.

Likewise, the quantitative and qualitative analyses of results from the second group, obtained in the first round of the questionnaire, showed difficulties in understanding some items, and even the theoretical concept and its pools. In this sense, it would have been positive to validate – both in clarity and relevance – the theoretical concept supplied and its pools, in order to determine if the connecting link established between the theoretical sphere (definitions) and the practical one (indicators) was acceptable.

A glossary of specific terminology could have also been included, an additional column to determine the ease to answer the item (due to lack of clarity, inaccuracy of the wording or simple ignorance) and an open field for comments in each question. This last improvement would have allowed the expert to point out the most problematic items, while he/she completed the questionnaire, and to explain the reasons therefor. Such information was lost since the final comment used to be too generic.

Some experts suggested that a more qualitative methodological approach based on interviews previous to the delivery of the questionnaire would have addressed many of the difficulties encountered. For example, if the questionnaire had been personally supplied to experts that were native from the UK

Table 4.6 Limitations faced regarding the validation of the instrument

Validation stages	*Limitations*	*Recommendations*
Stage 1. Selection and contact of international experts.	None.	None.
Stage 2. Design and online management of the instrument.	Slow answer of the second group. Difficulties to understand some items. No validation of the theoretical concept and its pools. Lack of a pre-test with a reduced sample of experts.	e) To include validation of the theoretical concept itself, besides its explanation (in clarity and relevance) and of its pools. f) To explain better the terminology used. g) To include an additional column to score ease to answer the item. h) To include an additional column in each item to leave open-ended comments. i) To adopt a more qualitative approach in the interviews with researchers. j) To conduct a pre-test.
Stage 3. Statistical analysis of results.	Some items suffered from lack of clarity in the first phase of questionnaire management.	k) Some recommendations from the previous stage are applicable here.
Stage 4. Final selection of the strongest indicators.	None.	None.

Source: Own elaboration

and/or the US, this would have reinforced the initial translation of the instrument. Likewise, if it had been checked whether the instructions included in the questionnaire were sufficiently clear and precise, this would have reduced confusion as to the purpose of the research and the tasks to be carried out by the researcher therein. Actually, all of it appeared to suggest the implementation of a pre-test or pilot study to obtain information on the operation of the instrument in real conditions. According to Fowler (1993, pp. 100–103) the best way to conduct a pre-test to a self-reported questionnaire is by using previous qualitative techniques. In our case, the pre-test was reduced to several technical tests in order to verify if the questionnaire was properly sent and received, if questions were properly registered or if data could be downloaded, among others. If the guidelines suggested by Fowler had been applied, the instrument would have been completed in the first place by a reduced group of experts from different countries in the presence of the team coordinators, who would have led a joint discussion to clarify any problematic aspect.

All these difficulties were somehow reflected in the third stage, in view of some Aiken's V coefficients obtained regarding clarity. Even though such difficulties were remedied later on, in the round carried out subsequently with the first group of experts, it would have been convenient to follow the recommendations suggested for the second stage.

6 Conclusions

The methodology adopted in the two research projects that were developed has successfully answered and fulfilled the main objectives of the study: to create and validate an instrument for criminal justice policy comparison that would enable to classify national crime control systems according to their socially exclusionary effects. In spite of facing certain limitations – that were to be expected given the diversity of the methodologies used in the various implementation phases over a long period of time – a very valid and reliable instrument for international comparison was obtained, which fills an important gap in criminal justice policy knowledge.

The set of 39 indicators proposed measures, in a clear, comprehensive and discriminatory way, many aspects of the criminal social exclusion, thus opening the door to analyses of comparative criminal justice policy that are more complex and useful than those traditionally focused on penal rigorism. Besides, the good results obtained have proved the suitability of the content validation method through the judgment of experts for the criminal justice policy research, as well as the relevance of Aiken's V test for the selection of robust indicators in large samples of experts. Likewise, the online management of the questionnaire did not show its traditional disadvantages.

As pointed out by Díez-Ripollés & García-España (2019, p. 25) the future implementation of this new tool in a high number of Western developed countries will allow to compare their respective national penal justice policies, and they may be classified in a social exclusion scale. The results obtained from the effective implementation of the instrument in subsequent phases will certainly provide relevant data on the instrument's operation and the additional methodological challenges faced by it.

In any case, it is to be expected that – in this advanced implementation phase – the instrument can already become a useful tool to place the different national penal justice systems before a mirror, to promote substantial changes towards a criminal justice policy management that is less socially exclusionary.

References

Aiken, L. (1980). Content Validity and Reliability of Single Items or Questionnaire. *Educational and Psychological Measurement*, *40*, 955–959.

Aiken, L. (1985). Three Coefficients for Analyzing the Reliability and Validity of Ratings. *Educational and Psychological Measurement*, *45*, 131–142.

Blasco, J.E., López, A. & Mengual, S. (2010). Validación mediante método Delphi de un cuestionario para conocer las experiencias e interés hacia las actividades acuáticas con especial atención al windsurf. *Ágora para la Educación Física y el Deporte*, *12*(1), 75–96.

Cabero Almenara, J. & Barroso Osuna, J. (2013). La utilización del juicio experto para la evaluación de TIC: El coeficiente de competencia experta. *Bordón*, *65*(2), 1–14.

Casas, F. (1989). *Técnicas de investigación social: los indicadores sociales y psicosociales (teoría y práctica)*. PPU.

Cordón, J. (2015). Analizando la V de Aiken usando el método score con hojas de cálculo. Available at: www.researchgate.net/publication/277556053_Analizando_la_V_de_Aiken_Usando_el_Metodo_Score_con_Hojas_de_Calculo (Last date accessed: 2023, November 5).

Crespo, T. (2007). *Respuestas a 16 preguntas sobre el empleo de expertos en la investigación pedagógica*. Editorial San Marcos.

Cruz, M. (2009). *El método Delphi en las investigaciones educacionales*. Editorial Academia.

Díez-Ripollés, J.L. (2011). La dimensión inclusión/exclusión social como guía de la política criminal comparada. *Revista electrónica de ciencia penal y criminología (RECPC)*, *13–12*, 1–36. Available at: http://criminet.ugr.es/recpc/13/recpc13-12.pdf (Last date accessed: 2023, November 5).

Díez-Ripollés, J.L. (2013). Social Inclusion and Comparative Criminal Justice Policy. *Journal of Scandinavian Studies in Criminology and Crime Prevention*, *14*, 62–78.

Díez-Ripollés, J.L. & García-España, E. (2019). RIMES: An instrument to compare national criminal justice policies from the social exclusion dimension. *International E-Journal of Criminal Sciences*, *1*(13), 1–27. Available at: www.ehu.eus/ojs/index.php/inecs/article/view/20866 (Last date accessed: 2023, November 5).

Ding, C.S. & Hershberger, S.L. (2002). Assessing Content Validity and Content Equivalence Using Structural Equation Modeling. *Structural Equation Modeling: A Multidisciplinary Journal*, *9*(2), 283–297.

Dunn, J.G., Bouffard, M. & Rogers, W.T. (1999). Assessing Item Content-Relevance in Sport Psychology Scale-Construction Research: Issues and Recommendations. *Measurement in Physical Education and Exercise Science*, *3*(1), 15–36.

Escobar-Pérez, J. & Cuervo-Martínez, A. (2008). Validez de contenido y juicio de expertos: Una aproximación a su utilización. *Avances en medición*, *6*, 27–37.

Escurra, L. (1988). Cuantificación de la validez de contenido por criterio de jueces. *Revista de Psicología*, *6*(1–2), 103–111. Available at: http://revistas.pucp.edu.pe/index.php/psicologia/article/view/4555 (Last date accessed: 2023, November 5).

Estévez-García, J. & Pérez-García, MJ. (2007). *Sistema de indicadores para el diagnóstico y seguimiento de la educación superior en México*. Asociación Nacional de Universidades e Instituciones de Educación Superior.

Fowler, F. (1993). *Survey Research Methods. Applied Social Research Methods Series* (2nd edition). Sage Publications.

Gable, R.K. & Wolf, M.B. (1993). *Instrument Development in the Affective Domain: Measuring Attitudes and Values in Corporate and School Settings*. Kluwer Academic Publishers.

García, L. & Fernández, S. (2008). Procedimiento de aplicación del trabajo creativo en grupo de expertos. *Energética*, *XXIX*(2), 46–50.

González Blasco, P. (1994). Medir en las ciencias sociales, in García Ferrando, M., et al. (comps.) *El análisis de la realidad social. Métodos y técnicas de investigación*. Alianza, 335–364.

Grant, J.S. & Davis, L.L. (1997). Selection and use of content experts for instrument development. *Research in Nursing and Health*, *20*(3), 269–274.

Hernández-Sampieri, H., Fernández-Collado, C. & Baptista Lucio, P. (2006). *Metodología de la investigación (cuarta edición)*. McGraw-Hill.

Hyrkas, K., Appelqvist-Schmidlechner, K. & Oksa, L. (2003). Validating an Instrument for Clinical Supervision Using an Expert Panel. *International Journal of Nursing Studies*, *40*, 619–625.

Lazarsfeld, P. (1985). De los conceptos a los índices empíricos, en Boudon, R., and Lazarsfeld, P. (eds.) *Metodología de las ciencias sociales*. Laia.

López, A. (2008). La moderación de la habilidad diagnóstico patológico desde el enfoque histórico cultural para la asignatura Patología Veterinaria. *Revista Pedagógica Universitaria*, *13*(5), 51–71.

López-Roldan, P. & Fachelli, S. (2015). *Metodología de la investigación social cuantitativa*. Universidad Autónoma de Cataluña.

Mehrens, W. & Lehmann, I. (1982). *Medición y evaluación en la educación y en la psicología*. Editorial CECSA.

Merino-Soto, C. & Livia-Segovia, J. (2009). Intervalos de confianza asimétricos para el índice la validez de contenido: Un programa Visual Basic para la V de Aiken. *Anales de Psicología*, *25*(1), 169–171.

Messick, S. (1989). Validity, En Linn, R.L. (ed.) *Educational Measurement*. American Council on Education, pp. 13–103.

Nunnally, J. (1973). *Introducción a la Medición Psicológica*. Paidós.

Oñate, M. (2001). Utilización del método Delphy en la pronosticación: Una experiencia inicial. *Aplicación del Método Delphy*. Available at: www.rieoei.org/deloslectores/804Bravo. (Last date accessed: 2023, November 5).

Penfield, R.D. & Miller, J.M. (2004). Improving Content Validation Studies using an Asymmetric Confidence Interval for the Mean of Expert Ratings. *Applied Measurement in Education*, *77*(4), 359–370. https://doi. org/10.1207/s15324818ame1704_2

Prieto, G. & Delgado, A.R. (2010). Fiabilidad y validez. *Papeles del psicólogo*, *31*(1), 67–74.

Rey Del Castillo, P. (2004). Nota metodológica sobre los indicadores del barómetro del CIS. *REIS*, *108*, 151–178.

Sierra-Bravo, R. (2008). *Técnicas de investigación social: Teoría y ejercicios (decimocuarta edición)*. Thomson Editores.

Skjong, R. & Wentworth, B. (2000). Expert Judgement and Risk Perception. Available at: www.researchgate.net/publication/265032303_Expert_Judgment_and_Risk_Perception (Last date accessed: 2023, November 5).

5 Implementation of the RIMES instrument in Spain

Elisa García-España

1 Introduction

As noted in previous chapters, the RIMES instrument is based on the conceptual model of Díez-Ripollés (2011, 2013), which aims to be an alternative to the strong political-criminal tendency to contrast the different national criminal control systems according to their greater or lesser punitive rigour. Instead, Díez-Ripollés opts for the criterion of social exclusion. According to him, a penal system is socially exclusive when it aspires substantially to achieve the innocuousness of the aforementioned groups, which implies ensuring that the suspect, convicted and exonerated person finds himself, after his contact with the penal institutions, in individual and social conditions in which it is more difficult for him to break the law or avoid being discovered.

To check whether the validated RIMES instrument could be implemented with reliable results, it was tested in the Spanish penal system before its application in other countries.

The specific objectives were several:

1 To design accurate response techniques to the 39 indicators, ensuring that these are an accurate reflection of reality (reliability).
2 To identify and resolve specific difficulties or 'bottlenecks' in responding to the 39 rules and practices (indicators) that make up the instrument.
3 Find the results obtained by the RIMES instrument for Spain.

The instrument that was applied in Spain was the original validated instrument, which contained 26 rules and 13 practices. Among these practices, the item 110 could not be answered in Spain and the item 52 could not be applied in the rest of the countries. Hence, in the final instrument, these practices were replaced by rules 99 and 46 respectively (see final instrument in the following pages). These rules were similar in content to the replaced practices, had also a high score in Aiken's V and are much easier to solve. In these pages we will explain the difficulties in solving practice 110 in Spain, which was finally replaced by rule 99. We will draw attention with an asterisk when we refer to the substituted items. The final results on the position of Spain in the

DOI: 10.4324/9781032661766-7

continuum have been found according to the final version of the instrument composed of 28 rules and 11 practices.

2 Implementation of the RIMES instrument in Spain

The RIMES instrument was applied in Spain as follows.

2.1 Procedure for compilation of information

The RIMES research team designed a way to proceed for the compilation of information to respond to each indicator, advised by methodology experts from the University of Malaga and the King's College of London. Particular attention was paid both to the design of an indicator response form or protocol and to organise the teams that would answer each indicator.

2.1.1 Form or protocol to respond to each item

To ensure that the response given was sufficiently substantiated and so that it could be subsequently reviewed by external experts, researchers collected the information in the protocol which appears in Table 5.1.

As can be seen, the form consists of eight sections: The first part includes the name of the researcher or researchers responding to the indicator, followed by the dates of response, review and final submission. This section allows to have information regarding the response process of that indicator and to identify the researchers in case of doubt or need for further review. In point 1 researchers should include the text of the item to be answered, its identifying number and whether it is a rule or a practice. Point 2 includes a brief description of the item's content which allows to clarify the response that is being sought. Point 3 is intended for the researcher to explain the steps that were needed (legal sources or empirical materials) to respond to that item, i.e., the methodology and techniques used in that case. Rules just show the regulation or bibliographic sources that have been used, while practices may simply include the secondary source of data used or, if this does not exist, an empirical approach must be designed to this end. In point 4 the item is answered in dichotomous form, with 'yes' or 'no', which must then include a convincing and well-founded explanation of the response. This is one of the key moments in the process of completing the item. Points 5 and 6 of the protocol refer to contributions that the researcher provides to the team for future graduation or weighting of the item. At the item's graduation, the information entered may help evaluate the greater or lesser capacity of that rule or practice to generate social exclusion, in such a way that if the answer is 'Yes', this can be specified as 'little', 'quite' or 'much'. If the answer is 'no', the graduation is not carried out. On the other hand, as regards weighting, information or recommendations are entered on the weight that each item may have on the RIMES instrument taken as a whole. Finally, the seventh and last point of the protocol leaves

Table 5.1 RIMES' item protocol

ITEMS PROTOCOL		
Researcher's name: **Starting date:** **Revision date:** **Submission date:**		
1. Rule or practice to research		
2. Brief description of contents		
3. Methodology a. Method of collecting information. Justification.		
b. Universe, and sample if required		
c. Lapse of time (five years recommended)		
d. Space boundaries (whole country recommended; some restrictions could apply)		
4. Results Why?	YES	NO
5. Relevant complementary information (specifically for graduating results).		
6. Suggestions for possible weighting of item		
7. Secondary sources		

room for the researcher to optionally provide other secondary sources that support his/her decision.

2.1.2 *Organisation of the work team*

In the quest for reliable answers, it was decided that each item would have a two-fold response, by two researchers of the team, who would not be in contact with each other for this task so as not to condition their replies. All responses were reviewed by a senior researcher acting as coordinator. All items were allocated at random. For such distribution to be equitable, an effort was made so that not only each researcher was assigned a similar number of items, but that said number of items was decided on the foreseeable difficulty in having them answered. As already explained, practices that require fieldwork are more difficult to respond than rules or other practices that may be answered with secondary data. Out of the 39 items, the team identified five practices that were particularly difficult. Taking those items into account, the distribution of the 39 items was made in two rounds, so that each item was assigned to two investigators. After deducting an item from the workload of researchers with more difficult items, the remaining researchers took care of 10 items.

A first attempt to respond to those practices considered more difficult showed that these required a different procedure from the rest: the difficulties encountered were hard to be overcome individually by the researchers. Hence, two different methodological strategies were designed to deal with two different types of items. The first strategy was aimed at the majority group of items, consisting of rules and practices that may be answered with secondary data. This group includes 25 rules and 9 practices (34 items). The second strategy aimed to solve the most difficult practices, which require fieldwork since there is no secondary data in Spain to answer them. These items are shown in Table 5.2.

The two strategies are set out below.

i) Procedure to respond to items in the first group:

The information regarding each item was collected separately by two team members, who did not share information with each other. Both were expected to get the same answer, even if the sources were different. This would make the answer more reliable.

To achieve this, it was decided that each researcher should consider how to address the item in question. The first three sections of the protocol, and the introduction should be completed and delivered to the senior researcher acting as coordinator. The latter had to review the proposal and then meet with each researcher separately to guide, clarify or deepen the methodological approach established in the protocol. After that first meeting, each researcher had to complete the protocol answering 'yes' or 'no', justifying it and proposing, where appropriate, criteria to graduate and weight the indicator. As an example, we provide the protocol of item 37, which was answered in an affirmative way in Spain (Table 5.3).

Table 5.2 Practices that require fieldwork

No.	Items
25	A significant number of mentally ill inmates serve their sentences in regular correctional facilities.
68	Family and intimate visits take place at intervals of over one month.
107	The media regularly disclose the full names, current addresses or pictures of ex-felons.
110*	Most companies with over 100 employees require a clean criminal record for recruitment.
126	Alien minor offenders are deported because of an offence.

Source: Own elaboration

Table 5.3 Protocol of item 37 in Spain

ITEMS PROTOCOL
Researcher's name: R-4 **Starting date:** 30/09/2017 **Review date:** 17/11/2017 **Submission date:** 5/12/2018 1. Rule or practice to research Item 37: The incarceration rate is higher than 120 inmates per 100,000 inhabitants. 2. Brief description of contents This item refers to a concept, the incarceration rate, which results from transforming the country's absolute data on prison population into a relative number per 100,000 inhabitants. The incarceration rate includes remand and sentenced prisoners. To conduct such arithmetic operation, the official population data of the country should be used as well as the official prison population. 3. Methodology a. Method of collecting information. Justification. Through secondary sources. And, more specifically, through: 1. the Spanish National Statistics Institute (Instituto Nacional de Estadística: INE) indicators (for demographic information). 2. Annual General Reports from the Spanish Prison Authorities (from 2010 to 2016). At the date of this document (October 2018) there's still no Annual General Report for 2017. Therefore, the average for this year will be calculated by adding the total prison population of every month and dividing it by the twelve months of the year, with data obtained from the National Prison Authorities' website. For such Authorities, the concept "prison population" refers to male and female population of any nationality, over 18 years of age and with a mental condition that allows them to be held responsible for their actions. The concept includes remand prisoners and sentenced prisoners. It also includes a third group of inmates included in the so-called "security measures", which are sentences served in a psychiatric facility (page 147 of the 2016 Annual General Report refers to two of these facilities in Alicante and Seville). In a later stage the Crime Observatory Report of 2009 may be used for comparisons among European countries and with the United States of America. In case it is necessary, the SPACE reports may also be used for European comparisons. B. Universe, and sample if required Not applicable c. Lapse of time (five years recommended) From 2010 to 2017. d. Space boundaries (whole country recommended; some restrictions may apply) Spain. 4. Results YES NO Why?

(*Continued*)

Table 5.3 (Continued)

ITEMS PROTOCOL

The following table includes three values for the Spanish situation in the 2010–2017 period: the general population, the prison population, and the incarceration rate.

Year	(A) Spanish population (millions of inhabitants included in the census by 1 January)	(B) Prison population (Annual average)	Incarceration rate (B/A *100,000).
2010	46,486,621	65,335	140.5
2011	46,667,175	61,851	132.5
2012	46,818,216	59,779	127.6
2013	46,727,890	58,427	125
2014	46,512,199	56,787	122
2015	46,449,565	55,415	119.3
2016	46,440,099	52,307	112.6
2017	46,527,039	59,978	128.9

Average for the whole period (2010–2017): 126 inmates per 100,000 inhabitants.

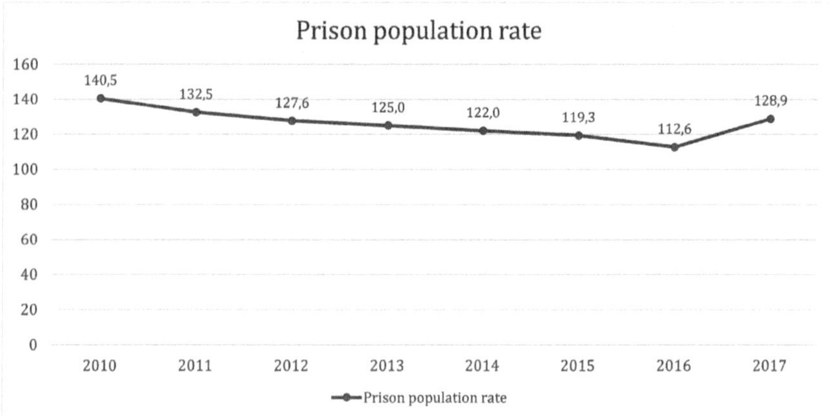

Line graph that shows Spanish prison population rate

Figure 5.1 Prison population rate

5. Relevant complementary information (specifically for graduating results).
According to the rate, specific scores could be established and added to the positive answers (1). For instance:
From 121 to 200: 0.25.
From 201 to 300: 0.50.
From 301 to 400: 0.75.
From 401 to 500: 1.
From 501 to 600: 1.25.
From 601 to 700: 1.50.
From 701 to 800: 1.75.
From 801 to 900: 2.

ITEMS PROTOCOL
6. Suggestions for possible weighting of item None 7. Secondary sources Spanish National Statistics Institute (Instituto Nacional de Estadística – INE): www.ine.es/dyngs/INEbase/es/categoria.htm?c=Estadistica_P&cid=1254735573206 Spanish Prison Authorities (Instituciones Penitenciarias): www.institucionespenitenciarias.es

Source: Own elaboration

When the coordinator considered that the item had been answered consistently and with reliable sources, it was submitted to the team for a complete review. For each item the following decisions were taken:

a. Whether the indicator had been correctly resolved or not. If it was properly resolved, the item was taken as definitely resolved, even if the researchers had used different procedures or sources. But if, after the discussion, the team concluded that, despite both investigators giving the same answer, the item had not been properly resolved, it was returned to them to look deeper into the issue and find a response that was better substantiated. On this occasion they could do it together. This occurred in few cases.
b. In the event of a discrepancy between the researchers, i.e., one answered the item in the affirmative and the other in the negative, the team, after studying and discussing the two protocols submitted, took the appropriate decision. An example of this scenario was item 55 regarding the existence or not of a specific prison regime for young adults. The discrepancy in this item came from the different consideration given to the terms 'specific prison regime'. Possible interpretations swung between considering that only the fact that young adults have different prison living conditions than other adults should be taken into account or understanding that they are asking whether there is a different whole prison regime. The team chose the first definition and decided to respond to this item in the negative in Spain, since both the General Organic Law on Prisons (Ley Orgánica General Penitenciaria) and the Prison Regulations (Reglamento Penitenciario) provide for the existence of different and separate departments for young adults.

2.1.3 *Procedure to answer the five most complicated items (practices)*

Researchers made a methodological proposal to the coordinator, separately. The latter submitted both proposals to the team, where they would be discussed until consensus was reached. This could mean one of the two methodologies was chosen or a new one was raised at the meeting. Then the project support technicians carried out the fieldwork according to the methodology decided by the research team. Once the fieldwork was completed, the researchers to whom those practices were assigned, with help from the support technicians, responded jointly to the item and submitted their answer to the coordinator, and then to the research team, for approval.

2.1.4 *Clarification of terminology*

Besides, throughout the process of approving item responses, the research team had to clarify some adverbs of frequency that were part of the item description. When applying the instrument in Spain, it became clear there was a need to specify those adverbs and keep a uniform criterion for future implementation of the instrument in other countries. For example, Practice 50 asks whether those sentenced to life imprisonment regularly serve more than 25 years. The question raised was how to define the term 'regularly'. In this case, the team decided that 'regularly' meant that over 35 per cent of those sentenced to reviewable permanent prison serve more than 25 years in prison.

2.2. *Techniques used for each item*

The research technique used for each item is set out below:

> The 28 rules that composed the instrument were answered considering the current legislation, the existing case law and doctrinal consultations. In some rules we found legal interpretation problems that had not been unequivocally resolved in Spain. In those cases, the goal was to adopt the majority position as regards such rule's interpretation. A clear example of this is Rule 99* ('Private employers which are not related to private security companies or to those working with children or vulnerable adults are entitled to request information about criminal records to potential employees'). After looking into whether employers may request to potential employees any information on criminal records not related to minors or vulnerable adults, it was concluded that in Spain there is no clear legal decision to prevent it, so the team understood that in Spain employers are entitled to ask their potential employees for criminal records, and the item was answered in the affirmative. Furthermore, Items 50, 52* and 81 are not applicable in Spain because, on the one hand, life imprisonment – referred to in Items 50 and 52* – is still very recent and not enough time has yet passed to assess it and, on the other hand, the preventive detention referred to in Item 81 has not been provided for in Spanish law. That is why these three practices do not occur in Spain (see Table 5.3).

a. Secondary data were used for the six practices for which there was information in Spain (see Table 5.4).
b. For the remaining four practices, a qualitative methodology was used in three cases (Items 68, 110* and 126), through interviews with key informants and using the saturation criterion in the selection of the interviewees.

Table 5.4 Secondary data used to respond to practices

Items	*Secondary data*
11. Discriminatory street police interventions (stop and search, arrests, frisks/body searches . . .) targeting specific groups occur regularly.	Results from empirical studies conducted by Spanish research groups
25. A significant number of mentally ill inmates serve their sentences in regular correctional facilities.	Official data and empirical research
37. The incarceration rate is higher than 120 inmates per 100,000 inhabitants.	Official data from prison institutions and INE (Spanish National Statistics Institute)
38. At least three quarters of the inmates are serving their sentences in closed prisons.	Official data from prison institutions
82. Over 30% of the prison population is in pre-trial detention.	Official data from prison institutions
121. Custodial sentences are one of the three types of sanctions which are most frequently applied to minors.	Official data from INE

Source: Own elaboration

Only in the case of practice 107 was necessary to use a quantitative methodology that was carried out through the analysis of online media content, as summarised in Table 5.5.

Practice 110* (whether most companies with over 100 employees require a clean criminal record for recruitment) was particularly difficult. An effort was made to answer this indicator taking account of three different methodological designs: the first consisted of connecting with key informants, i.e., with labour experts who might have knowledge about the practice in Spanish

Table 5.5 Empirical techniques for responding to practices categorised as difficult

Items	*Techniques*
68. Family and intimate visits take place at intervals of over one month.	Interview with prison officers through the snowball technique and personal contacts
107. The media regularly discloses the full names, current addresses or pictures of ex-felons.	Media content analysis
110*. Most companies with over 100 employees require a clean criminal record for recruitment.	Interview with key informants (randomness criterion from a stratified sample)
126. Alien minor offenders are deported.	Interview with key informants (saturation criterion)

Source: Own elaboration

companies of requesting criminal records from employees. An attempt was made to obtain a sample based on the saturation criterion, asking whether they knew – on the basis of their experience – of any business methods or techniques used to obtain the criminal records of job seekers. The experts consulted agreed that the data sought was very difficult to obtain and that the most feasible solution was trying to contact with human resources departments of the companies.

The second method was, therefore, to carry out fieldwork establishing contact with managers of the human resources departments of a sample of companies with over 100 employees. The starting point was a universe of 12,226 companies according to Camerdata (the Spanish Chamber of Commerce database). The sample – with a sampling error of 5 per cent and a degree of confidence of 95 per cent –, amounted to 372 companies throughout Spain. These were selected from the five autonomous communities which had more than 500 companies of over 100 employees (Madrid, Valencia, Catalonia, Andalusi, and the Basque Country), as all of them added up to 10,482 companies, i.e., 85.7 per cent of the total in Spain. The distribution was carried out on a proportional basis. Out of the total list of companies in each of those autonomous communities, the assigned number was chosen at random. Subsequently, a telephone contact was made with the human resources department of each of them and they were asked if their company usually requested criminal records to hire new employees. If the answer was affirmative, the reason for this was asked to classify each case according to whether it was supported by law. In four of the autonomous communities where fieldwork was conducted – all of those mentioned, except Madrid – there was a high rate of companies that refused to collaborate for different reasons. Among the companies that responded, most claimed they did not ask for criminal records. The ones that request them are companies working with minors or in the field of security and are therefore covered by legal provisions. However, those cases were out of the scope of this practice, since only companies which requested them outside of explicit legal provisions could be considered. Since the results of those four autonomous communities were very similar, completing the 160 companies in Madrid was not deemed necessary.

The third method consisted of going to the largest trade unions to provide us with contacts with the works council of the companies that made up the sample. The intention was to ask them if they were aware that the companies to which they belonged requested criminal records to hire new employees. We run into the drawback that, according to the Organic Law on Personal Data Protection, trade unions cannot provide the contact details of members of the works councils. On the other hand, trade unions branch out according to the type of activity, making it virtually impossible to find the company we were looking for if we did not contact the appropriate industry branch. In addition, even if the company has over 100 employees, it does not necessarily have a works council, as this depends on the will of employees. Although this approach could not be developed with the required methodological rigour, those trade unions with which contact was established said that they were not aware of any company requesting criminal records, except for hospitals and other authorised entities.

Once all these activities were carried out to respond to this item, the results obtained were not considered to be sufficiently conclusive, because of the methodological difficulties encountered. Besides, it was anticipated that similar problems would arise in other countries of the Western developed world. Hence it was decided to leave this item unanswered and to replace it with rule 99*. That decision was further endorsed because rule 99* concerned the same matter as practice 110*. Since it was a rule, it would be easier to respond both in Spain and in the other countries and, more importantly, this item obtained very good ratings in Aiken's V, which allows to preserve the validity of the instrument.

2.3 Graduation and weighting

Graduation of an item arises because, even if its answer is affirmative, it is noted that there may be very different levels of item's fulfillment depending on the country. An example of this is Item 37 ('the incarceration rate is higher than 120 inmates per 100,000 inhabitants'): according to the item's formulation in the RIMES instrument, it generates social exclusion when the incarceration rate is higher than 120 inmates per 100,000 inhabitants. A rate of 121 would entail an affirmative answer, but the item will be more expressive in cases where the incarceration rate reached 200 or 300 inmates per 100,000 inhabitants. Considerations included by researchers in this section on how to graduate the item will be filed for use when information is obtained from a considerable number of countries. Then we will proceed to make more refined scores of each of them, to insert them more accurately in a comparative scale referring to the degree of social exclusion.

Weighting was included in the protocol because it was thought that, at some point, we should give a different weight to the various items of the questionnaire, and that the team members should agree on the weight of each item. That is why it was important to collect the proposals of the different team members in view of the experience obtained with the first country where the instrument was implemented. It was later concluded that the weighting was already mathematically solved with the score obtained for each item in the validation carried out by the international experts. As we have already said, the weight of each indicator was achieved through the Aiken's V coefficient obtained in suitability (Díez-Ripollés and García-España 2019), which in all cases was equal to or greater than 0.73 and not greater than 0.96. The main advantage of this form of weighting is that it does not change the weight resulting from the items' validation by international experts, i.e., the average weighting of all of them is not distorted. Table 5.6 shows the weights of the different items, identified by their number, and grouped according to Aiken's V coefficient, as well as the distance among them, starting at the bottom of the

Table 5.6 Weighting of items according to Aiken's V

Item number	*Total*	*Weight or Aiken's V*
92, 93	2	0.96
36, 107 and 117	3	0.94
86, 88 and 101	3	0.92
126	1	0.90
1, 3, 91 and 99*	4	0.88
43 and 120	2	0.87
11, 79 and 113	3	0.85
2, 33, 38, 42 and 100	5	0.83
21, 35, 50, 55, 62 and 68	6	0.81
64, 74 and 121	3	0.79
22, 25, 37, 46*, 81 and 82	5	0.77
24	1	0.73

Source: Own elaboration.

table where item 24 has a weight of 0.73 up to the 0.96 of items 92 and 93 at the top of the table (Arenas-García 2021).

3 Results

First, we have advanced one of the results from the implementation of the RIMES instrument in Spain, which consists of removing practice 110* and replacing it with rule 99*. This result from the application and testing of the RIMES instrument has been of great relevance since it has allowed to identify the serious difficulties inherent to Item 110* to obtain a reliable and replicable response at international level. As noted earlier, this obstacle has been overcome by swapping an unreliable practice for a rule that is easier to answer and may be obtained more reliably. In any case the replacement could be done to the extent that Item 99* obtained good ratings on Aiken's V, thus allowing to preserve the validity of the instrument.

In the subsequent application of the RIMES instrument to four European countries and two US states, something similar occurred with respect to practice 52*. This was answered with a 'no' in Spain, as explained above, because the recent incorporation of the permanent revisable prison did not allow us to assess it. The attempt to answer this item in other countries has encountered serious difficulties, which has led to its substitution by rule 46*. This rule, which is easier to answer than practice 52*, also has a high score in the Aiken V, as can be seen in table 5.5. This decision following the application of RIMES in Spain slightly changes the result in this country, as practice 52* had a negative response, while in rule 46* the response is affirmative.

Moreover, the implementation of the RIMES instrument in Spain was settled with 30 items expressing social exclusion that were answered in the negative, against nine items that were answered in the affirmative. Table 5.7 shows which were those nine rules and practices according to their pool of origin.

Table 5.7 Items answered in the affirmative in Spain distributed by pools.

Pools	*Items*	*Rule or practice*
1. Control of public spaces	11. Discriminatory street police interventions (stop and search, arrests, frisks/body searches . . .) targeting specific groups occur regularly.	Practice
2. Legal safeguards	None	
3. Sentencing and sanction systems	37. The incarceration rate is higher than 120 inmates per 100,000 inhabitants.	Practice
	38. At least three quarters of the inmates are serving their sentences in closed prisons.	Practice
4. Harshest penalties	46*. A minimum of 20 years served is required before claiming release from life imprisonment.	Rule
5. Prison rules	None.	
6. Preventive intervention	79. The maximum statutory term for pretrial detention exceeds 3 years.	Rule
7. Legal and social status of offenders and ex-offenders	88. Aliens with residence permits may be deported if sentenced for any criminal offence either up to 1 year of imprisonment or to any other non-custodial sentence.	Rule
8. Police and criminal records	99*. Private employers which are not related to private security companies or to those working with children or vulnerable adults are entitled to request information about criminal records to potential employees.	Rule
	107. The media regularly disclose the full names, current addresses or pictures of exfelons	Practice
9. Youth criminal justice	121. Custodial sentences are one of three types of sanctions which are most frequently applied to minors.	Practice

Source: Own elaboration

Out of the 39 items that make up the RIMES instrument, the 9 items expressing social exclusion that materialised in Spain accounted for 23 per cent. The remaining 77 per cent represents items that were not confirmed in Spain.

The distribution of items answered positively in Spain is almost equal between practices and rules, namely five practices and four rules. The percentage of those practices in the instrument's total practices (n = 12) is 42 per cent, while the four rules answered in the affirmative represent 14.8 per cent of the total rules that make up the instrument, which are 27.

Taking into consideration the distribution in pools, in Spain there is at least one indicator expressing social exclusion in six of the nine pools. Pools 2 (legal safeguards) and 5 (prison regime) have all their items answered in the negative, i.e., there was no item expressing social exclusion in Spain. Pools regarding "sentencing and sanction systems" and "police and criminal records" have the highest number of items expressing social exclusion, with a total of two out of the five indicators in these pools.

Table 5.8 Final weight and by pools of Spain in social exclusion according to the RIMES instrument (values from 0 to 10 from least to most excluded)

Pools	*Weithting*
Spain's final weight	2.31
1. Control of public spaces	2.49
2. Legal safeguards	0
3. Sentencing and sanctions systems	3.83
4. Harshest penalties	2.35
5. Prison rules	0
6. Preventive intervention	2.68
7. Legal and social status of offenders and ex-offenders	1.97
8. Police and criminal records	5.10
9. Youth criminal justice	1.82

Source: Own elaboration

The four rules answered in the affirmative are distributed among the pools concerning 'harshest penalties', 'preventive intervention', 'legal and social status of offenders and ex-offenders' and 'police and criminal records'. For their part, the practices answered in the affirmative belongs to the pools concerning 'control of public spaces', 'sentencing and sanction systems', 'police and criminal records', 'youth criminal justice' and 'youth criminal justice' (see Table 5.7).

Spain's ranking on a continuum from least to most social exclusion, expressed from 0 to 10 and after applying the weighting to all the items, is 2.31 (table 5.8). On the other hand, the result of weighting by pools allows us to refine the most exclusionary aspects of Spanish criminal policy (table 5.8). The pool with the highest exclusion weighting in Spain, out of a maximum value of 10, is 'criminal and police records' (pool 8) with a score of 5.10, followed by 'sentencing system' (pool 3) with a score of 3.83. On the other hand, the pools with the lowest scores are 2 and 5 ('penal guarantees' and 'penitentiary system'), as their value is 0, i.e., they do not express social exclusion in Spain; this is followed by pool 9 ('juvenile justice'), with a score of 1.82.

4 Conclusions

With the implementation of the RIMES instrument in Spain some general conclusions can be reached regarding its replication in other countries. The results obtained also allow to assess the social exclusion generated by the Spanish criminal policy.

This approach proved to be useful and appropriate through the data collection protocol. Hence, it has continued to be used for the implementation of RIMES in other countries.

As has been explained, the application of the RIMES instrument in Spain has enabled us to locate and solve specific difficulties or bottlenecks when responding to the 39 rules and practices that composed the instrument. The reliability limitations detected in some practices have been addressed by designing various ways forward for the most complex practices and adapting the procedure to their difficulty. While most of the problems encountered have been overcome, these were insurmountable in a single case, resulting in the replacement of a practice (No. 110)* by a rule (No. 99*).

As for the results obtained in Spain with the implementation of the RIMES instrument, we can draw some interesting conclusions.

- A substantial majority of criminal policy indicators expressing social exclusion (30 items) do not occur in the Spanish case. Although the weighting criteria for the various items and pools have not yet been established or applied, we can offer – as a hypothesis – that an affirmative response in 9 of the 39 items (20 per cent of affirmative responses) may show that the Spanish penal system does not generate much social exclusion. We have based ourselves on the position it holds in the continuum made up by the extremes of greater or lesser social exclusion, where Spain is in the continuum's segment that is closest to the pole of less social exclusion (see Figure 5.2).
- Without considering results to be obtained from the application of the instrument in other countries, the position got by Spain seems to prove at a first glance that RIMES is sufficiently discriminating to the extent that it leaves room on both sides to place criminal policy systems from other countries that could generate more or less social exclusion than the Spanish one. In other words, and judging by the case in Spain, the instrument does not tend to take countries to one of the two extremes.
- Considering the number of rules and practices answered in the affirmative – both in absolute and in relative terms – we can say that in Spain the socially exclusionary effects are noticeable not so much in the rules as in a certain way of applying some of them. The Spanish prison policy has been internationally characterised by its enlightenment. This is somehow revealed by the fact that no item of the pool regarding 'prison rules' has been answered in the affirmative. As regards this pool, although it is true that the recent incorporation of the reviewable life imprisonment into the Spanish Penal Code has not allowed to answer the indicator related to its average duration, the items pertaining to the death penalty and the possibility of reviewing life imprisonment show a Spanish criminal policy that is far from the parameters of social exclusion. None of the indicators that make up the pool of

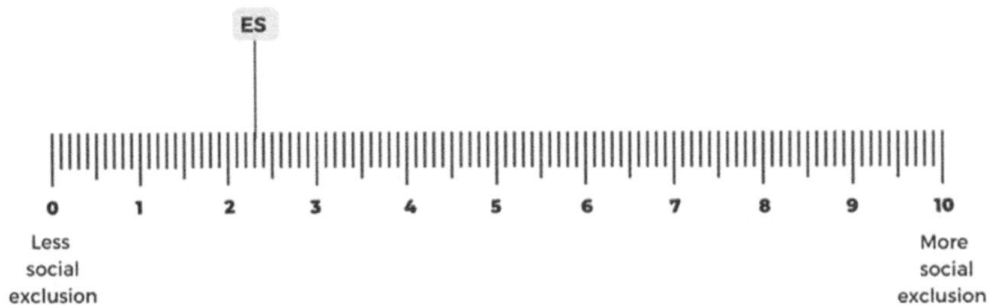

Figure 5.2 Spain's position in the continuum, from least to most social exclusion

'criminal safeguards' have been answered in the affirmative either, reflecting the fact that our penal system's safeguards structure is in good health.

- One of the results from the implementation of the RIMES instrument in Spain is that it corroborates the need to address the comparison of national criminal policies with an alternative model to punitiveness. It should be noted that the pool where more items have been answered in the affirmative has been the one referring to the 'sentencing and sanctions system'. In particular, the incarceration rate in Spain exceeds 120 per 100,000 inhabitants and at least three-quarters of the inmates are serving time in closed prisons. If the international comparison had been limited to the incarceration rate or to this and some other similar indicator, the Spanish criminal policy would have been labeled as rigorist. However, by using a more complex comparative model, which considers a greater number of criminal intervention measures -as is the case with the RIMES instrument – things look different. The Spanish criminal policy assessed as a whole, and regardless of subsequent comparisons with other countries, does not seem to be particularly exclusionary. This result calls into question some proposals that consider the incarceration rate to be a sufficiently comprehensive indicator for the purpose of characterising national criminal policies (Lappi-Seppälä 2008; Webster and Doob 2007).

Once this implementation has been explored in Spain, RIMES makes sense as an instrument for international comparison. For this reason, the RIMES team subsequently worked on the application of the instrument at the international level. In this book, we present comparative results from seven countries and states, in the hope that we have been able to demonstrate the virtues of this tool and its political-criminal usefulness.

References

Arenas-García, L. (2021). Constructing and validating an instrument to compare national criminal justice policies. *Revista Criminalidad de la Policía Nacional de Colombia*, 63(3), 107–125. https://doi.org/10.47741/17943108.313

Díez-Ripollés, J.L. (2011). La dimensión inclusión/exclusión social como guía de la política criminal comparada. *Revista Electrónica de Ciencia Penal y Criminología*, 13, 12. http://criminet.ugr.es/recpc/13/recpc13-12.pdf

Díez-Ripollés, J.L. (2013). Social inclusion and comparative criminal justice policy. *Journal of Scandinavian Studies in Criminology and Crime Prevention*, 14, 62–78.

Díez-Ripollés, J.L. and García-España, E. (2019). RIMES: An instrument to compare national criminal justice policies from the social exclusion dimension. *International E-Journal of Criminal Sciences, 1*(13), 1–27.

Lappi-Seppälä, T. (2008). Trust, welfare, and political culture: Explaining differences in national penal policies. *Crime and Justice*, 37(1), 313–387. https://doi.org/10.1086/525028

Webster, C.M. and Doob, A. (2007). Punitive trends and stable imprisonment rates in Canada. *Crime and Justice*, 36(1), 297–369. https://doi.org/10.1086/592807

Part II

AP-RIMES project

Results of the application of RIMES instrument in western jurisdictions

6 Pool 1

Control of public spaces

Pablo Rando-Casermeiro

1 Control of public spaces in the context of social exclusion

The first pool of the RIMES instrument is focused on the control of public spaces.

Criminal justice systems often make use of penal or "para-penal" control techniques (e.g., through administrative sanctioning law) to intervene in behaviour displayed in public spaces of cities by certain groups perceived as problematic. Very often, this type of control reaches people in situations of social exclusion, including ex-offenders. At other times, it is precisely the intervention of criminal control in public spaces that brings marginalised groups into contact with the criminal justice system *ex novo*, in so far as the behaviours conducted in public spaces that are intervened against may be defined as crimes in some of the countries or states under study – for example, vagrancy, loitering or prostitution (Doherty et al., 2008). In addition, certain police practices impacting on public spaces can contribute to the social exclusion of people considered suspicious or annoying (Von Hirsch and Shearing, 2000, 87). It is not unusual for a racial or ethnic bias to play a major role in this consideration of "suspected person" (Crocitti and Selmini, 2017, especially 108–109; García España, 2017).

In any of these cases, there is no doubt that, through the control of public spaces, penal control subsystems and the like can contribute to the social exclusion of individuals or, at the very least, to hindering the social integration of groups likely to come into conflict with criminal law – in short: suspects, offenders and ex-offenders (Díez-Ripollés, 2014, pp. 5, 6).

Our pool contains four items, numbered according to their order of appearance in the RIMES instrument. They are as follows:

1 Any person may be arrested for repeated street begging.
2 Any person may be arrested for repeated street loitering.
3 At its discretion, the police may enforce restrictions on specific individuals to access some public spaces (parks, squares, streets)
11. Discriminatory street police interventions (stop and search, arrests, frisks/body searches . . .) targeting specific groups occur regularly.

DOI: 10.4324/9781032661766-9

The first three items are rules, while the last one addresses a practice of the criminal control system (Díez Ripolles and García España, 2020, p. 689; García España and Díez-Ripollés, 2021, p. 263).

2 The control of public spaces pool

2.1 The process of building the public spaces pool

The four items that make up the first pool were definitively included in the RIMES instrument after a process that essentially consisted of two phases: a first one to identify rules and practices that generate social exclusion; and a second stage to validate such rules and practices by experts. Once the validation of experts had been obtained, a subsequent process was conducted for the screening of items by the research team, in order to reduce the instrument to more manageable dimensions (more details in Díez Ripolles and García España, 2020, pp. 674 et seq.).

In the first phase, the coordination team of the RIMES project initially produced a total of 35 items for the control of public spaces pool (RIMES Project, 2018, pp. 10–11). The team subsequently carried out a screening of items which resulted in a total of 28, divided into 11 practices and 17 rules, selected according to the scores obtained as regards completeness, extension and ease of access. The number of items was still too large so a new screening was decided on, now introducing the criteria of discrimination capacity and clarity.[1] In this way, 22 items were selected, including 12 rules and 10 practices (RIMES Project, 2018, pp. 26–27, 41, 47, 54).

The number of items in the control of public spaces pool still needed to be reduced, so, after a new selection by the team, the pool was finally made up of 12 items, comprising 8 rules and 4 practices (RIMES Project, 2018, pp. 58, 309). Those are the 12 items that passed to the second phase referred to above, i.e., the ones that were submitted to the assessment of international experts in two successive turns, together with the remaining items from other pools.

In the case of this pool, focused on control of public spaces, five of the items were validated by experts, specifically, three rules (items 1, 2 and 3) and two practices (items 9 and 11).

In a further process to reduce the instrument in order to improve its manageability, item 9 was discarded, as it had the lowest rating of the five.[2] This

1 Attached is a brief description of the five mentioned criteria: completeness (importance of the data), extension (this aspect is not too specific within pool), clarity (the item can be easily understood), ease of access (data is relatively easy to obtain) and discrimination capacity (it permits differentiation among the countries targeted by the study, according to the project) (RIMES Project, 2018, p. 8).

2 Item 9 obtained an Aiken's V coefficient of 0.72 in the first turn with international experts, and in the second turn it got 0.71. While a minimum of 0.70 was required for the item to be validated, the remaining four items had a considerably higher score (RIMES Project, 2018).

item, which dealt with a practice, was worded in these terms: "People are regularly arrested for soliciting prostitution on the street". Therefore, only four of the rules and practices related to the control of public spaces ended up being included in the final instrument: items number 1, 2, 3 and 11. The selection of the four items that were finally integrated into the instrument was made – as for the other pools that are part of it – according to the criteria of completeness, extension, ease of access, discrimination capacity and clarity. In conclusion, the items accumulating the highest combined score according to these five criteria were chosen, and the rest were discarded (further details in Díez Ripolles and García España, 2020, p. 677).

The four items that were finally chosen cover areas regarding the possibility of police detention for begging or loitering (items 1 and 2), as well as certain exclusionary and discriminatory police rules or practices (items 3 and 4). However, it is worth noting that, as mentioned above, a total of 35 items were considered as possible candidates for use in the instrument, which shows that the control of public spaces pool was very rich in content reflecting social exclusion. Thus, for example, a good number of items related to video surveillance, considered from different angles – such as the degree of discretion when used by the police or private companies, the prevalence of its implementation in urban areas or the possibility of its installation without prior signaling – were discarded. Other items related to the possibility of police detention for forbidden access to spaces open to the public, such as commercial areas or means of transport, were also considered.

Thirdly, the possibility of arrest for carrying out various activities in public spaces was also contemplated. Mention has already been made of loitering and begging, included in the instrument, or prostitution, which was finally discarded. However, the possibility of police detention for illicit street vending activities or the consumption of alcohol on public ways were also potential items that, in the end, were excluded from pool 1.

Finally, we must refer to various urban planning initiatives grouped around the ideas of defensible space and gentrification, which can generate social exclusion. Thus, for example, urban planning that does not promote socio-economic diversity in the areas of intervention, or the prevalence of demand for architecturally isolated residential areas with restricted access to non-residents. As we have already explained, the lower scores of all these potential items were the reason for their rejection (on this subject, see RIMES Project, 2018, 9–11).

2.2 *Discussion of selected items*

The first section includes the four items that make up the control of public spaces pool. In order to operationalise the selected items, a description was added so that the content of each one could be accurately understood. This would ensure that the results obtained in each country or state were homogeneous, irrespective of the team members working in each one of them.

Descriptions were prepared by a small number of members from the research team, and were then subjected to debate with the whole team.

In this section, we will address some aspects that were discussed regarding each item's description. Due to space constraints, we will only comment on those aspects that were particularly controversial in the debates among the team members.

In item 1, the discussion on the description wording dealt with how to properly limit the concept of begging. Cases in which begging did not in itself constitute an offence but was used as a means of committing other offences – such as fraud or neglect of minors – were finally excluded. As regards item 2, the team concluded that arrests for disobedience to law enforcement agents should be excluded. That is, a loitering detention would not be considered where the police order an individual to leave the place and, as a result of his or her fail to comply, he or she is arrested. Therefore, it is loitering itself that must give rise to a detention. In the case of item 3, since it was a rule and not a practice, it was concluded that there should be a legal authorisation to exclude from public spaces those individuals described in the item. In other words, the police could or could not – depending on the discretion attributed to them – expel such individuals from public spaces, but this procedure should always be covered by some regulation. Additionally, the possibility was raised that the item might be difficult to answer, since it refers to rules that are likely to be scattered across local regulations (RIMES Project, 2018, p. 294).

Finally, with regard to item 11, one of the main aspects under discussion was what should be understood by "regularly". The team concluded that the item would occur if police interventions targeted the groups described in the item disproportionately with respect to the majority population, irrespective of the temporal frequency with which this practice took place.

3 Methodology used to solve each item in the control of public spaces pool

3.1 Methodology used to solve the rules (items 1, 2 and 3)

Given that we are dealing with rules, the methodology mainly used has consisted of the search, compilation and study of the legal sources of each country or state, combining substantive and procedural legislation. Academic works and jurisprudence were also consulted in some cases where there could be room for interpretative issues.

As regards legal sources, it should be clear that both criminal and administrative legislation was taken into account, at all administrative levels that have regulatory authority: state, regional and local. In cases where begging prohibitions were contained in local ordinances, operational reasons advised to perform a sampling of them. Thus, in the case of item 2 applied to Italy, a consultation was made of the municipal ordinances of the ten most populated cities in the country. In the case of items 1, 2 and 3 concerning Spain, the sample was limited to the ordinances of all those municipalities with more than 200,000 inhabitants, i.e., 28 municipalities.

Sometimes, especially in view of the difficulty or impossibility of finding specific regulations regarding the content of the item, or in view of the persistence of aspects needing clarification, experts from some countries were consulted. This happened with items 2 and 3 in Germany and item 3 in Poland and California.

As a complementary method, in some cases it was useful to consult other Internet resources, such as news pages or media, in order to obtain guidance on the items' content.

3.2 Methodology used to solve the practice of item 11

This item aimed to find out whether discriminatory police practices – such as stops for identification, detentions or body searches – were regularly carried regarding certain population groups on the street, in each country or state.

The methodology used to respond to this item was mainly through secondary sources. We searched empirical studies and data sources on the content of the item, in each country or state, both from official institutions or other national or international organisations, as well as those emanating from academia.

As with the previous items, it was considered appropriate to resort to web resources – such as information or media pages, institutional portals or reports prepared by non-governmental organisations – in order to obtain guidance or complementary information on the subject under study.

In the specific case of Poland, and since there were doubts about the resolution of the item, experts were also consulted.

4 Results of items in the control of public spaces pool

Prior to the presentation of results regarding each item in the pool under study, we should devote a few lines to the question of its reliability. To ensure correctness of the response given to each item in the different countries and states analysed, each item was subjected to validation by different international experts.

Most of the answers to the four items were validated without further comments by the country experts who were responsible for reviewing the responses, thus making them reliable. However, the review of the experts sometimes led to the inclusion of complementary information, explanations, clarifications or fine distinctions. These observations were taken into account and the response protocols to the items were modified accordingly. Only in one case was the response or solution originally given by the research team to the item altered. It was item 3 regarding England and Wales: although the team initially replied that the police could not exclude certain people from public spaces at their discretion, the expert who validated the item concluded that the item did occur in the mentioned jurisdiction, based on various normative input he provided. The rest of the items kept the same answer.

With regard to the first item, and only in the case of Italy, some corrections were introduced concerning the appropriate citation of some legal changes. In item 2, the experts chosen for Germany and England and Wales reported the need to add additional information. As regards item 3, the response given to the protocol for Italy was also complemented by the incorporation of some legal changes after the expert's review, as occurred in item 1.

Item 11, which deals with the only practice included in the control of public spaces pool, received the largest number of comments from experts.

In the cases of Germany and Italy, the experts who reviewed the items provided additional information on data or studies regarding police identifications that had not been included by the team in the protocols for response to items; therefore, those studies and data were added. The New York protocol was also amended after its revision, this time to include jurisprudence regarding police identifications that had been omitted in the original reply to the item.

4.1 *Results by country*

The results obtained are detailed in Table 6.1 below, which shows whether or not the different items concur in each of the countries or states under study:

Table 6.1 Results of the control of public spaces pool, by item and country/state

	Germany	*California*	*Spain*	*Italy*	*New York*	*Poland*	*England & Wales*
Item 1	No	Yes	No	Yes	Yes	No	Yes
Item 2	No	Yes	No	No	Yes	No	Yes
Item 3	Yes	No	No	Yes	Yes	No	Yes
Item 11	Yes	Yes	Yes	Yes	Yes	No	Yes

Source: Own elaboration

The results show some striking contrasts. For example, while in New York and England and Wales all four items concur, in Poland none of them are present. This implies that Poland is the country generating the least social exclusion in the control of public spaces, followed by Spain, where only one of the items – number 11 – has been verified. Germany – with two concurrent items – would be in an intermediate place, while California and Italy – both with three out of four items present – would be placed in the area of greater social exclusion.

However, the location of the analysed countries and states on the continuum of social exclusion requires, in addition to the number of "yeses" and/or "nos" obtained in each item, the weighting of each of them. The scores regarding social exclusion obtained by the different states and countries are, from highest to lowest social exclusion, as follows: New York and England and Wales: 10; Italy: 7.59; California: 7.45; Germany: 5.04; Spain: 2.49; Poland: 0.

For a better display of the results, the following graph shows the location of each country or state on the continuum of social exclusion:

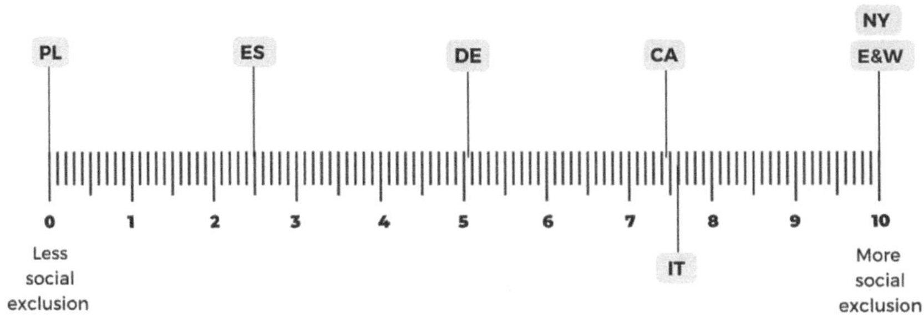

Figure 6.1 Position of countries on the continuum of social exclusion in terms of control of public spaces

4.2 *Brief explanation of the results*

Next, we will briefly review the content of the items, in order to get a more detailed understanding of the results obtained.

Item 1

As far as item 1 is concerned, we can easily see that begging is more frequently banned in Anglo-Saxon countries. Indeed, detention for begging is applicable in California, New York and England and Wales.

In the case of the two US states, it should be explained that the begging prohibition has been declared unconstitutional since it violates the fundamental right to freedom of expression enshrined in the First Amendment to the US Constitution (see Lauriello, 2016, and the cases *Schaumburg v. Citizens for Better Environment*, of 20 February 1980, and *Loper v. New York City Police Department*, of 17 June 1991). However, this has not prevented begging from being punished by criminal law at times, when it is considered that the benefits of incrimination justify the impact on freedom of expression (like in the case *Young v. New York City Transit Authority*, of 29 January 1990). In the United Kingdom, detention for begging behaviour is applicable as of an old Vagrancy Act of 1824. Although this conduct does not currently carry a prison sentence, it is a criminal offence punishable by a fine allowing the police to arrest the individual engaging in begging activities (Johnsen and Fitzpatrick, 2010, p. 1706). This old provision must be complemented with the "Anti-Social Behaviour Orders" (ASBOs), established by the Crime and Disorder Act of 1998 (Johnsen and Fitzpatrick, 2010, p. 1706; Larrauri Pijoan, 2007, p. 13; Villacampa Estiarte 2017, p. 43, Rando Casermeiro, 2019). This law was replaced by another one of 2014 (called "Anti-Social, Crime and Policy Act") that works in a very similar way to the previous one, in the issues that concern us here. These laws offer a very generic definition of what constitutes anti-social behaviour, namely any conduct likely to cause alarm, disquiet or annoyance to neighbours. With such a broad definition, it is not surprising that begging has ended up being defined as "anti-social behaviour" for the purposes of such legislation (Johnsen and Fitzpatrick, 2010, p. 1706).

The concurrence of item 1 in all Anglo-Saxon countries could be due to the survival of old vagrancy laws, which have been superseded in most continental European countries.

But this item is not only present in the Anglo-Saxon geopolitical environment. Italy, through the introduction of the so-called "Salvini decrees",[3] has also adopted the incrimination of begging (more details in Curi, 2019). However, this item is not found in the other continental European countries studied.

This does not mean that begging cannot be punished in these countries. Thus, Spain is a country where begging can be administratively sanctioned by municipal ordinances. Nevertheless, detention is not applied to such behaviour (arts. 490 et seq. of the Code of Criminal Procedure). In Germany, on the other hand, begging is not even considered an offence, let alone a criminal offence, as it was removed from the Criminal Code in 1976 (*Wissenschaftliche Dienste*, 2016).

Item 2

Similar conclusions should be drawn from the results of item 2. With the difference that, in this case, we find that the ban on loitering does seem exclusive to Anglo-Saxon countries. Table 6.1 shows clearly that police arrest for loitering is only present in the Anglo-Saxon area. In the case of the continental European countries under study, it should be stressed that loitering as such is not even defined as an infringement, in either the criminal or administrative spheres.

We know, however, that the ban on loitering is not foreign to the tradition of some continental European countries. Thus, for example, in the now repealed Spanish Law 16/1970, of 6 August, on Dangerousness and Social Rehabilitation, conduct akin to loitering was described which, even though it was not considered to be a criminal offence, was defined as a dangerous status that could lead to the arrest of the person considered dangerous. But it rather seems that in the two selected US states, as well as in England and Wales, the tradition of punishing loitering persists.

Item 3

Examination of item 3 reveals a break in the already mentioned trend: indeed, unlike the results obtained for items 1 and 2, there is no greater concentration

3 We refer to the Decree-Law 113/2018, of 4 October, on Urgent Measures on International Protection, Immigration and Public Security, and to the Decree-Law 53/2019, of 14 June, on Urgent Measures on Public Order and Security.

of "yeses" in Anglo-Saxon countries than in continental European countries. In the US, some legislation allows the police to discretionally exclude people from public spaces. Prohibitions of access are very often contained in administrative regulations or municipal codes (Goldstein, 2003; Herbert and Beckett, 2010, Díez-Ripollés, 2014).

The best-known case is the city of Seattle, where the so-called "parks exclusion orders" are applicable. These prohibitions of access, established for people who infringe the park's regulations, can last up to one year, and the offender may be subject to police arrest if he or she returns to the forbidden site (Herbert and Beckett, 2010 and 2017).

However, similar provisions were not found in the state of California. Besides, it should be noted that, although item 3 is also present in the case of the state of New York, police restrictions seem to be limited only to the common and open spaces of public housing projects.

As regards the other countries imposing discretionary police bans on access to public places, we note that, in the case of Germany, these prohibitions are simply based on a greater discretion granted to the police.[4] However, in the cases of England and Wales and Italy, these powers seem to stem from relatively recent legislative initiatives for security reasons. In the case of England and Wales, the legislation already mentioned for item one should be included in this brief summary: article 35 of the Anti-Social Behaviour, Crime and Policy Act, of 2014, allows uniformed police officers to exclude an individual from a certain place for a period of up to 48 hours, in two scenarios: First, if the officer thinks that such person has contributed, or is likely to contribute, either to the causation of alarm, annoyance or harassment towards neighbours, or to the perpetration of a crime or disorderly conduct. Secondly, if it is simply understood that expelling such individual can contribute to preventing the occurrence of any of those events. In these cases, the police only need the authorisation of a police inspector (art. 34) to proceed with the expulsion of an individual and/or to prohibit him or her from going to such place. Failure to comply with this order amounts to a criminal offence (on this, see Moss and Moss, 2019).

With regard to Italy, citizen security legislation passed in 2017 has granted discretionary powers on municipalities to order the expulsion from public spaces of certain individuals who engage in behaviour deemed "improper". This faculty is covered by the Minniti decree,[5] which empowers the Ministry of the Interior to allow municipalities to issue the so-called "urban DASPOs" for the aforementioned purpose. "DASPO" is an abbreviation of the words *Divieto di Accedere alle Manifestazioni Sportive*, i.e., an authorisation to exclude

4 See, for example, art. 38 of the *Bundespolizeigesetz*, of 19 October 1994; art. 16 of the *Polizeiaufgabengesetz* from Bavaria, of 14 September 1990.

5 This is the *Decreto-legge 17 febbraio 2017, n. 13, recante disposizioni urgenti per l'accelerazione dei procedimenti in materia di protezione internazionale, nonche' per il contrasto dell'immigrazione illegale.*

certain persons from access to sports facilities. Through the Minniti decree, this type of exclusion – stemming from sporting events – was extended to public spaces in general.

Therefore, in the case of England and Wales and Italy, these are recent trends that are not due to a geopolitical reason or to a different legal tradition in the various countries or states under study. As we can see from the brief examination of the countries where item 3 is present, there are different reasons – not always necessarily connected among them – that seem to account for the existence of this type of access prohibitions.

As can be seen in Table 6.1, police exclusions of individuals from public spaces have not yet reached Spain, California and Poland.

Item 11

Table 6.1 shows that item 11 is the most frequent one. Only Poland obtained a negative reply. In the remaining countries and states under study, police in one way or another engage in discriminatory practices in arrests, frisks, searches or stops for identification purposes. The review of empirical studies and/or official data that has been carried out shows that this reality is commonplace in virtually all countries and states.[6] The sources consulted confirm the existence of a police discriminatory bias beyond the simple finding that ethnic minorities are subject to police stops in a greater number of cases. Indeed, when control variables were introduced – especially those regarding police effectiveness, but also others of a sociodemographic nature – it was noted that the discriminatory component of police action persisted.

In view of this overwhelming result, perhaps it is worth to carry out a more detailed analysis of the only country where a negative answer was given: Poland. The initial problem we face in this country is the lack of specific studies available on the content of this item, so we studied various reports on the Polish situation with regard to it.

Thus, in a European Fundamental Rights Agency (FRA, hereinafter) report which used a sample of 500 Roma people in Poland, 20 per cent of the sample said that they had been questioned by the police. In addition, 51 per cent of

6 Although this is not the place to go into detail on this issue, we provide the following references pointing to discriminatory treatment by the police: For California: Lofstrom et al., 2018; Hetey et al., 2016; Chanin et al., 2016; Armentrout et al., 2007; Ayres and Borowsky, 2008. For New York: Gelman et al., 2007; Ridgeway, 2007; Goel et al., 2016. Only the study by Coviello and Persico (2015) found no discriminatory bias. In Germany there are no official data on the content of this item, something that has been criticised (Schicht, 2013, p. 34). However, qualitative studies such as the one by Pühl (2019), reveal that this item does occur in such country. Data from the "European Union Survey on Minorities and Discrimination" or EU-MIDIS –FRA, 2010–, point in the same direction. For Spain, see Wagman, 2005; Schmit and Pernas, 2008; FRA, 2010, p. 31; García-Añón et al., 2013; García-España et al., 2016. For Italy, see FRA, 2017, p. 70. For England & Wales, see Borooah, 2011; Miller, 2010; Parmar, 2011; Quinton, 2011. Only the study by Ariel and Tankebe (2016) shows more nuanced results but, on the whole, they suggest that the discriminatory bias discussed above exists.

the respondents believed they had been stopped by the police because of their ethnic origin, with this percentage being somewhat lower – although still significant (44 per cent) – in the case of stops carried out by the border control authorities (FRA, 2009, pp. 10–11).

In the second wave conducted by the FRA on minorities and discrimination (EU-MIDIS-II), a survey was carried out in Poland with a sample of new immigrants – a group of people who had arrived in this country in the last ten years – and the result was that 14 per cent of the sample had been stopped by the police in the last five years. Although only 1 per cent of the sample had perceived that the stop was because of their ethnic background, this percentage rose to 9 per cent when expressly asked about the last time they had contact with the police (FRA, 2019, p. 4).

These surveys are coupled with concerns about discriminatory policing practices expressed by the United Nations Committee on the Elimination of Racial Discrimination. The 2019 final report on Poland shows concern over "allegations of ethnically biased practices by law enforcement officials against Roma" (UN, 2019, p. 6).

However, these data and reports by themselves do not prove the existence of discriminatory police treatment, since there is no comparison with groups from the majority population. These doubts prompted the consultation of experts, which did not result in a clear answer. In short, we do not have enough data to say that the police engage in discriminatory practices on a regular basis, so Poland was the only country where this item was not answered with a "yes".

As a working hypothesis, the ethnic composition of the Polish population, much more homogeneous than that of other countries under study, is pointed out as a possible explanation for the negative response to this item.

5 Conclusions

5.1 Suitability of the items regarding the control of public spaces to measure social exclusion

Once the suitability of the RIMES instrument was verified from a general theoretical point of view, one of the questions faced by this study was the performance capacity of the instrument and, more specifically, of the control of public spaces pool in practice. In view of the results obtained in each of the items, we can draw the following conclusions, grouped around some of the criteria used to select the items.

In terms of the *discrimination capacity*, the results for each item allow us to differentiate between the seven countries or states under study. There has not been a case where an item occurred in all countries or, alternatively, did not occur in any country. Therefore, the items that make up this pool are suitable when applied to the different countries, from this point of view.

Secondly, according to the criterion of *ease of access* (i.e., that the data are relatively easy to obtain), we had some localised difficulties in very specific areas (for example, checking item 11 in Poland), but in the vast majority of cases there have been no serious difficulties in getting responses to each item.

5.2 *Social exclusion generated by the control of public spaces*

This paper was a partial application of the RIMES instrument to five European countries and two US states, in order to verify the social exclusion caused by the penal system in the specific field of control of public spaces.

As seen from the results obtained, there is a general trend in the two US states, as well as Italy and England and Wales, towards a greater social exclusion, while the rest of the European countries, in general, show a lower degree of social exclusion. In particular, the state of New York and England and Wales turn out to be the ones that would cause the greatest exclusion, since they are the only cases where our four items have been confirmed. California and Italy would be close, with a clear tendency towards social exclusion, with three of the four items of this pool present. All this is in line with the hypothesis of Díez-Ripollés (2011, p. 18), on the fact that the US would be among the countries with the highest level of social exclusion caused by penal systems. However, with regard to this specific pool, England and Wales in principle show greater social exclusion than the state of California. At the opposite end would be Poland, where none of the items is present, and Spain, where only one item of the four that make up the pool has been confirmed. Germany is positioned in an intermediate place.

It also seems clear that the prohibition of begging and loitering – and the consequent possibility of arrest by the police – would be more widespread, in general, in Anglo-Saxon countries, although this is not exclusive to that environment, as evidenced by item 1 concerning Italy.

Item 11 is the one with the most homogeneity. Discriminatory police practices are present in almost all the geographical areas analysed. In this sense, item 11 seems to be the one provoking the most social exclusion of the four under study. The widespread occurrence of ethnically biased police identifications or searches is therefore particularly worrying.

In any case, there is no doubt that, through the control of public spaces pool, the RIMES instrument has shown its usefulness in bringing to light the different degree of exclusion caused by the penal systems in the countries and states being compared and, with this, the instrument contributes to position them in a continuum of social exclusion.

Finally, it is noteworthy that, out of the seven countries and states analysed, most of them – specifically four – are highly exclusionary when using techniques to control public spaces. We therefore conclude that the RIMES instrument reveals how the control of public spaces can contribute significantly to social exclusion through the penal systems of Western countries. Only Poland, Spain and Germany seem to have low or intermediate levels of social exclusion.

References

Ariel, B. & Tankebe, J. (2018). Racial Stratification and Multiple Outcomes in Police Stops and Searches. *Policing and Society*, 28(5), 507–525. https://doi.org/10.1080/10439463.2016.1184270

Armentrout, M. et al. (2007). *Cops and Stops: Racial Profiling and a Preliminary Statistical Analysis of Los Angeles Police Department Traffic Stops and Searches.* California State Polytechnic University, Pomona and Loyola Marymount University.

Ayres, I. & Borowsky, J. (2008). *Study of Racially Disparate Outcomes in the Los Angeles Police Department.* U.S. Department of Justice, Office of Justice Programs.

Borooah, V. K. (2011). Racial Disparity in Police Stops and Searches in England and Wales. *Journal of Quantitative Criminology*, 27, 453–473. https://doi.org/10.1007/s10940-011-9131-0

Chanin, J. et al. (2016). *Traffic Enforcement in San Diego, California. An Analysis of SDPD Vehicle Stops in 2014 and 2015.* San Diego State University.

Coviello, D. & Persico, N. (2015). An Economic Analysis of Black-White Disparities in the New York Police Department's Stop-and-Frisk Program. *The Journal of Legal Studies*, 44(2), 315–359. https://doi.org/10.1086/684292

Crocitti, S. & Selmini, R. (2017). Controlling Immigrants: The Latent Function of Italian Administrative Orders. *European Journal of Criminal Policy and Research*, 23, 99–114. https://doi.org/10.1007/s10610-016-9311-4

Curi, F. (2019). Il reato de accatonaggio: "A volte ritornano". Il nuovo art. 669-bis c-p. del d.l. 113/2018, convertito con modificazioni dalla l. 132/2018. *Diritto Penale Contemporaneo.*

Díez-Ripollés, J.L. (2011). La dimensión inclusión/exclusión social como guía de la política criminal comparada. *Revista Electrónica de Ciencia Penal y Criminología*, 13, 12. http://criminet.ugr.es/recpc/13/recpc13-12.pdf

Díez-Ripollés, J.L. (2014). El control de los espacios públicos como técnica de exclusión social. Algunos contrastes regionales. *Revista Española de Investigación Criminológica*, 12, 1–28. https://doi.org/10.46381/reic.v12i0.82

Díez-Ripollés. J.L. & García España, E. (2020). RIMES: Un instrumento de comparación de políticas criminales nacionales desde la exclusión social (RIMES: An Instrument to Compare National Criminal Justice Policies from the Social Exclusion Dimension). *Política Criminal*, 15(30), 670–693.

Doherty, J. et al. (2008). Homelessness and Exclusion: Regulating Public Space in European Cities. *Surveillance & Society*, 5(3), 290–314. https://doi.org/10.24908/ss.v5i3.3425

FRA (2009). *Data in Focus. La población romaní.* Oficina de Publicaciones de la Unión Europea.

FRA (2010). *Por una actuación policial más eficaz. Guía para entender y evitar la elaboración de perfiles étnicos discriminatorios.* Oficina de Publicaciones de la Unión Europea.

FRA (2017). *Second European Union Minorities and Discrimination Survey. Main Results.* Oficina de Publicaciones de la Unión Europea.

FRA (2019). *Second European Union Minorities and Discrimination Survey. Summary of Main Results-PL.* Oficina de Publicaciones de la Unión Europea.

García Añón, J. et al. (2013). *Identificación policial por perfil étnico en España. Informe sobre experiencias y actitudes en relación con las actuaciones policiales.* Tirant lo Blanch.

García España, E. (2017). Extranjeros sospechosos, condenados y excondenados: un mosaico de exclusión social. *Revista Electrónica de Ciencia Penal y Criminología*, 19–15, 1–30.

García España, E., Arenas García, L. & Miller, J. (2016). *Identificaciones policiales y discriminación racial en España. Evaluación de un programa para su reducción.* Tirant lo Blanch.

García España, E. & Díez-Ripollés, J.L. (2021). La exclusión social generada por el sistema penal español: Aplicación del instrumento RIMES. *In-Dret*, 1, 259–281.

Gelman, A., Fagan, J. & Kiss, A. (2007). An Analysis of the New York City Police Department's "Stop-and-Frisk" Policy in the Context of Claims of Racial Bias. *Journal of the American Statistical Association*, 102(479), 813–823. https://doi.org/10.1198/016214506000001040

Goel, S., Rao Justin, M. & Shroff, R. (2016). Precint or Prejudice? Understanding Racial Disparities in New York City's Stop-and-Frisk Policy. *The Annuals of Applied Statistics.* 10(1), 365–394. http://dx.doi.org/10.2139/ssrn.2572718

Goldstein, E. (2003). Kept Out: Responding to Public Housing No-Trespass Policies. *Harvard Civil Rights-Civil Liberties Journal*, 38, 215–245.

Herbert, K. & Beckett, S. (2010). *Banished: The New Social Control in Urban America.* Oxford University Press.

Herbert, K. & Beckett, S. (2017). Banishment and the Post-Industrial City: Lessons from Seattle. *European Journal on Criminal Policy and Research*, 23, 27–40. https://doi.org/10.1007/s10610-016-9316-z

Hetey, R.C. et al. (2016). *Data for Change: A Statistical Analysis of Police Stops, Searches, Handcuffings, and Arrests in Oaklanda, Calif., 2013–2014.* Stanford University. SPARK: Social Psychological Answers to Real-World Questions.

Johnsen, S. & Fitzpatrick, S. (2010). Revanchist Sanitisation or Coercive Care? The Use of Enforcement to Combat Begging, Street Drinking, and Rough Sleeping in England. *Urban Studies*, 47(8), 1703–1723. https://doi.org/10.1177/0042098009356128

Larrauri Pijoan, E. (2007). Ayuntamientos de izquierda y control del delito. *InDret*, 3, 1–23.

Lauriello, A. (2016). Panhandling Regulation After Reed v. Town of Gilbert. *Columbia Law Review*, 116(3), 1105–1142.

Lofstrom, M. et al. (2018). *New Insights into California Arrests. Trends, Disparities and County Differences.* Public Policy Institute of California.

Miller, J. (2010). Stop and Search in England. A Reformed Tactic or Business as Usual? *British Journal of Criminology*, 50(5), 954–974. https://doi.org/10.1093/bjc/azq021

Moss, C. J. & Moss, K. (2019). Out of Sight: Social Control and the Regulation of Public Space in Manchester. *Social Sciences*, 8(5), 146. https://doi.org/10.3390/socsci8050146

Parmar, A. (2011). Stop and Search in London: Counter-Terrorist or Counter-Productive? *Policing & Society*, 21(4), 369–382. https://doi.org/10.1080/10439463.2011.617984

Pühl, K. (2019). *Racial Profilling. Erfahrungen, Wirkungen, Widerstand.* Rosa-Luxemburg-Stiftung.

Quinton, P. (2011). The Formation of Suspicions: Police Stops and Search Practices in England and Wales. *Policing & Society*, 21(4), 357–368. https://doi.org/10.1080/10439463.2011.610193

Rando Casermeiro, P. (2019). Modelos comparados de control local de espacios públicos, in: Izquierdo, M. and Alarcón Sotomayor, L (eds.). *Estudios sobre la ley de seguridad ciudadana*. Aranzadi.

Ridgeway, G. (2007). *Analysis of Racial Disparities in the New York Police Department's Stop, Question, and Frisk Practices*. RAND Corporation. Santa Monica. Arlington. Pittsburgh.

RIMES Project (2018). *Executive Report*. Unpublished.

Schicht, G. (2013). Racial Profiling bei Polizei in Deutschland. Bildungsbedarf? Beratungsresistenz? *Zeitschrift für internationale Bildungs- forschung und Entwicklungspädagogik*, 36(2), 32–37. https://doi. org/10.25656/01:10622

Schmit, M. & Pernas, B. (2008). *Pasos hacia la igualdad. El Proyecto STEPSS (Strategies for Effective Police Stop and Search)* en España. *Grupo de Estudios y Alternativas*, 21 (GEA 21).

UN (2019). *Observaciones finales sobre los informes periódicos 22 a 24 combinados de Polonia*. Comité para la Eliminación de la Discriminación Racial. Naciones Unidas.

Villacampa Estiarte, C. (2017). Municipal Ordinances and Street Prostitution in Spain. *European Journal on Criminal Policy and Research*, 23(1), 41–57. https://doi. org/10.1007/s10610-016-9313-2

von Hirsch, A. & Shearing, C. (2000). Exclusion from Public Space, in: von Hirsch, A., Garland, D. & Wakefield, A. (eds.) *Ethical and Social Perspectives on Situational Crime Prevention*. Hart Publishing.

Wagman, D. (2005). Perfil racial en España: Investigaciones y recomendaciones. *Grupo de Estudios y Alternativas*, 21.

Wissenschaftliche Dienste (2016). *Regelungen zu Bettelei*. Sachstand WD 7-3000-.

7 Pool 2

Legal safeguards[1]

Bertha Verónica Prado-Manrique

1 Social exclusion and legal safeguards

Criminal guarantees can be defined as the set of principles, rights and prerogatives that ensure respect for the dignity and freedom of persons who come into contact with the criminal justice system; at the same time, they seek to ensure the holding of a fair trial (Ferrajoli, 2000). In this sense, they are obligations that a constitutional state must fulfil to protect the freedom of the individual from excessive punitive intervention by the organs of criminal control (Villavicencio Terreros, 2017).

The welfare penal model characterises penal intervention as socially exclusive when it seeks to ensure that the person who comes into contact with the organs of criminal control finds it more difficult to break the law or that it is more difficult to avoid being caught (Díez-Ripollés, 2011, 2015). In this context, the social exclusion generated by the criminal justice system in terms of criminal guarantees is linked to the existence of rules or practices that aim to ensure that the experience of criminal proceedings is characterised by a particular rigour or severity. This may take the form of greater difficulty in accessing certain resources or services provided by the criminal justice system, such as free legal aid in criminal cases. This exclusionary character can also be seen in the failure to consider the specific needs or characteristics of the suspects, defendants, convicted or exonerated persons to whom the criminal justice system responds. For example, the fact that convicted persons in prison suffer from a mental disorder and require differentiated treatment (Díez-Ripollés, 2017).

The securitarian tendency of contemporary criminal policy reflects this socially exclusive tenor, as it prioritises the effectiveness of the criminal law and its mechanisms of prosecution and punishment. This political-criminal tendency seeks to guarantee security by relaxing the prerogatives that seek to protect personal freedom from arbitrary criminal intervention (Díez-Ripollés, 2005, 2013; Pérez Cepeda, 2007).

1 This chapter is also the result of grant PRE2019–088354 funded by MCIN/AEI/10.13039/501100011033 and by "ESF invest in your future".

DOI: 10.4324/9781032661766-10

As mentioned in previous chapters, the aim of applying the RIMES instrument in different countries is to construct a continuum that allows us to classify national penal systems as more or less exclusive, based on the effects that certain penal rules and practices produce on suspects, accused, convicted and ex-convicts (Díez-Ripollés and García España, 2019). In this chapter, we will focus on explaining the social exclusion generated by the pool of legal safeguards, based on the results obtained after the application of RIMES in the following European countries: Germany, Spain, Italy, Poland and England and Wales; and in two states in the United States: California and New York.

The process of constructing the pool of legal safeguards that is part of the RIMES instrument is explained below. It then discusses the methodology used to respond to each of the items that make up the analysed pool, and finally presents the results obtained for each item in each of the countries in which the RIMES instrument has been applied.

2 The construction of the legal safeguards' pool

2.1 Brief review of the pool construction process

The design, construction and validation of the legal safeguards pool went through different stages (Díez-Ripollés and García España, 2019; RIMES Project, 2018). The first phase in the construction of the RIMES tool was the identification and selection of penal rules and practices from different areas of the penal system that have been identified as factors of social exclusion, including those related to legal safeguards. The result of this search and selection was 236 indicators, of which 20 were those that initially formed the pool of legal safeguards. It is worth mentioning that these rules and practices were selected from a set of guidelines established by the RIMES team (RIMES Project, 2018).

Once the rules and practices had been identified, they were subjected to a first evaluation by the RIMES team, based on their adaptation to the criteria of completeness, extension, and ease of resolution. The score obtained by the indicators making up pool 2 placed it as the third best pool, with a score of 75.8 out of a maximum of 100. At the end of this first screening, pool 2 was reduced to 18 indicators, 6 rules and 12 practices by eliminating the indicators that obtained a score equal to or less than 4 in the sum of the scores of the three indicators evaluated. A second screening was then carried out, considering the discriminatory power and clarity of each item. On this occasion, the team decided to eliminate those indicators with a score of less than or equal to 1 in the completeness and discriminatory capacity criteria. Pool 2 remained with the 18 indicators from the previous stage. The next step was to carefully review the 18 indicators to identify and eliminate redundant items,[2] which resulted in the elimination of three of them (RIMES Project, 2018).

2 Minutes RIMES 23, of April 21, 2014.

The RIMES team then had to evaluate each of these indicators. On this occasion, the scoring criterion was the importance of the indicator in expressing social exclusion from the prison system. Once the scores were obtained, a consensus factor was developed based on the degree of acceptance by the judges of the indicator's ability to be exclusive. If a score greater than or equal to 75 was obtained, the evaluated indicator was considered to be exclusive. Similarly, a Delphi method was used by the research team to determine their experience in each of the dimensions of the penal system evaluated. The results obtained for pool 2 showed that the judges' knowledge of the items that make up the legal safeguards was mostly theoretical and not empirical (RIMES Project, 2018).

Once the RIMES team had completed its assessment of the items, the indicators selected were validated by international experts. Specifically, they had to assess the adequacy of each indicator to measure social exclusion according to the definition developed by the research team. The experts had to assess the extent to which each indicator reflected a penal system designed to incapacitate those who come into contact with it. For the validation, there were two profiles of experts, differentiated by their accumulated experience as researchers in the prevention or prosecution of crime, as well as their knowledge of the relationship between the identified areas of the criminal justice system and social exclusion (RIMES Project, 2018).

The current composition of pool 2 – and of the instrument as a whole – was the result of two phases of validation by nearly 100 international experts from 18 countries in Europe and North America. The 126 items were assessed for their suitability to measure social exclusion and for their suitability to the pool in which they were found. Once the results were available, the RIMES team made a final selection to obtain a smaller number of indicators that would allow the construction of an easily applicable measurement tool from a practical point of view. The criterion used for this last step was the value obtained in the V of Aiken. After this final selection, pool 2 of legal safeguards consisted of 4 items – 3 rules and 1 practice – out of the 39 items that make up the RIMES instrument (RIMES Project, 2018).

2.2 *Item descriptions in the pool of legal safeguards*

Once the final version of the RIMES instrument had been validated, each of its indicators was made operational by writing a description. For this purpose, the RIMES team drew on the pilot application of the instrument in Spain (García España and Díez-Ripollés, 2021). The discussion and acceptance of each description varied according to the topic addressed by the item and the complexity of each of them.

Item 21: the criminal justice system lacks indigent defense services

Item 21 refers to the lack of a system of free legal aid provided for persons accused of committing a crime, who do not have the financial means to pay for it. It is a rule, and its description defines the right of all suspects to free legal defense in criminal proceedings.[3]

Item 22: payment of court fees is legally required from defendant in order to get access to appellate review

Item 22 is a rule that refers to the existence of a rule in the criminal justice system requiring the payment of fees for filing a criminal appeal. The description of this item states that the payment of fees should be required as a condition for lodging an appeal in the first instance, and always in the case of criminal proceedings.[4]

Item 24: the regular term for police detention established by the law exceeds five days

Item 24 is a rule and seeks to determine whether the maximum period of police custody in a country exceeds five days. As a result of discussions on the elaboration of the description, detention periods for terrorism and organised crime have been excluded, as these are offences that are in most cases more complex to investigate. Administrative detention and detention of foreigners were also excluded as they are not linked to suspicion of having committed a criminal offence.[5]

Item 25: a significant number mentally ill inmates serve their sentences in regular correctional facilities

The drafting of the description corresponding to item 25 was particularly complex. As a practice aimed at verifying the effective response of the prison system to offenders suffering from a mental disorder or illness, the drafting of its description required several debates and rewrites. The first aspect to be defined was what was to be understood by a *significant number*. The team decided to operationalise this statement by 15 per cent, in line with the resolution and decision adopted when the issue was resolved in Spain.[6]

Subsequently, and because of the initial limitations and difficulties in responding to this item in Poland and England and Wales, it was decided to discuss its description again. On the one hand, it was necessary to operationalise the concept of *correctional facilities*. It was agreed that the existence of specialised therapeutic units within prisons would be included in this concept. On the other hand, it was necessary to define the universe of the item, which would finally allow the formula to be established to calculate

3 Minutes AP-RIMES seven, of October 30, 2019.

4 Minutes AP-RIMES seven, eight and eight, of October 30, November 20 and December 18, 2019, respectively.

5 Minutes AP-RIMES eight, of November 20, 2019.

6 Minutes AP-RIMES eight, of November 20, 2019.

the percentage required by the item. To this end, two alternative proposals were developed, depending on whether, on the one hand, only the semi-imputable and non-imputable offenders were taken into account, or, on the other hand, whether offenders suffering from a mental disorder and serving a prison sentence were also included.[7] The choice of one of the alternatives did not come quickly, so it was decided that each team would try to answer the question according to the two alternatives. After presenting and discussing their solutions, the second interpretation was chosen as it allowed the indicator to be resolved in all countries. Although the assumptions of addiction and drug dependence were excluded from this description, it was agreed to consider the definition of "person with mental illness" provided in each country analysed.[8]

3 Methodology used to answer the items of the legal safeguards' pool

Each of the items in pool 2 required the use of different methodological strategies. These were chosen on the basis of whether the item to be solved was a rule or a practice, and the reliability of the methodological technique used to identify the information required in each case.

On the one hand, the methodology used by all countries to resolve the rules that make up pool 2 – items 21, 22 and 24 – focused on the review of secondary sources. Firstly, both national and international legislation on the right to free defense was consulted. The review of constitutional, criminal and criminal procedural provisions was highlighted. Specific administrative provisions relating to the guarantees set out in the items were also consulted. Jurisprudence was also consulted to know the interpretation of the legal precepts contained in the rules and thus to be able to respond to the demands of the items. This happened in the cases of California and New York, where it was necessary to refer to the case law of the United States Supreme Court on the time limit for police custody in the absence of a prior arrest warrant.

A second source was the electronic portals of institutions linked to the penal system, which contained information on the characteristics of the rules on criminal guarantees. The third resource used was the review of scientific articles and reports by specialised organisations on specific aspects related to the items in this pool. Finally, on some occasions it was necessary to consult with experts as a methodological resource to clarify doubts or gaps in the legislation relating to the items in pool 2, particularly in cases where there were doubts about the interpretation of the legislation consulted, or where guidance was needed on references or statistical sources relating to

7 Minutes AP-RIMES 11, 12 and 15, of January 29, March 5 and April 1, 2020, respectively.
8 Minutes AP-RIMES 18, of May 13, 2020.

the subject of the item. This made it possible to obtain a more complete understanding of the provisions of the legislation of each of the criminal systems analysed.

On the other hand, item 25 is the only practice in the pool of legal safeguards. As can be seen from both the development process and the description of this item, the main stumbling block in resolving it was the ease of accessing empirical data to determine whether at least 15 per cent of the prison population serving a sentence in prison suffered from a mental illness. As was indeed found in each of the countries, it was not easy to find empirical information, so secondary sources of information were consulted to resolve this issue.

First, the relevant regulations – constitutional, criminal, penitentiary and/or sanitary – were reviewed with the aim of describing the mental health system in prisons in each of the countries analysed. Although this methodological strategy corresponds more to the solution of a rule than to that of a practice, it was considered relevant because it made it possible to contextualise the solution of the item and to explain the particularities of each specific case.

Secondly, official prison statistics were used to determine the characteristics of the prison population. Official data from other institutions were also examined in relation to what was requested by the item. It is worth mentioning the limitations of these data sources, which are related to the quality of the statistical information in each case. Either because the specific data required by the item are not collected, or because the methodology used to collect the information is not homogeneous over time, as can be seen from the protocols for England and Wales and Poland, respectively.

Thirdly, a search was carried out for articles on research or empirical studies that could shed light on the prevalence of convicted persons with a mental illness who were serving their sentence in prison. This search was supplemented, on the one hand, by information contained in reports by international organisations on living conditions in national prisons or by institutions responsible for ensuring compliance with the human rights of persons deprived of their liberty, as in the Polish case. Newspaper reports and news items about mentally ill persons in prison were also used to answer the item in Germany. Finally, and in a complementary way, case law was consulted. This was the case in Italy, where judgments about mentally ill people in prison and the possibility for them to receive specialised psychiatric care outside prison facilities were reviewed.

4 Results of the pool of legal safeguards

The general results of the application of the RIMES instrument, in terms of the pool of legal safeguards, are presented in Table 7.1. Specifically, it shows the response contained in the protocols adopted for each case and subsequently reviewed by international experts from each of the territories analysed.

Table 7.1 Results of pool 2: legal safeguards, by item and country

	Germany	*California*	*Spain*	*Italy*	*New York*	*Poland*	*England & Wales*
Item 21	No	No	No	No	No	No	No
Item 22	No	No	No	No	No	No	No
Item 24	Yes*	No	No	No	No	No	No
Item 25	Yes	Yes	No	Yes	Yes	No	Yes

Source: Own elaboration

Note: *The answer of the German item changed after the review by the experts. It will be explained in more detail in the corresponding section

The items that were answered negatively by all the countries were 21 and 22. Regarding item 21, it can generally be said that the criminal justice systems analysed recognise the right to free legal defense for those who do not have the financial means to pay for it. However, this does not mean that all countries regulate free legal aid in the same way. In some cases, there are requirements that must be met by persons who are accused of committing a crime or facing criminal prosecution. For example, in the Italian criminal law it is necessary to prove that the annual income of the accused does not exceed the amount of his or her tax declaration for the previous year. The English criminal justice system recognises criteria for determining eligibility for free legal aid, one of which is the financial resources the defendant has or receives.

The revisions made by the international experts to the resolution of this item in each country confirmed the responses obtained by the research team. In the cases of Germany and Italy, the experts provided additional resources to supplement the protocols of these countries.

For their part, the results of item 22 show that none of the countries in which the RIMES instrument has been used requires the payment of fees as a condition for filing an appeal at first instance. It can therefore be affirmed that the national legal systems guarantee access to the plurality of instances in criminal proceedings. However, it is striking that some countries provide for the payment of appeal fees, albeit after the appeal has been lodged and generally depending on the outcome of the appeal. This is the case in Germany, where the fees are paid when the judgment is enforced. Similarly, Polish law provides for the payment of fees after the appeal has been decided. Finally, in the English case, it is interesting to note the dissuasive tone of the wording of the rules concerning the appeal procedure, since in certain cases, and only if the appeal is dismissed, the payment of costs is required, although no fees are payable.

As with the resolution of item 21, the experts confirmed the answers obtained by the research team. And only in the German case was the corresponding protocol supplemented by additional information provided by the expert on the payment of costs, but not of fees. This addition was made to better explain the difference between costs and fees in the German legal system.

On the other hand, the resolution of item 24 allows us to observe the first case in which one of the countries would cause social exclusion. Although most of the penal systems analysed provide for police custody, the time limits foreseen for police custody do not exceed the time limit set by the item (five days). The standard period usually ranges from 24 hours (England and Wales, New York), 48 hours (Poland, California and Italy) to 72 hours (Spain). This provision is usually explicit, although in the case of New York, for example, state and federal case law had to be consulted to determine the maximum time limit for police arrests without a warrant. New York law provides that in such cases there should be no "unnecessary delay" in bringing the suspect before a judge. According to the New York Court of Appeals, this period should not exceed 24 hours, and according to the US Supreme Court, it should not exceed 48 hours.[9]

There are also exceptional cases of police custody, which allow for an extension of the normal time limit, but without exceeding the maximum time limit specified in the item. This is the case in the English criminal justice system, where the suspect may be detained for a maximum of 96 hours (four days) if there are valid reasons relating to the gathering of evidence to clarify the commission of an offence. It is worth noting that detention periods for terrorism or organised crime have not been considered, in line with the description drawn up by the AP-RIMES team.

On the other hand, the resolution of item 24 in the German penal system showed that the period of police custody of a person suspected of committing a crime could exceed the five days required by the item. Initially, the German RIMES implementation team considered that this item was not applicable as the period of detention of suspects before they are brought before a judge does not exceed 24 hours. However, upon review by the expert, the response to this item had to be modified. The expert noted that in some German Länder, the police can extend detention up to a maximum of 15 days if the release of the suspect is considered dangerous. In the other cases, the experts confirmed the answers given in the other penal systems analysed.

Finally, the results obtained for item 25 show that only in two countries – Spain and Poland – does the proportion of people serving prison sentences who suffer from a mental disorder, excluding cases of addiction and drug addiction, not exceed the 15 per cent required by the item, and was therefore answered in the negative. In the Spanish case, it is worth noting that, although this information was confirmed by the penitentiary institutions, the data provided on the prevalence of people with bipolar disorder or paranoid schizophrenia (4 per cent) did not correspond to the results of empirical research on the subject, according to which the prevalence ranged from 9.5 per cent to 13.8 per cent (Pérez Martínez, 2004). On the other hand, the Polish experience shows that, although the reliability of the statistics used is questionable, the data obtained indicate that the number of people serving prison sentences who are

9 We refer to the cases *People ex rel. Maxian v. Brown* (1991) decided by the New York Court of Appeals, and *County of Riverside v. McLaughlin* (1991) decided by the US Supreme Court.

under the "therapeutic regime" does not exceed 15 per cent. It is worth noting that this regime provides for the transfer of prisoners to specialised therapeutic units for their care, but these are located within penitentiary establishments, so they would be considered as *correctional facilities*, so they would be considered as *correctional facilities* according to the description of the item.

The remaining four prison systems would have answered in the affirmative, meaning that more than 15 per cent of the prison population has a mental disorder. On the one hand, it is possible to identify countries that would have reached this conclusion after consulting prison statistics, such as New York. Prison reports show that since 2014, at least 16 per cent of the prison population has been suffering from a mental disorder (New York State, 2014, 2015, 2016, 2017, 2018).

In the other territories analysed, the answer to the item was the result of a systematic interpretation of the information available in the sources consulted. A first example is the German case, where the answer was obtained indirectly. The team relied on the results of various empirical studies carried out in different German prisons, as there was no recent or historical statistical information on the status pf people with mental illness in prison. Similarly, in the Californian protocol it was possible to conclude, through the systematic interpretation of the empirical research consulted, as well as data from policy documents and legislative reports, allowed the conclusion to be drawn that the prevalence of prisoners with a mental disorder is the 15 per cent required by the item. In a similar vein is the Italian case illustrates how reality differs from the provisions of the Penal execution laws, according to which mentally ill inmates should serve their sentences in psychiatric hospitals.

The English case is another example of how the limitations of official statistics do not provide a reliable picture of the prevalence of people in prison who suffer from some form of mental disorder. To resolve this indicator, as in other countries, a review of empirical research on the subject had to be undertaken. Specifically, the team responsible for resolving this item highlighted the results of a longitudinal study carried out in 2005 and 2006 to determine the state of health of inmates sentenced to up to four years' imprisonment. These showed that 16 per cent of prisoners had some form of mental illness (Light et al., 2013).

The international experts also recognised the difficulty of responding to this item and validated the decision in almost all countries. The New York expert highlighted the tension between the wording of the item and the description developed by the AP-RIMES team. After consideration by the New York item response team, it was decided to note the expert's observation, but not to change the item response, as it had been resolved according to the description adopted by the AP-RIMES team.

To sum up and based on these general results, it is possible to compare the criminal justice systems analysed in terms of this specific pool. It can be affirmed that the penal intervention in Germany would be the most socially exclusive in terms of penal safeguards, as two items would have been answered in the affirmative, while Spain and Poland would be the least socially exclusive countries, with zero items expressing social exclusion. California, England and Wales, Italy and New York would be considered moderately exclusive in relation to the results obtained in the pool, as in all these cases the only expressive item of social exclusion would be item 25. This can be reflected by placing each territory on the continuum of social exclusion generated by the penal system in the basket analysed, as shown in Figure 7.1.

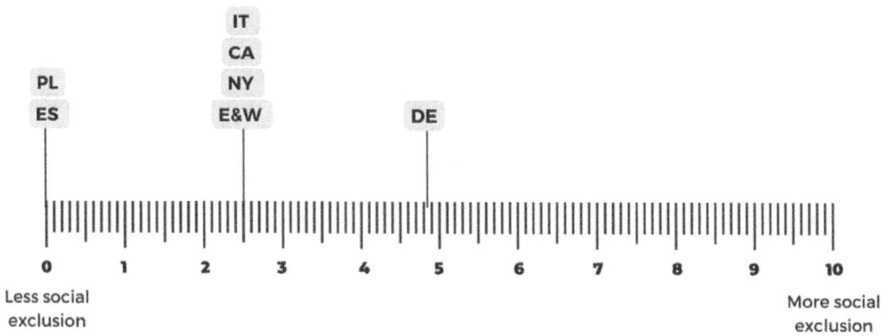

Figure 7.1 Position of countries on the continuum of social exclusion in terms of legal safeguards

5 Conclusions

In conclusion, firstly, the values of Aiken's V obtained for each of the items in pool 2 allow us to validate their usefulness and their ability to detect social exclusion in the field of legal safeguards.

Second, the results validated by the experts suggest that the penal systems analysed would generate little social exclusion in terms of criminal guarantees. From a global perspective, Germany would be the country with the most exclusionary penal system, while the penal systems of California, England and Wales, Italy and New York would be on a less exclusionary spectrum, and Spain and Poland would be at the extreme end of the spectrum with no social exclusion.

Thirdly, the items that possibly produce zero social exclusion are those that correspond to the rules of items 21 and 22. Thus, it could be affirmed that all of the criminal justice systems analysed comply with the recognition of the right to free criminal defence for those who cannot afford it, as well as the right to multiple instances, by not requiring the prior payment of fees in order to file an appeal. A lesser degree of social exclusion would be produced by the rule of item 24, since in the German case the maximum period of police custody would exceed five days, due to specific cases of particular gravity. On the other hand, the item that would produce the most social exclusion in the majority of countries would be the practice set out in item 25. This result shows that in five of the seven territories analysed, there is a tension between what is provided for in national and international legislation – differentiated treatment for sentenced persons suffering from a mental disorder – and what is observed in practice. One possible reason for this may be of a budgetary nature, namely the number of resources allocated to ensure special facilities for the accommodation of sentenced persons with mental disorders, rather than their incarceration in ordinary prisons.

Finally, although the results of the pool allow us to make distinctions between the countries in which the RIMES instrument has been used, it remains to look more closely at the discriminatory capacity of those items that were answered in the negative in all territories. We refer specifically to items 21 and 22. To a lesser extent, we also include item 24, which was also answered negatively in all countries except Germany. To achieve this, it is perhaps relevant to examine the differences in each of the national legislations analysed, with the aim of finding nuances that allow us to refine the political-criminal comparisons in terms of the socially exclusive effects of criminal intervention in terms of legal safeguards for suspects, defendants, convicted and ex-convicts.

References

Díez-Ripollés, J. L. (2005). De la sociedad del riesgo a la seguridad ciudadana: Un debate desenfocado. *Revista Electrónica de Ciencia Penal y Criminología*, *7*(1), 1–37. https://goo.gl/T75Q9d

Díez-Ripollés, J. L. (2011). La dimensión inclusión/exclusión social como guía de la política criminal comparada. *Revista Electrónica de Ciencia Penal y Criminología*, *12*(13), 1–36.

Díez-Ripollés, J. L. (2013). *El nuevo modelo penal de la seguridad ciudadana* (2 edición, pp. 69–102). Tirant lo Blanch.

Díez-Ripollés, J. L. (2015). *La política criminal en la encrucijada* (2a edición). B de F.

Díez-Ripollés, J. L. (2017). El abuso del sistema penal. *Revista Electrónica de Ciencia Penal y Criminología*, *19*(1), 1–24. https://goo.gl/snpZLr

Díez-Ripollés, J. L., & García España, E. (2019). RIMES: An instrument to compare national criminal justice policies from the social exclusion dimension. *International E-Journal of Criminal Sciences*, *13*, 1–27.

Ferrajoli, L. (2000). Garantías. *Jueces para la democracia*, *38*, 39–46.

García España, E., & Díez-Ripollés, J. L. (2021). La medición de la exclusión social generada por el sistema penal español: Aplicación del instrumento RIMES. *InDret*, *1*, 259–281.

Light, M., Grant, E., & Hopkins, K. (2013). *Gender differences in substance misuse and mental health amongst prisoners Results from the Surveying Prisoner Crime Reduction (SPCR) longitudinal cohort study of prisoners.* Ministry of Justice Analytical Series.

New York State. (2014). *Under custody report: Profile of under custody population 2014.* Department of Corrections and Community Supervision of the State of New York. https://www.prisonpolicy.org/scans/nydocs/UnderCustody_Report_2014.pdf

New York State. (2015). *Under custody report: Profile of under custody population 2015.* Department of Corrections and Community Supervision of the State of New York. https://doccs.ny.gov/system/files/documents/2019/09/UnderCustody_Report_2015.pdf

New York State. (2016). *Under custody report: Profile of under custody population 2016*. Department of Corrections and Community Supervision of the State of New York. https://doccs.ny.gov/system/files/documents/2019/09/UnderCustody_Report_2016.pdf

New York State. (2017). *Under custody report: Profile of under custody population 2017*. Department of Corrections and Community Supervision of the State of New York. https://doccs.ny.gov/system/files/documents/2019/09/Under%20Custody%20Report%202017.pdf

New York State. (2018). *Under custody report: Profile of under custody population 2018*. Department of Corrections and Community Supervision of the State of New York. https://doccs.ny.gov/system/files/documents/2019/09/Under%20Custody%20Report%202018.pdf

Pérez Cepeda, A. I. (2007). *La seguridad como fundamento de la deriva del derecho penal postmoderno*. Iustel.

Pérez Martínez, E. (2004). ¿Psiquiatría penitenciaria? *Revista española de sanidad penitenciaria*, *6*(3).

RIMES Project. (2018). *Executive Report*. Unpublished.

Villavicencio Terreros, F. (2017). *Derecho penal básico*. Fondo Editorial de la Pontificia Universidad Católica del Perú.

8 Pool 3

Sentencing and sanction systems

María Izco-Rincón

1 Introduction

Pool 3, which is analysed in this chapter, explores the sentencing and sanctions systems. As far as sanctions are concerned, the negative effects of imprisonment on offenders and their criminal careers are widely known in criminological literature, mainly as a result of their inability to achieve the rehabilitation of convicted persons or their adverse consequences for the respect of prisoners' human rights (Cid, 2010). However, following Díez-Ripollés (2017, 2019), despite the marked differences between incarceration rates in various countries, we are facing a situation where the imposition of prison sentences is becoming more and more widespread. In addition, maximum prison sentences are increasingly being raised for a wide range of offences and the prestige of short prison sentences is beginning to be restored, which, although traditionally criticised for their criminogenic effects and thus their adverse consequences on resocialisation, are now seen as tools with great intimidation power.

It is interesting to highlight the role of sanctions other than imprisonment, which are also analysed in pool 3. At European level, the Committee of Ministers of the Council of Europe has established the idea that prison should only be used *in ultima ratio*, i.e., only in those situations where it is certainly necessary to achieve the objectives of the punishment, promoting – through its recommendations – the use of alternative sanctions as a normal response to the commission of an offence, on the assumption that this types of sanctions respect the freedom of the individual, avoid the harmful effects of prison mentioned above and are able to achieve the aims of punishment, at least to a greater extent than imprisonment (Cid, 2010). However, as Díez-Ripollés (2017, 2019) points out, it should not be forgotten that the expansion of the phenomenon also means that those sanctions alternative to prison do not only to replace the latter, "but rather, criminal control is extended to areas where it did not reach or only reached occasionally" (2017, p. 10). The author also points out that, for example, fines have sufficient afflictive capacity to replace prison sentences for a wide range of offences. However, their excessive use can have socially exclusionary effects.

DOI: 10.4324/9781032661766-11

With regard to the sentencing system, Díez-Ripollés (2017, 2019) stated that it is undergoing important transformations in a significant number of legal systems, mainly due to the aggravation of sentences for recidivism. In addition, the author points out that one of the most repeated patterns in many recent legal reforms is the limitation of judicial discretion in sentencing, mainly as a result of the raising of the minimum sentence thresholds in the regulations or complex guidelines that should govern the judicial decision-making. All this is nothing more than an expression of the demands for "social segregation of the offender" (p. 14), disregarding the principle of proportionality, in order to try to keep the recidivist individual in prison for as long as possible, giving priority to retributive and innocuisation sentencing requirements.

With this, pool 3 aims to address different issues related to the social exclusion produced by the sentencing system and the sanctions system, such as the possibility of suspension of the judgment or enforcement of prison sentences, sanctions other than imprisonment in legal systems for less serious offences, alternatives to imprisonment in the case of non-payment of fines, the rate of imprisonment or the level of serving sentences in closed prisons.

2 The pool building process

2.1 The building of the pool

Initially, after screening with the criteria of completeness, extension and ease of access, pool 3 included a total of 38 items, having a score of 72.3 points in the completeness criterion, 64.4 in the extension criterion and 80.2 in the ease of access criterion. Then, and using the same three criteria, a second round was carried out with a screening that allowed to discard those items which had scored less than or equal to 4, thus resulting a total of 27 items (12 practices and 15 rules) in this pool. Given the high number of indicators, a new screening was carried out, this time using five criteria: the previous three together with the criteria of clarity and discrimination capacity. At this time, dated 24 March 2014, and after excluding those items with a score lower than 4 in the criteria, pool 3 was made up of a total of 19 items (12 rules and 7 practices). Then an in-depth analysis of each pool was carried out to extract a list of topics related to each dimension and check if some of them could be excluded. In other words, a monographic review of their extension was conducted. With this, on 3 April 2014, pool 3 was reduced to a total of 14 items (5 practices and 9 rules).

In a second stage, once the whole RIMES instrument was made up by 126 items thanks to the work of the research team, it was sent to 28 international experts for validation. They were asked to assess the adequacy of each item to measure social exclusion, as well as the clarity of their wording. They were specifically required to score with regard to the suitability and clarity of each item on a double Likert scale (from 1 to 5), in two consecutive rounds. At this point, 50 per cent of the 14 items of pool 3 were validated, and they were thus reduced to 7 items (4 rules and 3 practices).

Subsequently, the research team had to select a lower number of items that would allow to conform a more manageable instrument from the items validated by the experts in the second round. Specifically, items 32 and 41 were removed, although the research team was not in full agreement on this. In any case, the team understood that item 41 – on default imprisonment due to non-payment – would probably be very difficult to resolve and considered more feasible to adopt rule 36, dealing with the same issue and with an easier approach. Once the process was completed, pool 3 finally included items 33, 35, 36, 37 and 38, the two latter being punitive practices and the former ones, rules (RIMES Project, 2018).

2.2 *Presentation of the items that make up the pool*

Finally, pool 3 is made up of a total of five items: three of them are rules (specifically items 33, 35, 36) and two of them are practices (items 37 and 38). The research team approved the proposed definitions for each item with no need to discuss them.[1]

Item 33: *"In the case of prison sentences, neither probation as an alternative to sentencing nor suspended sentences are envisaged in the law"*

In short, the objective is to verify whether the legal system of the country under study provides for measures to suspend the judgement or the enforcement of prison sentences, i.e., the aim is to find out whether prison sentences can be suspended, either in the judgment or in the enforcement itself. It is interesting to note that the judicial decision to suspend the enforcement of prison sentences is based on the need to deal with first-time offenders, with no previous criminal record, and whose individualised prognosis suggests that they will not return to committing offences in the future as a result of their low criminal dangerousness. The main reasons taken into account have been the prison contamination that would occur as regards these first-time offenders and its negative effects on them, which would favour future offending. Thus, criminal dogma has traditionally advocated the existence of mechanisms to prevent the entry of persons with certain conditions, such as the example given here, by suspending the enforcement of the sentence, or by replacing it with different penal consequences that are less burdensome for the convicted individual.[2]

1 Minutes AP-RIMES No. 9, of 18 December 2019 and Minutes AP-RIMES No. 10, of 22 January 2020.
2 Protocol of item 33 in Spain.

Item 35: "The law lacks provisions for penalties other than prison (community service, fines, house arrest) in case of less serious felonies"

This item aims to verify whether the legal systems of the countries under study provide for penalties other than imprisonment for less serious offences. The team decided that felonies, cumulative penalties associated with imprisonment or penalties for legal persons would not be included under this item. With this, the research team stressed the relevance of describing what should be understood by "infringement of medium seriousness", concluding that they are equivalent to "less serious crimes".[3] For this reason, a detailed analysis of the legal provisions in each country must be carried out to determine what is meant by "less serious crimes" in each one of them.[4]

Item 36: "Default imprisonment is the sole alternative to non-payment of a fine"

This item refers to those cases in which the system only provides for imprisonment as the only alternative sanction for those individuals who cannot pay a fine imposed in a sentence.

Item 37: "The incarceration rate is higher than 120 inmates per 100,000 inhabitants"

In this case, the research team concluded the need to start from a broad concept of prison population, which takes into account both the sentenced prisoners and remand prisoners.

Item 38: "At least three quarters of the inmates are serving their sentences in closed prisons"

The goal of this item is to find out the number of inmates who are serving a custodial sentence in both first- and second-grade regimes, in closed prisons. This would exclude from the study those inmates in pretrial detention, serving in open correctional facilities, serving sentences in third-grade prisons or in detention centres for foreign nationals.[5]

3 Methodology used to solve the items

3.1 Methodology used to resolve rules 33, 35 and 36

It should be noted that, as these are rules, the main source of information used for their resolution by the research team was the legislation in force in each

3 Minutes AP-RIMES No. 70, of 9 May 2018.
4 Minutes AP-RIMES No. 17, of 29 April 2020.
5 Minutes RIMES No. 72, 6 June 2018.

country under study. At times, they had to complement it with a bibliographic and jurisprudential inquiry to clarify any interpretation issues.

With regard to item 33, criminal law sources were consulted in all cases at national level. In the case of Spain, procedural regulations were also used, specifically the Criminal Procedure Law (LECrim). In the case of England and Wales, and given the difficulties to interpret the regulations, the research team equally had to resort to the official website of the UK government which, among other issues, addresses and simplifies current legislation to make it understandable and easily accessible to citizens.

As to item 35, it is interesting to note the methodology applied by the researchers to resolve it in Spain, where a quantitative analysis of the provisions set forth in the Penal Code for less serious crimes was carried out, considering that such offences are those identified as "crimes of medium seriousness" by the item. The code states that less serious crimes are those punished with less serious penalties (art. 13.2), these being (according to art. 33.5): imprisonment from three months to five years, special barring up to five years, suspension from public employment and office up to five years, different deprivations of rights and prohibitions of different terms, the fine of more than three months, the proportional fine and community service from 30 days to one year. With this, the research team went to the special part of the Penal Code and carried out an in-depth analysis of the less serious crimes and the penalties prescribed for them. In addition, one of the researchers took into account other laws, such as the Criminal Air Navigation Law, the Organic Law of the General Electoral Regime, the Smuggling Law and the Exchange Control Law. As regards the other countries under study, their penal legislation in force was also consulted for the resolution of item 35. Besides, in England and Wales and Poland, an in-depth bibliographic review had to be carried out to obtain a detailed knowledge of the classification of crimes in such territories.

For the resolution of item 36, the team resorted to criminal law sources in all cases and, in Italy, also to constitutional rules. In some cases, the analysis needed to be complemented by resorting to jurisprudence, as for example in California and Italy (*People vs. Dueñas*, 2019 and Judgment 131/1979 of the Constitutional Court).

3.2 Methodology used to solve practices 37 and 38

Item 37 aims to find out the incarceration rate per 100,000 inhabitants in each country under study. To calculate the incarceration rate, the official population data of the country should be used as well as the official prison population.

In Spain, item 37 was resolved using secondary data obtained from two sources specifically: indicators from the National Institute of Statistics (INE) (for demographic information) and the monthly statistics of the Spanish Penitentiary Authorities (indicators from 2010 to 2017 on the website). The concept of prison population used in both data sources is the male and female population of any nationality, over 18 years of age and with a status that allows them to be held responsible for their actions. This concept includes remand prisoners and sentenced prisoners, as well as a third group of inmates serving security measures, mostly in psychiatric institutions. The research team also managed to analyse the time period 2010–2017.

To resolve the item in California, official sources were consulted to obtain data on the prison population and the total population of the State. With those data in hand, the incarceration rate was calculated by dividing the prison population by the total population and multiplying the result by 100,000. These data refer to the period 2014–2018.

In the case of Germany, item 37 was also resolved through secondary sources, namely from the Council of Europe Annual Crime Statistics – SPACE I 2018 data, covering the time period 2010–2018, in the same way as in Poland and Italy.

In England and Wales this item was resolved through secondary data obtained from the National Statistics Office and the Ministry of Justice for the period 2010–2018.

Finally, item 37 was resolved in the state of New York by using two secondary sources for data collection: the New York State Department of Corrections and Community Supervision and the US Census Bureau, for the period 2015–2019. An important particularity that should be noted is that the research team in charge of analysing this item in New York considered the concept of prison population in a broad sense, following the definition given by the United States, which combines "jail population" and "prison population".

With regard to item 38, this was resolved in Spain by using data available in the statistics published by the General Directorate of Penitentiary Institutions (DGIP) for the period 2013–2017, which is the last year for which data were available at the closing date of this item. It should be borne in mind that the closed prison facilities referred to by this practice correspond to the ordinary regime prisons in our country which – unlike the social insertion centres – imply a mode of serving the custodial sentence where the individual does not leave the establishment unless he has an exit permit granted by the treatment board of the centre. This corresponds to inmates who are in the first or second grade of treatment (art. 72.1 of the Penitentiary Organic Law 1/1979, of 26 September or LOGP). The data was obtained through the monthly statistics on prison population available on the DGIP website and a screening was carried out with the variable "treatment grade". The median value was taken for each year under study. The total number of inmates who were in the first and second grade (closed regime) for each year was calculated and compared with the numerical data corresponding to three quarters of the total number of inmates each year.

In the case of California, the Legislative Analyst's Office Report (nonpartisan Fiscal and Policy Advisor to the California Legislature) (2019) as well as the California Code of Regulations were used to obtain the data, for the analysed period 2015–2019.

In Germany there are regular statistics on the incarceration system. A special mention regarding this should be made to the document Prison System – Demographic and Criminological Characteristics of Prisoners as of 31.3 of the Federal Statistical Office (*Strafvollzug -Demographische und kriminologische Merkmale der Strafgefangenen zum Stichtag 31.3. of the Statistisches Bundesamt)*, which is produced annually by the state agency Destatis (2020). The research team consulted the latest available statistics, concerning year 2019, for the resolution of the item.

To resolve this item in Poland, the Polish Prison Statistics was used, together with other bibliographic sources of interest for the subject matter under research, which allow us to understand the classification system of prisoners in this country.

In the case of England and Wales, first of all it is necessary to know some particularities that justify the methodology used to resolve this item. Rule 7 of the Prison Rules in England and Wales allows to classify inmates on the basis of a wide range of factors such as age, temperament, background, etc. There are four security categories to classify male prisoners: category A, reserved for inmates whose escape would pose a danger to society and the state; category B, that includes inmates who – without requiring the above levels of security – should be prevented from escaping; category C, comprises inmates who are not considered capable of making an escape attempt but who cannot be trusted to be in open conditions, and category D, where prisoners who serve sentences in an open regime are classified (Garton Grimwood, 2015). With regard to women inmates, the classification is: category A, identical to the one for males; restricted status, for prisoners whose escape would pose a serious risk to the public and must remain in a safe accommodation; closed regime, includes inmates for whom an open regime is not appropriate; and open regime, for inmates that pose a low risk and can reasonably be trusted to be adequate for this category (PSI 39/2011). Thus, the object of study to resolve item 38 corresponds to categories A, B and C in the case of adult male prisoners, and category A, restricted status and closed regime, in the case of adult female prisoners. Once this decision was taken, it was necessary to find out which categories were lodged in each of the 121 prisons of the United Kingdom. To this end, using the "prison finder" tool on the official website of the UK Government, only those lodging inmates classified in the above categories were selected, excluding prisons that housed – only or jointly with other categories – inmates classified in category D, prisons that housed women – since they do not provide information on their classification – and prisons for juvenile offenders. Thus, the research for the resolution of item 38 focused on the male prison population (adults and young offenders over 18 years of age) who were serving sentences in categories A, B and C.

In Italy, the item was resolved by using the official statistics on prison population, secondary data and prison legislation in order to contextualise the overview of prison in this country. It is important to note that their penitentiary law divides the centres into: (1) preventive custody institutions; (2) institutes for the enforcement of arrests, (the latter) divided into detention centres and jails; (3) institutes in charge of serving security measures and (4) observation centres. On the other hand, the semi-open regime, regulated by article 48 of the Prisons Act (26 July 1975; No. 354), consists of granting inmates the possibility to spend part of the day outside the institution in order to take part in work, educational or social reintegration activities. For its part, the Ministry of Justice statistics include the total number of prisoners present and the regulatory capacity of prisons by region of detention. The difference between the total number of inmates and the number of inmates serving in a semi-open regime is also included. Therefore, this tool was used to resolve the item.

In the case of New York, the starting point was the concept of prison population in a broad sense, according to the definition of the United States, which combines 'jail population' and "prison population". The methodology used consisted of data collection from reports found in the website of prisonpolicy.org and the Vera Institute of Justice, together with official data from the U.S. Department of Justice, the National Institute of Corrections and the New York State Department of Corrections for the years 2020, 2019, 2018, 2016, 2015 and 2013. It should be mentioned that the main limitation found when trying to resolve this practice in New York was the impossibility to obtain a homogeneous data set that would allow information to be aggregated for the same period of time. The only way to overcome this challenge was to resort to data estimates instead of using exact numbers. For this reason, the reliability of the estimates built is precisely the main limitation of this research regarding the implementation of item 38 in New York.

It is worth noting that each item was reviewed by an expert in each of the countries under analysis, in order to verify whether the methodology used to resolve each item, as well as the results obtained, were correct.

4 Results obtained for each item

Table 8.1 shows the results obtained in each country and state under study regarding the fulfillment or not of the items at national level, after the investigations carried out by the Ap-RIMES team:

Table 8.1 Results of pool 3, by item and country

Item	*Germany*	*California*	*Spain*	*Italy*	*New York*	*Poland*	*England and Wales*
Item 33	No	No	No	No	No	No	No
Item 35	No	Yes	No	No	No	Yes	No
Item 36	No	Yes	No	No	No	No	Yes
Item 37	No	Yes	Yes	No	Yes	Yes	Yes
Item 38	Yes	Yes	Yes	Yes	Yes	Yes	Yes

Source: Own elaboration

With regard to the results obtained in the resolution of item 33, it should be noted that the response was negative in all countries, so that criminal legislations in all cases provided for the possibility of suspending the judgment or the enforcement of prison sentences. After reviewing the protocols, the experts only considered the need to expand the information provided in the case of Italy, where new articles of the Italian Penal Code were highlighted to complement the response to the item, without amending it.

In Spain, it was necessary to resort to the provisions of articles 80 et seq. of the Penal Code, which regulate the cases where the enforcement of prison sentences is suspended, although not the judgment. We should remember that this item covers the scenarios of both the suspension of the judgment and the suspension of the sentence enforcement. However, the research team agreed that the item was not met in Spain as only one of the conditions was fulfilled. Similarly, in the case of England and Wales,[6] where the Criminal Justice Act 1967 provides (article 39, first paragraph) that a court may suspend a prison sentence imposed for less than two years provided that during the period of the suspension order (up to three years) the individual does not commit any other imprisonable offence within the national territory. Prison sentences of less than six months may also be suspended as long as certain conditions are not met. Besides, if an offender is convicted of an offence punishable with imprisonment that was committed during the operative period of a suspended sentence, the court may, inter alia, order that the suspended sentence enter into force with the original term unchanged or may order that the sentence enter into force with the original term being replaced by a shorter term (article 40 of the Criminal Justice Act).

In the US states under study parole is provided for. Therefore, the item would not be fulfilled in either case. However, it is interesting to point out some existing nuances. Thus, in California, the item would not be met as there are two possibilities: parole as a way of enforcing a final sentence, and probation as an alternative to imposition of sentence (or judgment). In this sense, section 1203 of the Penal Code specifies that probation means suspension of the imposition or enforcement of a sentence and the order of conditional and revocable release into the community under the supervision of a probation officer. There is also a similar concept, that of "suspended sentence", which is a type of probation without supervision by a probation officer.

Similarly and pursuant to Section 65.00 of the New York State Penal Law, there are a number of criteria stating that, unless otherwise required, the court may sentence a person to a period of probation upon conviction of any crime if the court – taking into account the nature and circumstances of the offence, as well as the background, character and status of the defendant – considers that institutional confinement for the authorised term is or may be unnecessary for the protection of the public, the defendant needs guidance, training or

6 Minutes AP-RIMES No.12, of 5 February 2020.

assistance that can be supplied in supervision of probation or if such provision is not incompatible with the ends of justice. In any case, said probation shall not apply in the case of class A-I felonies, such as, for example, first-degree murder, terrorism offences or first-degree arson.

In the other European countries under analysis, the item was also not met as a result of the legal provision to suspend the sentence enforcement, although only in certain cases, mainly based on the length of the suspended prison sentence, or even associated with the crime committed. Thus, title 4 of chapter 3 of the German Criminal Code refers to suspended sentences on probation. Article 56.1 provides that if a person is sentenced to imprisonment for a period of less than one year, the court may suspend the enforcement of the sentence on probation if there is reason to believe that the sentence itself will serve as a sufficient warning to the convicted person and that he will not commit further offences, even if he does not serve the sentence. In making such a decision, the court must take into account the character and previous history of the convicted person, the circumstances of the offence committed, the circumstances of the convicted person, the conduct of the convicted person after the offence committed and the effects that could be expected after the suspension of the sentence. Suspended prison sentences of less than two years are also possible, provided that the above conditions are met and also bearing in mind the efforts of the convicted person to make restitution for the damage.

Similarly, the wording of article 60 of the Polish Penal Code lays down rules for mitigating penalties and even allows for conditional suspension of the sentence and suspension of the enforcement of said sentence by a probationary period. As stated in the fourth paragraph of such article, conditional suspension is allowed – at the request of the state prosecutor – if the term of imprisonment is less than 5 years, with the possibility of a probation period of up to 10 years.

In the case of Italy, item 33 is also not fulfilled since article 163 of the Italian Criminal Law provides that for those offences punished with a prison sentence not exceeding two years and/or a monetary penalty, the judge may order that the enforcement of the sentence be suspended for a period of five years in the first of these cases. On the other hand, article 168 bis states that in proceedings for offences punishable only by a monetary penalty or a custodial sentence not exceeding four years, the defendant may request a suspension of the trial with probation.

Item 35 was responded in the negative in all the countries analysed, except in the case of California and Poland. Following the review carried out by the experts, the Italian expert suggested referencing new regulations on the subject that would reaffirm the response given by the research team, as in the case of California, New York and Poland, where the expert considered that a new wording of the item was necessary to explain even more clearly the regulatory classification of offences in the country, while maintaining the response and the decisions taken by the research team.

In California and Poland this item is met. However, the reasons for accepting this conclusion are different, as in the case of California there is no legal penalty other than imprisonment for the offences described in the item while, in the case of Poland, alternative penalties to imprisonment are established for these crimes, but such penalties are not directly associated with them. It is interesting to note that in the Californian case, the research team highlighted the existence of a legal institution in force in the state that raised doubts when it came to resolving the item, the so-called "split sentences". Such institution allows the judge to sentence to an initial period of imprisonment and then to a second period of mandatory supervision, which is a special type of probation that allows the person to be released, under a series of conditions and supervision. Given the complexity of the issue, the entire research team decided in a meeting[7] that the kind of probation referred to in the split sentences is not subject to the analysis of item 35, since a legal provision for a penalty other than imprisonment cannot be considered.

On the other hand, the Polish Penal Code differentiates in its general part between serious crimes (art. 7.2) and minor offences (art. 7.3), depending on the harshness of the sentence associated with them. This classification does not directly identify with the object of item 35's analysis. However, three types of infractions may be found according to the penological response, i.e., the severity of the sanction prescribed: 1) the law only provides for different sanction options (direct sanctions) in those infractions punishable with up to two years in prison. In these cases, the court may choose between a fine, restriction of freedom or imprisonment, the latter being understood as the last resort (art. 58.1); 2) when the offence is punishable with imprisonment of between two and five years, the court may, instead of imposing this sentence, prescribe a fine or a custodial sentence of up to two years (section 58.3); and 3) when the offence is punishable with a custodial sentence of more than five years, there is no alternative or direct sanction to avoid imprisonment. The team agreed to equate the category of offences punishable with custodial sentences of between two and five years with "less serious offences",[8] therefore including any serious offence or minor offence that from a penological point of view is punishable with such sentence. The team, however, concluded that the item is met in Poland, since – even if the offence is subject to imprisonment of between two and five years, and the court may instead impose one of the mentioned alternatives – the truth is we are facing the possibility of a replacement of sentences, but not of direct sentences linked to less serious offences.

In the case of Spain, it was not difficult to define what the penal legislation means by less serious crime, since this term is literally used there. Thus, item 35 was resolved by concluding it was not fulfilled as there are sentences other than imprisonment for offences of medium seriousness in the country, such

7 Minutes AP-RIMES No.16, of 15 April 2020.
8 Discussion held in Minutes AP-RIMES No. 17, of 29 April 2020.

as alternative penalties and fines. The results obtained in Spain showed there was a total of 129 offences of medium seriousness that are not punished with imprisonment, 108 offences of medium seriousness that are punished with some alternative penalty to prison (in such cases, imprisonment is available) and 412 offences of medium seriousness that are always liable to prison, either solely or cumulatively. In conclusion, the number of cases in Spain where imprisonment is the sole or cumulative penalty is notoriously higher than in other countries.

In the other countries under study where the item is also not fulfilled, it was more complicated to detect which offences described in their legislation could be considered less serious crimes, as stated in this item. In the case of Germany, section 12, chapter 1, title 2 of the Criminal Code defines as "less serious criminal offences" (*Vergehen*) those unlawful acts that are punishable by a minimum sentence of short-term imprisonment or a fine. Hence, the research team is able to conclude that item 35 is not met in the German case, as penalties other than imprisonment for less serious crimes are provided for in its penal legislation.

It is important to highlight some particularities to be taken into account in the case of England and Wales, a territory where again this item is not fulfilled. Here offences are classified as: summary offences, either-way offences and indictable offences. The first are crimes that can be prosecuted on indictment and are less serious offences which are generally dealt with in the magistrates' courts, such as common assault, low-level shoplifting or road traffic offences. In the case of either-way indictable offences, the defendant is allowed to choose between a jury trial on indictment in the crown court and a summary trial in a magistrates' court. However, the choice may be overridden by the magistrates' court if the facts suggest that the sentencing powers of a magistrates' court would be inadequate to reflect the seriousness of the offence. These are more serious crimes, such as, for example, theft or drug-related offences. Finally, indictable offences are those of a more serious nature, in which the magistrates' court transfers the case to the crown court for prosecution. These include murder, rape and robbery. It is difficult to use the definition of this item in England and Wales, as the indicator states that the target of the analysis is sentencing for less serious offences, but these are not part of the legal categories established in this territory. Bearing all this in mind and considering that the vast majority of sentences are handed down by magistrates' courts, the analysis focused on summary offences and either-way offences. Specifically, the informal sentencing guidelines that provide orientation to magistrates' courts with their cases[9] were used and it could be concluded that in many cases the offences can be punished with a fine or a community order.

9 The statutory provision governing them is found in article 143 ("Determination of the seriousness of an offence") and article 167 ("Sentencing Guidelines Council") of the Criminal Justice Act 2003.

As far as Italy is concerned, article 39 of the Italian Penal Law specifies that offences are classified into crimes and minor offences, distinguishing according to the type of penalty provided for them in the penal code. Crimes are those for which a penalty of life imprisonment, imprisonment, and fine is prescribed, while minor offences are those for which a penalty of arrest and/or fine is prescribed (art. 17 of the Italian Penal Code). To the extent that even in the upper category of crimes, some of them are punishable by non-custodial sentences, it could be concluded that penalties other than imprisonment are prescribed for less serious offences in Italy. In addition to the above, there are other Italian laws that provide for alternative penalties in case of less serious offences such as, for example, Legislative Decree No. 274, of 28 August 2000, which provides for penalties such as fines, house arrest or community service, or art. 47 of the Law No. 354, of 26 July 1975, which provides for the transfer to the social services.

On the other hand, the Criminal Law of the state of New York (NYSPL) does not propose the same categories referred to by item 35. Instead, there is a distinction among felonies, misdemeanours, and violations. Subsequently, each category is subdivided into several subcategories. Felonies, for instance, are divided into five different categories, from A to E, with class A felonies being the most serious and class E felonies being the least serious. In addition, class A felonies are subcategorised into class A-I and A-II felonies. Misdemeanours range from class A to C (section 55.10, NYSPL). In view of all this, it is difficult to determine what is a less serious offence, in terms of item 35. We can interpret that minor offences are not serious offences, and we can also assume that class A and B felonies are serious crimes. In this tentative categorisation, we can say that class C, D and E felonies can be placed in the category of less serious crimes. But we are well aware that this is just a decision we have taken without any legal backing.

Pursuant to section 70 of NYSPL, incarceration is the default punishment for any felony. The same can be said for minor offences or even minor infringements. However, under section 60.1 of NYSPL, the judge may impose only a fine, as long as it is not a class B felony or any felony included in section 220 of NYSPL, which refers to specific drug-related offences. Bearing this in mind and following the previous categorisation, it can be deducted that there are alternatives to imprisonment for less serious crimes (category C, D and E offences and only when not related to drugs), therefore concluding that in the case of New York this item is not fulfilled.

In most of the countries and states analysed item 36 is not met, with the exception of California and England & Wales. In the first case, section 1205.a of the California Penal Code states that "A judgment that the defendant pays a fine, with or without other punishment, may also direct that he or she be imprisoned until the fine is satisfied". Although some judgments have shown that this section violates constitutional rights (see the case *People vs. Dueñas*, 2019) this is a punitive rule and, as a result of the existing legal provision, the team had to confirm that the item was met in California. However, it should be noted that, at the time of interpreting the item, the research team agreed to accept that the judge may have the possibility to order the imprisonment of the individual, which thus represents a faculty, but not an obligation.[10]

On the other hand, in England and Wales sentencing fines can be imposed by both the magistrates' court and the crown court. With regard to the former, it has the power to pass a custodial sentence if a person over 18 years of age has not paid the fine imposed in the sentence, and may prescribe payment of the fine immediately or in installments (article 75 of the Magistrates' Courts Act 1980). Annex 4 of said law prescribes a period of imprisonment in case of non-payment of the fine, depending on the amount of the latter. Thus, for example, if the fine exceeds 10,000 GBP the length of imprisonment will be 12 months. In the case of the crown court, the judgment shall specify the time period to be served in custodial sentence if the individual fails to pay the fine (article 139.2 of the Powers of Criminal Court (Sentencing) Act 2000). Again, there is a table with the equivalence between the period of imprisonment for non-payment of a fine, depending on the amount of the latter (art. 139.4 of the Powers of Criminal Court (Sentencing) Act 2000).

In Spain, it could not be confirmed that item 36 was met as a result of the provisions of article 53.1 of the Penal Code, which states that

> if the convicted person does not satisfy, voluntarily or by forced recovery, the fine imposed, he will be subject to a subsidiary personal liability of one day of deprivation of liberty for every two daily instalments not paid, which, in the case of minor offences, may be served by permanent localisation. The judge or court may also, with the consent of the convicted person, decide that the subsidiary liability be served by means of community service. In this case, each day of deprivation of liberty shall be equivalent to one day's work.

The response to the fulfilment of the item in Germany is negative to the extent that, although article 43 of its Penal Code specifies that in case of non-payment of a fine this must be replaced by imprisonment, currently article 293 of the Introductory Act to the Penal Code (*Einführungsgesetz zum Strafgesetzbuch* 1974 or EGStGB) provides that the German federal state governments may lay down rules to replace prison sentences with unpaid work.

The item is also not met in Poland, where imprisonment is not the only possible alternative in case of non-payment of a fine; restriction of freedom may also be imposed (arts. 45 and 46 of the Polish Executive Penal Code). However, we should note that the possibility of non-payment of a fine resulting directly in imprisonment, without first attempting to apply socially useful work, is limited to fines exceeding a certain number of daily units or particularly high amounts.

10 Minutes AP-RIMES No.17, of 29 April 2020.

In Italy, the item is not fulfilled. Article 136 of the Criminal Law lays down the modalities for the conversion of fines. Judgment 131/1979 of the Constitutional Court declared that the automatic conversion into a prison sentence as the only alternative to non-payment of a fine was unconstitutional. On the basis of the equality principle set forth in art. 3 of the Constitution, said judgment considered that there was a different treatment for rich and poor. At present it prescribes that non-payment of a fine shall be replaced by work or probation.

In New York, the item is also not fulfilled, as a result of the provisions of article 420 of the New York Criminal Procedure Law which addresses the issue of fines, restitution and reparation. Article 420.10 specifically refers to the methods for collecting fines. In principle, the sentence imposing the fine shall prescribe that the individual must remain in prison until the fine has been fully paid. However, it also specifies that the defendant shall have the right to apply to the court for re-sentencing according to the terms of subdivision five:

> In such case, if the court is satisfied that the defendant is unable to pay the fine . . . it must: a) adjust the terms of payment, or b) lower the amount of the fine . . . or c) where the sentence consists of probation or imprisonment and a fine . . . revoke the portion of the sentence imposing the fine . . . or d) revoke the entire sentence imposed and resentence the defendant.

Contrary to the rules that make up this pool, item 37 is met in most of the countries analysed, except in Germany and Italy. For its part, this item did not undergo any amendment as regards the response after the experts' review. However, small changes were suggested to improve the argumentation of the resolutions. Thus, in the case of New York, the expert stressed the need to specify the figures of prison population and in house-jail population. In the case of California, new sources of information on prison population were added, which further confirmed the response given by the research team as regards the item.

Nevertheless, it is true that, as mentioned above, the time periods covered in each case do not always coincide. It is very interesting to note that, although the item is met in 5 of the 7 countries under study (as they have more than 120 inmates per 100,000 inhabitants), the prison population rates are different. Considering that in all cases those rates are higher than foreseen in the item, and starting with the lowest, in the first place we have Spain, where the average is 144.4 inmates per 100,000 inhabitants for the period 2010–2017. The second place is taken by England & Wales, where the average for the period under analysis was 148.4 prisoners per 100,000 inhabitants. Poland is in the third place, with an average of 203.4 for the period 2010–2018. In fourth place we have California, where the average for the period 2014–2018 is 337.82 inmates per 100,000 inhabitants, a figure that is much higher than the previous ones. And finally, New York, a state where the prison population rate is notoriously higher than the rest, at 366.98 inmates per 100,000 inhabitants for the period 2015–2019, stands out.

Item 37 is not fulfilled, on the contrary, in either Germany or in Italy, where incarceration rates are below 120 per 100,000 inhabitants, with 82.75 in the former for the time period 2010–2018 and 101.9 in the latter for the same period.

The practice contained in item 38 is met in the 7 countries under study and, after the experts' review, they only proposed small amendments in the case of New York, suggesting to redefine the concept of prison population with which they worked, as well as for England & Wales, where they proposed to mention female inmates for the appropriate resolution of the item.

It is interesting to note that in no country was it possible to access data regarding the percentage of prisoners serving sentence in closed centres. For this reason and given the diversity of regimes in each country, types of detention facilities and available data on them, the research team considered it was important to conduct a careful analysis of the results found, country by country. At times, as in the case of Poland, due to the lack of the specific data needed for the resolution of the item, the research team resolved through logical deduction from other available data. Thus, in Poland, there are three categories of detention regimes: 1) closed prisons, 2) semi-open prisons and 3) open prisons. Open prisons in Poland account for 32.48 per cent of the total number of penitentiary centres. The team agreed to consider semi-open facilities as part of the closed prison regime.[11] According to Polish prison statistics, in February 2020 there was a total of 67,024 inmates in prison: 49.3 per cent (33,056 inmates) was serving sentences in closed prisons, 46.4 per cent (31,072 inmates) was in semi-open prisons, and only 2.3 per cent (1,770 inmates) was in open prisons. In conclusion, only 2.3 per cent of prisoners are currently serving sentences in open prisons, which means that more than three quarters of the inmates are serving their sentences in closed or semi-open prisons.

A similar deductive process was performed in the case of California where, according to the Legislative Analyst's Office Report (Petek, 2019) and the California Code of Regulations (article 10), the California Department of Corrections (CDCR) classifies inmates into two categories: 1) housing security level and 2) custody designation. The first generally refers to the type of facilities where inmates are lodged, which in turn are classified according to different levels of security (level I-level IV). For its part, the custody designation prescribes where inmates can go inside the prison during the day and what level of supervision they should be subject to (1- maximum, 2- closed, 3- medium A, 4- medium B, 5- minimum A and 6- minimum B). The CDCR has flexibility to apply different custody designations to inmates within the same level of housing security. This makes it extremely difficult to find out

11 Minutes AP-RIMES No. 22, of 8 July 2020.

which inmates are in a closed or open regime, according to the item's requirements. However, it is quite certain that medium A, closed and maximum level of supervision refer to lodging in closed prisons. Data from the Legislative Analyst's Office Report (2019) show that 68 per cent of inmates are in the medium A level, 10 per cent in the closed regime, and 5 per cent in the maximum level, adding up to a total of 83 per cent. Therefore, we must conclude that this item is met in California.

In Spain, this practice is fulfilled during the period under study (2013–2018), since at least three quarters of inmates serve sentences in closed prisons.[12]

In the case of Germany, again, item 38 is met and besides, it turned out to be a relatively simple item to solve because there are statistics that already handled data, clearly and unequivocally, on the issue addressed. Thus, according to information from the document Prison System – Demographic and Criminological Characteristics of Prisoners as of 31 March 2019, German prisons held a total of 50,589 inmates. Out of the total number, 43,275 prisoners were held in closed regime, so it is easy to conclude that more than three quarters of the total of inmates in Germany are serving a prison sentence in closed regime. This direct accessibility to data also occurred in Italy, where 98.22 per cent of the total prison population over 18 years of age is serving a prison sentence in one of the closed centres in such country.

Item 38 is also fulfilled in England and Wales where, in addition, thanks to the expert's review, it was possible to access a detailed review that allowed to obtain specific data on the male and female prison populations, something that did not happen in the other countries. Here, there are 102 male prisons (for adults and young offenders over 18 years of age), although in two of them (representing 1.96 per cent of missing data) it was impossible to find out how they were classified. For its part, the Offender Management Statistics – Prison Population Data Tool, specifically those data referring to December 2019, show the number of inmates per prison in said month. The number of male prisoners serving a sentence in some of the penitentiary facilities of England and Wales in categories A, B or C is 68,143. This result accounts for 89.72 per cent of the total male prison population over 18 years of age serving a sentence in one of the country's centres (75,954). On the other hand, in this territory there is a total of 12 prisons that house adult offenders, and only 2 of them operate as "open prisons". Through the analysis of data found with the mentioned tool, it was possible to obtain the number of female inmates in each prison for said month, although it is impossible to know how such women are classified. However, the number of women in open facilities in

12 It is important to report some limitations: data corresponding to February 2014 were not collected or computed as they were not available. Besides, data for July 2016 were not collected or computed in the total of that year, since the statistics of the General Directorate of Penitentiary Institutions only included information on Catalonia, and not on the rest of Spain. Therefore, this figure is much lower than that of the other months and years and would distort the operation. That is why it was excluded from the calculation.

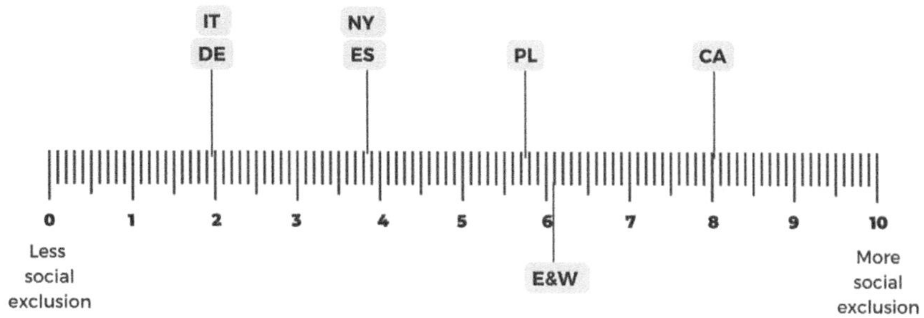

Figure 8.1 Position of the countries on the continuum of social exclusion as regards the sentencing and sanctions systems

December 2019 could be found: in Askham Grange there was a total of 105 women and in East Sutton Park, a total of 99 (making up a total of 204 women in open prisons). Since the total number of women in the different facilities throughout the territory was 3,654, if from this figure we subtract the number of women in open prisons (204), the result is that the total number of women in closed prisons is 3,450 (94.4 per cent). With this, we can conclude that the item is also fulfilled with respect to the female prison population.

Finally, New York was one of the countries where the resolution of item 38 was most complicated, although the team responded in the affirmative and the expert reviewer confirmed it. Obtaining a homogeneous data set was difficult, and the only way to overcome this limitation was to use data estimates instead of exact numbers. The results showed that the rates of imprisonment in closed facilities were so extremely high that, if a homogeneous real data set had been available, these figures would be very close to the estimates. Thus, after consulting numerous official data sources in New York state, the research team was able to approximate that, as regards 2018, the percentage of prison population in closed prisons was 96.84 per cent.

It is interesting to look at the data on the weighting carried out for each country under study in relation to pool 3 according to the answers obtained for each item. As can be seen in Figure 8.1, Germany and Italy are the countries that score lowest in social exclusion levels as regards the pool under analysis (specifically, 1.99 points out of 10). In the second place we find New York and Spain (with 3.83 points). In the third place Poland (5.76), followed by England and Wales (6.08) and, finally, California (8.01), which is the country with the highest social exclusion level, according to the results of implementing pool 3.

5 Conclusions

Pool 3 has the capacity to measure social exclusion by delving into important issues related to two of the three decisive moments of penal intervention, specifically the criminalisation of conducts and their penal prosecution. It is also considered that the consolidation of such issues in the penal control systems would determine their evolution towards exclusionary criminal policy models. The pool includes a set of items selected after a long process based on the work of the RIMES research team and that of a large number of experts in the field who, according to certain criteria, have considered that such items were suitable to evaluate, in an accessible way that allows for an in-depth study in each country to which the RIMES instrument is applied, the degree to which the different models of penal intervention in the countries analysed are moving, to a greater or lesser extent, towards a socially exclusionary approach.

From an overall perspective, the results obtained show that it is the punitive practices analysed (items 37 and 38) that occur with a significantly higher frequency in the countries under study than in the rules. Thus, in the case of practice 38, concerning the number of inmates serving sentences in closed prisons, this scenario is met in each and every one of the countries analysed. Something similar occurs as regards item 37 on the rate of prison population per 100,000 inhabitants, which is fulfilled in all the countries under study, except in Germany and England and Wales. In contrast, rule 33 is not met in any of the countries analysed, rule 35 is only met in California and Poland, and rule 36 only in the case of California and England & Wales. This shows how punitive practices, i.e., "the way in which different social agencies effectively react to behaviour or situations related to criminal control, whether or not in accordance with legal provisions" (García España and Díez-Ripollés 2021, p. 261), those which that occur most frequently with respect to punitive rules, i.e., those norms usually included in the legal-penal system that prescribe consequences for certain behaviours or situations related to criminal control.

The application of pool 3 in the countries analysed would therefore emphasise the discrepancy between what is provided for in the legislation and the effective implementation of issues related to penal intervention. Thus, for example, while most of the countries analysed provide for alternatives to imprisonment in the case of fines, the reality shows that prison population rates are very high in the regions under investigation in this case. This brings to light that punitivism or the punitive culture that tends towards the constant expansion of the penal system, considered as the only effective instrument against criminality, finds its main exponent in everything related to the penitentiary environment. Thus, according to Acevedo (2004), prison "has become the main or the only legal-criminal consequence of Western punitive systems; hence it fulfills a symbolic function of punishability" (p. 100). The costs of prison and its inability to resocialise have led to the emergence of proposals which, although for the most part fail to move away from the majority legal-penal conceptions, try to represent a viable alternative to prison. For this reason, alternative penalties to imprisonment have been raised, which are to a large extent the focus of this chapter. This is what is mainly revealed by the occurrence of practices in most of the countries under study, as compared to the rules. Despite the existence of legally provided alternatives to prison, our analysis has showed – assuming the limitations already pointed out – that imprisonment and the use of a closed regime continue to be the main instrument used by the punitive culture of the Western world.

It is also interesting to conclude that the items of this pool have a high discrimination potential in the countries analysed as – with the exception of item 33, which is not met in any country, and item 38, which, on the contrary, is fulfilled in all – the rest of the items show important differences among the countries under study. We suppose that this will be generalisable as the project progresses and the study sample is extended to other countries, for example, to non-Western areas.

Finally, and despite the fact that a global comparison among the different models of penal intervention in force in the countries analysed should only be conducted taking into account the results obtained in each of the pools, from a partial point of view, pool 3 points to California as the state with highest levels of social exclusion, as four of the five items that make up the pool are met here. The next countries with a higher score would be England and Wales and Poland, where three of the five items are fulfilled, followed by Spain and New York, where two items are met, and then Germany and Italy where only one of them is met.

References

Acevedo Matamoros, M. (2004). El sistema penitenciario en el contexto de la política criminal actual, Revista de Ciencias Sociales, *105*, 99–105.

Cid, J. (2010). La política criminal europea en materia de sanciones alternativas a la prisión y la realidad española: una brecha que debe superarse, *Estudios Penales y Criminológicos*, *30*, 55–83.

Destatis (2020). Strafvollzug-Demographische und kriminologische Merk- male der Strafgefangenen zum Stichtag 31.3. Destatis. https://www.statistischebibliothek.de/mir/receive/DESerie_mods_00000108

Díez-Ripollés, J.L. (2017). El abuso del sistema penal. *Revista Electrónica de Ciencia Penal y Criminología*, *19*(1), 1–24. Available at: http://criminet.ugr.es/recpc/19/recpc19-01.pdf

Díez-Ripollés, J.L. (2019). Overuse of the Criminal Justice System: Rules and Practices. *European Criminal Law Review*, *9*(1), 40–58. https://doi.org/10.5771/2193-5505-2019-1-40

Einführungsgesetz zum Strafgesetzbuch, 1974. https://www.gesetze-im-internet.de/stgbeg/BJNR004690974.html

García España, E., & Díez-Ripollés, J.L. (2021). La exclusión social generada por el sistema penal español: Aplicación del instrumento RIMES. *In-Dret*, *1*, 259–281.

Garton Grimwood, G. (2015). Categorisation of prisoners in the UK. *House of Commons Library*, *07437*(29), 1–14.

Offender Management Statistics (2019). *Prison Population Data Tool. Quarterly Prison Population.* https://www.gov.uk/government/statistics/offender-management-statistics-quarterly-january-to-march-2019

Petek, G. (2019). *Improving California's Prison Inmate Classification System.* Legislative Analyst's Office.

RIMES Project (2018). *Executive Report.* Unpublished.

9 Pool 4

Harshest penalties

Noelia Corral-Maraver

1 The role of harshest penalties in the context of social exclusion

In this chapter we will deal with pool 4, concerning harshest penalties. As we shall see, this pool includes items related to the most serious sanctions existing today in the different countries, namely the death penalty and life or long-term imprisonment. It is indisputable that both penalties are the greatest exponent of social exclusion in our criminal justice systems and that, therefore, they should be valued by the RIMES instrument.

The death penalty takes the notion of exclusion to its maximum extent, going as far as to physically eliminate the offender. This sanction has a long history but, fortunately, it is currently in decline,[1] due to the widespread opposition it arouses in large and diverse sectors of society (Arroyo Zapatero, Biglino Camplos, & Schabas, 2010).[2] Today this penalty has been abolished in most European and South American countries, although we cannot ignore the fact that it still remains in a large part of the world and even in some important Western countries.

On the other hand, we have life imprisonment or long or indeterminate prison sentences. Here we see a trend differing from that of capital punishment. As many countries have been abandoning the death penalty, they have embraced life sentences or long imprisonment sentences as a way of responding to certain types of serious criminality. Thus, we note that an ever-increasing number of countries have legislations where those convicted for certain offences can spend very long periods deprived of their liberty. These periods can easily exceed 25 or 30 years and, in some cases, extend over the whole life of the convicted. The way this type of punishment is configured varies considerably from one country to another. We find life sentences with no possibility

1 See Amnesty International's Global Report. Death sentences and executions 2020. www.amnesty.de/sites/default/files/2021-04/Amnesty-Bericht-Todesstrafe-2020-April-Englische-Version.pdf (last accessed on 2 November 2023).

2 See also the wealth of information contained on the website of the International Academic Network for the Abolition of Capital Punishment (REPECAP), available at: https://worldcoalition.org/es/ (last accessed on 7 July 2023).

DOI: 10.4324/9781032661766-12

of review or with a possible review, after a minimum period of time served. In any case, this type of sanctions is also a significant reflection of social exclusion, since it seeks the incapacitation of individuals, setting them apart from society for long periods of time.

The study of harshest penalties shows us how the government in office can react to punish individuals who commit the most serious crimes. There is no doubt that comparative law studies measuring such reactions are particularly relevant. In fact, maximum penalties are one of the aspects most used in national or comparative studies to try to evaluate the rigour of criminal legislation and there is a large number of academic works on this matter (among many others, Cavadino & Dignan, 2006; Tonry, 2007), which sometimes combine them with other easily accessible data[3] (Díez-Ripollés, 2019, pp. 43–44). Although, as we know, the RIMES Project aims to create a complex instrument for the comparison of criminal policies which is not only limited to partial and incomplete indicators (Díez-Ripollés & García-España, 2019, p. 2; Díez-Ripollés, 2019, pp. 40–41), the relevance of pool 4 and its indicators to measure social exclusion is undeniable.

2 The pool building process

2.1 Brief review of the pool building process

The pool we are dealing with in this chapter was initially quite large, since at the beginning it had a total of 13 items, which are listed below:

Item 42 Death penalty is legally available.
Item 43 Life imprisonment without release is legally available.
Item 44 Reviewable life imprisonment is legally available.
Item 45 Life imprisonment for mentally ill offenders is legally available.
Item 46 A minimum of 20 years served is required before claiming release from life imprisonment.
Item 47 The statutory maximum term of regular imprisonment exceeds 15 years.
Item 48 For some prison penalties sentence reduction is legally banned.
Item 49 Death penalty is imposed on ethnical or racial minorities, or on people in poverty in over 80 per cent of cases.
Item 50 Those sentenced to life imprisonment regularly serve more than 25 years.
Item 51 More than 5 per cent of all prison sentences are life imprisonment.
Item 52 Life imprisonment is imposed on ethnical or racial minorities, or on people in poverty in over 80 per cent of cases.

3 In this sense, it is common to use important but insufficient indicators, such as the incarceration rate per 100,000 inhabitants.

Item 53 On average, time spent serving prison sentences under a regular regime exceeds 80 per cent of the total sentenced term.
Item 54 Over 50 per cent of those sentenced to regular imprisonment get access to furlough after serving one third of the sentence.

The appropriateness of including so many items in the final instrument was already questioned in the first meetings and attention was drawn to possible overlaps between some of them. For example, overlaps can be seen between item 43 ("Life imprisonment without release is legally available") and item 44 ("Reviewable life imprisonment is legally available").

In the validation by experts, the overall rating of this pool was not too high and only 61.5 per cent of the items made the cut-off. All the items passed the screening for suitability, but only 5 of them passed the one for clarity. Items 48, 49 and 52 obtained a low score regarding clarity. Therefore, items 48 and 52 had to be rewritten and sent to the experts, for their second round, while item 49 was discarded by the team.

In the second turn of reviews by experts, the results obtained differ from those of the first round, as regards suitability and clarity of each item. In pool 4, one of the two modified indicators (item 52) is validated in the second turn (0.87), while item 48 still obtains a low score (0.63).

With these new results, the research team decided to further refine the list of indicators. For pool 4, the items with the lowest scores on the Aiken scale in the second round of expert reviews were rejected. Specifically, items 46 and 48 were discarded as they had obtained low results (0.77 and 0.63, respectively). Thus, finally this pool included 4 items, two rules (42, 43) and two practices (50, 52). Items 42 and 52 were approved unanimously and without discussion by the team, while items 43 and 50 aroused mild debate before being approved. We will see that, later on, the problems faced to resolve item 52 in most countries led to it being discarded and replaced by item 46.

2.2 Description of the pool's items

We will now focus on analysing those indicators of pool 4 that did pass through the methodological filters and were included in the final RIMES instrument. In addition to the aforementioned screenings carried out by the team and two revisions by experts, the research team then undertook the demanding task of explaining and clarifying each indicator so that they could be clear and operational for any external user. Next, we will see the wording and definition of each item that was finally included in pool 4,[4] as well as the main issues discussed by the team, if any.

4 The definitions are presented in English, as the RIMES instrument was validated in this language.

Item 42 (rule): death penalty is legally available

This item obtained good scores on Aiken scale, both in the first and second review by experts (0.88 and 0.83, respectively). Its description – which merely stated that it should be verified whether it was implemented in both wartime and peacetime – did not raise controversy among the research team and was approved without discussion.

Item 43 (rule): life imprisonment without release is legally available

This rule also obtained very high scores on the Aiken scale (0.90 and 0.87) and again, its description did not lead to discussions in the team, and thus was approved unanimously. Its definition merely specified that life imprisonment was considered non-reviewable when the judge or court could decree lack of review; in addition, temporary leaves were not considered as reviews of the sentence for the purposes of this item.

Item 50 (practice): those sentenced to life imprisonment regularly serve more than 25 years

Again, the scores obtained by this item – in this case a practice – on the Aiken scale were quite high, in both the first and second expert assessments, having scored 0.79 and 0.81, respectively.

Despite this, the subsequent description of this item by the RIMES team did raise some questions. Thus, it was discussed whether it was more convenient to use the term "usually" or "regularly" to measure the frequency of occurrence required for the item to be met. The second term was chosen. Then the question was also raised as to what should be understood by "regularly" here, since we are dealing with concepts that can be interpreted very differently by each expert or researcher. It was proposed that "regularity" should be considered to occur when the item was met in at least 35 per cent of cases and it was decided to review the existing scientific literature on the matter. This would provide a single criterion to solve the item. In the end, and with some other minor changes, the final description of the item was approved in a subsequent meeting.

Item 52 (practice): in over 80 per cent of life sentences those serving time are from an ethnic minority background or were living in poverty[5]

This has been one of the most problematic items for the team in the various phases of the project. As we have already seen, item 52 obtained poor results in the first round of international experts' assessment as regards clarity (0.67), which caused it to be reformulated and sent again for the second round, where it was finally validated (0.85).

5 The wording of this item was slightly changed by the team in order to improve clarity.

It was included in the final instrument, but the description process was not without controversies within the RIMES team, which were solved in various working sessions. The term "people in poverty" was debated, and the team considered using the definition of the World Bank in its latest report "Poverty and Shared Prosperity 2018: Piercing together".[6] However, it was agreed not to include an express mention of this report in the item's definition. As to the percentage of 80 per cent which the item requires to occur in a country, the research team discussed and decided that this percentage should be calculated over the total prison population of the country to be analysed. Nevertheless, as we shall see below when dealing with the methodology for item solving, this indicator proved to be very problematic and difficult to deal with, given the lack of data. For this reason, it was finally decided to remove it from the instrument and to replace it with item 46.

Item 46 (rule): a minimum of 20 years served is required before claiming release from life imprisonment

The RIMES team opted for this item as a substitute for item 52 over others that had been considered, such as item 48, due to its greater methodological robustness: it had obtained a score of 0.82 and 0.77 on the Aiken scale in the first and second rounds, respectively. This determined its selection, even if it meant replacing a practice (which are scarcer in the instrument) with another rule. Therefore, pool 4 finally included three rules and a practice.[7]

The description of this item did not prove to be particularly difficult, apart from some mentions that the first descriptions proposed were too generic and it was agreed to specify that the maximum of 20 years would also include the case of accumulation of sentences.

3 Methodology used to solve the items in each country

3.1 Methodology used to solve items 42, 43 and 46 (rules) in each country

These items were fairly straightforward to resolve in almost all the countries analysed, as it was usually only necessary to refer to the country's basic legislation or case law. It was normally enough to check the Constitution of the respective country. In other cases, a lower-ranking regulation had to be consulted – such as a norm with the status of law – like the penal code or a legislative decree. In some other cases, as for item 42 in New York, the response was obtained from a court decision.

6 This report established three steps of poverty according to the income level of the countries and the daily amount with which people can subsist: i) 1.90 USD per day; ii) 3.20 USD per day; and iii) 5.50 USD per day.

7 This also forced changes to be introduced in a previous study carried out with the RIMES instrument in Spain. See Chapter 5 of this book.

Sometimes legislation had to be supplemented by other secondary sources accessed on the Internet, such as news or articles published in the press. Occasionally, reports from government agencies or various associations or academic studies on the subject have been used. And, although exceptionally, some countries had to consult with experts.

3.2 Methodology used to solve items 50 and 52 (practices) in each country

These items are practices; therefore, collecting the data needed to solve them has been more complex. Since the regulatory sources were not enough, we had to go elsewhere to find not what was established by the law, but what was happening in reality.

In the case of practice 50, useful official documents could only be found in some countries. On the contrary, in most states there were no official data or statistics, or else they did not include information on what our item aimed to measure. Further searches were therefore required. Thus, in some cases, academic studies, reports from associations, NGOs or from EU governmental entities were found and they gave us relevant data. In others, various websites or press articles had to be used. On several occasions, expert advice was also required. In any case, it was possible to resolve the item in all countries except Spain, where this could not be done because not enough time had elapsed for the scenario of the item to be fulfilled.

With practice 52, however, the different teams in charge of fieldwork in each country found quite a lot of problems to resolve it. It soon became clear that there were difficulties in almost all countries to find data that could provide an answer. The item description required that more than 80 per cent of those sentenced to life imprisonment should belong to ethnic minorities or be living in poverty, and both qualities had to be taken into account. In some countries the teams were able to obtain data on ethnic minorities in prison,[8] with varying degrees of difficulty, but others were not so lucky.[9] In most cases, no relevant data could be found on poor people in prison.[10] Thus, after many inquiries, the item could only be resolved in the US states of

8 This was the case of England and Wales, where data could be obtained.

9 In the case of Germany, information was obtained on foreigners in prison, but as this does not necessarily correspond to the concept of ethnical or racial minority it was not accepted by the team. The same was true for Italy and Poland (the latter country does not have large niches of ethnic minorities in its population).

10 Such was the case of Germany, or England & Wales. The latter territory even submitted an official request to the British Government on the income of inmates in British prisons, but to no avail, since this data is not recorded in this country. In Italy there was no data, although it seems that most of those sentenced to life imprisonment were *mafiosi*, so it could be deduced that the item would not be fulfilled. In Poland, data could be found on people with limited resources in prison, but this concept was broader than the one required by the item's description ("poor" was identified with "working class").

California and New York.[11] Faced with these difficulties, the RIMES research team considered several options, such as the possibility of carrying out fieldwork to resolve the item or replacing it with another that would not be so troublesome. Finally, the decision was to discard it, since its accessibility was too low and it was inadequate to be part of a measuring instrument that claimed to be functional and user-friendly. Item 46 was chosen as a substitute, for its better scores, even if it meant changing one practice for another rule.

4 Results obtained by the items in each country

4.1 General issues

This section presents the results obtained in the resolution of pool 4's indicators. First, we have all the results ordered by country (Table 9.1) and then we conduct an analysis of the resolution of each item individually.

As we can see from the results of Table 9.1, here we have a pool that is useful for measuring social exclusion and drawing interesting conclusions. All the items of pool 4 have enough discrimination capacity, since all of them include countries responding "yes" or "no", and none of the items have been answered in the affirmative or in the negative in all countries. This pool has also not raised any particular problems as regards clarity for any of the working teams or for the expert reviewers.

The pool is highly reliable, as once the items had been resolved by the research team, they were reviewed by experts from each country. The experts replied with many comments in multiple directions, clearly differentiating the situation when it came to rules (items 42, 43 and 46) or to practices (item 50). Concerning the former, most rules have maintained their resolution after the experts' review and have generally not even required further clarification. Regarding item 42, only Italy and England and Wales have made minor additions to the item, without any major changes, and item 46 has been confirmed and not modified in any of the countries analysed. Item 43 has only been amended in Italy, where after the expert's review its resolution was changed.

Table 9.1 Results of pool 4, by item and country

	Germany	*California*	*Spain*	*Italy*	*New York*	*Poland*	*England & Wales*
Item 42	No	Yes	No	No	No	No	No
Item 43	No	Yes	No	Yes	Yes	No	Yes
Item 46	No	Yes	Yes	Yes	Yes	Yes	Yes
Item 50	No	No	No	Yes	No	Yes	No*

Source: Own elaboration

11 California made an estimate based on the percentage of ethnical minorities in prison, including – after discussing the matter with the rest of the RIMES team and making a decision – Latino people as an ethnic minority.

As for the practice, which involved greater difficulties, three countries did not require any modification (Germany, Italy, New York). However, three others (California, Poland and England and Wales) needed to introduce changes in the item after its review. In the case of California, this was just a slight amendment of the protocol to add additional sources. However, in Poland and the United Kingdom[12] the changes were profound and led to the modification of the item's response.[13]

Likewise, we have carried out a weighting based on the results and have proceeded to position the different countries in a continuum of social exclusion, according to their scores in this pool. Thus, we can see that Germany is the least exclusionary country, as it has responded to all the items in the negative, and therefore gets a score of 0 in the social exclusion continuum. Then comes Spain (with a score of 2.35), followed by Poland (with 4.82). Further to the right of the continuum would be New York and England and Wales (with the same score of 4.99). Then there is Italy (with a 7.46) and, finally, the country with the most social exclusion level would be California (with 7.52). All these results are shown in the following graph:

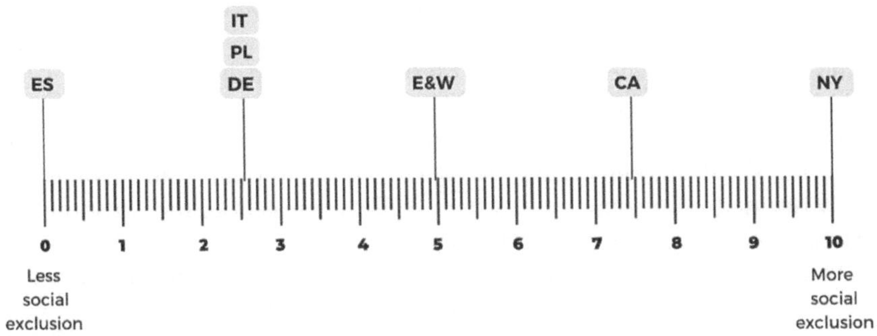

Figure 9.1 Position of countries in a continuum of social exclusion, as regards harshest penalties

The resolution of each item in the different countries analyzed will be explained in more detail below.

4.2 *Results obtained in item 42 (rule): death penalty is legally available*

Death penalty is the capital punishment that any legal system can foresee for criminal citizens and is, at the same time, the maximum exponent of the notion of social exclusion. In fact, it means the definitive exclusion of the offender from society, by punishing him or her with the deprivation of their

12 In fact, all the data analysed in this study does not correspond to the whole of the United Kingdom, but to the territories of England and Wales.

13 All this is further explained below, in the resolution of each item.

own life. Fortunately, this penalty has gradually fallen into disuse in much of the world. Most of the countries analysed by the RIMES instrument do not have the death penalty in force, so they do not fulfill the item.

In Spain, the death penalty is expressly prohibited by article 15 of the Spanish Constitution, although this provision leaves open the possibility that it could be applied through military criminal laws in war times However, years later, Organic Law 11/1995, of 27 November, abolishing the death penalty in war times, also declared that the death penalty was abolished in the Military Penal Code. For this reason, there is currently no such penalty in any case in this country.

In Italy, this penalty disappeared in August 1944, after a legislative decree abolished it, replacing it with life imprisonment.

Something similar happened in the United Kingdom, where the capital punishment was repealed in 1965, by the Murder (Abolition of Death Penalty) Act, which also replaced it with life imprisonment.

In Germany, as a result of its history and its division after the Second World War, the death penalty was in force for different time periods. In the western side, the Federal Republic of Germany, this sentence was abolished a few years after the end of the Second World War, with the adoption of its new Constitution in 1949 (article 102), which is still in force today. However, in the side under Soviet control, the German Democratic Republic, the capital punishment was retained for a longer term, and was finally abolished in 1987. When the German reunification took place after 1989, the Constitution of 1949 became applicable to the whole territory and with it, the prohibition of imposing the death penalty was extended. Thus, although some *Länder* formally retained it for some time in their regional legislation, the constitutional mandate prevented it from being applied.[14]

In Poland, the death penalty was formally maintained until the entry into force of its current Criminal Code in September 1998, although it had been on stand-by since the entry of the country into the democratic system in 1989. In such Criminal Code, this punishment disappeared and was replaced by life imprisonment.[15]

As we know, the death penalty is still used in the United States of America, although not in all its federal states. In New York this sentence has been used for a long time, and has been eliminated and reinstated on several occasions. It is currently not in force, since it was abolished in 2007 after a ruling of the New York Court of Appeal[16] which declared it was incompatible with the Constitution of such state.

14 The last German federal state to symbolically remove it from its legal system, after a referendum, was Hesse in 2018. Today it is currently formally abolished in the whole territory.

15 Besides, a few years later this country signed international instruments where it committed itself to repeal it both in times of peace and war. See Protocols to the European Convention on Human Rights, no. 6 (abolishing the death penalty in peacetime) of 2000, and Protocol no. 13 (abolishing the death penalty in all circumstances) of 2014.

16 It is the decision of the New York Court of Appeals in *People v. LaValle*.

However, the death penalty is currently in force in California. It is prescribed in the ordinary Penal Code for certain particularly serious crimes, such as treason or murder in the first degree.[17] California also has a Military Penal Code that applies this sanction for some criminal offences. It is the only case of the countries analysed where the item is met.

4.3 Results obtained in item 43 (rule): life imprisonment without release is legally available

The response to item 43 (rule) is not as homogeneous as that of the previous rule. There are three countries where this item is not met, i.e., they do not have non-reviewable life sentences, but there are also four countries where we can say it is fulfilled.

Starting with the former group of countries, we note that in Spain today there is any non-reviewable life sentence. There, an important reform of the Penal Code in 2015 introduced the so-called "permanent reviewable prison" (*prisión permanente revisable*), which is a kind of life sentence. However, as mentioned in its name and detailed in several articles of the Code, it provides in any case for the possibility of reviewing the sentence after serving a certain period, which varies depending on the crime or crimes committed.[18]

German law also includes a sentence of life imprisonment (*lebenslange Freiheitsstrafe*), although there is always the possibility of reviewing the sentence after a period of 15 years served (section 57.a of the German Criminal Code, *Strafgesetzbuch or StGB).*

In Poland, the Criminal Code includes – among its sentencing options – life imprisonment (article 32.5). The Polish Code provides for the possibility of a review of this sentence after 25 years have been served (article 78.3), so we must conclude that there is always the possibility of revising the sentence (Kładoczny & Wolny, 2013, p. 40; Stańdo-Kawecka, 2014, pp. 242–259). However, we should note that at the time of writing this paper the situation is not final. In 2019, the Polish Parliament passed an amendment to the Penal Code increasing the periods for review from 25 to 35 years and, as regards this item, it also provided for a non-reviewable life imprisonment sentence.[19] This measure was highly questioned and there were protests from legal practitioners, academics and civil society, so the president of the republic sent the

17 Although in 2019 the death penalty in the civil sphere was temporarily suspended in California by a decision of the Democratic Governor, Gavin Newson, it has not been repealed, so it remains in force today. News item from *The New York Times*, available at: www.nytimes.com/2019/03/12/us/california-death-penalty.html (last accessed on 5 July 2023).

18 This will be detailed later, with the resolution of item 46 (see below).

19 The annual report of the Helsinki Foundation for Human Rights of 2018 has also been consulted. Available at: www.prison-insider.com/files/9614b50a/fp_pologne_en.pdf (last accessed on 7 July 2023).

reform for study to the Polish Constitutional Court.[20] The matter is still pending resolution. The decision of this court or any legal changes it may cause could imply a change in the resolution of the item, because – if it confirms the reform and decides that it in accordance with the Constitution – we would find that item 43 would be fulfilled in Poland, as it would include a life sentence without the possibility of review.

As to those countries where there are non-revisable life sentences, we find Italy in the first place. The resolution of this item changed after the expert's review, going from "no" to "yes". Although the Italian Penal Code states that life imprisonment may be reviewed after 26 years have been served, in certain cases convicts are excluded from this benefit (*ergastolo ostativo)*, such as, for example, convicts who do not cooperate with the authorities. Thus, there are currently mafia members sentenced to life imprisonment to whom the review cannot be applied. This was appealed before the Italian Constitutional Court, which ruled on 15 April 2021 that such penalty was against the Constitution and called on the Italian Parliament to amend the criminal law appropriately within one year. This sets May 2022 as the date by which the penalty of *ergastolo ostativo* should disappear from the legal system of this country. For this reason, although it seems that this situation may change in the near future, for the time being, the answer to this item would be in the affirmative.

Secondly, there is the state of California whose Penal Code specifies that life imprisonment with no possibility of reviewing the conviction (*parole*) shall be imposed in certain particularly serious cases. Its determination will depend on the type of crime involved and the specific provisions of the laws regarding the execution of sanctions.

Third, the state of New York also has a non-reviewable life sentence which can be applied, under the New York Criminal Code, to certain crimes, including first-degree murder, second-degree murder, and aggravated murder.

Finally, in the United Kingdom we also find a way of applying non-reviewable life imprisonment, which there is called "whole life order". This is an order issued by the judicial authority stating that the person sentenced to life imprisonment has no possibility of reviewing his or her sentence or accessing parole, so they must remain in prison until their death. Such order is issued in particularly serious cases, where aggravating circumstances concur. In short, we can conclude that in this country the item is fulfilled, as judges have the discretion to turn the sentence of ordinary life imprisonment (with periods for review) into a penalty without the possibility of review (through the issuance of a whole life order). This clearly violates the European Convention on Human Rights and does not heed the existing convictions handed down by the European Court of Human Rights against this country for its life imprisonment sentence.

20 This information has been extracted from both the report of the United Nations Committee against Torture of 2019, and personal communications of Polish professors who are experts in the criminal field.

4.4 *Results obtained in item 46 (rule): a minimum of 20 years served is required before claiming release from life imprisonment*

As to the results of item 46 in each country, we should bear in mind that among the countries that have a sentence of life imprisonment, at least reviewable (all those analysed here). But we must now look at the time periods in which the respective Criminal Laws allows access to the first review of the sentence and check whether or not this occurs after 20 years have been completed.

We only find one case where the answer to this item is negative, since the time frame of the first review does not reach such term: Germany. Here, the statutory period for a convict of life imprisonment to be eligible to apply for parole is 15 years. There are no exceptions to this rule and a review always takes place within this period (Dessecker, 2017),[21] although it may of course be decided not to release the offender and to wait for further periodic reviews. Therefore, the rule described in the item is not met in Germany.

The other countries analysed do met the item. In Spain, the regulation of life imprisonment establishes a complex system of access to prison benefits and parole. The period varies depending on the crimes committed and whether it is a case of accumulation of sentences. Thus, in order to be eligible for suspension of the sentence (probation), a person convicted to reviewable life imprisonment must serve as a general rule 25 years of imprisonment (article 92.1 of the Spanish Criminal Code). However, according to article 78 bis, this period increases if the conviction is for multiple crimes and depending on the type of crime committed (it is increased in the case of terrorism or organised crime). In such cases, the terms can reach up to 28, 30 or 35 years of serving the sentence.

In Poland, article 78.3 of the Criminal Code prescribes that a person sentenced to life imprisonment may review his sentence after serving 25 years. This goes beyond what is described in the item's description. In addition, as already mentioned in the previous section, the new reform of the Polish Criminal Code plans to further extend these periods up to 35 years in some cases.[22]

In Italy, the review of life imprisonment and eligibility for parole occurs after serving 26 years. Prison benefits, such as a semi-confinement regime or third grade, are applicable once the inmate has served 20 years. In any case, the terms of the item description are also met here.

This item is also fulfilled in California, where the reviewable life sentence establishes different periods to allow apply for parole. A general term of seven years is set, in the first place, but this does not apply when the law establishes a different period, which occurs for certain serious crimes. Thus, for example, if

21 Information extracted from the report *Die Vollstreckung lebenslanger Freiheitsstrafen. Dauer und Gründe Der Beendigung Im Jahr 2015–2017*, 2017. Available at: https://krimpub.krimz.de/frontdoor/deliver/index/docId/39/file/bm-online9.pdf (last accessed on 2 November 2023).

22 As noted in the previous section, this amendment is pending review by the Polish Constitutional Court.

a person has been sentenced to a prison term ranging from 25 years to life for first-degree murder, the review may not take place until 25 years of the sentence have been served.[23] These time periods are longer in the case of convicts with various sentences and can reach up to 21 years in prison. Therefore, the limits set by item 46 are exceeded.

In the state of New York, those sentenced to reviewable life imprisonment must generally serve a term of not less than 15 and not more than 25 years. However, there are other legally prescribed time limits, depending on the offence and circumstances. In the case of first-degree murder, the period that must elapse to be eligible to apply for parole ranges between 20 and 25 years. But in some cases, these periods can go up to 40 years. With this in mind, we can say that, frequently the time needed for lifers to be eligible for parole exceeds 20 years, so the item would be fulfilled here.

Finally, we have the case of the United Kingdom, where there is a complex and casuistic regulation to determine the term after which life sentences can be reviewed. For example, in the case of murder by means of a knife or weapon brought to the scene with premeditation, the first review of the sentence cannot take place before having served 25 years.[24] There are numerous scenarios like this one, where the time needed to be eligible for parole exceeds 20 or 25 years. Therefore, the response to the item in this country is also in the affirmative.

4.5 *Results obtained in item 50 (practice): those sentenced to life imprisonment regularly serve more than 25 years*

Regarding this item, it should be borne in mind that now it is no longer a question of looking at the rules set forth in the different legislations, but rather of checking what actions are taken regarding the release of those sentenced to life imprisonment. Indeed, despite the fact that each country provides for a series of minimum time periods to access the reviews – which, as we have seen, are very variable – this does not prevent there being cases where inmates remain in prison after those deadlines have expired, probably because the reviews had a negative outcome. During the analysis of this practice the research teams have had greater difficulties than in previous items, as it has not always been easy to find data on the average prison stays of those sentenced to life imprisonment. In some cases, this data does not exist because 25 years have not yet elapsed since this penalty was included in the criminal system of such country or state. In others, there is simply no official data because the country in question does not collect it or it becomes difficult to find information on persons convicted

23 Information available at: www.socalcriminallawyer.com/parole-california/ (last accessed on 7 July 2023).

24 See the report "Offender Management Statistics (2019)" of Prison Population Data Tool, available at: https://assets.publishing.service.gov.uk/media/5d372e73e5274a400af813e4/prison-population-data-tool.xlsx (last accessed on 7 July 2023).

so many years ago. Despite these limitations, most countries have been able to resolve this item.

Again, we find Germany among the countries where this item is not fulfilled. In this country there is no official data on this issue, although we have found an interesting academic study from which we were able to extract the necessary data (Dessecker & Hoffmann, 2019). This work analyses the country's prison data over a period of 14 years, from 2002 to 2017. It appears that the average length of prison stays for those convicted to life sentence is about 19 years. It is therefore considered that this item is not met here, as it does not reach the 25 years required.

It is worth noting that in California – a state where all the previous items have been fulfilled – this item, on the contrary, must be answered with a "no", as in practice those convicted to life sentence normally have access to freedom before they have served 25 years. This conclusion can be drawn from a report analysing the prison population in 2018,[25] which includes those sentenced to life imprisonment, with or without review. This study claims that the average stay of those sentenced to reviewable life imprisonment in this state is 24.6 years, and 19.9 years in case of life imprisonment without revision. Therefore, from the data we have we can conclude that, on average, they do not exceed 25 years in prison.

In New York, the work team found it very difficult to obtain information, despite consulting multiple sources, but finally managed to obtain data through a personal consultation with experts from the Vera Institute of Justice. According to this organisation, the percentage of those sentenced to life imprisonment who serve more than 25 years is 14.13 per cent, while the rest do not reach that length of time. For this reason, we can conclude that this item is not met in this state either, as it is a low percentage.

In the United Kingdom, numerous problems were also found in accessing official sources to resolve practice 50. Although at first the team tried to answer the item with some media sources, which established that over 80 per cent of those sentenced to life imprisonment in the United Kingdom had served more than 25 years in prison, the expert's review led them to rethink this answer. Thus, they were able to find official data, based on the response by the British Ministry of Justice to a request for information made by an association (Full Fact Organisation).[26] According to this, the number of inmates sentenced to life imprisonment who in the period 2010–2018 had been released only after 25 years was 168, which was only 9.17 per cent of the total. It was therefore decided to change the resolution of the item and consider that it is not fulfilled in England and Wales.

25 See "Offender data points. Offender demographics for the 24-month period ending December 2018", available at: www.cdcr.ca.gov/research/wp-content/uploads/sites/174/2020/01/201812_DataPoints.pdf (last accessed on 7 July 2023).

26 Freedom Information request (FOI) 191007006 (Ministry of Justice; DASD-JSAS). Information available at: https://fullfact.org/crime/how-long-do-murderers-serve-prison/ (last accessed on 7 July 2023).

On the other hand, among the countries with an affirmative answer to this item we have Italy. As seen in the resolution of previous items, the Italian Penal Code prescribes that those sentenced to life imprisonment in this country must serve at least 26 years before being eligible for parole. For this reason, we should expect that most cases will serve more than 25 years old. However, a partial reduction of the sentence (of 90 days per year) is possible for good behaviour. There is no official data on how many of those sentenced to this penalty receive a sentence reduction. Therefore, this is not enough to answer the item and the research team has resorted to other sources, such as press reports, from which we can draw the conclusion that the length of life sentences served in Italy is very high.[27] More relevant, however, is a report carried out in 2019 by the European Parliament on life imprisonment in the different Member States, stating that since 2010, the number of people sentenced to life imprisonment in Italy accounted for 4 per cent (representing 1,735 convicts at the end of 2017) of the total prison population. It seems that 70 per cent of these never qualify for parole on the basis of dangerousness criteria.[28] Despite the fact that in Italy there are no exact data, it can be deduced from the above that in general (both by the law and by the practice of not granting reviews), the 25 years of imprisonment are exceeded, so this item is fulfilled.

In Poland, the Penal Code itself already prescribes that the review of life sentences begins after 25 years of serving. This code dates from 1997, so those sentenced to life imprisonment by this regulation will only complete 25 years in prison in 2022. However, this sanction was also applied to those previously sentenced to the death penalty (since it was finally abolished with the adoption of this Code, as explained in item 42). In the latter case, there are prisoners who have already been able to serve 25 years of the sentence before having access to parole (Stańdo-Kawecka, 2014, pp. 242–259).[29] Specifically, a research study claims that at the beginning of 2020 there were 5 inmates sentenced to life imprisonment who had served 25 years of deprivation of liberty and one who had died in prison. But in 2019 the total number of people sentenced to this maximum penalty was 460. Out of these, only 5 had already served more than 25 years (1 per cent of the total), 64 had served at least 20 years (14 per cent), 185 inmates had served at least 15 years (40 per cent) and the rest, 206 convicts, had served less time than that (45 per cent) (Klimczak & Nielaczna, 2020). Therefore, although we can say

27 El País newspaper reported in an article that in Italy out of 1,540 convicts sentenced to life, about 100 had asked Pope Benedict XVI for help and that several humanitarian organisations had tried to intercede with the Italian State on this issue. However, this is a low percentage of the total number of convicts and not enough to conclude that the item is met. See El País newspaper, issue of 21 January 2015, available at: https://elpais.com/politica/2015/01/21/actualidad/1421871492_173347.html (last accessed on 7 July 2023).

28 See the European Parliament resolution A8-0251/2017 on prison systems and conditions reaffirms the role of the EU, available at: www.europarl.europa.eu/doceo/document/E-8-2019-001555_EN.html#def3 (last accessed on 7 July 2023).

29 See also Helsinki Foundation for Human Rights, 2018 Report.

that the percentage of prisoners who have served more than 25 years – clearly sentenced before 1997 to the death penalty, replaced by life imprisonment – is today too low, the rest of the convicts have not yet reached the time required to serve 25 years. According to the assessment of the country's experts, the answer to this item should be "yes", as it seems that it is common for convicts who reach this period to exceed it. In fact, the resolution of this item was modified by the experts' advice.

Finally, in Spain, it is not possible at the moment to answer to this item. The reason is that the reviewable life imprisonment was introduced very recently (in 2015) and before that there was no equivalent penalty. In fact, the sanction that replaced death penalty in this country when it was repealed in 1978 was imprisonment for up to 30 years, but– until now – there was no indeterminate penalty. Given the short time that has elapsed since the reform came into force, we will not be able to have data for many years yet. If this sentence is maintained, we will have to wait at least until 2040 to find out whether the period served in practice exceeds 25 years.

5 Conclusions

After analysing the items of pool 4 in the different countries we can conclude that this is a relevant pool, as well as quite useful to measure social exclusion in the different countries or states. Indeed, the importance of the pool's theme is not in question. The harshest penalties provided for the most serious crimes are the pinnacle of the sentencing system of each country. They represent the maximum level of severity to which the state can punish the most serious violations of the rules of social coexistence. In this sense, they are an important and unavoidable indicator of social exclusion.

Access to reliable data may be the main difficulty in this pool. In general, this has not been particularly difficult in the case of rules, 42, 43 and 46. However, item 50 has proved complex to resolve, given that it is a practice and due to the scarcity of official data on the subject.[30] In spite of everything, most of the research teams have been able to solve it and in only one case, in Spain, has it been impossible to answer it, although not for lack of data, but because not enough time has elapsed for the indicator to be fulfilled. This, however, does not detract from the relevance of the item, as it is important to note the difference between the rules and their practical application in the different countries.

Another point that deserves to be highlighted in this pool is that there have been three occasions where an item had to change its response after being evaluated by the national experts. Thus, in Italy, item 43 went from "no" to "yes" after the expert's review; the same happened with item 50 in

30 As we already pointed out, the same problems to access data occurred with item 52. In that case, the difficulties could not be overcome, which is why that item was discarded and replaced by item 46.

Poland, which also changed from "no" to "yes"; and with item 50 in England and Wales, which changed from an initial "yes" to a final "no". Item 50 – a practice, quite complex and difficult to access – has presented the greatest complications, and there were errors or inaccuracies that had to be solved by the experts. On the other hand, some indicators of this pool may change their resolution in the near future, because there is a high probability of a legal reform affecting them. This is the case of item 43 in both Italy and Poland. In fact, this is normal and does not constitute a failure of the RIMES instrument. We are simply dealing with issues that are under discussion in certain countries, where they generate strong political and constitutional controversies, so such legislative changes are to be expected.

Next, we will point out some interesting assessments that can be extracted from the data obtained in the different countries, which are shown in Table 9.1. We do not have any case where the same indicator has been answered in the affirmative or negative in all states, so all of them have discrimination capacity. Therefore, if we look specifically at each country, the indicators regarding harshest penalties allow us to distinguish varying degrees of social exclusion. This has been graphically represented above, in the continuum of social exclusion.

In this sense we can note that Anglo-Saxon countries, i.e., the United Kingdom or, more specifically, England and Wales, and the two US states of New York and California, are the ones which, according to this instrument and with respect to the results of pool 4, are the most socially exclusionary. Indeed, in these countries item 43 is met, which – after item 42 on capital punishment – is the one describing the most severe and exclusionary sanction: the non-reviewable life imprisonment sentence. This conclusion is no less important for being expected. It confirms that the general impression we may have from academic readings on comparative criminal policy – where these states are presented as more rigorous and exclusionary – is true. California is clearly the most excessive state in this respect, with items 42, 43 and 46 being fulfilled, and scoring 7.52 in the social exclusion continuum. In other words, it has the death penalty, non-reviewable life imprisonment and provides for reviewable life sentence, but with terms often exceeding 20 years of serving before being eligible for parole. It is followed by New York and England and Wales, with a score of 4.99, which do not provide for the capital punishment, but where items 43 and 46 are met.

Among the continental countries, we are astonished to see how Italy scores very high in terms of social exclusion, as items 43, 46 and 50 are answered in the affirmative there, with a score of 7.46 on the social exclusion scale, although we know that the resolution of item 43 may change, as its current non-reviewable prison sentence has been overturned by the Constitutional Court. In any case, there is definitely a great trend towards great punitive rigorism in this country. Something similar happens in Poland, a country that does not score so high in the continuum, with 4.82, but where the conservative drift of the Government in recent years also translates into a clear increase of harshest penalties. With regard to it, we may consider item 43 on non-revisable life imprisonment which, although not currently fulfilled, would be met in the near future. As said, it has been reformed by the polish legislator and this issue is pending resolution by its Constitutional Court. This has also influenced item 46 in that country.

At the other side we have Germany, a country where none of the items is responded in the affirmative, with a score of 0 points in the continuum. This renders it, with respect to pool 4, the least exclusionary of the countries we have analysed. Spain's results are moderate or low on the social exclusion scale, having scored only 2.35. However, we should bear in mind that these data are not fully conclusive, as it was not possible to respond to item 50.

Yet, it should be noted that the results of item 50 have been interesting and somewhat surprising. We found very exclusionary places – as in the case of California – where, despite expectations, this item was not met. So, we can say that, in practice, there is some punitive moderation (although limited, since the times of serving analysed by the indicator are very long). The same happens in England and Wales and in New York, where the item is not fulfilled either. However, in other countries, such as Italy or Poland, this item is met. This shows the relevance and necessity of including practices – and not only rules – in the instrument, since it often happens that the former help us get a more reliable picture of how legal systems work in reality.

In short, the results of pool 4 are significant and its items are useful to draw relevant conclusions regarding comparative criminal policy. It is undeniable that the RIMES instrument provides a good starting point for further research works and could continue to yield interesting results if applied to other countries. Likewise, the experience described here could act as an incentive to conduct more criminological studies in relation to maximum sentences, either at a national level or from a comparative perspective. As we have seen, there is often a lack of data – official or not – to help us understand criminal rules or practices that are very relevant to measure social exclusion.

References

Arroyo Zapatero, L., Biglino Camplos, P. & Schabas, W. (2010). *Hacia la Abolición Universal de la Pena Capital*. Tirant lo Blanch.

Cavadino, M. & Dignan, J. (2006). *Penal Systems. A Comparative Approach*. Sage Publications.

Dessecker, A. (2017). *Die Vollstreckung lebenslanger Freiheitsstrafen. Dauer und Gründe der Beendigung im Jahr 2015*. KrimZ (BM-Online; Bd. 16) Wiesbaden BM-Online, Band 9. https://krimpub.krimz.de/frontdoor/deliver/index/docId/39/file/bm-online9.pdf

Dessecker, A. & Hoffmann, A. (2019). *Die Vollstreckung lebenslanger Freiheitsstrafen. Dauer und Gründe der Beendigung in den Jahren 2016 und 2017*. Wiesbaden KrimZ BM-Online, Band. 16. https://www.krimz.de/fileadmin/dateiablage/E-Publikationen/BM-Online/bm-online16.pdf

Díez-Ripollés, J.L. (2019). Overuse of the Criminal Justice System: Rules and Practices. *European Criminal Law Review, 9*(1), 40–58. https://doi.org/10.1017/9781780688398.004

Díez-Ripollés, J.L. & García-España, E. (2019). RIMES: An Instrument to Compare National Criminal Justice Policies from the Social Exclusion Dimension. *International E-Journal of Criminal Sciences, 1*(13), 1–27. www.ehu.eus/ojs/index.php/inecs/article/view/20866

European Parliament (2017). Resolution A8–0251/2017 on prison systems and conditions reaffirms the role of the EU. Available at: www.europarl.europa.eu/doceo/document/E-8-2019-001555_EN.html#def3

Helsinki Foundation for Human Rights Report (2018). *Criminal Detention in the EU – Conditions and Monitoring. Country Report Poland.* https://fra.europa.eu/en/databases/criminal-detention/criminal-detention/monitoring-reports-and-statements?country%5B%5D=189

Kładoczny, P. & Wolny, M. (2013). *Prison conditions in Poland.* European Prison Observatory. www.prisonobservatory.org/upload/Prison_Poland.pdf

Klimczak, J. & Nielaczna, M. (2020). *Extreme Criminal Penalties: Death Penalty and Life Imprisonment in the Polish Penal and Penitentiary System.* Archiwum Kryminologii, T. XLII, nr.1.

Offender Management Statistics (2019). *Prison Population Data Tool. Quarterly Prison Population.* https://assets.publishing.service.gov.uk/media/5d372e73e5274a400af813e4/prison-population-data-tool.xlsx

Stańdo-Kawecka, B. (2014). Poland, en Drenkhahn, K., Dudeck, M. and Frieder Dünkel, F (eds). *Long-Term Imprisonment and Human Rights* (pp. 218–235). Routledge.

Tonry, M. (ed.) (2007). *Crime, Punishment and Politics in Comparative Perspective. Crime and Justice 36.* University of Chicago Press.

United Nations (2019). Report of the United Nations Committee against Torture. https://tbinternet.ohchr.org/_layouts/15/TreatyBodyExternal/TBSearch.aspx?Lang=en&TreatyID=1&DocTypeID=27

10 Pool 5

Prison rules

Lorea Arenas-García

1 Introduction

This chapter analyses the process of selection, validation, screening and application of the indicators that make up the fifth pool of the RIMES instrument called "prison rules". All of them measure very diverse and specific aspects of the social exclusion generated by criminal policy in prison settings, and are founded theoretically on the works by Díez-Ripollés (2011, 2013, 2017) and Díez-Ripollés and García-España (2019), in line with the existing literature on the subject (Nilsson, 2003; Drake, 2011; Liebling, Durie, Stiles & Tait, 2011; Jewkes, Crewe & Bennett, 2016; Van Ginneken, Sutherland & Molleman, 2016; MacDonald, 2018; Auty & Liebling, 2020). The author points out that in the last two decades, the regime of enforcing prison sentences has been moving towards social segregation and the inocuisation of inmates, while extolling its retributive and intimidating value. This would explain the over-representation of disadvantaged people in prison – mainly ethnic or racial minorities, or poor, illegal foreigners – that are treated, or rather managed, as if they were residues or social waste. This is also helped by other elements such as: the relegation of resocialisation measures, the hardening of living conditions in prison, the difficulties to access parole and appeal prison decisions, the rise of private prisons, the use of uniforms, the normality of high-security prisons, the construction of large-capacity prisons ("macroprisons"), the overcrowding, etc. The policies behind such rules and practices intentionally seek to worsen the material conditions and prison regime of inmates by reducing his or her capacities, or hindering the exercise of their rights, which aggravates the distressing and stigmatising nature of the penalty, thus generating greater exclusion (Díez-Ripollés, 2017, pp. 16–17). This paper addresses the latter aspect by examining the pool building in the different stages of creation and validation of the RIMES instrument, the descriptions drafted by the research team to operationalise its measurement on a practical level, the application itself and the results of such instrument in Germany, California, Spain, Italy, New York, Poland and England and Wales, as well as methodological issues regarding completeness, extension, clarity, ease of data access

DOI: 10.4324/9781032661766-13

and discrimination capacity of indicators, which are very used at the time of implementing the different research projects carried out to date.

2 The pool building process

The fifth exclusion pool contained 19 indicators (13 rules and 6 practices) out of the 126 that made up the instrument to be validated, so it was the most extensive. Such items dealt with very different issues in relation to the penitentiary system, such as, among others: access to prison benefits, exercise of other rights not affected by the sentence, review of penitentiary decisions, free legal aid, family or intimate visits, imposition and duration of disciplinary sanctions, use of coercive means, separation of inmates, overcrowding and suicides. Once the questionnaire was administered, the second group of international experts validated 14 indicators (10 rules and 4 practices) with an Aiken's V coefficient higher than 0.70 for suitability, with items 58, 65, 66, 67 and 69 being excluded for failing to meet the cut-off threshold. The experts considered it was particularly exclusionary that no legal provision was made for the exercise of rights not affected by the sentence, for ending the sentence without access to parole, and for requiring the payment of fees in order to review penitentiary decisions or living conditions. On the contrary, the compulsory wearing of uniforms, the application of a more severe regime for certain convicts solely because of the nature of the offence committed, the cohabitation of first-time offenders with repeat offenders or not having access to parole unless civil liability was satisfied, were considered less exclusionary issues.

Once the second screening of items to reduce the instrument was completed, another five items were removed from the pool (numbers 56, 59, 61, 70 and 72), leaving a total of nine indicators (six rules and three practices) for subsequent validation. Table 10.1 shows a comparison of the validation results from both groups of experts (one and two), with the indicators ordered from highest to lowest, according to the score obtained as regards suitability for the exclusion of the second group.

At this time, the experts of the first group established an upper limit as regards suitability for exclusion lower than the one granted by the second group. In other words, the indicator that obtained the highest score did not exceed 0.81 in Aiken's V coefficient (items 55, 62 and 68) while, in the first turn, a higher validation was reached (between 0.82 and 0.89 in Aiken's V) for items 60, 62, 64 and 73. However, the experts of the first group did not consider the latter as the most exclusionary items. So, there were differences between the groups as regards setting the level for exclusion. Despite these variations in both turns, a very large number of items was validated and almost complete in the second turn (64 out of 65 items), which prompted the research team to restart a screening procedure of indicators. The methodological criteria adopted were very similar to those agreed in the previous reduction of the instrument, ensuring a minimum of three items per pool (between rules and practices). In the pool we are dealing with, four items were selected

Table 10.1 List of items validated for clarity, suitability (for exclusion and within the pool) and by group of international experts

Type	*Items*	*Second group (Aiken's V)*		*First group (Aiken's V)*		
		Clarity	*Suitability*	*Clarity*	*Suitability (exclusion)*	*Suitability (pool)*
R	55. The system lacks a specific prison regime for young adults.	0.78	0.80	0.96	0.81	0.90
P	68. Family and intimate visits take place at intervals of over one month.	0.82	0.80	0.98	0.81	0.92
R	62. The law lacks statutory provisions regulating inmates' legal assistance for penitentiary matters.	0.75	0.82	0.79	0.81	0.88
R	64. The law requires payment of fees by the inmate before claiming judicial review of penitentiary decisions.	0.80	0.84	0.77	0.79	0.88
R	60. Statutory mandates fail to include safeguards to inmates' rights which are not affected by the sentence (i.e., educational and occupational needs, cultural activities, religious assistance).	0.72	0.89	0.65	0.73	0.77
P	73. Over 20% of inmates serve their sentences without getting access to parole.	0.78	0.86	0.77	0.69	0.65
R	57. Solitary confinement may exceed 15 consecutive days.	0.86	0.75	0.83	0.67	0.94
P	71. The prison overcrowding rate exceeds the average European rate by 30%.	0.73	0.71	0.81	0.67	0.81
R	63. The system lacks a judicial review process for relevant decisions made by the prison administration on living conditions or prison regime.	0.79	0.83	0.90	0.60	0.81

Source: Own elaboration

with an Aiken's V value equal to or greater than 0.79: this requirement was met by items 55, 62, 68 and 64. In addition, the final selection of all of them was approved unanimously in group discussions. So, in the subsequent application of the instrument, we had three rules that covered issues such as the existence of a specific prison regime for young adults (55), whether there was a legal provision for free legal aid to inmates regarding penitentiary matters (62) and whether the legal system required the payment of fees by inmates before claiming the review of prison decisions (64). Likewise, the pool included a single practice that sought to verify whether family or intimate visits took place at intervals of over one month (68). It can be seen, therefore, that this final selection of items meets the criterion of extension by covering different topics in very comprehensive, clear and suitable items.

3 Description of items

This section contains the descriptions drafted for items 55, 62, 64 and 68 (mentioned above), based on the information generated in successive group meetings and summarised in the minutes and the manual.

The description given for *item 55* clarifies that the *criminal justice system* does not provide for a specific prison regime for young adults based on their age, and "young adults" should generally be understood as those between the ages of 18 and 21. It is also noted that special attention should be paid to the appropriate age range used in each country under study.

The researchers who dealt with the indicator in Spain already raised the first doubts on what should be understood by the term "prison regime". In this regard, it was questioned whether the fact that there are specific rules for women implies that they have a different regime from that of men, whether this happens in the case of foreigners or repeat offenders, or whether the mere existence of specific facilities for minors would imply that they have a different regime. At the time of applying this item in New York, California and Germany, doubts arose about the concept of "young adults" and the fact that they were convicted by either the adult or the juvenile penal system. In this sense, and to ensure completeness and clarity in the measurement of exclusion, it was argued that this indicator refers to the fact that the penitentiary system has specific rules on the treatment of young-adult convicts, and not to the fact that they are prosecuted under juvenile criminal law. That is, the item seeks to identify young people who – having attained the age of criminal responsibility and after been tried as adults – are subject or have access to a specific penitentiary regime. Only to the extent that they have done so can they be considered young adults, despite the fact that the enforcement of the sentence provides for them to be placed in centres for minors. In the event that they are judged as minors, this item would not be fulfilled. This implied that the teams in California and Germany had to be very precise about the age of criminal responsibility and the functioning of their penal system, since in both territories the judge had some flexibility to prosecute the person as an adult or a juvenile on the basis of guidance criteria and specific circumstances. However, whether one option or the other was chosen, a mitigated regime could be applied, that included serving the sentence in juvenile centres. Hence the answer to this item was negative.

With respect to *item 62*, the description specified that "penitentiary matters" should be understood as relevant issues, such as: probation, disciplinary procedures, change of regime, etc. The description was very clear for the whole team and, thanks to this, it was approved unanimously.

According to the description of *item 64*, the indicator refers to the legal provisions that require the inmate to pay fees before claiming review of the penitentiary decisions taken by the prison authorities. Although in a first discussion the description was approved by the team due to its clarity, when it was applied in Spain, several clarifications had to be made: the costs of legal assistance (lawyer) were not included, nor those regarding police custody; if payment is required but there is a free system for inmates with economic difficulties, this does not mean that the item is not met, because it is, since there are fees; and if there are differences among different territories regarding fees, it will be understood that there are fees when more than 50 per cent of the territories charge them.

Perhaps *item 68* generated the most controversy, probably because it dealt with a practice. The description was discussed in several meetings and it was agreed that the indicator would be met when family or intimate visits to inmates, or any of them, took place at intervals of over one month, as well as when both or one type of such visits were not carried out at all. In other words, for the item to be fulfilled, either both assumptions had to be met, or there had to be no provision on either of them. Besides, the group of "inmates" should be understood in a broad sense (including preventive ones), and the meetings mentioned could not be virtual, but with personal contact.

It was also clarified that intimate visits could be of a sexual nature and take place with people with whom there was – or not – a previous relationship. This included both visits between couples and those with prostitutes. In order to establish a limit that would allow to confirm fulfillment of this item, it was decided that if more than 35 per cent of the visits occurred at intervals of over one month, this would be exclusionary. Here it was necessary to clarify two issues: the calculations had to be made with respect to inmates who had requested such visits, i.e., leaving out those not interested in receiving them; and for the interval, the time elapsed between one visit and the next for the same inmate had to be taken into account.

4 Application of the instrument

In general, the rules have required to a greater extent a method based on consultation of secondary sources of information (FSI), either by reviewing only legislative texts (FSI-L) – such as regulations, codes of various kinds,

Table 10.2 Methodology used to solve each item of the pool, per country

Country	*Item 55*	*Item 62*	*Item 64*	*Item 68*
Germany	FSI	FSI-L	FSI-L	FSI
California	FSI-L	FSI	FSI	FSI
Spain	FSI-L	*Ad hoc* methodology	FSI-L	*Ad hoc* methodology
Italy	FSI	FSI-L	FSI	FSI
New York	FSI-L	FSI-L	FSI-L	FSI
Poland	FSI	FSI	FSI-L	*Ad hoc* methodology
England & Wales	FSI	FSI-L	FSI	FSI

Source: Own elaboration

constitutions–, or through broader systematic searches of scientific works, reports, official websites, etc. On the contrary, practices have often required the design of an *ad hoc* methodology, as is the case with practice 68. As shown in the table below, rules 55, 62 and 64 were resolved by the teams through secondary sources of information that, at times, were only legal, although indicator 62 in Spain required a different approach, as happened with practice 68 in Germany, Spain and Poland.

The secondary sources consulted for the resolution of each item in the different countries are detailed below, as well as the *ad hoc* methodology proposed for items 62 and 68.

In *Germany*, the research team solved all items by consulting FSI, although practice 68 required a more complex search and analysis due to the lack of official data. For item 55, the German Juvenile Court Act (*Jugendgerichtsgesetz)* and the report by Matthews, Schiraldi & Chester, 2018, were analysed; for item 62, the Prisons Act (*Strafvollzugsgesetz* or *StVollzG*) and the Code of Civil Procedure (*Zivilprozessordnung* or *ZPO)* were consulted; and for item 64, the review focused on the Law on Penal Execution and Reform and Prevention Measures with Deprivation of Liberty (*Gesetz über den Vollzug der Freiheitsstrafe und der freiheitsentziehenden Maßregeln der Besserung und Sicherung*), as well as the Code of Criminal Procedure (*Strafprozeßordnung*).

As regards item 68, a review of the Prisons Act mentioned above showed that inmates were entitled to receive visits at regular intervals of at least one hour per month, although the team needed to consult various documents and news items on the Internet in order to find out the practical application of this legal provision. This revealed that, in practice, different rules were applied depending on the region where the prison was located. In this regard, the team gathered information that confirmed this disparity. For example, some inmates were entitled to two hours of visits per month, with a maximum of four visits of 30 minutes per month[1]; others had a monthly quota of two hours

1 Prison Insider: www.prison-insider.com/countryprofile/prisonsgermany-en?s=contact-avec-l-exterieur#contact-avec-l-exterieur (Last date accessed: 2023, November 5).

with the possibility of arranging for another two in the case of minor children[2]; and in some other cases, four 30-minute visits per month were provided for.[3] However, such variability did not alter the fact that the normal regime of visits took place at intervals of less than one month. In order to establish whether the visits were of an intimate or sexual nature, it was necessary to review academic works and testimonies of inmates due to the lack of legal provisions and official data on this matter.

With respect to California, item 55 was resolved by consulting the California Welfare and Institutions Code, as well as the official website of the California Division of Juvenile Justice (DJJ). For item 62, a review was carried out of the Constitution of the United States, the official website of the California Judiciary, the California Judicial Branch (which contains a specific section on free legal aid), the California Legislative Information official website and other resources found through Google. For item 64, a consultation was conducted of the Prison Litigation Reform Act 1996; and for item 68, we reviewed the California Code of Regulations (title 15, sections 3044 and 3170–3179), as well as the Adult Inmate Visiting Guidelines[4] from the California Department of Corrections and Rehabilitation.

In *Spain*, item 55 was resolved according to the provisions set forth in Organic Law 10/1995, of 23 November, on the Criminal Code; in Organic Law 5/2000, of 12 January, regulating the criminal responsibility of minors; in Organic Law 1/1979, of 26 September, General Penitentiary; and in Royal Decree 190/1996, of 9 February, approving the Prison Regulations. As regards item 62, its resolution was carried out via two channels, proposing an *ad hoc* methodology for the second of them. In the first, a review of legislative texts was carried out, such as: Law 1/1996, of 10 January, on free legal aid; Royal Decree 996/2003, of 2 December, on the regulation of free legal aid; Royal Decree 1455/2005, of 2 December, on free assistance to victims of gender violence; Royal Decree-Law 3/2013, of 22 February, on fees in the Administration of Justice and free legal aid system; and other regulations on free legal aid at the level of the autonomous communities and collaboration agreements between the Directorate General for Prisons and Bar Associations. In the second track, some of the legal sources mentioned above were examined, but with a special focus on Royal Decree 658/2001, of 22 June, approving the General Statute of the Spanish Legal Profession and the statutes approved by each provincial bar association, as well as the regulations of the Prison Legal Advice and Assistance Services (SOAJP). This last legislative

2 Justiz-ONLINE: www.jva-duesseldorf.nrw.de/infos/index.php (Last date accessed: 2023, November 5).

3 Berliner Justizvollzug: www.berlin.de/justizvollzug/anstalten/jva-tegel/erste-informationen/ (Last date accessed: 2023, November 5).

4 California Department of Corrections and Rehabilitation: www.cdcr.ca.gov/visitors/prepare-to-visit/ (Last date accessed: 2023, November 5).

provision was relevant because the Bar Associations, together with the Prison Legal Advice Services, are key figures in the provision of free legal aid. In turn, as the services are set up and managed by the Bar Associations, it was considered appropriate to locate the latter (a total of 83) in order to find out how they managed free legal aid, and to ascertain whether they had indeed created mechanisms to provide and guarantee such aid regarding prison issues.

For item 64, we used Law 10/2012 on Court Fees, amended by Royal Decree-Law 3/2013, of 22 February; and for item 68 an *ad hoc* methodology was proposed due to the lack of data. This consisted of making random telephone calls to various prisons throughout the country (n=10), with the exception of Catalonia, to contact the treatment deputy directors, as they are familiar with the information regarding the management of visits.

In *Italy*, to resolve items 55 and 62, the research team reviewed the rules on the penitentiary system and the execution of custodial measures and limitations of freedom (*Norme sull'ordinamento penitenziario e sulla esecuzione delle misure privative e limitative della liberta)*, of 26 July 1975, No. 354. For item 64, a consultation was carried out of Presidential Decree No. 115 (*Decreto del Presidente Della Repubblica)*, of 30 May 2002, articles 74 to 141, and the Italian Code of Criminal Procedure (*Codice di procedura penale)*, No. 27, of 24 April 2020, as well as other secondary sources (Arena, 2000; Perego, 2017; European Committee for the Prevention of Torture and Inhuman or Degrading Treatment or Punishment (CPT), 2020). Finally, data regarding practice 68 were extracted from the CPT reports (2017 and 2020) based on visits made to the prisons of Biella, Milano Opera, Saluzzo and Viterbo in 2019, and to those of Ascoli Piceno, Como, Genoa, Marassi, Ivrea, Sassari and Turin in 2016 (CPT, 2017). In total, these 11 prisons accounted for about 10 per cent of the Italian prison population (in 2016 the prisons visited by the CPT had 3,084 inmates, out of a total of 53,495 inmates; and in 2019 these figures were 2,812 and 60,611 respectively). However, conjugal visits were not provided for and did not occur in practice (Talini, 2018, 2020).

With respect to *New York*, item 55 was resolved by consulting the Correction Law from New York State, information from the Vera Institute of Justice and the Rules of the City of New York, the latter being also used to resolve indicator 62. For item 64, the New York Civil Practice Law and Rules 2006 was revised. As to practice 68, it could be determined in Directive DIR 4500 DTD 4/2/2011of the Corrections and Community Supervision Department of NYS, that the Family Reunion Program (FRP) intended to bring the inmate and his or her family together in a private, home-like environment to strengthen family ties. These visits could last from one to three days and include sexual visits. The only information available on the frequency of those visits was contained in Senate Bill S5588, submitted on 8 May 2019 by Senator Velmanette Montgomery, which modified the guidelines given by the FRP.

In *Poland*, the Executive Penal Code (*Ustawa z dnia 6 czerwca 1997 r. Kodeks karny wykonawczy*) and the 2016 report by Daniluk and Mierzwińska-Lorencka were consulted for item 55. While for items 62 and 64, the

Constitution of the Republic of Poland (*Konstytucja Rzeczypospolitej Polskiej*) and the Executive Penal Code were revised, together with reports prepared by Kładoczny and Wolny (2013) and the Helsinki Foundation for Human Rights in 2018, for indicator 62. In the case of item 68, a mixed methodology was proposed, on the basis of personal interviews and FSI reviews. As regards the former, experts in the field were called upon to do so, in particular the professors Krzysztof Krajewski[5] and Kladoczny.[6] With regard to the latter, the search focused on the complaints of institutions, NGOs and inmates. Analyses were carried out of reports on Poland by the Helsinki Foundation for Human Rights (2018), the Prison Insider,[7] the European Prison Observatory,[8] as well as press reports from the CPT (2014, 2018) and others relating to such visits.

To respond to item 55 in *England and Wales* we consulted the Criminal Justice Act 1982 and various reports and official websites (Allen, 2013; McGuire & Arriaza Conde, 2016; Ministry of Justice, 2013; National Offender Management Service, 2015; The Young Offender Institution Rules 2000 No. 3371[9]; Parliament United Kingdom[10]; Ministry of Justice, 2021[11]). For items 62 and 64, we reviewed the Criminal Legal Aid Act 2013 and other guides and documents drafted by official bodies that helped with its interpretation (Ministry of Justice, 2023) and the official website of the government.[12] As regards practice 68, and as in other countries, there was no official data. A research on prison visits in the UK by McCarthy and Adams (2017) stated that: "There is little demographic information on family-inmate status, let alone on the number of visits received over the course of a sentence". It was found that only family visits were legally allowed, the frequency of which was known thanks to the study conducted by Hutton in 2017, after reviewing the existing literature on the subject.

5 Director of the Department of Criminology at the Jagiellonian University since 2006.

6 Expert in criminal law, criminal procedure and Polish penitentiary system. Since 1990 he works at the Criminal Law Institute of the Faculty of Law and Administration at the University of Warsaw. At the Helsinki Foundation for Human Rights, he coordinates the Legal Intervention Programme which deals with the provision of legal advice and assistance to victims of human rights violations in Poland, in particular to those imprisoned. In 2014, he signed the European Prison Observatory's report on prison conditions in Poland.

7 Prison Insider: www.prison-insider.com/files/9614b50a/fp_pologne_en.pdf (Last date accessed: 2023, November 5).

8 European Prison Observatory: www.prisonobservatory.org (Last date accessed: 2023, November 5).

9 The Young Offender Institution Rules 2000 No. 3371: www.legislation.gov.uk/uksi/2000/3371/article/26/made

10 Parliament United Kingdom. Parliamentary Business: www.parliament.uk/business/ (Last date accessed: 2023, November 5).

11 Ministry of Justice 2021: http://data.parliament.uk/WrittenEvidence/CommitteeEvidence.svc/EvidenceDocument/Justice/Young%20adult%20offenders/written/22021.html#_ftn3 (Last date accessed: 2023, November 5).

12 Government of the United Kingdom: www.legislation.gov.uk (Last date accessed: 2023, November 5).

5 Results

Once the methodological procedure established in the protocols was developed, each item was resolved by answering in the affirmative or negative as regards the existence of the rule or practice involved. In addition, the responses were subsequently analysed by international experts, and all of them were accepted. In the pool we are dealing with, rule 55 was only answered with a "yes" in New York; rule 62 in California and New York; and rule 64 in California and New York, as well as in England and Wales. Undoubtedly, the indicator that brought together the largest number of positive responses was item 68, since it occurred in all countries except Spain (see Table 10.3). It should therefore be noted that all the exclusion measured by the first three items of the pool correspond to US states and, to a lesser extent, to England and Wales.

At first glance the country with the highest number of "yeses" is New York and, at the opposite end would be Spain, with the largest number of "noes". However, to accurately place countries on an exclusion continuum, their relative position has been calculated on a scale of 0 to 10 – where 0 means less exclusion and 10 is the highest exclusion level. As shown in Figure 10.1, and from the point of view of this pool, Spain is the least exclusionary country (with a score of 0), followed at an equal distance by Italy, Poland and Germany (2.52 points). These countries are far from reaching a midpoint of exclusion – which would entail 5 points – i.e., the middle of the scale, so their exclusionary level is low. On the other hand, England and Wales (4.97 points), has a medium level of exclusion, and is the third most exclusionary territory. While the states of California (7.48 points) and New York (10 points) are the most exclusionary territories of this pool.

However, to identify trends in the exclusion expressed by each country it is necessary to examine why some items get a larger number of positive responses, or else they do not show a clear exclusion trend, as there is a balance of "yeses" and "noes".

In this regard, rule 55 is not confirmed because in most countries the particular needs of young adults are addressed by adjusting the prison system to their cognitive and evolutionary development. This is not the case in New York where, despite the fact that the New York City Department of

Table 10.3 Results of pool 5, by item and country

	Germany	*California*	*Spain*	*Italy*	*New York*	*Poland*	*England & Wales*
Item 55	No	No	No	No	Yes	No	No
Item 62	No	Yes	No	No	Yes	No	No
Item 64	No	Yes	No	No	Yes	No	Yes
Item 68	Yes	Yes	No	Yes	Yes	Yes	Yes

Source: Own elaboration

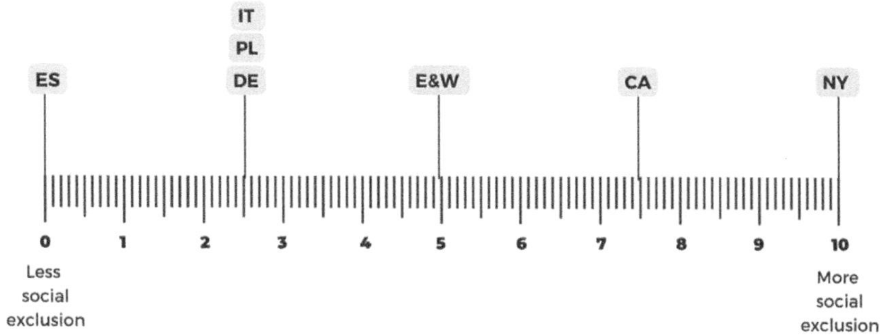

Figure 10.1 Position of the countries within a continuum of social exclusion in terms of prison regime

Corrections applies a specific regime in certain cases,[13] there is no such provision for young people at state level, so that the majority of young inmates are serving sentences under the same conditions as adults.

With regard to item 62, in California the sixth amendment to the United States Constitution establishes the right to counsel in criminal proceedings. The US Supreme Court ruled that people who cannot afford legal fees are entitled to have a public defender free of charge. However, all the above refers to the right to a lawyer before and during the trial, but not after, once the inmate is in prison. According to the official website of the US Congress, the Prison Litigation Reform Act of 1995 requires inmates to pay court filing fees in full, although they can pay in installments if they do not have sufficient resources.

No statutory provisions on legal aid were found in New York. As mentioned in the Jailhouse Lawyer's Handbook (NLG-CCR, 2010, 4), prison matters are considered civil in nature and, for this type of cases – unlike criminal cases – there is no right to a lawyer free of charge. Hence, there is an extensive network of legal aid for inmates regarding penitentiary issues provided by organisations such as Prisoner's Legal Services of New York.[14]

With respect to item 64, California requires appellate fees for the judicial review of federal prison decisions, but not for state prison decisions. The federal law enacted in 1996, called the Prison Litigation Reform Act (PLRA), limits inmates' access to the courts by imposing full and mandatory payment of the fees to challenge any prison situation or decision. However, it provides for the possibility of paying the fee in monthly installments if the prisoner does

13 In 2013, such department approved rules that provided for the application of a specific regime for young adults with sentences of up to one year in local prisons. Such provision is regulated in section 1, chapter 1, title 40, of the Rules of the City of New York.

14 Prisoners' Legal Services of New York: https://plsny.org. (Last date accessed: 2023, November 5).

not have the means to pay in advance. In practice, an initial amount of 20 per cent of the recognised income is required and monthly installments of such percentage until the fee is fully paid.

In New York, if an inmate wishes to contest a decision taken by the prison administration, – such as denial of parole or solitary confinement – he or she may do so through the special procedure of article 78 of the New York Civil Practice Law and Rules (NYCPLR). This article is used to appeal the administrative decision of a local or state agency, deemed illegal, before the New York State Supreme Court. Such appeal must fulfil some requirements, one of which is payment of 190 dollars, unless the inmate claims – via an affidavit – that he or she does not have the resources for it.

In England & Wales inmates must pay some legal costs (if they want a lawyer[15]) and court fees for using their services. The Criminal Legal Aid Act helps inmates to pay such expenses and, as referred to in several sections of article 12,[16] must be interpreted in the terms described in article 15, where legal assistance depends on the economic eligibility of the individual. Inmates must have a low income and very limited savings or other assets in order to obtain legal aid. They must also pay the mentioned fees, the amounts of which have been set in advance[17] (Ministry of Justice, 2021, 4), although they can be exempted from such payments or reimbursed in cases of low income.

Finally, item 68 is the most exclusionary practice in almost all countries. The table below shows whether family or intimate visits take place at intervals of less than one month or, in other words, if the item is not met. As can be seen, in practice all countries comply with this requirement when it comes to family visits, but this is not the case for intimate visits.

In *Germany*, article 24 of the Prisons Act, establishes that: "(1) Inmates shall be allowed to receive visits at regular intervals. Their total duration will be at least one hour per month. Everything else in this regard shall be governed by the institution's regulations". In practice, visitation rules differ according to the location of the prison within Germany, and each correctional facility (*Justizvollzugsanstalt or JVA)* has different regimes, i.e., there are variations among the states (*länder)*. However, this does not happen with intimate visits,

15 However, prisoners may represent themselves at the Parole Board hearing if they do not have a lawyer.

16 (2) The conditions (for obtaining legal aid) are that a person must: (f) require advice and assistance related to the treatment or discipline of such person in a prison, juvenile institution or secure training facility (other than with respect to actual or anticipated proceedings regarding personal injury, death or damage to property); (g) be subject to proceedings before the Parole Board; (h) require advice and assistance related to representation in connection with a mandatory life imprisonment sentence or other probation review; Prescribed conditions.

17 Requirements are, specifically: £154 to apply for leave for judicial review at the beginning of the case; £385 to apply for a refusal of permission to be reconsidered at an oral hearing; and £770 for a full court hearing (i.e., if the court grants leave to the case), although this amount is reduced to £385 if the inmate has already paid £385 to have the leave reconsidered at an oral hearing.

Table 10.4 Results of item 68 by type of prison visit – family or intimate – by country

Countries	*Family visits at < 1-month intervals*	*Intimate visits at < 1-month intervals*	*The item is met*
Germany	Yes	No	Yes
California	Yes	No	Yes
Spain	Yes	Yes	No
Italy	Yes	No	Yes
New York	Yes	No	Yes
Poland	Yes	No	Yes
England & Wales	Yes	No	Yes

Source: Own elaboration

because a clear periodicity is not established and the centres do not always have available rooms. In addition, some JVAs lack sufficient material means (adequate rooms).

In *California*, the visits that the research team defines as "family visits" would be those considered as visits – with and without contact – [and] those visits which we call "intimate" are called "family visits" by them. The California Code of Regulations governs family visits (title 5, section 3170.1), and allows inmates to share space with up to five visitors and have limited physical contact with them (kissing and/or hugging at the beginning and end of the visit, and holding hands during the visit). They take place on visiting days (Saturdays, Sundays and four public holidays during each year), with a maximum of 12 hours a week (title 15, section 3172.2). As for intimate visits (title 15, section 3177), these take place in private facilities (apartments), last 30 to 40 hours approximately and are restricted to immediate family members of the inmate (parents, children, siblings, legal spouses or unmarried partners). They are considered a privilege (title 15, section 3177.b), generally reserved for inmates who work at the facility and have professional training and who, in practice, enjoy them once every three or five months.

In *Italy*, the law establishes different visiting regimes depending on the level of security in which the inmate is classified. If security is average, they can receive up to six one-hour visits per month; if security is high, up to four one-hour visits per month; and if they are inmates under the "special detention regime" (art. 41 bis), i.e., terrorists and people belonging to the mafia, they can only receive one visit per month, without personal contact. The only empirical information on this issue is found in the CPT reports, whose findings confirm that such legal oversight is complied with in practice. However, Italian criminal policy is exclusionary as it does not provide for conjugal visits (Talini, 2018, 2020).

In *New York*, as in California, "family visits" are in practice intimate visits, and they are also called "night" visits. They are enshrined in article 220, chapter IV, of title seven of the Official Compilation of Codes, Rules and

Regulations of the New York State (NYS) and in Directive DIR 4500 DTD. 4/2/2011 of the Corrections and Community Supervision Department of NYS. Although those visits are provided for and take place in a private home-like environment (flats, caravans or modular units), what is exclusionary is that, in order to apply for this programme, inmates must comply with certain requirements related to the time spent in prison and their behavioural record, which in practice means that the decision to grant it takes up to 5 weeks to be communicated.

In *Poland*, according to the law all inmates have the right to family visits and, as in Italy, their periodicity depends on the level of security in which the inmate is classified. If security is high, two one-hour visits per month are established; if it is average, the number of visits rises to three; and in the case of low security, the number of visits is unlimited. According to a report by the Helsinki Foundation for Human Rights, visits take place in large and noisy rooms, shared with many inmates. Besides, there are difficulties to visit a relative (mother, brother, etc.) who is serving a sentence in a different block of the same facility or in a different prison (CPT, 2014, 2018; Prison Insider).[18] There are also long waiting times and queues of visitors outside the establishments due to lack of reservation lists (CPT, 2014, 2018). However, despite the above, there is no evidence to suggest that the frequency established by the law for this type of visits is not being complied with.

With regard to intimate visits, referred to in the Polish Penal Executive Code (article 138.1 to 138.3), an inmate may be compensated with or awarded the right to additional or longer visits, the right to an unsupervised visit and the right to visits in a separate and more private place. As for what we know about these in practice, the European Prison Observatory, in its report on prison conditions in Poland (Kładoczny & Wolny, 2013), expressed concern that not all prisons had facilities for unsupervised visits. That is why the European Prison Observatory mentioned that, in some prisons, inmates could not receive this prize. The situation seems to be improving in recent years due to the implementation of the Prison Service Modernisation Programme for 2017–2020[19] and the declarations of the spokesperson of the Bydgoszcz Prison Service in 2020. According to her, "intimate visits are available 2–3 times a month. However, even the most deserving person cannot receive this award if his loved one is not his wife". Likewise, according to the deputy director of the Włocławek prison in 2009, the average waiting time for intimate visits was about two months.

18 Prison Insider: www.prison-insider.com/fichepays/prisonspologne-2019?s=vue-d-ensemble#vue-d-ensemble (Last date accessed: 2023, November 5).

19 The main objectives of this Modernisation Programme have been: to improve the security of prisons and detention centres, to improve the working conditions of staff, to modernise the treatment system and to modernise the infrastructures. See: Director General of the Polish Prison Service: https://justice-trends.press/the-polish-prison-modernisation-programme-as-a-turning-point/ (Last date accessed: 2023, November 5).

Finally, in ***England and Wales***, according to the Prison Rules 1999 (section 35.2), "A convicted prisoner shall have the right: (. . .) (b) to receive a visit twice in each four-week period, but only once in each period if so decided by the Secretary of State". This is the basic legal requirement, and any additional visits depend on the institution and the incentives and privileges granted to inmates.

Until September 2017, "privileged" visits were regulated by a system of incentives called Incentives and Earned Privilege (IEP), intended for inmates whose behaviour was responsible and participative. In this way, inmates had access to additional visits according to their classification levels, these being: basic level (with less privileges), standard level (for inmates who behave correctly) and improved level (intended for those who for three months show a commitment to their rehabilitation and an abandonment of crime). In relation to this, Hutton (2017) pointed out that, in practice, there were frequency differences among prisons and that almost all inmates received two one-hour visits per month, and this number could increase if they were rewarded for good behaviour.

Conjugal or intimate visits that may have a sexual nature are prohibited for reasons of security and maintenance of prison order. Some courts have supported these grounds by stating that if married inmates are allowed to carry out their married life inside the prison, security and order would be seriously jeopardised. The impossibility of many inmates to have sexual relations with their partners for paternity purposes and the difficulties to access artificial insemination techniques are issues mentioned in some judgments of the European Court, as both practices violate article 8 of the Human Rights Act, regarding the right to family and privacy (see: Grand Chamber Judgment of Dickson v. the United Kingdom 873 4.12.2007).[20]

In short, practice 68 is not fulfilled in most countries because visits – and especially sexual visits – take place at intervals of more than one month, they are configured as a discretionary prize or reward and not as a right, only married inmates or de facto partners have access to intimate visits, and they are prohibited in order to maintain order and security inside prisons.

6 Conclusions

The indicators that make up the fifth pool of the RIMES instrument were considered by international experts as the most valid – as regards suitability and clarity – to measure social exclusion, as they had obtained an Aiken's V coefficient higher than 0.79. In this way, the methodological criteria of completeness and clarity developed by the research team were validated, while

20 European Court of Human Rights. Grand Chamber Judgment of Dickson v. the United Kingdom, 873 4.12.2007. Available in: www.globalhealthrights.org/wp-content/uploads/2018/05/Case-of-Dickson-v-the-United-Kingdom-United-Kingdom-2007.pdf (Last date accessed: 2023, November 5).

others (extension, ease of data access and discrimination capacity) were used to reduce the questionnaire at different stages of the research. Prior to the application of the instrument in different territories, i.e., during the drafting of the descriptions that further operationalised (and clarified) the validated indicators, doubts arose again with relation to the criteria of completeness, extension and discrimination capacity. In item 55 the debate was generated among the teams of Spain, New York, California and Germany around the concept of young adults and the type of penal system (adult or juvenile) that condemned them. However, in item 62 no debates were generated. And in item 64 several issues related to completeness had to be clarified during the pilot application in Spain regarding the costs that were included or not in the fees, the presence of bonuses for people without resources and the territorial diversity. Clearly, item 68 caused the greatest debate among all the teams, probably because it was a practice and because it measured two variables (family visits and intimate visits) that had to occur together in order to confirm the item. In addition, it was necessary to specify and contextualise concepts that were closely related (inmate, visitor, independently, etc.) and establish a minimum percentage for the practice to be fulfilled, as well as other time parameters.

The criterion "ease of data access" was put into practice during the search for information to complete the protocols, which greatly conditioned the methodological design of each item. In this sense, the consultation of secondary sources of information – both legal and of various kinds – was enough to respond to indicators 55, 62 and 64, all of them being accessible on the Internet and allowing *ad hoc* methodological designs to be proposed in the Spanish case. On the contrary, difficulties were found in all countries to collect data regarding practice 68 through FSI, due to the lack of statistics and/or official reports. It was therefore necessary to conduct personal interviews with experts and prison officials in Spain and Poland.

With regard to the results, these were considered valid and reliable by the international experts who carried out the subsequent review of the protocols, which gave greater weight and robustness to the methodological procedure used to achieve them. Once this circumstance was overcome, it was noted that the state of New York was the most exclusionary of the pool, followed by California and, at some distance, England and Wales. Consequently, it can be concluded that there is an exclusionary tendency in criminal policies regarding prison matters in the territories referred to and a less exclusionary one in Germany, Poland and Italy, with Spain being the only country with an exclusion equal to 0. It should be noted that the affirmative answer to item 68 is the one that determines that Germany, Poland and Italy are exclusionary in equal measure, and that such item is configured as the most exclusionary of the entire pool, largely due to the restrictions and prohibitions that are applied to intimate or sexual visits.

Finally, although the items that make up the pool have made it possible to discriminate between European countries and US states, it is worth asking whether the discrimination capacity of those items that receive the largest number of "noes" (item 55) or "yeses" (item 68) is sufficient, and whether incorporating more indicators from the same pool would allow us to identify nuances among the criminal policies of Germany, Poland, Italy and Spain. These are, therefore, very descriptive results that allow us to glimpse a clear exclusionary trend in the criminal policies of the United States, but a deeper and more complex explanation of this reality would be required if it is to become the basis for future hypotheses and research studies.

References

Allen, R. (2013). *Young adults in custody. The way forward.* The Transition to Adulthood Alliance. Available at: https://t2a.org.uk/wp-content/uploads/2016/02/T2A-Young-Adults-in-Custody_V3.pdf (Last date accessed: 2023, November 5).

Arena, D. (2000). Instituciones, modalidades y tendencias del sistema de ejecución penal italiano: Elementos para su comparación con la experiencia penal española. *Revista electrónica de ciencia penal y criminología*, 2.

Auty, K. M. & Liebling, A. (2020). Exploring the Relationship between Prison Social Climate and Reoffending. *Justice Quarterly*, *37*(2), 358–381. https://doi.org/10.1080/07418825.2018.1538421 (Last date accessed: 2023, November 5).

Daniluk, P. & Mierzwińska-Lorencka, J. (2016). Responsibility of a Juvenile for a Prohibited Act under Polish Law. *International and Comparative Law Review*, *16*(2), 99–115. https://doi.org/10.1515/iclr-2016-0017

Díez-Ripollés, J. L. (2011). La dimensión inclusión/exclusión social como guía de la política criminal comparada. *Revista electrónica de ciencia penal y criminología (RECPC)*, *13*(12), 1–36. Available at: http://criminet.ugr.es/recpc/13/recpc13-12.pdf (Last date accessed: 2023, November 5).

Díez-Ripollés, J. L. (2013). Social Inclusion and Comparative Criminal Justice Policy. *Journal of Scandinavian Studies in Criminology and Crime Prevention*, *14*, 62–78.

Díez-Ripollés, J. L. (2017). El abuso del sistema penal. *Revista Electrónica de Ciencia Penal y Criminología*, *19*(1), 1–24. Available at: http://criminet.ugr.es/recpc/19/recpc19-01.pdf (Last date accessed: 2023, November 5).

Díez-Ripollés, J. L. & García-España, E. (2019). RIMES: An Instrument to Compare National Criminal Justice Policies from the Social Exclusion Dimension. *International E-Journal of Criminal Sciences*, *1*(13), 1–27. Available at: www.ehu.eus/ojs/index.php/inecs/article/view/20866 (Last date accessed: 2023, November 5).

Drake, D. (2011). The 'Dangerous Other' in Maximum-Security Prisons. *Criminology & Criminal Justice*, *11*(4), 367–382. https://doi.org/10.1177/1748895811408836

European Committee for the Prevention of Torture and Inhuman or Degrading Treatment or Punishment (CPT) (2014). Report to the Polish Government on the Visit to Poland in 2013. Available at: https://rm.coe.int/1680697928 (Last date accessed: 2023, November 5).

European Committee for the Prevention of Torture and Inhuman or Degrading Treatment or Punishment (CPT) (2017). 23. Report to the Italian Government on the Visit to Italy Carried Out by the European Committee for the Prevention of Torture and Inhuman or Degrading Treatment or Punishment (CPT) from 8 to 21 April 2016. Available at: https://rm.coe.int/16809986b4 (Last date accessed: 2023, November 5).

European Committee for the Prevention of Torture and Inhuman or Degrading Treatment or Punishment (CPT) (2018). Report to the Polish Government on the Visit to Poland in 2017. Available at: https://rm.coe.int/16808c7a91 (Last date accessed: 2023, November 5).

European Committee for the Prevention of Torture and Inhuman or Degrading Treatment or Punishment (CPT) (2020). 2. Report to the Italian Government on the visit to Italy carried out by the European Committee for the Prevention of Torture and Inhuman or Degrading Treatment or Punishment (CPT) from 12 to 22 March 2019. Available at: https://rm.coe.int/16809986b4 (Last date accessed: 2023, November 5).

Jewkes, Y., Crewe, B. & Bennett, J. (2016). *Handbook on prisons.* Routledge. https://doi.org/10.4324/9781315797779

Helsinki Foundation for Human Rights Report (2018). Criminal Detention in the EU – Conditions and Monitoring. Country Report Poland. Available at: https://fra.europa.eu/sites/default/files/fra_uploads/poland-criminal-detention-country-study_en.pdf (Last date accessed: 2023, November 5).

Hutton, M. A. (2017). Prison Visits and Desistance: A Human Rights Perspective. In Hart, E. L. & Van Ginneken, E. F. J. C. (eds.) *New perspectives on desistance. Theoretical and empirical developments* (pp. 187–209). Springer.

Kładoczny, P. & Wolny, M. (2013). Prison Conditions in Poland. *European Prison Observatory.* Available at: www.prisonobservatory.org/index.php?option=com_content&view=article&id=13:prison-conditions-in-poland&catid=13&Itemid=116#CONTACTS

Liebling, A., Durie, L., Stiles, A. & Tait, S. (2011). Revisiting Prison Suicide: The Role of Fairness and Distress. In Liebling, A. & Maruna, S. (eds.) *The effects of imprisonment.* Routledge, Taylor & Francis Group.

MacDonald, M. (2018). Overcrowding and Its Impact on Prison Conditions and Health. *International Journal of Prisoner Health, 14*(2), 65–68. https://doi.org/10.1108/IJPH-04-2018-0014

Matthews, S., Schiraldi, V. & Chester, L. (2018). Youth Justice in Europe: Experience of Germany, the Netherlands, and Croatia in Providing Developmentally Appropriate Responses to Emerging Adults in the Criminal Justice System. *Justice Evaluation Journal 1*(1), 1–23. https://doi.org/10.1 080/24751979.2018.1478443

McCarthy, D. & Adams, M. (2017). Prison Visitation as Human 'Right' or Earned 'Privilege'? The Differing Tales of England/Wales, and Scotland. *Journal of Social Welfare and Family Law, 39*(4), 403–416. https://doi.org/10.1080/09649069.2017.1390292

McGuire, J. & Arriaza Conde, A. M. (2016). Intervención con menores en conflicto con la ley. Reino Unido. In Nieto Morales, C. (ed.). *La intervención comparada con menores en desprotección y en conflicto con la ley en diferentes países.* Dykinson.

Ministry of Justice (2013). Transforming Management of Young Adults in Custody. Available at: https://consult.justice.gov.uk/digital-communications/young-adults/user_uploads/transforming-management-of-young-adults-in-custody.pdf (Last date accessed: 2023, November 5).

Ministry of Justice (2021). EX50A: May 2021. Available at: www.gov.uk/government/publications/fees-in-the-civil-and-family-courts-full-list-ex50a

Ministry of Justice (2023). Administrative Court Judicial Review Guide 2023. Available at: https://www.judiciary.uk/courts-and-tribunals/high-court/administrative-court/administrative-court-judicial-review-guide-2022/

National Lawyers Guild (NLG) and the Center for Constitutional Rights (CCR) (2010). The Jailhouse Lawyers Handbook. Available at: http://jailhouselaw.org/ (Last date accessed: 2023, November 5).

National Offender Management Service (2015). Better Outcomes for Young Adult Men. Evidence Based Commissioning Principles. National Offender Management Service. Available at: https://assets.publishing.service.gov.uk/government/uploads/system/uploads/attachment_data/file/462169/Better_Outcomes_for_Young_Adult_Men__P1_1_.pdf (Last date accessed: 2023, November 5).

Nilsson, A. (2003). Living Conditions, Social Exclusion and Recidivism Among Prison Inmates. *Journal of Scandinavian Studies in Criminology and Crime Prevention*, *4*(1), 57–83. https://doi.org/10.1080/14043850310005321

Perego, B. (2017). "Magistratura di sorveglianza, questa sconosciuta". Torna il carcere: XIII Rapporto sulle condizioni di detenzione. Available at: www.antigone.it/tredicesimo-rapporto-sulle-condizioni-di-detenzione/04-magistrati-di-sorveglianza/ (Last date accessed: 2023, November 5).

Talini, S. (2018). *La privazione della libertà personale. Metamorfosi normative, apporti giurisprudenziali, applicazioni amministrative*. Editoriale Scientifica.

Talini, S. (2020). Prison Leave in Italy: Legislation and Practical Application Is the Italian Regulation on Prison Leave Ensuring the Constitutional Purpose of Punishment? *European Journal on Criminal Policy and Research*, *26*(2), 159–176. https://doi.org/10.1007/s10610-019-09432-4

Van Ginneken, E. F., Sutherland, A. & Molleman, T. (2016). An Ecological Analysis of Prison Overcrowding and Suicide Rates in England and Wales, 2000–2014. *International Journal of Law Psychiatry*, *50*, 76–82.

11 Pool 6

Preventive intervention

Elena Casado-Patricio and Cristina Güerri

1 Introduction

Preventive intervention consists of the preemptive detention of individuals based on notions of dangerousness. Such detentions can take place either before the trial ("pre-trial detention") or after the sentence has been served ("preventive detention"). Both types of preventive intervention have experienced significant abuse in a number of countries over the last few years (Díez-Ripollés, 2019).

On the one hand, pre-trial detention is a common resource in many countries, where it can be used for extended periods of time. Detention of suspects should be used exceptionally and be directed towards ensuring their prosecution, as a widespread and insufficiently justified use of this measure can have a negative impact on the confidence and perceived legitimacy of the criminal justice system.

On the other hand, the preventive detention of ex-convicts who are still considered dangerous after the completion of their sentences is undergoing a period of relegitimisation, as can be seen in the fact that many countries have established new grounds of dangerousness and are allowing indefinite post-conviction detention. Such post-sentence internment entails recognising the failure of the prison system to rehabilitate and leads to the temporary or permanent social exclusion of ex-convicts.

Although these forms of preventive intervention can be considered a sign of the expansion of preventive justice (Zedner and Ashworth, 2019), it is also relevant to consider the social exclusion effects they have on the individuals to whom they are applied (Díez-Ripollés, 2019). Thus, pre-trial detention represents the interruption of an individual's life (personal, labour, etc.) when we do not yet know whether or not this person will be convicted; and preventive detention extends – sometimes indefinitely – the situation of social exclusion generated by the custodial sentence.

Therefore, in the RIMES instrument we shall focus on the two expressions of preventive intervention mentioned above: pre-trial detention of those suspected of committing criminal offences and preventive detention of ex-convicts who are still considered dangerous after serving their sentence, which are the two indicators included in pool 6.

DOI: 10.4324/9781032661766-14

Specifically, the indicator on pre-trial detention takes into account the extent to which these detentions before the trial are used (item 82) and what is the legal limit imposed by judicial systems on their length (item 79); and the indicator on preventive detention analyses whether, according to the legal regulations of the country under study, it can be for indefinite periods or has limits (item 74) and what is, in practice, the average term of this type of confinement (item 81).

In this way, pool 6 on preventive intervention studies the exclusionary effects of the penal system on two of the four groups analysed in the RIMES project (Díez-Ripollés, 2011): defendants to whom pre-trial detention is applied and ex-convicts who are kept locked up by the imposition of an internment after their sentence has been completed.

2 The pool building process

This section refers to the process of building pool 6, on preventive intervention, since the beginning of creating the instrument until its implementation in different countries. In other words, we shall review the different phases which this pool went through until being finally made up of the current four items.

As seen in the appropriate chapter, in a first phase a number of rules and practices were selected in order to design a research tool with capacity to measure the social exclusion generated by the Spanish penal control system. Specifically, in this first phase there were successive meetings to establish a list of rules and practices, and at the beginning pool 6 included 27 items. Subsequently, this list was screened in successive rounds until the pool was composed of 4 items in the final instrument.

The first screening to reduce the number of rules and practices was based on the criteria of completeness (importance of the data), extension (that the aspect is not too specific within the pool) and ease of access (that the data is relatively easy to obtain). In the first round of this screening, pool 6 was made up of 27 items which were assessed from 0 to 4 by the judges, according to the three mentioned criteria.

Then a second round was carried out to reduce the number of items, using the same three criteria. In both rounds, those items whose total scores were less than 4, when adding up the scores obtained for the three criteria, were discarded. Thus, the pool now consisted of 12 rules and 11 practices. In other words, the pool was reduced by 4 items in these two rounds. Specifically, two items were discarded that referred to the imposition of pre-trial detention in cases that raised social alarm, another about deaths during post-sentence internment and a final one about the impossibility of offering specific treatment in post-sentence detention. These items were removed because they did not meet the criteria of completeness, extension and ease of access. That is, because data related to them were not considered to be easy to obtain, they were too specific within the pool and not relevant for measuring exclusion.

In a second screening, the criteria of discrimination capacity (which allows to differentiate among the countries to which, according to the project, the study is targeted) and clarity (ease of understanding of the item) were added to the previous criteria. In this case, each item was also assessed in the same manner (from 0 to 4). At the time of reducing the number of items after this screening, the team decided to remove from the pools all items that had scored 0 or 1 for completeness and discrimination capacity. With this screening, the number of items in pool 6 was not reduced.

However, it was necessary to keep reducing the number of items. The team decided to conduct a new analysis of each pool in order to draw up a list of issues in each dimension and to check whether there were topics that could be excluded. In short, the aim was to carry out a monographic review of its scope. For this purpose, a scheme was used which showed in detail everything that each rule should contain, in order to have it as a reference when individualising and discarding issues within each pool. It was decided: 1) to leave only those items that scored 3 or 4 (the maximum scores); 2) to remove, after reviewing them previously, those items with 0 or 1 for exhaustiveness; 3) to remove, after reviewing them previously, those items with 0 or 1 for discrimination capacity; and 4) to study those items that were not in the former scenarios.

At this stage, the rules and practices that were not validated in relation to preventive intervention addressed aspects such as, among others, the lack of legal criteria to impose preventive detention, that it could have a term equal to the penalty prescribed for the offence of which he or she is charged, or that foreigners or persons belonging to minorities were more represented among remand detainees than nationals. In the case of items about post-sentence detention, the team decided to exclude some that referred to the legal provision of post-conviction imprisonment on grounds of dangerousness or for first-time offenders, another that prescribed the mandatory imposition of this measure for certain offences, or the item referred to serving the sentence in a regular correctional facility. After this analysis by criteria and issues, pool 6 was made up of 12 items (6 rules and 6 practices).

The next step taken was to draft a questionnaire with the total of items in all the pools so that the judges could assess each rule and each practice, in a Likert scale going from 1 (little weight or relevance to measure exclusion) to 7 (a lot of weight or relevance to measure exclusion). The result of this process to identify the most characteristic items of each pool by the research team was then submitted to validation by international experts. 91.60 per cent of the items in pool 6 were validated, this being the pool with the highest percentage of validation.

The only items that were not validated by experts were two practices (P) and two rules (R):

- P: Over 5 per cent of individuals sentenced to imprisonment additionally serve preventive detention.
- P: Pre-trial detention is as long as the sentence term imposed by the court or longer in at least 5 per cent of cases.

- R: Preventive detention is legally established for offences other than violent crimes.
- R: Individual dangerousness of preventive detainees is reviewed every two years or more.

After the final validation by international experts was carried out, it still had a number of items that hindered the dissemination and administration of the instrument. Specifically, after this phase pool 6 included eight items. Therefore, the research team selected a lower number of items than the validated total in order to obtain a more manageable instrument, following the previously explained criteria. After this process, the final version of pool 6 was made up of four items: two rules (74 and 79) and two practices (81 and 82).[1]

3 Description of the pool's items

The AP-RIMES project began in 2019. The research team was divided into sub-teams to apply the instrument to the seven selected countries or territories. First, the items of each pool were defined and drafted in English, and in the case of pool 6, they were as shown in Table 11.1:

Table 11.1 Definition of the items in pool 6.

Items	*Definition*
Rule 74	Preventive detention may last for an unlimited period of time.
Rule 79	The maximum statutory term for pre-trial detention exceeds 3 years.
Practice 81	The average length of preventive detention exceeds 5 years.
Practice 82	Over 30% of the prison population is in pre-trial detention.

Source: Own elaboration

Next, we proceeded to clarify how each definition would be interpreted in order to check whether or not the items were fulfilled.

Two doubts were raised in those indicators concerning pre-trial detention. Rule 79 raised the question of whether the maximum legal term for pre-trial detention referred to the ordinary limit or included the exceptions permitted by law. In this case, the research team agreed that the item is also fulfilled when pre-trial detention does not exceed three years as a general rule, but there are regulations which, in specific cases, allow this period to be exceeded.

Originally the description of practice 82 included a second paragraph, so the item was worded as follows: "The item is only met when over 30% of inmates in pre-trial detention are subject to this measure for more than 5 years on average". This proposal generated debate around the word 'average' because

1 Minutes No. 55 of the RIMES project meetings, 9 February 2017.

it was seen as introducing an additional parameter (the average length) that was not included in the definition of the item that had been validated by experts. For that reason, the team decided to delete the second paragraph of the description.

With regard to the indicators on indefinite post-conviction detention, some doubts arose as to which places and forms of detention should be taken into account; an issue that affected both Rule 74 and Practice 81.

Thus, it was discussed whether indefinite home confinement should be taken into consideration when resolving the items. To this end, it was concluded that the item only refers to those who are part of the prison population, leaving house arrests out of it.

It was also discussed what would happen if, while initially a post-conviction detention was imposed, this was later relaxed towards supervision where the individual was proving that he or she could live in society. After considering this issue, the research team decided to differentiate between "preventive supervision" and "preventive detention", and it became clear that the item referred to the latter case, given that keeping a person under home supervision is a relaxation of the institution and would be less exclusionary than what is described in the item.

4 Methodology used to implement the items

This section will focus on the methodology used to solve each item of pool 6 in the seven countries or territories where the instrument has been tested: California, England and Wales, Germany, Italy, New York and Poland, including also Spain.

With respect to item 74 on post-conviction detention, as it is a rule, the most commonly used methodology to resolve it in each country was legislative revision and, in some cases, secondary sources were also used.

Specifically, as regards Spain, New York, California and Germany, their respective penal codes were consulted, as well as the specialised regulation on this matter in each country, and the rulings of the European Court of Human Rights and the Constitutional Courts.

In Poland, for its part, a review of the specific regulations was also carried out and, in addition, two reports were used: the Report of the Polish Government on the visit to Poland conducted by the European Committee for the Prevention of Torture and Inhuman or Degrading Treatment or Punishment and the 2016 Report on Human Rights in Poland. An expert from the University of Krakow was also contacted in this country.

Finally, in England and Wales and Italy, in addition to regulations, scientific research was used as a methodological novelty to resolve this item (see, for example, Lévai, 2013; Ogg, 2015; Pighi, 2008; Slobogin, 2012).

As in the previous item, the methodology used for rule 79 on pre-trial detention in the seven countries was the analysis of legislation, usually the

Code of Criminal Procedure, complemented in some of them by consulting secondary sources or experts for a better interpretation of the regulations.

Specifically, in Spain and Italy consultation of their respective Criminal Procedure Codes was enough to resolve the item, while in Germany the doctrine was revised (Putzke, n.d.), and in Poland experts were contacted from the Jagiellonian University (Magdalena Grzyb and Krzysztof Krajewski) to confirm whether or not the criminal procedure code allowed to extend pre-trial detention beyond three years.

In New York, the Criminal Procedure Law was also consulted, although it only determines the cases in which "commission to the custody of the Sheriff" (equivalent to pre-trial detention) can be applied, but not its maximum limits. For this reason, regulations on the preventive prison reform (2019 Bail Reform) and secondary sources (Center for Court Innovation, 2019) were also consulted to verify that there were no additional rules to the Criminal Procedure Code that would limit pre-trial detention.

In England and Wales the rules consulted were the Prosecution of Offences Act 1985 and the Custody Time Limits Regulations 1987.

Finally, the case of California required the consultation of Senate Bill No. 10 of 2018 (which determines in which cases pre-trial detention can be applied), and of the rules that cover and govern the right to a speedy trial (Constitution of the United States, Constitution of California and Penal Code of California), since this right could entail a limit to the length of pre-trial detention.

The resolution of practice 81 required reviewing the official statistics of the countries under study. This was the case with New York and England and Wales. In those countries where statistics did not exist, or were not comprehensive enough to answer the item, secondary sources were used to resolve it.

For example, previous investigations were used in Germany (e.g., Dessecker, 2013; Dessecker and Leuschner, 2019) as official statistics did not provide information on the average length of pre-trial detention. In the case of California, in addition to official statistics, experts on this issue were contacted from California National University and the Office of Data Management to confirm the interpretation of such data. In Poland the item was resolved by contacting the Prison Service and an expert on the subject from the University of Krakow.

Finally, the cases of Spain and Italy differ from the other countries. In the Spanish case, it was not necessary to seek information on this item as when resolving rule 74 it had been noted that this practice could not be met because it has no place in the Spanish legal system. In the case of Italy, the item could not be resolved because the Italian prison administration did not have the required statistical information.

Finally, with regard to practice 82, it has been possible to resolve it in all countries by consulting statistics, although in the two US states these data have been extracted from reports by non-governmental organisations rather than from official statistics.

In the cases of Germany, Italy and Poland, information from the SPACE I annual reports 2014 to 2019 of the Council of Europe's crime statistics portal has been used.[2] In these reports pre-trial detainees are defined as persons suspected of having committed a criminal offence who are detained by court order without having been convicted, in line with Recommendation Rec(2006)13 of the Committee of Ministers of the Council of Europe.

In Spain, the statistics from the General Secretariat of Penitentiary Institutions for the years 2012 to 2018 were used. To calculate the percentages, the number of pre-trial detainees (excluding convicts to which remand custody would apply)[3] has been taken into account in comparison with the total prison population.

For England and Wales, statistics have been used from Her Majesty Prison Service (HMPS) of the Ministry of Justice, which manages custodial sentences in this territory, for the years 2015 to 2019. For HMPS, the category of detainees on remand includes both prisoners who have not yet gone to trial ("untried") and those who have been convicted but do not have a final sentence yet ("convicted unsentenced"). To resolve this item, only the category of "untried detainees" has been used.

Finally, in order to know the number of pre-trial detainees with regard to the total incarcerated population in the states of California and New York, it has been necessary to obtain information from both jails (where remand prisoners and those sentenced to short sentences are held) and prisons (where those convicted to long periods of custody sentences are held).[4]

With regard to California, jail data used are from the Board of State and Community Corrections and prison data are from The Sentencing Project, and refer to the 2015–2019 period. As to New York, the same period has been studied and information on jails comes from the Vera Institute of Justice, while information on prisons also comes from The Sentencing Project.

5 Results of the items in each country

The results of pool 6 after implementing the RIMES instrument in each country and the review of all the protocols by experts[5] are shown in Table 11.2 below.

2 No report was published for 2017.

3 It was decided not to include convicts with another criminal case pending trial, as the reason for their imprisonment was that they were already convicted and not that they should now be placed in pre-trial detention, so they are outside the scope of analysis of this item. Minutes No. 73 of the RIMES project meetings, 22 June 2018.

4 Minutes No. 37 of AP-RIMES project meetings, 30 April 2021.

5 In pool 6, most of the items remained unchanged after the experts' review. The only item that modified its answer after verification was rule 74 in Italy. In this case, the expert pointed to a ruling of the Italian Constitutional Court that helped to interpret the legislation, in such a way that the response to the item changed from affirmative to negative. In the remainder of the items and countries the response did not change after the review by experts, but these revisions

Table 11.2 Results of pool 6, by item and country

	Germany	*California*	*Spain*	*Italy*	*New York*	*Poland*	*England & Wales*
Item 74	Yes	Yes	No	No	Yes	Yes	No
Item 79	Yes	Yes	Yes	Yes	Yes	Yes	Yes
Item 81	Yes	Yes	No	-	No	Yes	Yes
Item 82	No	No	No	No	No	No	No

Source: Own elaboration

Below we elaborate on the response offered for each item in each country.

In relation to rule 74, the results showed that the item was fulfilled in four countries: California, New York, Germany and Poland. And the item was answered in the negative in Spain, Italy and England and Wales.

With respect to the countries where the item was met, in California, according to the Prison and Parole Law Handbook and the laws for mentally disturbed offenders and sexually violent predators, there are two types of civil commitments in a psychiatric hospital after the end of a prison sentence. Each confinement has its own eligibility and release criteria. On the one hand, commitment for mentally disturbed offenders was created with the intention of providing a mechanism for holding and treating prisoners with serious mental illness who are considered dangerous. In the first instance, this commitment lasts for one year, but can be renewed as many times as necessary, upon proposal from the district attorney, and can be for an indefinite period.

The other type of civil commitment in California is provided for violent sexual predators in Department of State Hospitals (DSH). Two requirements are needed for this: that the person has committed a sexually violent offence and that he or she has a current mental disorder that makes it likely that he or she will participate in sexually violent criminal acts in the future. This confinement will last until said person can successfully prove to a court or jury that his or her hospitalisation is not necessary to protect public safety. In other words, such commitment can also last a lifetime and, therefore, the research team concluded that in California item 74 is fulfilled.

In New York, the Sex Offender Management and Treatment Act was passed in 2007, creating a process to handle certain sex offenders under the civil jurisdiction. For the convict to be placed in a secure treatment centre it is necessary to follow the procedure specified in section 10 of the Mental Hygiene Law. Specifically, section 10.10 provides that each year the "respondent" (i.e., the confined person) has the opportunity to obtain an application for discharge and release. Therefore, as we can see, there is no time limit, nor a maximum term for such civil commitment, so the response to this item is New York is in the affirmative.

did allow to complete the justifications for the responses given, such as item 74 in England and Wales, item 81 in Germany, or item 82 in Poland.

In the German case there is a preventive internment after the conviction – which can be applied cumulatively on the prison sentence – whose duration is not established by law and must be resolved by the court at the sentence or after it, which may vary according to the cases and circumstances. However, while it is true that until 2002 this confinement after the sentence could not last more than ten years, as of that year the limit is removed and an indeterminate period is established when the court considers that there is a risk of committing other offences. This lack of limits generated controversy with the European Court of Human Rights and the Federal Constitutional Court. For this reason, the German Parliament passed a law on the federal implementation of post-conviction confinement, with guidelines that came into force in June 2013. But these reforms did not change the possibility of such internment being for an indeterminate period.

Finally, in Poland post-conviction internment can be prescribed on the basis of the Law on Procedure against Persons with Mental Disorders Posing a Danger to the Life, Health or Sexual Freedom of Other Persons which the Polish Parliament adopted in November 2013. According to this law, persons who meet all the following conditions may be placed in a closed establishment for an unlimited time: a) serve a prison sentence in a "therapeutic unit"; b) have a mental disorder (i.e., learning disability, personality disorder or "sexual preference disorders", especially paedophilia); c) the disorder is of such type or intensity that repetition of a prohibited violent act is at least very likely; and d) the punishment for such an offense would be at least 10 years in prison. These individuals may be subjected to "preventive supervision" (in the outside community) or placed at the National Centre for the Prevention of Antisocial Behaviour. Confinement is carried out by court decision at the request of a prison director along with the opinion of a psychiatrist and a psychologist, as well as information on the results of therapy and resocialisation. Therefore, rule 74 is also fulfilled in Poland.

However, this rule is not met in three other countries. Thus, in Spain the item is not met as there are no post-sentence measures of internment, nor civil confinements based on the commission of a criminal offence. The Penal Code provides for security measures after serving the sentence, but in no case is there any provision for internment.

In Italy, on the other hand, the Penal Code establishes a minimum limit for post-conviction preventive detention, but there is no maximum limit. For its part, article 1.1.c of Decree Law No. 52, of 31 March 2014, specifies that "security measures, including placement in residences for compliance purposes, may not last longer than the time prescribed for the custodial sentence for the offence committed". The Italian Constitutional Court (judgment No. 83/2017) noted that the upper limit established by art. 1 is applicable to all detention security measures. Therefore, in Italy the item is not met since there is no indeterminate post-conviction confinement.

Finally, in England and Wales, imprisonment for public protection was a form of indeterminate punishment introduced by article 225 of the Criminal

Justice Act in 2003 (with effect from 2005) by Labour Home Secretary David Blunkett. This prison sentence for public protection was abolished by the coalition government on 3 December 2012, describing the system as "non-defendable". However, the change was not made retrospectively. In conclusion, although from 2005 to 2012 unlimited imprisonment for criminal dangerousness was legally available and there are people serving this penalty, the item is not met in England & Wales because it is now abolished.

As shown in Table 11.2, rule 79 is fulfilled in all cases. This is because, despite the fact that in many cases there are limits of less than three years for pre-trial detention (for example, Germany or Spain), there are always exceptions allowing this period to be exceeded. Besides, in the two US states there are no time limits in the legislation regarding pre-trial detention, the duration of which is at the discretion of the judge.

In Germany, the Code of Criminal Procedure provides for the possibility of pre-trial detention (sections112 and 112.a), the maximum duration of which will generally be six months or one year depending on the case (sections 121 and 121.a). However, it is possible to extend the period of pre-trial detention beyond these limits, without the law specifying any additional maximum. The doctrine stipulates that a maximum limit of 2/3 of the sentence that could be imposed on the accused is usually applied (Putzke, n.d.).

In California, there is a system of pre-trial detention for suspected criminals that relies on judicial discretion and risk assessment tools. However, the rule governing the possibility of imposing pre-trial detention (Senate Bill No. 10, of 2018) does not set any limit on its duration. The right to a speedy trial has been considered to be a limit for pre-trial detention, as the Californian Penal Code imposes a maximum of 60 days to hold trial after arrest (section 1382 PC). However, the same rule allows the court to extend the detention period if there are "good reasons" to justify it, but does not specify any maximum limit for this extension.

In Spain, the Constitution states that the law must establish a maximum duration for pre-trial detention (art. 17.4) and this aspect is developed by the Criminal Procedure Law. Article 504 specifically stipulates that pre-trial detention may not exceed a period of two years, but exceptionally the judge or court may agree to an extension of up to two additional years in certain scenarios, which would imply a period of four years in pre-trial detention.

In Italy, the maximum length of pre-trial detention depends on the sentences that can be imposed for the offence for which the detainee has been charged. In this sense, the maximum limit prescribed by the Code of Criminal Procedure is six years for offences for which permanent imprisonment may be imposed (art. 303.4).

In New York, the Criminal Procedure Law provides for three procedures to ensure the defendant's appearance at the trial, one of which is "commission to the custody of the Sheriff" (section 510.10), which is equivalent to pre-trial detention. However, this rule only specifies the cases to which this type of detention can be applied (section 510.30), without setting limits on its duration. Since the other sources consulted (see section 3.2) do not stipulate a maximum period for pre-trial detention either and its duration depends on judicial discretion, this item is considered to be fulfilled.

In Poland, the Code of Criminal Procedure sets a limit of two years to the duration of pre-trial detention (art. 263.3), although additional – and unlimited – extensions are allowed at the discretion of the judge (art. 263.4). The experts consulted (see section 3.2) state that pre-trial detention of up to 6 years has occurred when applying this regulation, although nowadays this is rarely the case, after several convictions of the Polish government by the European Court of Human Rights.

In England and Wales, the Prosecution of Offences (Custody Time Limits) Regulations 1987 stipulate different periods for pre-trial detention depending on the type of offence charged and the stage of the criminal proceedings (section 4), with a maximum permitted of 182 days. However, the Prosecution of Offences Act 1985 allows the court to extend the period of pre-trial detention and stipulates no limit to this extension (section 22), so the time spent in pre-trial detention can exceed three years.

Practice 81, on post-conviction confinement, occurs in most countries, namely Germany, England and Wales, Poland and California. However, this item is not met in New York and Spain. On the other hand, in Italy the item could not be resolved because there are no statistics about it and the experts consulted by the team explained that there are no records on this issue.

Germany is among the countries where the item is fulfilled. The first study found regarding this country (Dessecker, 2013) shows that almost half of the inmates (46 per cent) spent less than 5 years serving a post-sentence detention, and another 20 per cent of inmates spent from 5 to 10 years. As the author affirms, the average duration of post-conviction internment in 2011 was more than 5 years and 4 months. In 2014, people serving a post-conviction detention had already served an average of 3.5 years. However, in that year those who had been released had spent an average of 14 years and 4 months of post-conviction internment. In 2015, those who at the time were confined after the sentence had been in detention for almost 4 years, and those who had already been released had been confined for an average of 10.5 years (Dessecker and Leuschner, 2019).

In England and Wales – as already seen in item 74 – imprisonment for public protection as a form of preventive detention was abolished in 2012, but the change was not made retrospective. The report "Prison Sentences for Public Protection" of 2019, states that 64 per cent of inmates for public protection remain detained indefinitely five years after the expiry date of their sentence. Therefore, we must conclude that in England and Wales this item is also fulfilled because post-conviction confinements exceed five years.

In Poland for its part, the National Mechanism for the Prevention of Torture (hereinafter, NPM) conducted a visit in February 2019 to the National Center for the Prevention of Antisocial Behaviour (hereinafter, NCPAB). In its report, the NCPAB described that "since the beginning of the facility's existence, only one patient left the centre". In a similar vein, the expert who was consulted – a criminologist and expert in penitentiary law from the University of Krakow – informed in a personal communication that since 2014, when the first man was interned in the NCPAB, she had no knowledge of anyone being released. Despite the contradiction between the NPM (only one person released) and the expert (no one released), both sources agree on the idea that release of persons confined in the NCPAB is not a common practice since the beginning of its activity.

In California, the 2019 Annual Report of the California Sex Offender Management Board examined the implementation of the sexually violent predator act. According to the report, detainees are interned at Coalinga State Hospital for an average of six years, and one in four current detainees have been confined there for more than ten years.

However, in New York, according to data presented by the New York Office of Mental Health (2017), the average duration of stay in treatment facilities was 38.4 months (3.2 years). In the latest available report, referred to 2018, the average stay in safe treatment facilities was 46.2 months (3.9 years).

Finally, in Spain the legislator has not used custodial sentences of an indefinite nature to be imposed after completion of the prison sentence to those accountable or partially accountable. Freedom under surveillance has only been provided for to deal with the possible dangerousness of those who have already served their prison sentence. Hence, since there is no rule for this, it cannot occur in practice and therefore, item 81 is not fulfilled in Spain.

As can be seen in Table 11.2 regarding rule 82 on pre-trial detention, none of the countries reach 30% of the prison population in pre-trial detention, although we can see differences among the seven countries analysed. In two of these countries the proportion of persons in pre-trial detention was less than 10 per cent: Poland (7.9 per cent on average, between 2014 and 2019) and England & Wales (with percentages ranging between 7 and 9 per cent for the years 2015 to 2019).

In Spain, the percentage of people in pre-trial detention ranges between 13 and 16 per cent for the years 2012 to 2018. California is also in this range, as its pre-trial detainees for the period from 2015 to 2019 represent, on average, 12.85 per cent of the total prison population in the state.

In the case of Italy, the average number of pre-trial prisoners compared to the total prison population was 17.02 per cent for the years 2014 to 2019, while in Germany, the average is 19.16 per cent of pre-trial prisoners for the period 2013–2019.

Finally, the state of New York is the only case under study that exceeds 20 per cent of the prison population in pre-trial detention. This percentage is exceeded in all the years analysed (2015–2019), with the average for this period being 21.99 per cent.

If we take the results of pool 6 jointly for each country and weight them using the scores obtained after the experts' review, we can place them in a "continuum" from lowest to highest social exclusion, as shown in the following image:

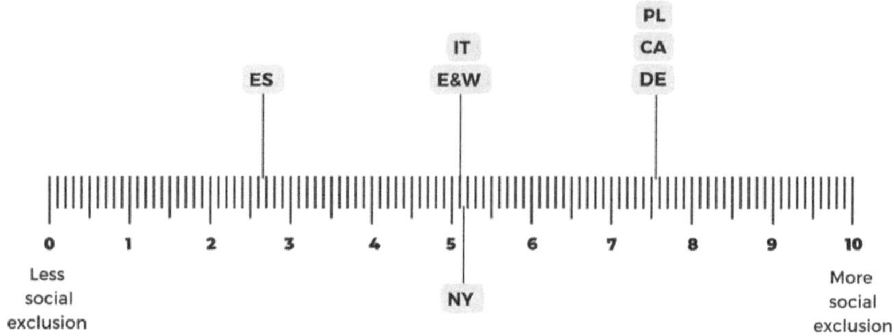

Figure 11.1 Position of the countries within the continuum of social exclusion in terms of preventive intervention

In view of the results, we can conclude that Spain is the country that generates the least social exclusion through preventive intervention. In an intermediate position we find Italy,[6] England and Wales and New York, while Germany, California and Poland are at the opposite end of the continuum, with the highest social exclusion.

6 Conclusions

In this chapter we have analysed pre-trial detention and internment after completion of the sentence as indicators of an exclusionary criminal policy in the area of preventive or security intervention.

With regard to confinement after the conviction, analysis of the regulations (item 74) and their practical application (item 81) shows significant differences among countries.

In the first place, we find the most exclusionary countries: Germany, California and Poland, where the legislation allows for an indefinite confinement after the sentence has been completed and, in addition, practice shows us that, when this measure is applied, inmates spend on average more than five years serving it. Secondly, New York also has a socially exclusionary rule that allows for indefinite internment after completing the sentence, but in practice security internments do not exceed five years on average.

On the other hand, since 2012 England and Wales do not allow for indefinite detention after completion of the sentence. However, despite such abolishment, this provision was not made retrospective and in practice people interned before that date are serving a post-conviction detention of more than five years on average. In other words, England and Wales do not generate social exclusion with current regulations on indefinite confinement after

6 We place Italy at an intermediate point due to the impossibility of resolving item 81. If item 81 were not fulfilled in Italy, this country would be at the head of the least exclusionary countries, along with Spain.

conviction, but in practice it continues to generate exclusion due to the non-retrospective nature of its rule.

In Italy, on the other hand, indefinite post-conviction detention is not allowed by law. However, it has not been possible to verify whether in practice exclusion is not generated either, exceeding five years of post-sentence confinement. Finally, Spain differs from the other countries under study because it does not allow for post-conviction internment.

With regard to the clarity of this indicator, we must say that during its implementation we found some problems regarding the translation of "internment after completion of the sentence" into English as "preventive detention". For example, in the case of Italy, when various experts were asked about data, it was difficult to convey exactly what we were looking for: one expert referred us to pre-trial detention data, while another informed us on security measures for those not subject to criminal liability. This suggests that it might have been more appropriate to use a different term, such as "post-conviction detention" (Zedner and Ashworth, 2019, p. 436).

In the case of pre-trial detention, we have found that all the countries under study have regulations that allow for imprisonment pending trial for more than three years (item 79), but they do not abuse its use, as those in pre-trial detention in no case represent more than 30% of the prison population (item 82). However, some clarification is appropriate in both cases.

All the countries analysed have regulations that allow to extend pre-trial detention for more than 3 years, although in many cases this is only permitted exceptionally. Thus, Germany, Spain and Poland have a lower ordinary limit (one year in the case of Germany, two years in Spain and Poland). The case is different in Italy (up to six years for those accused of an offence that can lead to permanent imprisonment) and the United States (the law does not specify a maximum duration of pre-trial detention in either New York or California, where the only limits stem from the right to a speedy trial and can be extended indefinitely at the discretion of the judge). This suggests that the decision to include exceptions (see Section 3), while consistent with the instrument's purpose of measuring the exclusionary potential of pre-trial detention regulations, has diminished our ability to discriminate among the countries assessed so far.

Regarding the proportion of pre-trial detainees, although no country exceeded 30 per cent, differences can be established: in two cases the percentage of pre-trial detainees is less than 10 per cent (Poland and England and Wales), while the majority are between 10 and 20 per cent (Spain, California, Italy and Germany), with New York being the only region that exceeds 20% of pre-trial detainees over the period analysed. The fact that the response to item 82 was not affirmative in any of the countries studied was to be expected, since the European median for the use of pre-trial detention is 25 per cent and the global median is 29.5 per cent (Walmsley, 2020). However, this same data also underlines that this item has the potential to discriminate as the instrument is applied to more countries.

In short, pool 6 of the RIMES instrument has allowed us to compare the social exclusion generated by the use of preventive intervention in the different countries analysed, with the result that Spain is the country that generates the least social exclusion with these measures, while Germany, California and Poland are the most exclusionary.

References

Center for Court Innovation (2019). *New York's Bail Reform Law. Summary of Major Components.* New York: Center for Court Innovation.

Dessecker, A. (2013). *Lebenslange Freiheitsstrafe und Sicherungsverwahrung. Dauer und Gründe der Beendigung in den Jahren 2011 und 2012 mit einer Stichtagserhebung zur lebenslangen Freiheitsstrafe.* Wierbaden: Kriminologische Zentralstelle.

Dessecker, A. & Leuschner, F. (2019). *Sicherungsverwahrung und vorgelagerte Freiheitsstrafe. Eine empirische Untersuchung zur Ausgestaltung der Unterbringung und des vorhergehenden Strafvollzugs.* Wierbaden: Kriminologische Zentralstelle.

Díez-Ripollés, J. L. (2011). La dimensión inclusión/exclusión social como guía de la política criminal comparada. *Revista electrónica de ciencia penal y criminología*, 13, 1–36.

Díez-Ripollés, J. L. (2019). Overuse of the Criminal Justice System: Rules and Practices. *European Criminal Law Review*, 9(1), 40–58.

Lévai, M. C. (2013). Indefinite Sentencing in Criminal Law: A Human Rights Perspective. Thesis doctoral. Retrieved from www.etd.ceu.edu/2014/levai_marianna.pdf.

Office of Mental Health of New York (2017): "2016 Annual Report on the Implementation of Mental Hygiene Law", available in https://apps.omh.ny.gov/omhweb/forensic/bsoect/somta-annual-report.pdf

Ogg, J. T. (2015). Preventive Justice and the Power of Police Transfer. *Preventive Justice and the Power of Policy Transfer*, 127–149.

Pighi, G. (2008). Sistemas penales comparados: Medidas de seguridad. Italia. *Revista Penal*, 14, 238–241.

Putzke, H. (n.d.). "Untersuchungshaft", in Kriminologie-Lexicon. Retrieved September 21, 2021, from www.krimlex.de/artikel.php?BUCHSTABE=U&KL_ID=197

Slobogin, C. (2012). Preventive Detention in Europe, the United States and Australia. Vanderbilt Public Law Research Paper Working Paper, (12–27), 12–20.

Walmsley, R. (2020). World Pre-trial/Remand Imprisonment List. Fourth Edition. World Prison Brief. Retrieved from www.prisonstudies.org/sites/default/files/resources/downloads/world_pre-trial_list_4th_edn_final.pdf

Zedner, L. & Ashworth, A. (2019). The Rise and Restraint of the Preventive State. *Annual Review of Criminology*, 2, 429–450.

12 Pool 7

Legal and social status of offenders and ex-offenders

María Contreras-Román

1 Introduction

The deprivation of political, civil or social rights of convicts and former convicts due to the imposition of a sentence, particularly imprisonment, is an increasingly widespread phenomenon. We are not talking about deprivations of rights that are imposed as a principal penalty or as an accessory punitive consequence related to the nature of the offence committed or linked to the sentence serving regime. We refer to removal of rights that stem compulsorily or optionally from the mere fact of having been convicted of an offence or a group of offences unrelated, or only slightly related, to the right being deprived (Díez-Ripollés, 2014).

Among the political rights we could include the right to vote, to stand for election, to sit on a jury or to reside legally in a country. Civil rights refer to the right to marriage, the right to parental authority, the right to adopt, the right to enter the civil service, the right to take up a job or group of jobs, the right to contract with the public administration and the right to obtain a driver's licence. Social rights include access to social benefits, social housing, scholarships or other educational assistance, and health programmes. All this is without prejudice to the fact that such deprivations of rights may be included in the sentence as a penalty, measure or criminal consequence, or may be imposed through other civil or administrative legal instruments (Díez-Ripollés, 2014).

These additional deprivations of rights, or collateral consequences of conviction in Anglo-Saxon terminology, have until recently gone unnoticed or have been neglected by legal operators. Hence some scholars have referred to them as 'invisible criminal sanctions'. Invisible because they are the brief object of attention in criminal law decisions, which usually focus on the main penalties to be imposed for existing or newly created offences. Invisible because at the judicial stage of sentencing, they are the object of minimal consideration, either because they are automatically generated from the imposition of the main penalty, or because they will arise from non-criminal legal provisions applied simultaneously or subsequent to the imposition of the sentence (Díez-Ripollés, 2014; Travis, 2002).

DOI: 10.4324/9781032661766-15

A reflection based on these sanctions brings us to the issue of social exclusion. It is difficult to understand these reactions from the perspective of retributionism, as they bear little or no relation to the type of offence committed and its seriousness. In fact, some countries with a strong rigorist trend make little use of them. Nor does intimidation, at least in general, seem to play a decisive role here: sanctions whose threat of being imposed is often unknown, and whose existence is discovered by convicts as they are suffered are not very intimidating. Obviously, the most commonly used reason is the need to address the dangerousness of the perpetrator. However, when they are applied indiscriminately, without taking into account the particularities of the offenders and their behaviour, they become immoral incapacitating sanctions (in line with this, see Díez-Ripollés, 2014; Hoskin, 2017; Bennett, 2017; and Brown, 2020).

The socially exclusionary effects already produced by imprisonment, or submission to penal control in general, are reinforced by an additional supervision that can exceed the term of the main sentence and makes it more difficult for convicts and ex-convicts to access political and social participation and the benefits of the welfare state. Instead, these groups become criminally governed, involving social agents outside the penal justice system, such as electoral or immigration authorities, various administrative and jurisdictional bodies, employers, landlords or those responsible for educational or health administration, among others. In fact, it is frequently said that they are not sanctions but administrative measures of social control (Díez-Ripollés, 2014).

The desocialising effects of this are easy to identify and understand. The deprivation of civil and social rights of convicts and ex-convicts places them at a disadvantage compared to other citizens when it comes to developing their vital projects within the respect of social standards. These deprivations pose serious difficulties to the maintenance or configuration of family or community ties, to the improvement of their life expectancies through education or employment, or to the relief they may need when facing extreme social situations. The negative consequences caused by all this in preserving the social integration achieved until then or in its improvement – which is one of the essential purposes of the sentence – seem obvious. In fact, all these obstacles produce or aggravate the social exclusion of convicts and ex-convicts and, therefore increase the risk of criminal repetition (Uggen & Manza, 2002; Travis, 2002; Petersilia, 2003; Mele & Miller, 2013; Colgate Love, 2005; Uggen et al., 2006; Pinard, 2010; Díez-Ripollés, 2014).[1]

1 See Uggen and Manza (2002, p. 796); Travis (2002, pp. 19, 23, 25–27); Petersilia (2003, pp. 105, 136–137); Mele/Miller (2013); Colgate Love (2005, pp. 2, 4); Uggen et al. (2006, pp. 281–310); Pinard (2010, pp. 467–468, 506–511). Díez-Ripollés (2014).

2 The pool building process

The starting point of the pool building process was the 36 rules and practices that, out of the 236 identified in the previous project, related to the legal and social status of offenders and ex-offenders. After their assessment by the research team according to a scoring system of 1 to 5 points on a Likert scale, based on criteria of completeness, extension, ease of access, discrimination capacity and clarity, the 12 items with the best scores (9 rules and 3 practices) were selected to move on to the validation phase by international experts.

2.1 Validation of the items proposed for the pool

In the first phase, the experts validated – according to the criteria of clarity and suitability – 8 of the 12 items proposed for this pool, with this being the fourth pool with the highest percentage of validation at this stage (66.6 per cent). Seven of those items were rules and only one was a practice. Although they obtained good scores for suitability, items 86, 88 and 91 got low scores for clarity, so their wording was reviewed by the team before proceeding to the second phase of validation.

In a second round, the experts validated seven of the eight items proposed. The only practice that had reached this stage (item 97 regarding convicts of non-traffic related criminal offences who are deprived of the right to drive after serving their sentence) did not pass the validation, so this is the only pool of the nine included in the RIMES instrument that consists only of rules. The problems of clarity of items 86, 88 and 91 were overcome in this second phase with the new wording.

2.2 Final composition of the pool with the validated items

Out of the seven items validated by experts, the research team decided to include five of them in the final instrument. Items 92 (deprivation of access to public housing) and 93 (deprivation of access to social benefits) had obtained the highest scores for clarity and suitability and were approved by the team in the first round (item 93 was approved unanimously without debate and item 92 was provisionally approved after discussing the importance of housing as an essential issue for any citizen). Items 91 (deprivation of the right to employment), 86 (deprivation of the right to vote) and 88 (expulsion) were provisionally approved in the second round and ratified in the third, after an intense debate on the importance of the different items of this pool and their greater or lesser completeness (importance of the data), extension (not too specific), ease of access (to information), and discrimination capacity (to differentiate them among developed Western countries).

The interpretation of the scores obtained by the final items of this pool within the international experts' assessment of suitability to measure social exclusion as regards the set of items included in the RIMES instrument, drives us to underline that items 92 and 93 were those with the highest Aiken's V coefficient score of the whole instrument (with 0.96), followed by items 86 and 88 (with a score of 0.92) and item 91 (with an Aiken's V of 0.88). Only eight items in the instrument had a coefficient similar to or higher than these items, which proves the good consistency of the indicators that make up this pool.

2.3 *Final description of each item*

The description drawn up by the research team for each item is briefly detailed below, which also includes a comment on the main issues of the research team's discussion.

> *Item 86 (rule): those sentenced to up three years of imprisonment for any criminal offence may be deprived of the right to vote for over four years after serving their sentences.*

This item refers to disenfranchisement in national, regional or local elections for those sentenced to up to three years in prison. It was decided that disenfranchisement included all types of offence, as long as the penalties fulfilled the general conditions described by the item. Finally, it was specified that the item would be fulfilled when either the judicial or the administrative bodies had power to deprive convicts of their rights as a result of said conviction; but imposing such a decision was not mandatory.

> *Item 88 (rule): legally resident foreigners may be deported if they receive a custodial sentence up to one year or a non-custodial sentence.*

This item covers the expulsion of foreigners that are legally resident in a country for the commission of an offence punishable by imprisonment for up to one year or any non-custodial sentence. Deportation may occur before, during, or after the alien has served his sentence. It is not required that the enforcement of the deportation be carried out effectively, as the exclusionary feature would be in the legal possibility of imposing this deportation on the foreign citizen.

> *Item 91 (rule): those sentenced to up to three years of imprisonment are prohibited from doing certain jobs not connected with their offences or with law enforcement for a period of more than five years after their sentence has been completed.*

This item refers to those sentenced to up to three years imprisonment, or any other non-custodial sentence, being disqualified from taking certain jobs, which are not related to the offence committed. It was decided to leave out of the item the disqualifications for work regarding civilian security (either public or private security).

Item 92 (rule): those sentenced to up to three years of imprisonment for any criminal offence are not eligible for public housing for a certain period after having served their sentences.

This item refers to the prohibition for those sentenced to up to three years in prison or any other non-custodial sentence, to be chosen as beneficiaries of social housing programmes offered by the state. The ineligibility can be caused by any type of offence.

Item 93 (rule): nationals sentenced to imprisonment for any criminal offence are not eligible for welfare benefits for a certain period after having served their sentences.

This item refers to the ineligibility of nationals of a state sentenced to imprisonment to be recipients of social benefit programmes offered by the various public bodies, at state, regional or local level. The item will be fulfilled when the power to prevent access to social benefits rests with judicial or administrative bodies.

In the process of describing the items that make up this pool, the issues that raised most debate in the team were, firstly, the type of penalties covered by the expression "sentenced to up to 3 years of imprisonment" (items 86, 91 and 92), having opted for a broad interpretation which includes custodial sentences up to a three-year limit (three years included) and non-custodial sentences[2]; and secondly, the expression 'for a certain period after having served their sentences' (items 92 and 93), having chosen not to specify for how long the deprivation of the right needs to be in place, deeming it is sufficient that this occurs to understand that there is exclusion, and to leave the assessment of the amount of time for a later graduation phase.

On the other hand, during the process of resolving the items it has been necessary to revise the descriptions in order to determine the number of offences for which the disqualifications must take place to understand that the items are or not fulfilled. Thus, the team insisted that to resolve items 88 and 91 it was enough to detect some offences for which disqualification or deportation is prescribed, while for items 86, 92 and 93 the prohibition or disqualification must be for all offences that fulfil the general conditions of the linked sanction.[3]

2 The decision on the type of penalties covered by the item was widely discussed (minutes No. 17 and No. 18), as although the item's wording only mentions expressly imprisonment of up to three years, part of the team defended an extensive interpretation to also consider direct penalties other than imprisonment. Supporters of a literal interpretation argued that this distorted the wording validated by the experts, but it was finally accepted that the possibility of depriving those sentenced to penalties other than imprisonment of the right to vote is clearly more exclusionary and fits into the idea of light sentences.

3 Minutes No. 17.

The team also discussed whether the exclusion referred to in each item must be mandatory or whether it is enough when left at the discretionary power of the authorities[4]: thus, items 86, 88, 92 and 93 specify that it is sufficient for the possibility to exist without the imposition of it being compulsory, while item 91 requires such imposition to be mandatory. These elements of item operationalisation, while rendering more complex the process of reaching a univocal decision about whether or not the item is met in each country, allow us to obtain very rich information to grade the different levels of exclusion that can be found.

3 Methodology used to resolve the items in each country

As this is a pool composed of rules only, the general methodology used to resolve the items has been normative analysis. Since disenfranchisement can be regulated in both criminal and administrative legislation, a wide range of rules had to be revised. In those cases where interpretation doubts arose, the research team consulted academic works, jurisprudence or country experts.

The review of the completed protocols by national experts confirms the reliability of the responses given by the team to this pool's items, whose answers have remained the same in all cases. It has only been necessary to supplement or clarify some information in two items regarding Italy (items 92 and 93) which, in any case, have not changed their initial conclusions.[5] With regard to the methodology used to resolve item 86 on disenfranchisement, criminal legislation was consulted to check whether deprivation of the right to vote was envisaged as a direct or accessory penalty for all convicts or for some of them. Likewise, electoral legislation was consulted to ascertain whether being a convict or an ex-convict is a reason for disenfranchisement.

As to the methodology used to resolve item 88 on deportation, an analysis was carried out of both criminal legislation – to check whether the expulsion of resident foreigners is prescribed as a penalty (either as a direct penalty or as a substitution for it) – and the legislation on aliens – to find out whether having been convicted is stipulated as a cause for administrative expulsion.

With regard to the methodology used to resolve item 91 on disqualification from work, the criminal legislation has been examined to check whether disqualification to perform certain jobs is specified as the main or accessory penalty, as well as labour legislation, to ascertain whether having a criminal record is considered a cause for exclusion. In some countries, labour legislation is

4 Minutes No. 28.

5 After the expert's review in Italy, the protocol for item 92 was supplemented with regional legislation and that of item 93 was supplemented with two explanatory paragraphs.

covered by a single labour code, while in others it has been necessary to review a wide range of regulations on the access to different professions.

Concerning the methodology used to resolve item 92 on public housing, the criminal legislation has been analysed to verify whether deprivation of the right of access to social housing is provided for as the main or accessory penalty, as well as the administrative legislation, to find out if having a criminal record is stipulated as a cause of exclusion in the requirements that applicants for public housing must meet. In some countries such administrative legislation is set forth at regional level, while in others it is local, so (as in the previous item) the team had to revise the legislation of a sample of regions or municipalities to ensure that the response to the item is sufficiently representative of the country's population.

Finally, with regard to the methodology used to resolve item 93 on social benefits, criminal legislation in all countries has been reviewed to ascertain whether deprivation of the right to obtain subsidies or public assistance is prescribed as a principal or accessory penalty. Likewise, the administrative legislation regulating such aid was revised, to find out whether having a criminal record is envisaged as a cause for exclusion among the requirements that applicants must meet. When such administrative regulations were regional or local, the team had to review the legislation of a sample of regions or municipalities to ensure that the response to the item is sufficiently representative of the country's population.

4 Results

The following table summarises the results of the analysis, specifying which countries reach the level of exclusion measured by each item.

As can be seen, the exclusion of convicted and ex-convicted resident foreigners by deportation (item 88) is common in all countries, except in Italy. The labour exclusion of ex-offenders (item 91) is met in four of the six countries analysed, with Spain and Italy being the least exclusionary. The exclusion of ex-offenders from the right to social housing (item 92) is fulfilled in two of the three countries in the Anglo-Saxon context, but in none of the countries with a continental tradition. The exclusion of ex-offenders from the right to vote (item 86) is only met in Poland, and the deprivation of ex-offenders from

Table 12.1 Results of pool 7, by item and country

Item	*Germany*	*Italy*	*Spain*	*Poland*	*England & Wales*	*California*	*New York*
Item 86	No	No	No	Yes	No	No	No
Item 88	Yes	No	Yes	Yes	Yes	Yes	Yes
Item 91	Yes	No	No	Yes	Yes	No	Yes
Item 92	No	No	No	No	Yes	No	Yes
Item 93	No	No	No	No	No	No	No

access to social benefits (item 93) is not fulfilled at the level of exclusion measured by the item in any of the countries under study.

In a country rating, Poland, England and Wales and the state of New York have turned out to be the most exclusionary, with three items answered in the affirmative by each of them, followed by Germany, with two affirmative responses. Spain and California with only one item in the affirmative, and Italy, with none, are among the least exclusionary countries (or states) in this pool.

As to the results of item 86, Spain turned out to be the least exclusionary country regarding this item. Persons sentenced to prison have all their fundamental rights recognised both in the Spanish Constitution (art. 25.2) and in the Penitentiary Law (art. 3).[6] For its part, the Electoral Law stipulates that those convicted by a final judicial sentence to the main or accessory penalty of deprivation of the right of suffrage while they are serving the sentence (art. 3) do not have such right, without specifying whether this refers to the right to vote (active suffrage) or to stand as a candidate (passive suffrage). But as the Penal Code only prescribes the deprivation of passive suffrage (art. 39), we can state that in Spain neither the criminal legislation nor the electoral legislation deprives offenders or ex-offenders from the right to vote.

In England and Wales, the Electoral Law specifies that during the time inmates are serving a prison sentence they are deprived of the right to vote.[7] This deprivation does not affect either persons in pre-trial detention or those on probation. Once the convict is released from prison, he automatically regains his right to vote, even during parole. In California[8] and New York,[9] election laws also prescribe deprivation of voting rights only during the time of serving the prison sentence, although in these states such disenfranchisement does extend to the period of probation (Penal Reform International, 2016). However, since 2018, in New York the governor has the discretionary power to restore voting rights to those released on parole through a pardon (Executive Order 181).

6 Art. 3 of Organic Law 1/1979, of 26 September, on General Penitentiary, specifies that: 'Inmates may exercise civil, political, social, economic and cultural rights, without excluding the right of suffrage, unless they are incompatible with the purpose of their detention or the serving of the sentence'.

7 Article 3 of the Representation of the People Act 1983.

8 In California, Election Code Amendment Act No. 2466 of 2016 specifically addresses the right of convicts to vote (chapter 757). In particular, it defines 'imprisoned' as currently serving a state or federal prison sentence – so it does not affect those serving time in county jails, those convicted of a misdemeanour, or the sentencing of minors – and it defines 'probation' as a period of supervision by the Department of Corrections and Rehabilitation.

9 In New York, the Electoral Law (section 5–106) specifies that no person who has been convicted to prison for felony may register to vote or vote in an election, unless the maximum prison sentence has expired or he has been released from parole.

In the case of Italy[10] and Germany,[11] disenfranchisement is part of the catalogue of ancillary penalties that can be imposed during and after completion of the sentence, but only for specified offences related to national security. Despite this, while disqualification cannot be imposed as a consequence of any offence, as required by the definition, the item is not fulfilled in either of these two countries.

In Poland, deprivation of the right to vote is included in the catalogue of criminal measures of deprivation of public/civil rights (art. 40.1 of the Penal Code), its period can range from 1 to 10 years and the term does not begin to run until the main prison sentence has been served (art. 40.3). This deprivation may be imposed by the court in cases of imprisonment sentences of at least three years and for an offence committed with a particularly reprehensible intent[12] (art. 40.2). As the lower limit of the penalty implying disenfranchisement coincides with the upper limit set in the item's description and refers to any offence (although that particular reproachability is required), we can say that, as per the rule, Poland is the most exclusionary country regarding this item. However, in practice, it seems that this penal measure is used rather infrequently, and the vast majority of inmates in Polish prisons

10 In Italy, the Constitution recognises the right to vote for all persons of legal age, but provides for three exceptions, among them that the person has been convicted of a criminal offence by a final judgment (art. 48). However, this is not a general consequence for all convicts but, as developed in Decree No. 223 implementing the Electoral Law of 1967, it applies only to specific cases: a) some are disenfranchised only for the duration of the situation leading to the disqualification: this is the case for those sentenced to life imprisonment, those subject to a temporary ban from holding public office, those subject to preventive measures, those who are subject to custody or probation measures or a prohibition of residence in one or more municipalities or in one or more provinces (art. 2); and b) others are deprived of the [right to] vote for a period of five years after serving the prison sentence or security measure: this is the case for those convicted of certain specifically mentioned offences. Most of them imply a custodial sentence of more than three years, although two gambling-related offences draw attention, both of which carry lower penalties. In any case, in the event of a specific type of offence, the item is not fulfilled.

11 In Germany, the Federal Elections Law stipulates that a person shall be disqualified from voting if so provided for in a court decision (section 13.1), which is explicitly provided for in the Criminal Code and the Federal Constitutional Court Law as an accessory penalty and for a duration of two to five years when the offence committed is one of those specifically indicated, most of them linked to national security. Specifically, disqualification from voting will be imposed as an accessory penalty to those convicted of offences against peace, high treason, endangering the democratic state under the rule of law (section 92.a), treason and endangering external security (section 101), preparing a war of aggression and high treason against the Federation, attacks against bodies and representatives of foreign states (section 101), interruption of the electoral process (section 107), fraud in connection with elections (section 107.a), coercion or bribery of voters (section 108), sabotage against the means of defence (109.e) and intelligence activity endangering national security (109.f).

12 A somewhat vague formulation of its evaluative nature, which eventually gives judges broad discretion, although the meaning is more or less restricted by the jurisprudence of the courts of appeal and the Supreme Court (Professor Krajewski, personal communication).

(around 99 per cent) are not deprived of their right to vote either during or after their stay behind bars (Professor Krajewski, personal communication).

With regard to the results of item 88, all the countries analysed provide for the expulsion of convicted foreigners on the grounds of national security interests, but there are substantial differences in the cases in which this interest is defined by each legislation and the foreigners on whom it may be applied.

In Italy, the legislation on aliens provides for the possibility of expelling foreign convicts in three different ways, one of which fits within the penalty limits set by the item.[13] However, Italian law specifically provides for a residence permit as a ground for exemption in all cases (art. 19.2.b), so that in Italy the expulsion of foreign convicts is only possible when foreigners are in an irregular situation.

In Poland, England and Wales and Germany foreigners can be deported if they are sentenced to prison of up to one year or even to non-custodial sentences, although in the case of resident aliens, the law requires an additional effort of individualisation. Thus, in Poland, in the case of foreigners with a residence permit for family reasons, the period of stay and the existence of cultural and social ties with the country of origin must be assessed.[14] In England and Wales, when foreigners have legally resided in the country for most of their life, an assessment must be made of whether they are socially and culturally integrated and whether there are major obstacles to their integration into the country to which they are proposed to be deported.[15] And in the

13 In Italy, Legislative Decree No. 286, of 25 July 1998, 'Consolidated text of the provisions concerning immigration regulations and rules on the status of foreigners' provides for expulsion: a) as a security measure in cases of flagrante delicto or offences specifically listed in the Penal Code, also needing a declaration of social danger (art. 13); b) as an alternative to imprisonment, where the offence must be intentional, the custodial sentence cannot exceed two years and the requirements for conditional suspension of the sentence must not be met (art. 16.1–4); and c) as an alternative to imprisonment when the penalty is already in the enforcement phase and, after having served part of the sentence, less than two years remain for its completion (art. 16.5–6).

14 In Poland, the legislation on aliens (art. 302 et seq.) contemplates the possibility of imposing an obligation to return to their country of origin, inter alia: a) When the foreigner is entered on the 'list of aliens whose stay in the territory of the Republic of Poland is undesirable', which occurs if he is sentenced by a final judgment to pay a fine or serve a prison sentence for an intentional offence or a tax offence, without a minimum duration being required; or b) when the foreigner is sentenced to a custodial penalty subject to enforcement, and there are grounds for his/her transfer to serve the sentence abroad. An exception is made for aliens with a residence permit issued on the basis of a Schengen visa for tourism, humanitarian reasons, foreigners that must appear in person before a Polish public authority and EU citizens with permanent or long-term residence, but the deportation of the rest is accepted, including those with residence permits for family reasons (although in the latter case an effort of individualisation is required).

15 In England and Wales, several regulations provide for the possibility of deportation of convicted non-British citizens. Firstly, the Immigration Act of 1971 specifies that the secretary of state has the power to issue an expulsion order against a non-British citizen if it is considered that such deportation is in the public interest (section 3.5), which may happen if, on reaching the age of 17, the foreigner is convicted of an offence punishable by a custodial sentence and

German case, no distinction is made according to whether the foreigners have a residence permit or not, but it is for the Federal Office for Migration and Refugees to assess whether it is in the public interest to expel them, in each particular case, weighing the interests in the departure of the alien against their individual interests in remaining in federal territory.[16]

In Spain, the deportation of convicted foreigners is stipulated both in criminal and in aliens' legislation. In the first case, it is specified as a judicial substitute for prison sentences of more than one year imposed on a foreign citizen (art. 89 of the Penal Code). While in the Law on Aliens, it is established as a cause for expulsion that the foreigner has been convicted, inside or outside Spain, for an intentional conduct that in Spain is punishable by imprisonment of more than one year (art. 57.2). Both cases are applicable to resident and non-resident foreigners, although in criminal cases a greater effort of individualisation is required when the foreigner is a legal resident, especially when he has lived in said country for more than 10 years.[17] In the event of administrative expulsion of convicted aliens, the Supreme Court has interpreted that expulsion 'is appropriate when the penalty referred to in art. 57.2 is that provided for in abstract in the Penal Code for the offence committed, and not the

---

in his/her conviction the court recommends deportation (section 6). Secondly, the Borders Act 2007 (section 32.5) reiterates this discretion, specifying that the person must be a 'foreign offender' sentenced to imprisonment for at least 12 months. Thirdly, the Immigration Rules (part 13, art. 398) describe three scenarios within the penal field where a foreigner can be deported in the public interest: a) the alien has been sentenced to a prison term of at least four years; b) the alien has been sentenced to imprisonment of less than four years, but at least 12 months; or c) the alien's offence has caused serious harm or he is a persistent offender who shows a particular disregard for the law, irrespective of the penalty. In cases b) and c), personal circumstances must be considered (art. 399).

16 In Germany, the Law on Residence, Economic Activity and Integration of Foreigners in the Federal Territory (section 53) prescribes that a foreigner whose stay endangers public security and order or other significant interests of the Republic shall be expelled if, after weighing the interests in the foreigner's departure against his individual interests in remaining in the federal territory, taking into account the particular circumstances, there is a public interest in the alien's departure. No distinction is made on whether the foreigner has a residence permit or not, but the competence to assess whether it is in the public interest to expel the foreigner in each particular case lies with the Federal Office for Migration and Refugees. The same law specifies that there is a particularly serious public interest when the foreigner has been sentenced to imprisonment or a period of juvenile custody of: a) at least two years for one or more intentionally committed offences or pre-trial detention has been ordered in connection with the most recent conviction; or b) at least one year for one or more intentionally committed offences against life, physical integrity, sexual self-determination or property, or for resisting enforcement officers if the criminal offence was committed using violence, using a threat of danger to life or limb, or with guile.

17 '*The substitution shall not be carried out when, in view of the circumstances of the criminal offence and the personal circumstances of the perpetrator, particularly his roots in Spain, deportation is deemed as disproportionate*' (art. 89 of the Penal Code): these are requirements which, while limiting the application of expulsion regarding resident foreigners, do not exclude it, and in fact, the possibility of expelling also residents was introduced as a novelty in the 2015 penal reform (García-España, 2017).

specific penalty imposed on the person affected by the sentence',[18] so it could happen that the specific penalty imposed is less than one year (for example, if there is a sentence of conformity or if some mitigating factor is applied) and expulsion could still be carried out. That is why the research team considers that this possibility generates the level of exclusion measured by the item.

In the United States, the federal Immigration and Nationality Act ('INA') specifies that any alien living in the country can be deported if convicted of certain crimes, called deportable offences. No distinction is made between resident foreigners and non-resident foreigners. Five categories of deportable offences are established, at least two of which match or exceed the exclusion limits set out in the item: a) crimes of moral turpitude (fraudulent, deceptive or harmful), with a penalty of one year or more[19]; and b) crimes of domestic violence, stalking, child abuse or trafficking in human beings,[20] regardless of the penalty. Some offences in the latter category are even punishable, under the state criminal codes of California and New York, with non-custodial sentences (for example, in New York, the offence of child abandonment committed by someone without a criminal record, art. 260).

The results of item 91 show that in all the countries analysed, labour disqualifications for taking certain jobs are prescribed, both in criminal and labour law. In any case, the levels of exclusion set in the item are not fulfilled through the criminal system, either because the time limit of disqualification is less than five years or because, even exceeding that time limit, a link is established between the type of employment for which he is disqualified and the type of offence committed.[21]

18 Judgment of 31/05/2018 of the fifth section of the Administrative Chamber of the Supreme Court *www.iustel.com/diario_del_derecho/noticia.asp?ref_iustel=1178021*

19 There is no list of cases involving moral turpitude (CIMT), but this feature is decided on a case-by-case basis. In general, offences that involve behaviour that is fraudulent, deceptive or harmful to others are usually considered as such. Judges often classify in this category crimes such as murder, rape, robbery, kidnapping, homicide, aggravated assault, spousal abuse, child abuse, incest, bigamy, paternity fraud, lewd acts on a child, arson, prostitution, pimping, fraud, driving under the influence of alcohol without a license, criminal threats, failure to register as a sex offender, perjury, drug offences or receiving stolen property. Crimes that receive this classification have additional consequences beyond the typical criminal penalties, especially immigration, employment and reputational consequences. Source: www.aerlawgroup.com/resources/crimes-involving-moral-turpitude/ (consulted on 23/09/2021).

20 The categories of deportable offences under federal legislation are completed by: i) aggravated offences; ii) serious drug offences; and iii) offences involving firearms or related to espionage, sabotage, treason or sedition, where the penalty exceeds five years, or a violation of the Military Selective Service Act or the Trading with the Enemy Act.

21 In Italy, disqualification has the status of an accessory penalty (art. 19) and may entail the prohibition from holding public office – which is automatic and perpetual in the case of prison sentences of more than five years, discretionary and not exceeding five years in the case of prison sentences of three to five years (art. 29) – and the exercise of other professions, arts, industry or commerce requiring a special licence – in which case the prohibition may not exceed five years (art. 30). But in all cases, it is required that the offence was committed with abuse of office or profession, or in violation of the duties inherent to them. In Spain, the

In order to understand the level of labour exclusion of ex-convicts in different countries, it is more interesting to analyse their employment regulations: In Italy, all the specific labour regulations consulted establish a connection between crime and employment (bankruptcy law, law on forensic professions, rules on health advertising and repression of abuse in the health profession, provisions on price regulation or law on financial intermediation), so the level of exclusion measured by the item is not fulfilled.

In Spain, Germany, England and Wales, New York and Poland, in addition to being banned from related jobs, disqualifications are also prescribed for jobs unrelated to the offence, but while in Spain the item is not met because the disqualification period does not exceed five years,[22] in the case of Germany, England and Wales, New York and Poland it does: either because the criminal conviction implies the loss of the 'suitability' required by certain professional regulations for reappointment (like in Germany), or because the criminal record is required to be expunged and the time periods to apply for this are very long, even for sentences of less than three years' imprisonment (such time period is five years in New York, seven years in England and Wales, and ten years in Poland). We shall analyse in more detail the regulations in each country where the item is fulfilled.

In Germany, the Labour Code provides for disqualification from certain jobs, but the item is not met because there is either a link between the offence

penalty of disqualification may be special (in relation to jobs related to the offence, art. 40 of the Penal Code) or absolute (definitive deprivation of public jobs and posts held by the convicted person or of obtaining them, art. 41 Penal Code), applicable as an accessory penalty to a prison sentence of ten years or more (art. 55 PC) or as the main penalty for a set of specified offences. Of these, only those committed by an authority or civil servant in the exercise of his position are subject to a disqualification exceeding the limits set out in the item. In Germany, this may be imposed as a main penalty in cases of professions and trades related to the offence when there is a risk of recidivism, even for life (art. 70), and as an accessory penalty when there is a prison sentence (automatically if it is more than one year, or at the discretion of the court, if it is less in certain specified cases (art. 54)). This penalty implies deprivation of exercising a public office, shall begin to run when the main sentence is served and affects civil servants of the state administration or the judiciary, and also those whose work has a public purpose (art. 45), including by assimilation notaries, tax advisors, auditors or lawyers, but in any case, it will always have a duration within the five-year limit set by the item.

22 In Spain, following the exhaustive review carried out by Larrauri (2013), labour regulations provide for three different formulas to exclude ex-convicts: i) Express mention of the need to have no criminal record; ii) Express mention of the need not to have been disqualified from practicing the profession by a final judgment; and iii) Express mention of the need not to have been convicted by a final judgment within the previous five years. In the first case would be, for example, civil servants, and according to the regulations governing the expungement of criminal records in Spain, those convicted of prison sentences of up to three years may cancel them before the five-year period stipulated in the item. In the second case, the item would not be fulfilled either, as it involves deprivation of exercising professions related to the offence committed. The third case would be that of professions related to public security, expressly excluded from the item, or that of casino employees, in which case the exclusion does not exceed the period of five years after the conviction required by the item.

and the job (e.g., deprivation of access to jobs related to children and youth welfare for those convicted of sexual offences against minors (art. 72)), or they are jobs related to public safety (e.g., the police, where it is not possible to be admitted with a criminal record, regardless of the offence committed and when it was committed, even if the conviction was under juvenile criminal law). However, for civil servants or notaries, a criminal conviction (irrespective of its length) implies in practice the loss of the 'suitability' that the specific administrative regulations of these professions require for reappointment (Krausnick, 2020; Miermeister, 2020). Thus, the research team considered that the item is fulfilled in Germany.

In England and Wales, bans on accessing or performing certain jobs are also linked to the existence of a criminal record. According to the Rehabilitation of Offenders Law 1974, a criminal record is deemed 'spent' after a 'rehabilitation period' which begins to run after the completion of the full sentence and whose length varies according to the type of penalty. During the 'rehabilitation period' there are no prohibitions on applying for a job, only the obligation to inform the employer about the ex-offender's criminal record, which may or may not refuse the person access to work at his or her discretion. Once the rehabilitation period has elapsed, the ex-offender is considered rehabilitated and the law requires that they be treated as if they had never committed an offence. As a result, it is not necessary for a person to disclose the conviction when applying for most jobs and it is illegal for an employer to refuse to hire a person because of a past conviction. However, the rehabilitation periods (reformed in 2012) exceed the five years stipulated in the item for convictions of less than three years.[23] In addition, an Order of 1975 (amended in 2013) provides for a set of jobs exempted from the application of the Corrections Law by allowing prohibitions to perform certain jobs unrelated to the offence committed, even if the rehabilitation period has ended.[24]

In Poland, the absence of a criminal record is a common requirement for employment, at least for civil servants, security workers, those working with minors and in the financial sector.[25] In general, there is a link between the type of work and the type of offence that gave rise to the criminal record, but in the case of civil servants, this connection is unnecessary: any kind of criminal

23 Rehabilitation periods shall be one year in the case of community penalties, two years in the case of imprisonment of less than six months, four years in the case of prison sentences between six and 30 months, seven years in the case of prison sentences of 30 months to four years, and perpetual in the case of prison sentences of more than four years (Legal Aid, Sentencing and Punishment of Offenders Act 2012, section 139).

24 This would be the case for activities that involve working with children (including health professions), as well as those related to national security (including the provision of services in airlines or in the Atomic Energy Authority). Order of 1975, according to the 2013 reform.

25 Polish Penal Code (arts. 39 to 43), Law of 24 May 2000 on the National Criminal Register, Polish Labour Code, Law of 21 November 2008 on Civil Service, Law of 13 May 2016 on Counteracting Threats of Sexual Offenses, Law of 24 October 2017 on Amending the Financial Sector Legislation.

record for an intentional or fiscal offence would prevent a person from being recruited. According to the Polish rules on expungement of criminal records, when the penalty imposed is imprisonment of up to three years – which is the one relevant for the item – removal will take place by legal mandate 10 years after the sentence has been served. It can only take place earlier if requested by the ex-convict, which is a discretionary decision of the court, so the item is clearly met.

In the United States, the Civil Rights Act of 1964[26] makes employment discrimination against people with criminal records illegal, although federal law does prohibit those with records from entering the armed forces or law enforcement agencies. In any case, these jobs would fall outside the scope of the item. Specifically, in California no law prevents ex-offenders from taking a job, except for prohibitions on occupations related to certain criminal conduct, such as working with children if they have been convicted of a sexual offence, or obtaining a business licence if convicted of an offence related to the functions or duties of the company or profession within the previous seven years.[27] In all other cases, labour discrimination against ex-offenders is illegal in California.[28]

With regard to New York, the Corrections Act also prescribes specifically that it is not allowed to deny former convicts the possibility of having a job after serving their sentence, although it provides for exceptions: 1) if the work is directly related to the offence for which the person was convicted; or 2) if the hiring of the person poses a risk to the property, safety or welfare of specific individuals or to the general public.[29] On the other hand, some state laws regulating jobs that require some type of licence or permit establish prohibitions or restrictions for those with a criminal record: sometimes related to the offence committed (for example, in the case of work related to people with mental disabilities),[30] and sometimes not (for example, to obtain a licence as a supplier of gambling or bingo equipment[31] or to participate in a funeral home[32]). So, there would be some jobs for which the exclusion would be fulfilled. And while there are mechanisms by which convicted persons can apply for reinstatement of their rights (through a certificate of relief of disabilities for first-time offenders or a certificate of good conduct for others), a specific period must have elapsed since the last sentence was served: up to five years in the case of sentences of up to three years in prison[33] (this limit is within the

26 The US Civil Rights Act of 1964. www.eeoc.gov/statutes/title-vii-civil-rights-act-1964.
27 California Business and Professions Code, sections 480–489.
28 Assembly Bill No. 1008.
29 Correction Law, articles 752 and 753.
30 Mental Hygiene Law, section 31.16.
31 General Municipal Law, section 189.a. https://codes.findlaw.com/ny/general-municipal-law/gmu-sect-189-a.html.
32 Public Health Law, section 3450. https://codes.findlaw.com/ny/public-health-law/pbh-sect-3450.html.
33 https://doccs.ny.gov/certificate-relief-good-conduct-restoration-rights (consulted on 01/10/2021).

item). In addition, applying for the certificate does not guarantee that it is obtained.

Regarding the results of item 92, it should be noted that in Germany and Poland there are no regulations excluding people with a criminal record from access to the public housing system, although in the case of Poland, the experts report that there is a significant problem of homeless ex-convicts in the country because the social housing system is underdeveloped. In Spain, people with a criminal record are not excluded either, but exceptionally it is possible to find some regulations from the municipal registers of housing applicants that exclude those convicted of misappropriation offences. In Italy, most regions do not stipulate the exclusion of persons with a criminal record from public housing, although others exclude those convicted for serious offences or certain offences related to the right of which they are deprived, and there is even a region that excludes those convicted for any offence to prison sentences of less than two years or to community services. We will take a closer look at each country, rating them from least to most exclusionary:

In Germany, where there is a highly developed system of public housing and social assistance for housing, federal regulations establish some requirements for access, such as income limits or administrative conditions for legal residence, work permits, etc., but no mention is made of any restriction of access due to previous convictions or criminal records.[34] This federal legislation is supplemented by the regional laws of the different German Länder, but none of the regional laws consulted includes restrictions for the mentioned reason. On the websites of the associations that provide advice on public housing or social assistance there is also no reference to any limitation on the basis of criminal convictions. Consultation with the National Working Group for Assistance to Offenders (BAG.S)[35] confirms that those who had served a prison sentence are not excluded from access to public housing in Germany (Maike Weigand, personal communication).

In Poland, the penal law does not include any option to deprive convicts of the right to public housing. As far as administrative regulations are concerned, and according to the experts consulted from the Jagiellonian University of Krakow, there is no formal rule or provision explicitly prohibiting ex-convicts from accessing any kind of social benefit, although in practice it is difficult to obtain such benefits even for 'normal' people, due to the shortage of this type of housing and to long waiting lists, which generates a serious problem of homeless ex-convicts (Prof. Krajewski, personal communication). Studies with homeless people and their experience with access to social housing reveal that some have had interactions with the law that include imprisonment, which

34 Housing Promotion Act (WoFG).

35 BAG.S (*Bundesarbeitsgemeinschaft für Straffälligenhilfe*) is an institution specialised in social assistance to persons who have served a prison sentence and in promoting public awareness of the tasks of integration and resocialisation of ex-offenders (https://bag-s.de/die-bags/portrait/)

proves that, although few, some people with a criminal record manage to access public housing in Poland (Prof. Grzyb, personal communication).

In Spain, the concept of 'social housing' means 'officially sponsored housing' (Royal Decree 31/1978, Royal Decree 2066/2008), which is defined as a type of housing with a limited price and partially subsidised by the public administration, aimed at promoting citizens with lower incomes to acquire or rent decent and adequate housing at prices affordable to their possibilities. The state legislates on the features of social housing and specifies which social groups can be considered beneficiaries, with a right to preferential protection, but it is the regional governments that must establish the specific requirements for those wishing to acquire social housing, and they have set up municipal registers of applicants for officially sponsored housing. The fact of having a criminal record for any offence does not appear as an impediment to apply for social housing in any of the regional regulations consulted (Andalusia, Madrid, the Basque Country, Catalonia, Asturias, Castilla-La Mancha or Valencia regions). Nevertheless, having a record for misappropriation or damage to public housing does appear as an exclusion criterion in some ordinances that regulate municipal registers in the provinces of Seville and Córdoba (this is the case of the Ordinances of Seville, Tocina, Gelves, Carrión de los Céspedes, Lora del Rio or La Carlota).[36] In any case, it only affects these municipalities that are not representative of the population as a whole and only for those convicted of a particular type of offence, so the level of exclusion required by the item is not met.

In Italy, access to social housing is regulated regionally. Most of the regional regulations consulted do not exclude convicts (Lombardy, Lazio, Emilia-Romagna, Sicily, Puglia, Basilicata, Calabria and Piedmont), although others do when convictions were for serious offences whose penalty exceeds the one described by the item (Campania and Liguria)[37] or for certain types of offences linked to the right that is deprived (Abruzzo),[38] which is also left out of the item. There is only one region where the exclusion affects those convicted of minor offences that have nothing to do with the right of which they are

36 The ordinance of Seville specifies that in housing allocation preference will be given to those who have not been convicted by a final judgment in a criminal proceeding for misappropriation or damage to social housing. The municipal ordinances of Tocina, Gelves, Carrión de los Céspedes and Lora del Río have the same wording: *'None of the members of the family or cohabitation unit who want to be entered in the Municipal Register of Social Housing Applicants may [. . .] have been convicted by a final judgment in criminal proceedings, for misappropriation or damage to social housing'*. Only the ordinance of La Carlota specifies that this exclusion criterion will be valid for five years.

37 Access to public housing is prohibited for those convicted of intentional offences to sentences of more than seven years in the region of Campania, and more than five years in the region of Liguria (*Regolamento Regionale 28 of ottobre de 2019, n. 11* (art. 9) and Law 10/04 (art. 3)).

38 Access to public housing is prohibited to those convicted in the last five years for offences of land encroachment or building encroachment, punishable by prison sentences of one to four years (art. 633 of the Italian penal code). Regional Law of 3 November 2017, n. 39, art. 25.2.b.

deprived (Veneto),[39] but since this region only represents 8 per cent of the Italian population, it is concluded that the item is not fulfilled in Italy.

In England and Wales and the United States, where the social housing system is highly developed, ex-convicts can be excluded from it for more than five years after the sentence has been served, even if the penalty was less than three years in prison, because the exclusion from public housing is linked to criminal records and the periods for expungement in these countries are very long. In any case, regulations specify that such exclusion is not automatic, but rather at the discretion of the local public housing authorities, after each case is individually analysed.

In England and Wales, national legislation for the allocation of social housing stipulates that preferential rights for access to social housing will be granted to homeless people, people living in unhealthy, overcrowded or unsatisfactory conditions, people in need of moving for medical or welfare reasons, and people who need to move to a particular area to avoid hardships, so convicted persons are not excluded.[40] However, local authorities have the power to remove people from the waiting list on the basis of past anti-social behaviour, in which case it applies the Rehabilitation of Offenders Act 1974 that, while specifying that a 'spent' sentence (one whose rehabilitation period has already elapsed) must be treated as if the offence had never been committed. However, it prescribes rehabilitation periods that allow those convicted to prison sentences of up to 6 months to be excluded for 2 years; those convicted to between 6 and 30 months, for 4 years; those convicted to prison sentences from 30 months to 4 years, to be excluded for 7 years; and those convicted to longer prison sentences, perpetually. Thereupon, the exclusion measured by the item is fulfilled in England and Wales.

In the United States, the social housing programme is designed to help low-income families find housing within their financial means through a system of vouchers given to beneficiaries.[41] The programme is managed by each state's public housing authority, which receives funding from the Department of Housing and Urban Development. Federal regulations stipulate a set of grounds for rejecting applicants (having been evicted from social housing within the last three years for drug-related reasons, being on the sex offender register for life, having been convicted of manufacturing methamphetamine in public housing, current illegal use of drugs or abusing alcohol in a manner that interferes with living in the public housing community).[42]

39 Access to social housing is prohibited to those who have been convicted of intentional crimes in the last 10 years for an offence punishable by imprisonment of more than two years and to those who in the last five years have been convicted of offences of contempt (arts. 290, 291 and 292 of the Penal Code) or for offences of illegal use, possession and/or carrying of weapons (art. 21.b-ter), punishable by a fine.

40 Housing Act 1996 (part 6), as amended by the Homelessness Act 2002 and the Law on Local Government 2011.

41 https://eligibility.com/section-8/california-ca-section-8-benefits

42 Quality Housing and Work Responsibility Act of 1998.

To these federal grounds for exclusion, local regulations in each state add others. In the case of the state of California, local regulations in San Diego[43] and San Francisco,[44] for example, stipulate that all potential adult household members must pass a criminal background check by the public housing authority before the final eligibility assessment, and in both cities, there is a list of specified offences for which possible exclusion is prescribed. Although the list of offences is quite extensive, the item's requirement that exclusion be for any offence is not met. In any event, involvement in such criminal activities does not automatically exclude the possibility of accessing or remaining in social housing, but the competent authority has the discretion to consider the circumstances in each particular case, including the seriousness of the case, the degree of involvement or culpability of individual members of the family, and the effects of the denial or termination of assistance on other family members who were not involved in such activities.

Exclusion from access to public housing for more than five years is also possible for persons sentenced to up to three years in prison in at least three of the largest cities in New York state, but unlike California – where there is a list of specified offences – here exclusion can be for any offence, either because a direct link is established between the type of sentence and the period of exclusion (as in New York City),[45] where exclusion seems mandatory unless the family reunion programme applies, or because even if there is a specified list of offences, it includes the possibility for the authorities to consider any other offence (as in Yonkers or Buffalo),[46] which puts federally subsidised housing out of reach for many applicants with criminal records (Tran-Leung, 2015, p. 23).

43 In the case of San Diego, it is expressly mentioned that participation in violent or drug-related criminal activity within the past five years that posed a threat to the health, safety or right to peaceful enjoyment of public housing of other residents or employees of the public housing authority and that resulted in a conviction, arrest or eviction from housing, shall be verified (Housing Authority of the County of San Diego, Public Housing Admissions and Continued Occupancy Policy, 2018).

44 In the case of San Francisco, it is specified that drug-related or violent criminal activity, illegal possession of firearms, criminal activity that posed a threat to the health, safety or welfare of other tenants, criminal sexual conduct, incest, child abuse or arson in the past five years shall be verified (San Francisco Housing Authority, Admissions and Continued Occupancy Policy, 2016).

45 In New York City the exclusion period is directly established according to the severity of the convictions: six years for class A, B or C felonies, five years for class D or E felonies, four years for class A misdemeanors, three years for class B or unclassified misdemeanours (Bae et al., 2016, p. 9). Therefore, it includes even minor offences, often punished by less than three years' imprisonment or non-custodial sentences. To address this exclusion, the New York public housing authority together with the VERA Institute of Justice launched in 2013 a 'Family Reentry Program' so that some convicts could be eligible for public housing, although it is only available for a selected group of convicts and not for all of them (Ianelli 2020).

46 In Buffalo, those convicted of property offences, disorderly conduct, crimes of violence against persons or drug-related offences are specifically excluded and authorities are empowered to consider any other activity, with no express retroactive period specified.

With regard to the results of item 93, we should note that deprivation of the right to receive public assistance is stipulated in the criminal and administrative legislation of all countries, but only for those convicted of offences related to the right of which they are deprived. In some countries, like England and Wales, it is possible to deprive of some benefits unrelated to the offence while the sentence is being served, but the right is restored once the sentence has been completed, although sometimes additional conditions may be imposed, such as participation in a programme or treatment. This exclusion is not even met in California or New York, because both states have distanced themselves from the Clinton anti-drug policy that perpetually excludes from social benefits those convicted for drug offenses. On the contrary, in all the countries consulted, ex-convicts seem to be among the groups of preferential social care due to their particular vulnerability.

In Spain, the Penal Code prescribes disqualification from obtaining public subsidies and assistance as an accessory penalty for natural persons convicted of offences against the Public Treasury and against Social Security, which can last up to eight years, even if the prison sentence imposed as main penalty is shorter (art. 305.2 et seq.). However, insofar as a link is established between the type of offence and the disqualification, the level of exclusion described by the item is not fulfilled. The same connection is required in the administrative legislation consulted.[47] Apart from these cases, social benefits are available to former prisoners. The case of unemployment benefits is particularly noteworthy, the right to which applies to all former convicts who have served prison sentences of more than six months, although obtaining such benefits is sometimes subject to certain requirements that the released person must fulfil (request for forgiveness, satisfaction of civil liability for sexual offences, terrorism, etc.) (General Law on Social Security, art. 274.2).

Germany has a comprehensive and consolidated social legislation, contained in the Social Code. It specifies, in article 9, that

> anyone who is unable to earn a living or help himself in special circumstances and does not receive enough help from others is entitled to personal and financial assistance that corresponds to his special needs, enables him to help himself, allows him to participate in the life of the community and ensures him a decent living.[48]

47 a) General Law on Subsidies denies the status of beneficiary or collaborating entity to those who have been convicted of offences of prevarication, bribery, embezzlement of public funds, influence peddling, fraud and illegal exactions or urban planning offences (art. 13.2); b) A multitude of local regulations make assistance to entrepreneurs or self-employed individuals conditional on the beneficiary not having been convicted of those same crimes; c) The General Law on Social Security deprives convicts of the right to obtain certain benefits, such as those regarding widowhood or orphanhood, for the commission of an intentional homicide offence against the partner or parents of the person claiming this benefit (articles 231 to 234).

48 Social Assistance *(Sozialgesetzbuch* – SGB), book I, section 9.

From the review of the requirements established to access the assistance described in this code, we may affirm that there are no legal restrictions to exclude those who have been convicted. This is confirmed by the National Working Group for Assistance to Offenders (BAG.S), which states that anyone who cannot cover their living expenses on their own can apply for benefits to ensure their livelihood (personal communication).

In Italy, the Penal Code does not contain among the accessory sanctions (described in Chapter 3) any prohibition of access to aid or subsidies. The labour regulations do include the accessory sanction, for the duration of the sentence, of revocation of the benefits that the convicts may be entitled to in the event that he is convicted of offences of terrorism or criminal organisation.[49] The requirements for access to the nine types of social benefits described on the website of the National Social Welfare Institute have also been consulted, but none of them excludes persons who have served their sentences, although conditions are imposed on applicants which, in practice, a former offender may not be able to fulfil (for example, to access the wage integration fund the applicant must have actually worked at least 90 days in the production unit for which the application is made).

In Poland there is no formal rule stipulating that ex-convicts are not eligible for social benefits, rather the contrary. Poland recognises that people who have just been released from prison may have problems integrating into society (finding a house, a job, etc.), so they are expressly covered by social assistance under the same conditions as other vulnerable persons (orphans, homeless, disabled, refugees, etc.).[50] The problem may be that many, or most, ex-convicts do not meet other requirements to receive the various benefits (it also depends on time spent in prison, previous criminal career, etc.), but this is related to realities and not to formal rules (Prof. Krajewski, personal communication).

In England and Wales the social benefit system was reformed in 2012 to simplify the six types of provisions existing at the time and replace them with a single type of benefit, the universal credit, which is a monthly payment for people who are unemployed or working but have low incomes.[51] As regards convicts, the legislation differentiates between those in prison (preventive or convicted), who are disqualified from obtaining the universal credit – although they may be entitled to housing benefits and child tax credit – and those that

49 Specifically, Law of 28 June 2012, No. 92 (*Disposizioni in materia di riforma del mercato del lavoro in una prospettiva di Crescita*) refers to the following offences included in the Italian Penal Code: associations for terrorist purposes, including international or subversion of the democratic order (art. 270 bis), attack for terrorist or subversive purposes (art. 280), kidnapping for terrorist or subversive purposes (289 bis), mafia-type association, including foreigners (art. 416 bis), political-mafioso electoral exchange (art. 416 ter) and massacre (art. 422).

50 www.asylumineurope.org/reports/country/poland/content-international-protection/social-welfare

51 Welfare Reform Act (2012). www.legislation.gov.uk/ukpga/2012/5/contents

are released, who can apply for access to universal credit as soon as they leave prison.[52]

In the United States, the Personal Responsibility and Work Opportunity Reconciliation Act (known as the Welfare Reform) passed in 1996, during the Clinton administration, established a lifetime ban on access to federal food stamp and cash assistance programmes for anyone convicted of a drug-related offence. In 1998, after numerous protests, Congress allowed states to decide whether or not they wanted to participate in this policy. In the case of the state of California, the lifetime ban was in effect until 2015 but then was eliminated, although there may still be some temporary impact on access to certain public assistance programmes for those convicted of serious drug offenses, for being on the run or for failing to comply with probation.[53] In any case, the prohibition does not prevent them from receiving support for dependent children. The remaining persons with a criminal record are eligible for the food programme (CalFresh), the medical assistance programme (MediCal) and the employment programme (CalWorks), although additional conditions may be required to access them, such as participating in treatment for addictions or proving active job search.[54]

The federal prohibition of lifetime exclusion of those convicted of serious drug offences is also not in force in New York State where social assistance is available to people in poverty and covers different types of benefits aimed at covering basic human needs: supplemental nutrition assistance programme ('food stamps'), cash assistance, temporary assistance for needy families, medical assistance. Some public benefits are suspended while the sentence is being served, others are not, but in any case, the affected person can reapply for them once released (Kovel, 2015).[55] In the case of New York, the only exception seems to be the conviction for social assistance fraud, where those convicted may lose welfare aid, but since there is a link between the offence and the right that is deprived, the exclusion measured by the item is not met here.

As can be seen from the graph, New York State, England and Wales and Poland are the most exclusionary jurisdictions in terms of depriving prisoners and ex-prisoners of their civil and social rights, as they accumulate the highest number of affirmative responses.

52 In fact, there is a guide published by the British government to support prison leavers that clarifies in detail how to apply for such credit: *"Prison Leavers: a guide to Universal Credit"*. www.gov.uk/government/publications/universal-credit-and-prison-leavers/supporting-prison-leavers-a-guide-to-universal-credit

53 Drug Policy Alliance (2015). https://drugpolicy.org/blog/california-lifts-ban-public-assistance-people-drug-convictions

54 California Department of Social Service. Changes for People with a Prior Felony Drug Conviction. https://www.cdss.ca.gov/cdssweb/entres/forms/English/Temp3005.pdf

55 Kovel, M. (2015). *The Consequences Of Criminal Proceedings In New York State, A Comprehensively Updated Guide for Criminal Defense Attorneys, Civil Legal Services Attorneys, and Other Reentry Advocates.* The Bronx Defenders. https://www.reentry.net/ny/library/item.76898-Consequences_of_Criminal_Proceedings_in_New_York_State_August_2014_The_Bron

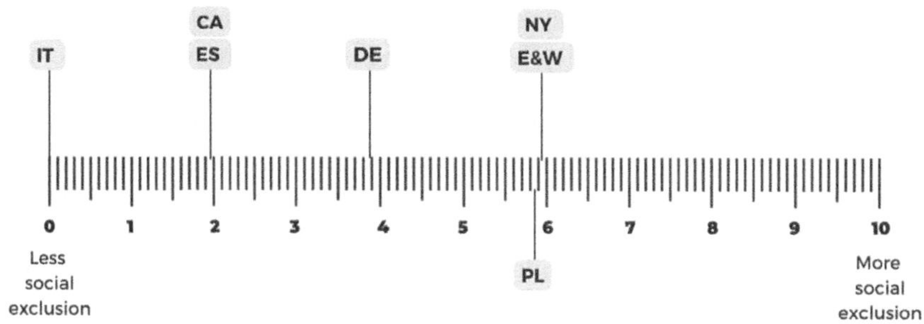

Figure 12.1 Position of the countries in the continuum of exclusion, according to pool 7

5 Conclusions

The analysis of national regulations through the rigorous operationalisation of each item in the RIMES instrument has allowed us to acquire an excellent understanding of the level of exclusion of former convicts as regards their political, labour and civil participation and their access to the resources of the welfare state in each country. Therefore, we may conclude that the exclusion of foreign convicts and ex-convicts is the most common in the countries studied, followed by labour exclusion and exclusion from access to social housing. On the other hand, exclusion from the right to vote is not common in these same countries, nor is deprivation of the right to receive social benefits, although additional conditions for access may be imposed on convicts and ex-convicts that do not exist for non-convicted persons.

The analysis process has not been easy. The fact that deprivation of each right may be regulated in criminal or administrative legislation implies the need to locate, handle and understand a wide range of laws (penal, electoral, foreigners, labour, public housing and social benefits) that are not always easy to access, especially when the texts are not available in English. In addition, the fact that competence to regulate access to the rights under study often falls on regional or municipal authorities, has forced us to repeat the search for information at multiple geographical levels in order to find out a response that may be representative of the country.

On the other hand, since the requirements established in the items' definitions are so precise regarding the type of offences and penalties, the term of the deprivation or the type of discretion authorities have for their application, it was necessary to understand very well all the potential assumptions to be able to decide in a well-founded way which ones fit into the requirements of the item and which ones, although maybe also exclusionary, do not reach the level of exclusion measured by the item. This aspect leads us to reflect on the discrimination capacity of the items in this pool, because if we only look at the final result of implementing the instrument, some exclusions that may affect a significant number of ex-convicts may remain hidden. A good example of this would be the case of exclusion of access to public housing in San Francisco (United States), where the list of offences for which people with a criminal record can be deprived of the right to social housing is extremely extensive, although it is not 'for any offence'.

Finally, it is important to highlight that as this pool is only made up of rules, we have not been able to delve into how they are applied in practice. It would be interesting to have the opportunity to study this aspect in depth in the future, especially in those cases where the rule raises the need for legal operators to make an effort of individualisation, taking into account the personal and social circumstances of the individuals before taking their decision. This is a key aspect, in line with those authors who warned that if these deprivations of rights are applied indiscriminately, they become sanctions, which are not only exclusionary, but also immoral.

References

Bae, J., Dizerega, M., Kang-Brown, J., Shanahan, R., & Subramanian, R. (2016). *Coming Home. An Evaluation of the New York Housing Authority's Family Reentry Pilot Program*. Vera Institute of Justice.

Bennett, C. (2017). Invisible Punishment Is Wrong – But Why? The Normative Basis of Criticism of Collateral Consequences of Criminal Conviction. *The Howard Journal of Crime and Justice*, 56(4), 480–499. https://doi. org/10.1111/hojo.12230

Brown, J. M. (2020). Collateral Legal Consequences of Criminal Convictions in a Society of Equals. *Criminal Law and Philosophy*, 15, 181–205. https://doi.org/10.1007/s11572-020-09544-7

Colgate Love, M. (2005). *Relief from the Collateral Consequences of a Criminal Conviction: A State-by-State Resource Guide*. William s Hein & Co.

Díez-Ripollés, J. L. (2014). Sanciones adicionales a delincuentes y exdelincuentes. *InDret*, 4.

García-España, E. (2017). Extranjeros sospechosos, condenados y excondenados: un mosaico de exclusión social. *Revista Electrónica de Ciencia Penal y Criminología*, 19(15), 1–30.

Hoskins, Z. (2017). Criminalization and the Collateral Consequences of Conviction. *Criminal Law and Philosophy*, 12, 625–639. https://doi.org/10.1007/s11572-017-9449-2

Ianelli, J. (2020). New York City's Public Housing Rules Could Force Many Released Prisoners into Homelessness. *The Appeal*. Available at: https://theappeal.org/new-york-public-housing-decarceration/

Kovel, M. (2015). *The Consequences Of Criminal Proceedings In New York State, A Comprehensively Updated Guide for Criminal Defense Attorneys, Civil Legal Services Attorneys, and Other Reentry Advocates*. The Bronx Defenders. https://www.reentry.net/ny/library/item.76898-Consequences_of_Criminal_Proceedings_in_New_York_State_August_2014_The_Bron

Krausnick, B. (2020). *Bundesbeamtegesetz Kommentar*, § 24, 20a ed. Kyvsgaard, B. (2004). Youth Justice in Denmark. *Crime and Justice*, 31, 349–390. https://doi.org/10.1086/655344

Larrauri, E. (2013). ¿En qué empleos se exigen los antecedentes penales? *Revista Electrónica de Ciencia Penal y Criminología*, 15, 1–14.

Mele, C., & Miller, T. A. (2013). Collateral civil penalties as techniques of social policy. In *Civil Penalties, Social Consequences* (pp. 9–26). Routledge.

Miermeister, F. (2020). *Bundesnotarordnung Kommentar*. C.H. Beck Verlag. 5a edition.

Penal Reform International (2016). *The Right of Prisoners to Vote: A Global Overview*. Penal Reform International. https://cdn.penalreform.org/wp-content/uploads/2016/08/The-right-of-prisoners-to-vote_March-2016.pdf

Petersilia, J. (2003). *When Prisoners Come Home*. Oxford University Press.

Pinard, M. (2010). Collateral Consequences of Criminal Convictions: Confronting Issues of Race and Dignity. *New York University Law Review*, 85, 457–534.

Tran-Leung, M. (2015). *When Discretion Means Denial: A National Perspective on Criminal Records Barriers to Federally Subsidized Housing*. Sargent Shriver Center on Poverty Law.

Travis, J. (2002). Invisible punishment: An instrument of social exclusion. In Mauer, M., & Chesney-Lind, M. (eds.) *Invisible Punishment. The Collateral Consequences of Mass Imprisonment* (pp. 15–36). The New Press.

Uggen, C., & Manza, J. (2002). Democratic Contraction? Political Consequences of Felon Disenfranchisement in the United States. *American Sociological Review*, 67(6), 777–803.

Uggen, C., Manza, J., & Thompson, M. (2006). Citizenship, Democracy and the Civic Reintegration of Criminal Offenders. *Annals of the American Academy of Political and Social Science*, 605(1), 281–310.

13 Pool 8

Police and criminal records

Juan Antonio Aguilar-Jurado

1 Introduction

The eighth pool of RIMES, on police and criminal records, provides a suitable framework of analysis that matches the purpose of the instrument, since it is an area where it is possible to identify rules and practices that can generate socially exclusionary effects on the groups under study. In this sense, some authors have warned of the harmful consequences that can result from having a criminal history in some countries. In particular, individuals with criminal records may be deprived of certain social, political and civil rights, mainly related to access to employment and to public benefits (Larrauri and Jacobs, 2011; Díez-Ripollés, 2014). Similarly, the disclosure of criminal records is a violation of the right to privacy, and may even have a negative impact on the right to the presumption of innocence (Larrauri, 2014). All of this places the persons concerned in a position of exclusion with respect to the rest, in turn undermining their possibilities of resocialisation and reintegration into society.

Certain items, such as the legitimacy of specific players to request criminal records, the ease of access to them by any citizen, and the media treatment of the personal data of ex-offenders – which are the ones that make up this pool – can be perfectly analysed empirically, and allow comparisons to be established among the countries under study, to the extent that such items are verified or not.

For all these reasons, we are dealing with a pool that is essential for the task of measuring the exclusion generated by states, since the way in which countries manage the police and criminal records of their citizens – as regards their accessibility and capacity for discrimination or impairment of rights – can lead people to positions of exclusion and social alienation.

2 The pool building process

At the beginning of the project, the pool of this chapter consisted of seven items (four rules and three practices), which were as follows:

Item 99: private employers which are not related to private security companies or to those working with children or vulnerable adults are entitled to request information about criminal records to potential employees.

DOI: 10.4324/9781032661766-16

Item 100: anyone may request information about other people's criminal records without needing to argue grounds established by law.

Item 101: the criminal records of any citizen are legally accessible through Internet.

Item 102: law enforcement authorities are obliged to report the whereabouts of some ex-felons to the community or NGOs.

Item 106: private employers which are not related to private security companies or to those working with children or vulnerable adults regularly request information about criminal records to potential employees or to the relevant public bodies.

Item 107: the media regularly disclose the full names, current addresses or pictures of ex-felons.

Item 110: most companies with over 100 employees require a clean criminal record for recruitment.

In the validation carried out in the first turn by the experts, all the items obtained good scores with respect to the criteria of suitability and clarity, except item 106, which got an Aiken's V coefficient for clarity below 0.70 (0.52). After the validation results and once the second turn was completed, it was decided that the items to be included in the final instrument were numbers 100, 101, 107 and 110. With regard to the latter, the team discussed whether it should be included, as it might be excessively difficult to respond. But it concluded that, despite being a complicated item, its response was feasible (RIMES Project, 2018, p. 294 and 302). However, during the application of the RIMES instrument in Spain, this item presented important methodological difficulties related to data access, so the results obtained were not deemed conclusive. It was noted that these problems would probably arise when working on the item in the other countries, so it was finally decided to replace it with item 99, taking into account that the latter addresses the same issue as item 110 and that, in addition to being easier to answer as it is a rule, it had obtained good Aiken's V values (García-España and Díez-Ripollés, 2021, p. 275). After all this, the pool definitively consisted of items 99, 100, 101 and 107.

The items that finally make up this pool are described below. These descriptions were drafted and discussed by the entire team in work meetings, to clarify the meaning of each item and avoid any confusion. The descriptions shown here are from the project manual.

Item 99: private employers which are not related to private security companies or to those working with children or vulnerable adults are entitled to request information about criminal records to potential employees.

With regard to item 99, it was discussed whether the phrase "or are in contact with them" (referred to minors) was too generic, and it was decided to maintain the wording, since in this way the item includes more exclusionary assumptions. The need to clarify the concept of "vulnerable adults" was also raised, and it was determined that, if during the resolution of this item there were problems in this regard, it would be discussed again. And this was finally not necessary. In addition, the possibility that this item was too extensive was discussed, to the effect that its description could include elements of other items not included in the final instrument, and there was a possible duplication with item 100. The team agreed to retain the original wording as it saw no problems in such aspects.

Item 100: anyone may request information about other people's criminal records without needing to argue grounds established by law.

As for the description of item 100, the original wording included the term "corporation" in the first paragraph; and it was decided to remove it. The concept of "grounds established by law" was also clarified indicating that, if it was necessary to pay a moderate fee to have access to a criminal record, this would be deemed to be included in the item.

Item 101: the criminal records of any citizen are legally accessible through internet.

Regarding the description of item 101, a possible overlap with item 100 was raised, but it was concluded that the latter refers to requesting criminal records in an office or through the Internet, while item 101 refers to the fact that the records are available and accessible to anyone on the Internet, without the need the submit an application to the administration. With regard to cases where payment is required in order to access the criminal register, it was mentioned that this should be a significant amount. Doubts were also cleared up regarding the type of criminal record included in this item. It was agreed that the description should be supplemented with the phrase "the item is also met when only some kinds of criminal records are accessible".

Item 107: the media regularly disclose the full names, current addresses or pictures of ex-felons.

Finally, in the description of item 107, the core issue was about the implication of the term "regularly", deciding on a minimum percentage of news items containing personal information about ex-offenders out of the total number of news items about ex-offenders for the item to be fulfilled: 35 per cent. Besides, for the cases of California and New York, the question was raised about whether to resort to state or federal media. It was decided that the former should be taken into account, given that in the project both states were considered as countries, excluding emblematic cases that could have media coverage in several states. The description remained unchanged after this discussion.

3 Methodology used to solve each pool's item in each country

Item 99

The methodology used to solve this item has been similar in each of the countries studied. Specifically, current legislation has been consulted, together with certain reports, scientific articles and Internet pages on the subject.

In Spain, we revised Royal Decree 95/2009, of 6 February, regulating the system of administrative records to support the Administration of Justice, and Organic Law 7/2014, of 12 November, on the exchange of information on criminal records and the recognition of criminal judgments in the European Union. Two scientific articles were also consulted: one by Professor Larrauri and another one by Professor Rovira i Sopeña.

In Germany, the Central Criminal Register Act and the Register of Educational Measures (Bundeszentralregistergesetz or BZRG) were revised. That is where the different types of criminal record certificates are established and where entities and individuals can apply for them, among other things. A consultation has also been carried out regarding the Federal Data Protection Act (Bundesdatenschutzgesetz or BSDG), which sets certain limits on the processing of this kind of information. Finally, some Internet websites containing information on this matter were examined.

In California, a simple search with respect to regulations was carried out on the official website of California Legislative Information, and the item was resolved on the basis of the provisions set forth in Assembly Bill No. 1008, approved in 2017.

As regards Italy, the revision mainly focused on Presidential Decree No. 313, of 14 November 2002, concerning criminal records, European criminal records, the register of administrative sanctions resulting from offences and related pending charges (Decreto del Presidente della Repubblica 14 Novembre 2002, n. 313. Testo unico delle disposizioni legislative e regolamentari in materia di casellario giudiziale, di anagrafe delle sanzioni amministrative dipendenti da reato e dei relativi carichi pendenti). In addition, some websites were consulted to complement and clarify such regulation's content.

In New York, a major review of the current regulations has been carried out. At state level there is no specific legislation regarding the issue expressed in the item (although the so-called New York State Correction Law and Executive Law 296 have been analysed). Therefore, the regulations referred to the city of New York have been consulted; specifically, the Fair Chance Act and Executive Order 151.

As far as Poland is concerned, information has been collected, first from the websites of the National Register of Convicted Persons (Krajowy Rejestr Karny or KRK) and the Register of Sex Offenders (Rejestr Sprawców Przestępstw na Tle Seksualnym); and secondly, from the following regulations: Labour Code (Kodeks Pracy), Law of 24 October 2017 on Amendments to the Financial Sector's Legislation (Ustawa z dnia 24 listopada 2017 r.

o zmianie niektórych ustaw w celu przeciwdziałania wykorzystywaniu sektora finansowego do wyłudzeń skarbowych), and Law of 13 May 2016 on countering sexual offences threats (Ustawa z dnia 13 maja 2016 r. o przeciwdzialaniu zagrozeniom przestepczoscia na tle seksualnym).

Finally, in England and Wales different sources were also examined, mainly legislation and public reports. Specifically, the Police Act 1997, the EU General Data Protection Regulation (GDPR) (Regulation 2016/679), the Rehabilitation of Offenders Act 1974, as well as the Disclosing Criminal Records guide, and the report "Unlock for people conviction. A question of fairness. Research into employers asking about criminal records at application stage".

Item 100

This item was resolved in a similar way to the previous one, i.e., by reviewing the legislation on the subject, although some official websites have also been consulted.

In Spain, a significant number of regulations have been consulted, specifically: the Criminal Procedure Law, the Criminal Code, Organic Law 39/2015, of 1 October, on the common administrative procedure of Public Administrations, Law 19/2013, of 9 December, on transparency, access to public information and good governance, Organic Law 15/1999, of 13 December, on the protection of personal data, amended by Law 62/2003, of 30 December, and Royal Decree 1720/2007, of 21 December, approving the Regulation for the development of Organic Law 15/1999, as well as Instruction 1/1998, of 19 January, of the Data Protection Agency, regarding the exercise of rights of access, rectification and cancellation (Spanish State Gazette -BOE- No. 25, of 29 January).

In Germany, a re-examination of the Central Criminal Register Act and the Register of Educational Measures was enough, as it allowed to find the response to this item without major complications.

In California, Megan's Law was analysed. This is a federal law regulating information about the criminal records of sex offenders. As a complement, a random search was carried out on the official website of Megan's Law for the State of California, under the Department of Justice, to verify if anyone can access such criminal records.

With regard to Italy, the methodology used was practically the same as that of item 99: a review of Presidential Decree No. 313, of 14 November 2002, concerning criminal records, European criminal records, the register of administrative sanctions resulting from offences and related pending charges.

As for New York, two official websites were inspected: the Office of Court Administration (OCA) – which has a search engine called New York Statewide Criminal History and Record Search (CHRS) – and the New York State Records.

In Poland, a methodology similar to that of item 99 has also been used. Consultations focused on the websites of the National Register of Convicted

Persons and the Register of Sex Offenders, as well as Law of 29 August 1997 on the Protection of Personal Data and the National Criminal Records Act, of the year 2000 (Ustawa z dnia 24 maja 2000 r. or Krajowym Rejestrze Karnym).

Finally, in England and Wales, only the EU General Data Protection Regulation (GDPR) (Regulation 2016/679) has been revised, which sufficed to obtain responses to the item.

Item 101

The methods used to solve this item have not differed substantially from those used previously. The techniques used have again consisted of revising regulations and consulting official websites.

In Spain, the Penal Code, Organic Law 15/1999, of 13 December, on the protection of personal data, and Royal Decree 95/2009, of 6 February, regulating the system of administrative records to support the Administration of Justice have been consulted.

In Germany, reference has been made to the legislation discussed in previous items, especially as regards the Federal Data Protection Act.

In California, on the one hand, regulations on this matter have been consulted; specifically, the Public Records Act, the Penal Code, and Megan's Law. On the other hand, a revision was made of two websites that allow access to the criminal records of third parties: the California State Records site and the official portal of Megan's Law for the State of California.

As far as Italy is concerned, Presidential Decree No. 313, of 14 November 2002, concerning criminal records, European criminal records, the register of administrative sanctions resulting from offences and related pending charges has been further revised and, in addition, a consultation has been carried out of the Visureinrete website, which contains information on the application process of such records.

With relation to New York, a revision was conducted of the New York State Public Officers Law, and of the governmental website the New York State Department of Criminal Justice Services, as well as – like for the previous item – the New York Statewide Criminal History Record Search (CHRS) and the New York State Records.

In Poland, the methodology used has been very similar to that of the previous item: the websites of the National Register of Convicted Persons and the Register of Sex Offenders have been consulted, as well as the Law of 13 May 2016 on countering the sexual offences threats.

Finally, in England and Wales, the EU General Data Protection Regulation (GDPR) (Regulation 2016/679) has been revised again, and a consultation was undertaken regarding two criminal record databases, the Police National Computer (PNC) and the Police National Database (PND), as well as the website of the Criminal Records Office (ACRO).

Item 107, which represents the only practice of this pool, is one of the most complex indicators of the entire RIMES instrument, as, by its very nature, it requires a great effort, including the search and filtering of news items, their subsequent review, categorisation and analysis of the results. The methodological procedure has been subject to important discussions by the team and, although each country has had to adapt to its particularities, a standard strategy for dealing with the item has been established. Such strategy essentially consists of using the national news search engines (of each country) and, with a keyword – usually "offender" or "ex-offender" – in the appropriate language, accessing the amount of resulting news. Subsequently, each news item is reviewed and classified one by one, according to the following colour criteria: gray, news that are relevant due to their context; orange, news referring to ex-offenders, but not disclosing personal information; green, news that comply with the item; red, news not referring to ex-offenders; blue, news that are not available. Finally, to obtain the percentage of news that disclose personal data of ex-offenders, and thus respond to the item, the following formula is used:

$$\% = \frac{n = news \in greencolour}{N = newsonex - offenders\left(greencolour + orangecolour\right)} 100$$

In Spain, the MyNews tool has been used, which is an electronic media library of modern printed press including more than 1,400 sources of printed and digital press. A search was conducted for news items of 2015 to 2017, alternating months, and using the keyword "condenado" (convicted). The search was limited to local and regional newspapers, as they are more likely to contain personal information about the ex-offenders, given the proximity of the events covered by such news. A total of 20,835 news items were analysed (6,772 from 2015, 6,611 from 2016 and 7,452 from 2017).

In Germany, the Press Reader search engine was used, as using ProQuest International Newsstream was impossible, since it only accessed a very limited number of national newspapers. A news search was conducted from 2018 to 2020, using the keyword "verurteil" (convicted), with the selected regional newspapers Rheinische Zeitung and Abendzeitung München. Due to the huge amount of news found, only six months per year were reviewed, alternating months. The total news items finally revised was 1,391 (487 from 2018, 525 from 2019 and 379 from 2020).

In California, the ProQuest Central tool was used, which included an extremely large number of news stories from newspapers worldwide. In this case, a news search was carried out from 2017 to 2019. Instead of using the term "ex-felon" (ex-offender or ex-convicted), the keyword "felon" (offender or convicted) was used, since the latter includes the former, while otherwise it does not. Out of the total available newspapers, namely: East Bay Times, Los Angeles Times, The Mercury News, Inland Valley Daily Bulletin, San Gabriel Valley Tribune, Visalia Times-Delta, Redlands Daily Facts, The Press

Democrat, Orange County Register, Pasadena Star-News, Daily Press and The Examiner, those discarded were: Los Angeles Times, The Press Democrat, Daily Press and The Examiner, since they are not regional newspapers and also cover news from other states and countries. Orange County Register was discarded as it did not provide the full text of the news. After the selection, 991 news items were analysed (368 from 2017, 325 from 2018 and 298 from 2019).

Regarding Italy, a search was made firstly of regional newspapers, among which only the Gazzetta del Sud was chosen, because it is one of the most important in southern Italy, and because it is the only one that allows a simple search based on keywords. The term used was "condannato" ("convicted"). Then, since there was no time filter, the news items corresponding to the years 2017, 2018 and 2019 were manually identified. Finally, they were reviewed, alternating the months. There was a total of 746 news items (232 from 2017, 221 from 2018 and 293 from 2019).

In New York, the ProQuest International Newsstream tool was used, conducting a news search with the keyword "felon" (as in California), for the years 2017 to 2019. The search found the following newspapers: New York Post, New York Times, New York Daily News, Rochester Democrat and Chronicle, The Journal News, and Newsday. The first of these, New York Post, was discarded, as it could not be downloaded. In addition, from the New York Times only news items referring to the state of New York were taken into account. In spite of all this, the final sample of news reviewed amounted to 433 (122 from 2017, 203 from 2018 and 108 from 2019).

Handling the item in Poland applied a more unique methodological procedure, and entailed, in general, greater difficulties than in the rest of the countries, mainly at the time of obtaining a significant news sample. First, we contacted Barbara Błońska, assistant professor in the Department of Criminology and Criminal Policy at the Institute of Social Prevention and Rehabilitation at the University of Warsaw, so that she could provide advice on the most relevant Polish newspapers, as well as on the keywords needed to obtain the best results in the news search. The newspapers chosen were Gazeta Wyborcza, SuperEkspres and Fakt, and the keywords, "były przestępca", "przestępca" and "kryminalista" ("ex-offender"); "były skazany", "skazany" and "skazaniec" ("ex-convict"); "były więzień" ("ex-prisoner"); "wypuszczony z więzienia" and "zwolniony z więzienia" ("released from prison"). The use of the ProQuest tool was ruled out, as it only gave access to a single national newspaper. Conversely, and as in Germany, the PressReader tool was decided to be used, because it includes national and regional newspapers. Secondly, we selected the news found for the period from 2017 to 2019. The total of news finally reviewed was 77. Since this figure was particularly low, it was discussed in some meetings of the team. In the end it was decided that the number was sufficient, since the methodological procedure had been correctly applied and the analysed news items were in line with the general trend.

To conclude, in England & Wales the search engine ProQuest International Newsstream was also used. News from 2017, 2018 and 2019 were accessed using the keyword "convicted". The term "felon" was not used, as it is rare in British English. The Northern Echo was selected, which is a very relevant newspaper covering both national and regional news. Finally, 678 news items regarding this territory were reviewed (281 from 2017, 204 from 2018 and 256 from 2019).

4 Results of the pool's items in each country

This first section includes global results, and later on, the results of each item will be analysed individually, in successive sections.

Table 13.1 shows the findings obtained after solving the items of this eighth pool:

Table 13.1 Results of pool 8, by item and country

	Germany	*California*	*Spain*	*Italy*	*New York*	*Poland*	*England & Wales*
Item 99	Yes	Yes	Yes	No	Yes	Yes	Yes
Item 100	No	Yes	No	No	Yes	Yes	No
Item 101	No	Yes	No	No	Yes	Yes	No
Item 107	Yes	Yes	Yes	Yes	Yes	No	Yes

Source: Own elaboration

The items with the lowest discrimination are numbers 99 and 107, since they have been answered in the affirmative in all countries, except 99 in Italy and 107 in Poland. Item 100 is met in California, New York and Poland, while it is not fulfilled in Spain, Germany, Italy and England & Wales. Item 101 is met in California, New York and Poland, but is not fulfilled in Spain, Germany, England and Wales and Italy. These two latter items are, therefore, those with the greatest capacity for discrimination.

Figure 13.1 shows a graph with the position of countries on a continuum of social exclusion, according to the weighting of this pool:

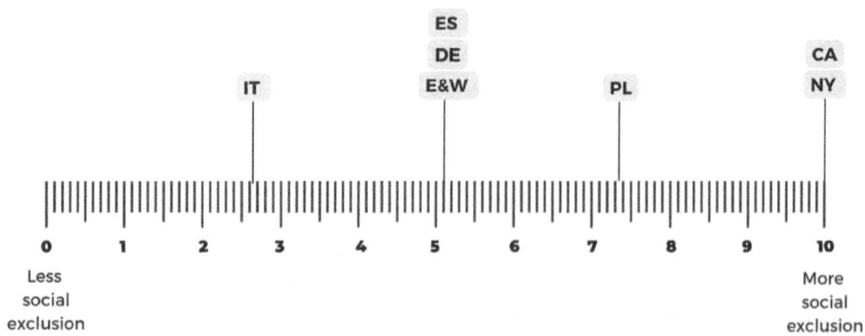

Figure 13.1 Position of countries within the continuum of social exclusion in terms of police and criminal records

In this scale from 0 to 10 – where 0 means "less social exclusion", and 10 "more social exclusion" – we can see that California and New York are placed at the end of greatest exclusion (with a score of 10), followed by Poland (with 7.37), then by Spain, Germany and England (5.1), and finally by Italy (with only a score of 2.63).

Item 99

In Spain, the law does not expressly prohibit companies from requesting the criminal records of prospective employees, although it is not entirely clear whether this means there is a right to request such information. Rovira i Sopeña (2016) has studied the judicial rulings on this matter and concludes that, although there is not much jurisprudence in this regard, all the judgments are in favour of requiring criminal records in personnel recruitment processes. That is why this item is met in Spain.

In Germany, according to article 30 et seq. of the Central Criminal Register Act and the Register of Educational Measures, there are three types of criminal record certificates that can applied for: one for private matters, that can only be required by private entities; one for public matters, that can be required by the State administrations; and another, a specific one, necessary for people working with minors. The first one matches the description of the item. Therefore, in Germany the law allows any private company to request a criminal record certificate from potential employees. However, Article 26.1 of the Federal Data Protection Act states that the information requested must relate to the job in question. Thus, the answer to this item is affirmative in this country.

As for Poland, according to the provisions of the Law amending the Financial Sector's Legislation, any private company may require a criminal record certificate from potential employees. This certificate cannot be older than three months, and must reflect that the candidate has not been convicted of the following offences: crimes against property, those related to the protection of documents and information, to economic security, to financial exchanges, infringement of market rules or payment services. Besides, companies can reject a job applicant if he or she refuses to deliver this certificate. Therefore, this item is fulfilled in this country.

In the case of England and Wales, private companies may request the criminal records of potential workers for the professions listed in the Rehabilitation of Offenders Act 1974: health professions, financial sector employment, jobs related to the legal sector and the veterinary profession.[1] There is also the possibility of requiring a criminal record certificate outside of these cases, but only with regard to those convictions that have not yet reached the period of time established by the law ("unspent convictions"), and that cannot be deleted from the records. In these cases, according to the General Data Protection

1 Professions related to minors, vulnerable adults and private security are also included, but these are left out of the item.

Regulation, the need to obtain and verify this information must be justified. Therefore, this item is answered in the affirmative.

In California private companies are allowed to ask for a criminal record certificate from future workers, with the exception of entities with more than five employees, which can only do so at the end of the process, according to Assembly Bill No. 1008, which establishes what is commonly known as "ban the box" (removing the criminal background check box on job applications). Therefore, in California this item is also fulfilled.

In New York, although there is no specific legislation prohibiting companies from requesting a criminal record certificate from potential workers, Executive Law 296, in its article 15, establishes that rejecting an applicant simply because he or she has a record is a discriminatory practice. In turn, article 23 of the New York State Correction Law includes a number of elements that companies must take into account before discarding a candidate who has a criminal record, such as the time that has elapsed since the offence was committed, its seriousness and whether the person has reports proving their rehabilitation, among others. Besides, as in California, companies are prohibited – through the Fair Chance Act – from investigating criminal records at the beginning of the selection process ("ban the box"). Thus, this item is met.

Finally, in Italy, according to Presidential Decree No 313, of 14 November 2002, concerning criminal records, European criminal records, the register of administrative sanctions resulting from offences and related pending charges, a criminal record certificate may only be requested for persons applying for a job whose activity involves frequent contact with minors, excluding any other case. Consequently, this item is not fulfilled in Italy.

Item 100

In Poland, in addition to what has been said in item 99 regarding private companies, only some public entities and institutions may access any criminal record of certain persons (in general, those opting for certain public jobs, related to the justice system or the education system, among others), according to article 6 of the National Criminal Records Act. Any other citizen can only consult the criminal records related to sexual crimes, through the Register of Sex Offenders, created in 2016, where one of its parts is publicly accessible, and anyone can view information about this type of offences and their perpetrators. Therefore, this item is met.

This item is also answered in the affirmative in California, since Megan's Law allows anyone to access the criminal records of sex offenders, free of charge and without having to justify their purpose. Through a random search on the official website of Megan's Law for the State of California, it has been proved that it is indeed possible to visualise such information. Specifically, the following data can be obtained: name and picture of the individual, date of birth, sex, height, weight, eye colour, hair colour, ethnicity, article of the penal code infringed, description of the offence, year of conviction and year of release.

In New York there is also the possibility for anyone to access the criminal record of a third party, at least through two different ways. On the one hand, via the New York Statewide Criminal History Record Search (CHRS), paying a fee of 95 dollars. On the other hand, through the New York State Records, paying only 15 dollars for the consultation. No justification is necessary in any of the two cases, so this item is met.

In Spain, article 136.4 of the Criminal Code establishes that criminal records are not public. Likewise, according to articles 5 and 6 of Royal Decree 95/2009, of 6 February, regulating the system of administrative records to support the Administration of Justice, criminal records are only accessible to courts, certain police units, and to those persons who wish to consult their own background. Therefore, this item is not met in Spain.

With regard to Italy, the aforementioned Presidential Decree No. 313, of 14 November 2002, concerning criminal records, European criminal records, the register of administrative sanctions resulting from offences and related pending charges, prevents anyone from accessing the criminal records of a third party, this being only possible for private companies that work with minors, as we saw in item 99. That is why this item is not fulfilled here.

In Germany, article 30.4 of the Central Criminal Register Act and the Register of Educational Measures stipulate that, in general, criminal record certificates may only be sent to the person to whom such record relates. However, they may be issued to a third person in a professional context related to the supervision, care, education or training of minors (article 30a). In addition, article 41 authorises certain government agencies and other bodies of the justice system to access the criminal records of any individual, and article 42a allows access to this information for scientific purposes. Therefore, the item is not fulfilled.

Finally, in England and Wales no citizen can access the criminal record of a third party without complying with the requirements established by the General Data Protection Regulation. In essence, those conditions mean that only those who are authorised to do so (official bodies or private companies, as seen in item 99) can obtain such records. For this reason, the item is not met here.

Item 101

In Spain, as already mentioned, criminal records are not public, and allow limited access to judges, prosecutors and judicial police, as well as to the person concerned. In short, and according to the Spanish legislation, criminal records are not available to the public, so this item is not fulfilled.

In Italy, as seen in items 99 and 100, Presidential Decree No. 313, of 14 November 2002, concerning criminal records, European criminal records, and the register of administrative sanctions limits access to the records of third parties; only authorised entities are allowed to do so, i.e., private companies whose work activity involves frequent contact with minors. Therefore, there are no public lists on the Internet and, for this reason, the item is not fulfilled in this country.

In Germany, as can be seen from items 99 and 100, access to citizens' criminal background is very limited, so not everyone can access the criminal records of others. However, due to a very mediatic case of sexual abuse of a child in the state of Saxony, a few years ago, there was a proposal to create a public list of sex offenders, although to date this has not been successful, mainly because it is contrary to the Federal Data Protection Act. That is why this item is not fulfilled.

As for England and Wales, this item is not met, given that citizens cannot access the criminal records of third parties. And, besides, although there are two police databases that collect the criminal background of citizens – the Police National Computer (PNC) and the Police National Database (PND) – neither of them has an Internet portal.

Regarding Poland, as seen in item 100, there is a Register of Sex Offenders, created in 2016, which has a website where anyone can view the criminal records of this type of offenders, for free. Mind you, the information that can be consulted is limited to records on offenders convicted of rape of children under fifteen years of age and repeat sex offenders. However, the answer to this item is in the affirmative.

As to California, the Public Records Act states that "Californians have the right, under the Public Records Act of the State and the California Constitution, to access public information managed by state and local government agencies, including the Department of Justice". However, criminal records are not considered public records, so in principle, citizens can only access their own criminal history, and not that of others. But as seen in item 100, Megan's Law, allows anyone to consult the criminal records of sex offenders through its website and, in addition, other Internet portals, which do not belong to the public sector, such as California State Records, offer anyone the possibility of accessing an extensive background database. Thus, the item is fulfilled.

Finally, in New York, according to article 6, section 84, of the New York State Public Officers Law, any citizen may access public records held by government agencies, including law enforcement authorities. Criminal histories are part of those records, and as seen in item 100, they are available on the Internet to any citizen who wants to consult them, for example, in the New York Statewide Criminal History Record Search, or on the website of the New York State Records. Therefore, this item is fulfilled.

Item 107

In Spain, the percentage of analysed news items containing personal information about ex-offenders over the total news about ex-offenders, largely exceeds 35 per cent in all the years under study: 87.7 per cent in 2015, 66.6 per cent in 2016 and 100 per cent in 2017. This item is therefore fulfilled.

In Italy, the item is also answered in the affirmative, with very high percentages of news disclosing personal information of ex-offenders: 100 per cent in 2017, 95 per cent in 2018 and 100 per cent in 2019.

In the case of Germany, the same percentage amounts to 42.3 per cent in 2018, 45.2 per cent in 2019 and 34.4 per cent in 2020. Since the parameter to be taken into account was 35 per cent, it was decided that this item was fulfilled.

In England and Wales such percentages are also very high: 95.6 per cent in 2017, 92.6 per cent in 2018 and 95.4 per cent in 2019, so the item is met.

As far as California is concerned, this percentage is well above the 35 per cent established as baseline. Specifically, it is 95.4 per cent in 2017, 92.5 per cent in 2018 and 89.4 per cent in 2019. Therefore, the personal data of ex-offenders are frequently disclosed in the media, so the item is fulfilled here.

As for New York, the percentages are as follows: 75.9 per cent in 2017, 75 per cent in 2018 and 70.5 per cent in 2019. Therefore, the item is met.

Finally, in Poland, of all the news items analysed, none was classified with the green colour, so this item is not met.

5 Conclusions

We can say that, in general, all the items of this pool have an important discrimination capacity, since none of them has been answered in the positive or negative ("yes/no") in all countries at the same time. That is why this pool is adequate or suitable to measure social exclusion in the area covered by it – police and criminal records. Only items 99 and 107 have been answered in the affirmative in all but one country, so they are the least discriminatory. These items refer to the legitimacy of private companies to request a criminal record certificate from future employees, and to disclose personal information of ex-offenders in the media, respectively. Hence, both aspects that generate social exclusion are frequent in the countries analysed. The remaining items – 100 and 101 – show more varied results or, in other words, they are the ones that discriminate the most in the entire pool.

The results obtained after analysing the items that make up this pool allow us to detect a number of trends. The most exclusionary territories are California and New York, where all the analysed items are fulfilled. Therefore, the management conducted by these states of their citizens' criminal records is certainly worrying, and matches what some authors – such as Larrauri, Jacobs and Díez-Ripollés – had already pointed out. They are followed by Poland, with three out of four items fulfilled, and then Spain, Germany and England and Wales with two out of four. The least exclusionary country in this respect is Italy, where only item 107 is met. In this context, Presidential Decree No. 313 offers great regulatory protection regarding access to criminal records, something that is lacking in the remaining countries under study, particularly the two North American states.

It is difficult to evaluate the results according to whether the items are rules or practices, since this pool consists of three rules (99, 100 and 101) and only one practice (107), although it is true that, out of the three rules, only one (99) generates social exclusion at the same level as the practice, where all countries but one, meet the item (85.7 per cent). Instead, the remaining two rules produce, in general, little social exclusion, since only three out of the seven analysed countries fulfill the item (42.8 per cent).

In short, the items of this pool show relevant differences in the levels of social exclusion applied in the countries under study, which is a good indicator that this pool is adequate from a perspective of criminal policy analysis.

References

Díez-Ripollés, J.L. (2014). Sanciones adicionales a delincuentes y exdelincuentes. *In-Dret*, 4.

García-España, E. & Díez-Ripollés, J.L. (2021). La exclusión social generada por el sistema penal español: Aplicación del instrumento RIMES. *In-Dret*, 1, 259–281.

Larrauri, E. (2014). Are Police Records Criminal Records? *European Journal of Crime, Criminal Law and Criminal Justice*, 22(4), 377–395. https://doi.org/10.1163/15718174-22042055

Larrauri, E. & Jacobs, J. (2011). Reinserción laboral y antecedentes penales. *Revista Electrónica de Ciencia Penal y Criminología*, 13(9), 1–25.

RIMES Project (2018). *Executive Report.* Unpublished.

Rovira, M. (2016). *Antecedentes penales y mercado laboral.* [Doctoral Thesis, Universitat Pompeu Fabra]. Institutional repository – Universitat Pompeu Fabra.

14 Pool 9

Youth criminal justice

Fátima Pérez-Jiménez

1 The role of youth criminal justice in the context of social exclusion

In the theoretical presentation of this study, we have analysed the different goals and arguments driving each decision taken to formalise the research project at hand. Looking at this broad content from the specific perspective of criminal justice system for juveniles, we highlight some of the elements that justify the inclusion of this pool's subject matter in the investigation and how its results can contribute to the debate on criminal policy.

A selection criterion has been the inclusion of indicators covering different moments of those measures aimed at criminal prosecution. The focus on identifying the individuals that a society decides to leave out of this penal response is understood as essential for this purpose. This legal penal decision determines at what point in a person's life this system of formal social control becomes susceptible of falling on him. Whether and when formal criminal control is activated is very decisive for the process of encouraging minors not to repeat criminal behaviour. In 1985 the General Assembly of the United Nations approved the so-called "Beijing Rules"[1] where the need to establish an age of criminal responsibility was agreed upon, bearing in mind the cognitive and emotional maturity of minors. The range established was between 7 and 18 years of age so as to take into account the diversity of legal, cultural, political, social and economic systems of the states. With the UN Convention on the Rights of the Child in 1989 and subsequent resolutions of the Assembly (45/112 and 45/113 of 1990) the need for differentiating the social response given to crimes and misdemeanours committed by minors of a certain age, compared to that established for adults, was universally recognised and consolidated. Article 40.3 requires signatory states to set a minimum age below which the person is presumed not to have the capacity to infringe the criminal law. Subsequently, the UN Committee on the Rights of the Child, in its General Comment no. 10 (2007) on the Rights of the Child in Juvenile Justice (chapter IV, no. 32), states that "a minimum age of criminal responsibility

1 United Nations Standard Minimum Rules for the Administration of Juvenile Justice.

DOI: 10.4324/9781032661766-17

below the age of 12 years is considered by the Committee not to be internationally acceptable". Despite this recommendation, the issue is not peaceful and is not welcomed by all countries for various reasons (Abrams et al., 2018).

Once a society specifies, or not, the relevant age for this formal penal control, the treatment to be accorded to the juveniles is one of the areas of criminal proceedings that can lead to a wider discrepancy in procedural decisions among countries. So is confirmed by Zimring and Langer (2015) in their global comparison study, which in turn verify the extension and strength of consolidation of this treatment differentiated from that of adults in national legal systems. These options range from the way in which the specific criminal proceedings are carried out at each stage and the guarantees attached to them, to the nature and content of the possible sanctions and their way of being enforced.

Currently, the comparative criminal policy discussion on juvenile justice revolves around the assessment of which penal systems as a whole, or which specific tools within each system, promote the successful treatment of juvenile offenders so that they return to a law-abiding behaviour (Dünkel, 2014). This focus includes the issues addressed by the five items that international experts and the research team have entered into the youth justice pool as exclusion criteria. Therefore, the results of this pool in the different countries will allow us to contribute to the criminal policy discussion by generating a classification that will make it possible to discriminate among the diverse approaches.

2 The pool building process

2.1 Brief review of the pool building process

The RIMES instrument designed by the researchers for validation by international experts consisted of 126 items, and the pool related to juvenile criminal law included 13. These items were identified and developed by the coordinating team as aspects that generate social exclusion within juvenile justice. The low number of items included in this pool meant that the team did not have to perform any screening to reduce their number before their assessment by international experts, as happened in other pools. The aspects to be addressed related to the existence of a specific criminal justice system for minors and the age of its application, the custodial sanctions, the suspension of the judgement or its enforcement, the criminal records and the expulsion of foreign minors.

To validate these items, they were submitted to the opinion of international experts in two successive rounds. In the first, this pool obtained a very high percentage of validation, with 86.6 per cent, and no item was removed from the pool. In the second round, 11 items made the cut, with an Aiken's V coefficient ranging between 0.71 and 0.94, and remained in the pool, thus revealing the adequate measurement capacity of these indicators. The following items were not considered as exclusionary: "adult criminal justice applies to everyone who is 15 years old or older" and "less than 10% of all custodial sanctions to minors benefit either from probation as an alternative to sentencing or from suspension of sentence".

In the last step, the coordinating team selected only five items so that the final instrument was more manageable for its administration. This pool finally included items 113, 117, 120, 121 and 126, by unanimous decision of the entire research team, with none of the items generating any debate. The selection criterion was to choose those who had obtained the highest score in Aiken's V – three rules and one practice – and the sixth best valued item corresponding to another practice, to balance both types of items in the pool. The values of these items were between 0.79 and 0.94.

The definitive issues of this pool are fixed around the age set for differentiated sanctioning treatment of juveniles, the custodial sanction, the criminal records and the expulsion of foreign minor offenders.

2.2 *Description of the items finally included in the pool*

Each of the items has been specified individually in more detail so as to operationalise the issue referred to by it. The initial description and clarification of its content have required the task of explaining and specifying some aspects that had to be taken into account when investigating whether such rule or practice was fulfilled in each of the countries under study.

Below we revise the process of describing and explaining each item from the start of the work. In general, they are very clear items and discussions due to different perceptions have been very scarce.

Item 113 (rule): youth justice applies to children who are 12 years old or younger

The detailed description emphasises that those civil or administrative systems that protect disadvantaged minors are not considered within juvenile justice. This item will only be deemed to be validly fulfilled if the juvenile penal justice system can be applied to minors of 12 years of age or younger.

Item 117 (rule): youth justice provides custodial sanctions of over 10 years

The wording of this item obtained a high score in the criteria of completeness, extension, ease of access, discrimination capacity and clarity by the research team members (4 out of 4), without this opinion being changed in any of the subsequent rounds and was approved for inclusion in the final instrument without discussion. The international experts also did not comment on its wording.

Those researchers that carried out the fieldwork in Spain proposed to explain this item by specifying that the juvenile criminal law had to contain custodial sentences of more than 10 years. For its part, the description made to initiate the fieldwork at international level stated that juvenile justice was understood as the criminal justice or tutelary system that deals with the prosecution, trial and imposition of penal sanctions or correction after the commission of an offence by minors of criminal age. Custodial sanctions are described as those that can be imposed by the juvenile justice system for a period of more than 10 years for one or more cumulative sanctions.

Item 120 (rule): minors' criminal records keep legal effects after reaching the age of majority age

This item was rated with a 3 in completeness and a 4 in extension and ease of access in all opinion rounds, and also reached the maximum score as regards clarity and discrimination capacity. Such assessment meant the inclusion of the item with the same wording in the final instrument.

The description of the item was approved without discussion by the team, the only detail concerning clarity being that the consequences of the conviction as a juvenile were only to be taken into account if they influenced the sentence imposed at the age of majority, regardless of any other legal consequences that might follow. A criminal record refers to a child's or adolescent's history of prior convictions, whether or not that record has been expunged. The legal age or age of majority refers to the legally established minimum age for criminal responsibility as an adult.

Item 121 (practice): custodial sanction is one of the three most common sanctions applied to minors

This item was also rated in all criteria with the highest score except in the last round, where its assessment as regards extension obtained a 3.

Given the very specific practice to which this element refers, the proposed explanation focused only on clarifying that this practice seeks to verify whether custodial sentences are one of the three types of sanctions which, in practice, judges impose and enforce more frequently in the five years analysed by the study, regardless of what is included in the text of the law.

Item 126 (practice): alien minors are deported. because of an offence

The wording of this item has changed slightly throughout the project. Its first draft was: "*At least 10% of juvenile offenders are expelled*". In the first and second rounds the judges accorded to this item a 3 for completeness and extension, and a 1 for ease of access. In the review, the first two criteria obtained a 4, as well as discrimination capacity and clarity. In view of the low score on the criterion of ease of data collection, the team decided to change its wording by omitting the percentage.

Those female researchers who carried out the fieldwork in Spain noted a possible lack of discrimination capacity of the item, since the Convention on the Rights of the Child, signed by the majority of states, specifies that foreign minors cannot be expelled, although family reunifications can be carried out. They also stressed the limited ease with which data could be obtained, which was confirmed by those conducting the fieldwork in several other countries.

The description for the international fieldwork underlined that a foreign minor is one who lives in a country of which he or she is not a citizen. A conviction by the juvenile justice system following the commission of an offence must result in the expulsion of the minor. This deportation can take place before the sentence or educational measure begins to be served, during the sentence or after its completion, and it does not matter if the expulsion occurs when the juvenile has already reached the age of 18, thus improving the completeness and clarity of the item. This practice is considered to be fulfilled whenever the judicial or administrative bodies of a country may deport foreign minors due to the mentioned reason, but it is not required that such decision be compulsory.

3 Methodology used to solve the items in each country

For the resolution of the rules, the specific laws or regulations of each territory on juvenile justice and the penalties to be imposed on minor offenders have been used in a general way, and in the case of England and Wales, the guidelines for juvenile sentencing courts – which specify the decisions to be taken by judges – were also consulted. In most cases, this enquiry was enough to resolve the item. As regards the two situations where the legal texts gave rise to doubts, academic experts on the subject in each country were consulted.

For their part, the practices have been resolved in the five European countries and the two US states by resorting to the official statistics that the official institutions of each territory had published on measures or penalties imposed to minors. Reports and statistics from ministries, departments and official institutions related to youth were also consulted and information was obtained from key informants. The period taken into account to explore the information related to these practices is five years from the most up-to-date data available in each country on the subject under study.

After resolving the items in all countries, the international experts reviewed the way of obtaining the information and the results achieved, and none of them made any relevant comment that would lead to their revision. This suggests that the data obtained regarding the elements analysed in pool 9 is highly reliable.

4 Results of the pool's items in each country

The results for pool 9 are presented below in an aggregated form. Table 14.1 shows the positive or negative responses to each item in each country or state.

As can be seen, the items in this pool give rise to answers in both directions. There is a unanimous positive response to allowing custodial sentences of more than 10 years for minors in all countries, except in Spain. Only in two

Table 14.1 Results of the pool according to each item and country

	Germany	*California*	*Spain*	*Italy*	*New York*	*Poland*	*England & Wales*
Item 113	No	Yes	No	Yes	Yes	No	Yes
Item 117	Yes	Yes	No	Yes	Yes	Yes	Yes
Item 120	Yes	Yes	No	Yes	Yes	No	Yes
Item 121	No	Yes	Yes	No	Yes	No	No
Item 126	Yes	Yes	No	No	Yes	No	Yes

Source: Own elaboration

countries – Spain and Poland – are the criminal records generated as minors not taken into account in possible sentences as adults. In the case of the rule on criminal age limits, only Germany, Poland and Spain do not provide for the application of criminal law to minors under 12 years of age. There are also three countries – Italy, Poland and Spain – where foreign minors who have been convicted of a criminal offence are not deported. In four territories – England and Wales, Poland, Italy and Germany – custodial sentences are not one of the most common sanctions applied to this population group.

If these results are analysed according to the positive or negative response in each country and these results are weighted, a "continuum" emerges that allows to classify them as regards the exclusion generated by their juvenile justice systems. Criminal policies in youth justice in Spain and Poland are positioned with the lowest score of social exclusion indicators, as compared to those applied in the states of California and New York which fulfil the maximum number of exclusionary indicators, as pointed out by one of the hypotheses of the theoretical framework. The rest of the European countries under study are positioned in an intermediate situation: Germany and Italy show some elements that reveal the presence of exclusionary policies, while England and Wales is also marked by a high level of social exclusion in the response of their penal system to juvenile offenders (see Figure 14.1).

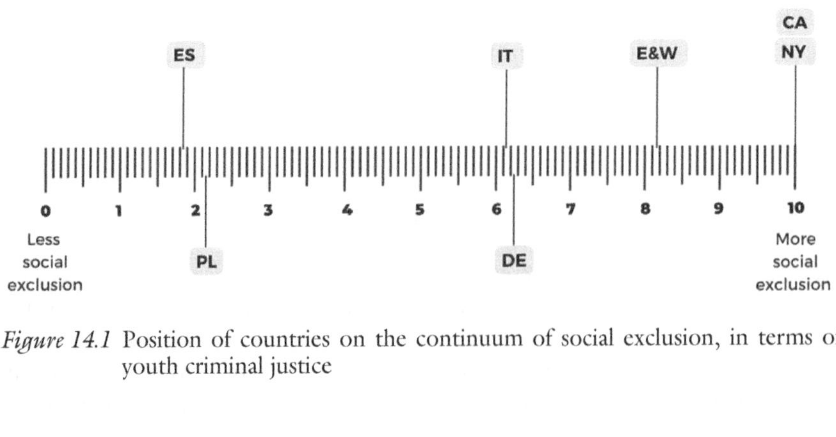

Figure 14.1 Position of countries on the continuum of social exclusion, in terms of youth criminal justice

5 Brief description of each indicator's results

Item 113: youth justice applies to children who are 12 years old or younger

The limits in the age of criminal responsibility are disparate in the countries studied. In the states of New York and California, as well as in Italy, England and Wales, the criminal justice system applies to children aged 12 or younger who have committed a crime. In Germany, Poland and Spain this is not the case.

The age of criminal responsibility in England and Wales and Northern Ireland is 10 years. The term "juvenile delinquent" refers to individuals aged between 10 and 17, while individuals aged between 18 and 20 are referred to as "young adult criminals". Young adults are convicted as adults, but serve their sentences in special and more adapted conditions. Juvenile justice, therefore, applies to those aged between 10 and 17, and the proceedings take place in either the Youth Court or the Crown Court, depending on the type of offence committed, in particular its seriousness.

In Italy there is no juvenile criminal law separate from that of adults. According to article 97 of the Italian Penal Code, minors under 14 years of age are not subject to any form of criminal prosecution, they are considered not responsible. In fact, it is specified that juvenile jurisdiction is applicable from the age of 14 to the age of majority at 18 – diminished responsibility – provided that the minor has the capacity to understand. Although minors under the age of 14 are not subject to criminal prosecution, when they are considered socially dangerous, the judge may apply a judicial security measure of internment in a centre or probation. In these cases, only the danger of committing acts of a certain gravity can justify the deprivation of personal liberty. It should also be borne in mind that, although in Italy there is no substantive juvenile criminal law, there is a specific procedure for minors with important implications in the regulation provided for in the Criminal Code. This is DPR n° 448, of 22 September 1988 (*Disposizioni sul processo penale a carico di imputati minorenni*), which is complemented by the co-ordinating and transitional rules contained in Decree-Law n° 272, of 29 July 1989. In DPR n° 448, the educational needs of the minor are constantly present and become the predominant purpose. Priority is given to the idea that the minor is a subject to be recovered and not punished, so that the main objective would be to return him or her to society in conditions of maturity and responsibility.

In the State of New York this issue is established as follows: the New York Family Court Act defines a juvenile delinquent as a child over the age of seven and under the age of eighteen who has committed a criminal offence which, if committed by an adult, would be a criminal offence. This age limit was changed in October 2019, when the Raise the Age legislation raised the age of criminal responsibility as an adult to 18: formerly, sixteen- and seventeen-year-olds were also considered adults.

In the State of California, the age of criminal majority is 18 and the lower age limit is 12. The California State Law stipulates that a youth must be at least fourteen years old in order to be charged as an adult in a criminal court. However, there is no law that prevents girls and boys from being charged and tried in the juvenile justice system, and they can be arrested and detained. The principle applied in these cases is that of the "best interests of the child". In said State, children under the age of 12 may be liable for crimes in specific situations, but they are not normally sent to the Division of Juvenile Justice (DJJ), since the law states that appropriate measures will be taken to care for and protect those children only when necessary, avoiding any intervention whenever possible, and using the least restrictive alternatives through available school, health and community services.

These results show that the recommendation made by the UN in 2008 not to establish a minimum age below 12 years to request criminal responsibility is not accepted in some countries and states. It is noted that all Anglo-Saxon countries agree on this point, but it is not exclusive to this tradition, as this is also the case in Italy. An outstanding feature is that in England and Wales and New York an age is established (seventeen) below which the minor who has committed an offence will not receive any punishment. This shows that the legislator of these territories considers that there are certain ages at which a child does not have the capacity to infringe the criminal law, as set out in article 40.3 of the Convention on the Rights of the Child. In Italy this lower limit does not exist and in California, although the law establishes 12 years as the lower age limit, there are exceptions and interventions are conducted with younger individuals. This may be due to the fact that the motivation or interest in formally responding to minors who commit offences and are under 14 and 12 years of age respectively, is an educational interest: It will be carried out in those cases where the offending behaviour has been serious and it is considered necessary, by using the least coercive means.

Item 117: youth justice provides custodial sanctions of over 10 years

As regards this rule on the duration of penalties, the legislation of all the countries studied establishes the deprivation of liberty of more than ten years, with the sole exception of Spain.

In the six countries or states where this exclusion criterion is promoted, the dynamics for its inclusion are the same: the young person must have committed very serious offences for the judge to consider a custodial sentence for over ten years.

In this common scenario there are differentiating elements. Thus, in Poland the criminal law applicable to minors is of a tutelary nature, and the measures imposed are therefore of an indefinite duration. If the young person, after reaching the age of 21, has not achieved the educational objectives, he or she can be transferred to a prison. California coincides with this European country in the indefinite duration of the penalties, with the limit that the minor cannot be institutionalised for longer than the maximum period stipulated for adults. Germany and Italy reserve this possibility for cases where the offence committed was homicide or manslaughter. For their part, New York and England and Wales have a wider catalogue of offences that can result in the minor being sentenced to more than 10 years' deprivation of liberty, but all of them are offences of the utmost gravity. The latter region stands out for the possibility of sentencing a minor to life imprisonment: if the Crown Court considers that a long-term sentence will not provide the necessary public protection or if, after the commission of a murder, a detention during Her Majesty's pleasure is declared.

These exceptions are not included in Spanish law: The Organic Law 5/2000, of 12 January, amended by the Organic Law 8/2006, of 4 December, expressly imposes an insurmountable limit of ten years to be served in a closed detention centre for young people aged sixteen and seventeen, without prejudice to adding a subsequent probation measure.

Item 120: minors' criminal records keep legal effects after reaching the age of majority

After consulting the laws of the different countries regarding the criminal records of minors and their effect when they come of age in order to specify the rule of item 120, it is noted that there was a majority of positive replies. Only in Poland and Spain does recidivism for crimes committed during minority have no legal consequences in adulthood, due to the tutelary nature of the Polish model and because judges of adults are banned from accessing any criminal records generated during the age of minority, in the Spanish case.

In Germany, England and Wales, Italy and the states of New York and California, the legislation provides for the criminal records of minors to be taken into account, but for different reasons that are described below.

In Italy, only sentences of deprivation of liberty imposed during minority cases will count as criminal records in adult cases, even if they had been suspended on a conditional basis.

In New York, the New York Family Court Act establishes that the criminal records of minors can be taken into account by a judge sentencing an adult, with the only exclusion of any records as a minor that had been already cancelled. And in California, the so-called Three Strikes Law, explicitly authorises the use of any sentence imposed on minors as one of these three occasions of recidivism to be taken into account when increasing the prison sentence as an adult, in the terms provided for in this law.

In England and Wales, the time limit criterion is the determining factor in this matter. Criminal records of minors are subject to periods of rehabilitation. For the duration of such rehabilitation period, a sanction is listed as "unspent", which means that it can be reported to any potential employer or other body or institution. Besides, the Criminal Justice Act of 2003 states that when the judge is assessing the seriousness of an offence committed by a young person who has one or more previous convictions, the court must decide whether to treat each of those previous convictions as an aggravating factor for the current case, taking into account the nature of the previous offence and the time that has elapsed.

Finally, in Germany, if the criminal records relating to a conviction remain in the Central Criminal Registry or in the Register of Educational Measures, they retain their legal effect after the offender reaches the age of majority and can influence the sentences of adults, as this effect depends on their removal from the Federal Central Criminal Registry or the Register of Educational Measures (*Bundeszentralregistergesetz*). The decisive issue for a possible legal effect is the removal from the register and not a certain age or the age of majority, for which a gradual system of prescription periods is established according to the length of the minors' sentences.

As we can see, different criteria are taken into account for this issue regarding criminal records: the nature of the offence or the time elapsed since it was committed, which is revealed in the possible expiration or cancellation of its validity. In some legal systems, the judge of adults must take this information into account while, in others, his/her decision is discretionary.

Item 121: custodial sanction is one of the three most common sanctions applied to minors

Item 121 must assess the punitive practice regarding the quantitative intensity of imposing an internment measure.

Research into this practice showed that in the states of New York and California, as well as in Spain, detention is indeed one of the top three sanctions applied to minors convicted of a criminal offence, but in England and Wales, Poland, Italy and Germany this is not confirmed.

In the latter group of countries, the most frequently imposed measures are community service, socio-educational tasks, behavioural conditions and fines, among others. The situation in Italy is perhaps worth highlighting, where the sanctions that can be imposed on minors are the same as those for adults, with no differentiated catalogue.

The statistical data from the Family Courts and Youth Parts of criminal courts in New York include all minors that have been tried in them, whether juvenile delinquents or juvenile offenders. The sanctions typically imposed in this jurisdiction are only three. Between 2014 and 2018, only conditional suspension, probation and detention were imposed. Until 2018, the most frequently imposed sanction was probation, followed by deprivation of liberty in significantly fewer cases. It should be noted that deprivation of liberty can be executed in a variety of institutions, including those under the Department of Social Services.

In California, four out of every five minors arrested are referred to the Juvenile Probation Department. Those cases that reach the juvenile courts may face penalties with a wide range of consequences, but during the period studied (2014–2019) and according to the report "Juvenile Justice in California 2019", placement in a closed county facility was the second most common sanction imposed on juvenile offenders. This report provides data on minors sanctioned by both juvenile and adult courts.

The Spanish situation is similar to that of the latter state: The law applies a fairly broad catalogue of sanctioning measures for minors found guilty, but the internment measure in its different regimes (open, semi-open, closed or therapeutic) was the second most frequent quantitative measure imposed by juvenile courts between 2015 and 2019.

An issue that should be considered in these results is the percentage difference between the imposition of deprivation of liberty and the other most frequently imposed measures. For example, probation in Spain was imposed in 40 per cent of cases and detention in 16 per cent of them; in New York, detention accounted for 22 per cent of cases compared to conditional suspension, representing 67 per cent.

Item 126: alien minors are deported because of an offence

The last item included in this pool proposes to analyse a punitive practice: foreign juvenile offenders are expelled.

Research findings on this practice reveal that international responses vary. In California, New York, England and Wales and Germany, alien juvenile offenders are expelled, while in Spain, Poland and Italy, they are not. The presentation of these results will be somewhat more detailed than in previous items, as these data were difficult to obtain in almost all countries, and their nuances need to be taken into account.

In California, deportation is one of the measures that both the Juvenile Probation Department and Juvenile Courts can impose on minors who are detained and sent to the juvenile justice system. Its number has declined in recent years, going from fourteen in 2010 to none in 2019. The provisions of these courts are not considered a conviction under federal immigration laws, which is a necessary condition for expulsion on grounds of a criminal action. However, according to the Immigration and Nationality Act, expulsion can be a consequence imposed by the "bad acts" carried out or by a specific behaviour (US Code: Conduct-based and non-conduct-based grounds for deportation) and can lead to a decision of expulsion if committed by a non-US minor, and the following is namely specified: drug use, violation of a domestic violence protection order, or misrepresenting US citizenship. This is what leads to the deportation of these minors after they have been arrested and brought to the juvenile justice services.

The legal situation in New York is the same, as the convictions by juvenile courts in this state are also not considered a sufficient condition for deportation of a person under 18 years of age. Thus, the Matter of Devison states that juvenile proceedings are not criminal in nature, their acts are not offences and the fact that a minor has offended is not a conviction requiring his or her expulsion. However, as in California, according to the Immigration and Nationality Act some behaviours qualified as "bad acts" can lead to the decision of expulsion if committed by a non-US minor. The specific number of deportations is not clearly specified in official statistics. Information was found in the Historical Data on Immigration and Customs Enforcement, that provides data for the period between 2003 and 2016. According to this source, three foreign minors were deported for pretending to have US citizenship in 2005, 2006 and 2010. In order to confirm this information, an academic expert on the subject, Professor Clairissa Breen, from the University of Buffalo, was consulted and she specified that the majority of expulsions of foreign children in the state of New York are due to their being treated as adults when they are tried for committing an offence, and they are also expelled due to misconduct, although this rule is usually only applied to unaccompanied minors. It can be concluded that minors are being deported for this reason in New York, but it is not possible to know the specific number of minors affected.

In England and Wales, the removal process for minors does not differ in its essential elements from that for adults, which is set forth in the UK Border Act 2007, the Immigration Act 1971 and the "Early Removal Release Scheme" included in the Criminal Justice Act 2003. It must always be taken into account whether the expulsion decision is in the interest of society, and there is no exception for minors either. The Immigration Act specifies the protocol for minors in the document "Managing Foreign National Offenders Under 18 Years Old". Due to his or her offending behaviour, the juvenile must be considered as posing a significant risk to society upon release. It is also specified that expulsion is not normally to be carried out until the minor has reached the age of 18, unless such departure from the country is carried out with an adult family member or there is evidence of appropriate reception conditions in his or her country of origin. The statistics on the application of the Immigration Act do not differentiate between persons expelled for committing an offence and those who are removed for public interest reasons. The number of minors expelled has decreased over the years, but these types of actions continue to occur: in 2018 there were 26 children under 14 years of age, and 3 aged between 14 and 17.

In Germany, the situation is in line with the above-mentioned countries in that juvenile offenders have been expelled, but it is also impossible to provide specific figures on annual cases. The Law on Residence, Economic Activity and Integration of Aliens 2008 (*Gesetz über den Aufenthalt, die Erwerbstätigkeitund die Integration von Ausländern im Bundesgebie – AufenthG*) states that if a foreigner has endangered public security, public order or other interests significant to the country, he or she shall be expelled after weighing the public interest in expulsion against the individual's interest in remaining in the country. The public interest in removal becomes significant if the juvenile has received a custodial sentence of at least two years for the commission of one or more offences; if the sentence has been of at least one year for a crime against life, physical integrity, sexual freedom or property, committed in a series of cases or for assault or resistance to the authority. One of the individual interests taken into account in this balance proposed by the law is the underage status. German police data show that juvenile migrants do commit criminal offences. However, there is no official data detailing whether or not they have been subsequently expelled as a result of this offence. The opinion of various experts has therefore been sought for quality information, namely Professor Axel Dessecker, Deputy Director of the German Centre for Criminology and Dr Thomas Hohlfeld, representative for migration and integration issues in the DIE LINKE section of the German Parliament. Both agree that deportation orders are indeed issued against juvenile offenders in the country, although not even through parliamentary questions is it possible to know the specific number of minors who have actually left Germany for this reason.

In Spain, Organic Law 5/2000 on the criminal responsibility of minors does not provide for expulsion as a sanctioning measure for foreigners found guilty. This possibility is also not included in the Law on Foreigners. However, since this item is a practice, an exploration has been carried out with qualitative methodology to verify the situation. Key informants from the police, the judiciary, public prosecutors, civil society, child protection centres, detention centres and the Spanish Ombudsman were asked individually and with specific questions. The answers were unanimously negative: In Spain, minors convicted of a criminal offence are not deported.

In Poland, the Criminal Law on Minors 1982 also does not provide for expulsion as a sanctioning measure after the commission of a criminal offence and, therefore, police statistics on juvenile sanctions do not report any such action. Consultation with experts (namely Witold Klaus, a lecturer at the Institute of Legal Studies of the Polish Academy of Sciences and a researcher at the Migration Research Centre from the University of Warsaw) confirms that the commission of an offence by a minor aged 16 or under does not generate a criminal record, so that he or she cannot be expelled for committing a penal offence either. The situation is slightly different for 17-year-old boys and girls: Although expulsion is not included in the Criminal Code as a sanction, a residence permit can be refused for this reason. However, this possible situation cannot be included in the content of this item, because it would be an indirect and administrative consequence of the conviction and not a cause for a direct deportation order.

In Italy, Legislative Decree n° 286, of 25 July 1998, as consolidated text of the provisions regarding immigration rules and the status of foreigners, states that the expulsion of aliens under the age of 18 is not permitted, unless authorised by the Ministry of the Interior for public order or national security reasons. This ministry's statistics show that foreigners are expelled in Italy for suspected international terrorism, but these data are not broken down by age. To find out if this practice is carried out with minors, Massimiliano Bagaglini, Head of the organisational unit "Deprivation of Liberty and Migrants", at the National Ombudsman Office *(Ufficio del Garante Nazionale dei Diritti)*, was contacted. He confirmed there were no statistics on this matter in any public institution, not even the one which he belongs to. Furthermore, he stated that in all the previous years no communication had been received reporting the deportation of a foreign juvenile offender, and so it could be deduced that such expulsions had never been carried out with this population group.

The clearest conclusion that can be drawn from the work carried out is that these deportations are very rare in all the countries and states where they are actually conducted and that their incidence is in decline. It should be noted that in most of the territories studied it was necessary to rely on the opinion of experts and key informants to ascertain the reality, as only Anglo-Saxon countries collected these data in official statistics, and not always in a clear way.

6 Conclusions

In this section, we will first review to what extent these items have revealed their suitability to measure social exclusion from the theoretical criteria used in their preparation and validation and, secondly, the social exclusion which the analysis of these five items has brought to light.

6.1 Suitability of the pool

As to the six criteria used throughout the building of the RIMES instrument by the research team and the international experts,[2] we can state that all of them are present in a favourable way in this pool's items. These five indicators obtained a high score in Aiken's V coefficient in the experts' assessment of clarity, suitability and adequacy for the pool, and the fieldwork conducted has confirmed in practice the high ratings of these three aspects, since no problem has arisen in this regard.

The high discrimination capacity of these indicators should be emphasised in view that different responses were obtained for all of them in the countries under study.

As to the other criteria taken into consideration, only the ease of access to information has been refuted in the case of item 126 with respect to the expulsion of foreign minors. This possible difficulty was already noticed in the discussions of the research team and was confirmed during the conduct of the work, as explained above.

This pool is therefore suitable to be applied to the diverse juvenile justice systems with the objective of measuring the social exclusion they provoke.

6.2 Social exclusion revealed after the study

The results show two very different positions. At the most-exclusion end are placed New York and California: in these states all items were answered in the

2 Completeness, extension and ease of access (research group). Clarity, suitability and adequacy to the pool (international experts).

affirmative, without exception. At the opposite end, but not as strongly, are placed Spain and Poland, where only one item was answered in the affirmative in each country. Italy, Germany and England and Wales have more intermediate positions, but also with differentiated features. The latter territory reveals a high capacity for exclusion in the field of juvenile justice, as only the practice concerning the use of custodial sentences was answered in the negative. Italy and Germany are further away from the exclusionary extreme, with only two negative responses.

It can be concluded that the juvenile justice systems of Anglo-Saxon countries display a high level of social exclusion, with the two US states leading the way, which confirms the hypothesis advanced in the theoretical framework of this study (Díez-Ripollés, 2011).

Another important aspect to underline is that the items that allow for the most discrimination among countries were three: the two practices (the common use of custodial sentences and the possibility of expelling foreign juvenile offenders from the country) and one rule (the application of the juvenile justice system to minors under the age of 12).

But there were also indicators that showed very similar – although not unanimous – trends in all countries: the rule concerning the possibility of imposing a custodial sentence of more than 10 years and the one referring to the use of criminal records generated during minority of age to aggravate sentences as an adult. In the first, only one country received a negative response, and in the second there were two. The information obtained on the basis of these two rules leads us to reflect on one of the main indicators that make up this pool: the differential treatment of minors with respect to those of adults.

Of the three rules included in this pool, these two have in common that they focus on the lack of a differential treatment between juvenile and young offenders and adult offenders, either by the length of detention or by the consideration of their criminal history. They differ from rule 113 in that the latter tries to find out whether there is a population group to which the criminal law does not apply at all, even in an adapted manner. The fulfilment of these two rules in a large number of countries shows that many societies, even if they choose to treat juvenile offenders differently, in a global way, sometimes consider that they should be treated more similarly to adults. Nevertheless, the resolution of the items in this group of countries shows that these normative decisions are taken in cases of young people who have revealed serious or very serious criminal activity.

This leads us to reflect on the limitation of any attempt to classify complex realities and which is also revealed here. Dichotomous answers leave out the richness of reality. In this pool, this situation is revealed in several indicators: the expulsion of foreign juvenile offenders occurs very rarely in the countries where it is applied; the custodial sentence is enforced at a much lower rate than other community measures; and the treatment of minors as adults only occurs if the offences committed have been very serious, which is not usual in this population group.

Therefore, the overview shown on the "continuum" of social exclusion as regards juvenile justice with the countries analysed tending more towards this extreme, must be tempered and interpreted bearing in mind the unique contents of some responses. This scenario is similar to that disclosed by the few studies of comparative criminal policy in juvenile justice worldwide (Dünkel, 2015; Tonry and Chambers, 2011), which emphasise the need to take into account both legislation and practice in the implementation of juvenile justice, as it is often the specific decisions and actions carried out on a day-to-day basis that reveal the true nature of juvenile justice in each country.

In any case, it must be asserted that the detailed information in the seven territories concerning each of the punitive practices and rules relating to juvenile justice has allowed us to obtain comparative results that reveal the effectiveness of the RIMES instrument as an element of international criminal policy comparison from the perspective of social exclusion.

References

Abrams, L. S., Jordan, S. P., & Montero, L. A. (2018). What Is a Juvenile? A Cross-National Comparison of Youth Justice Systems. *Youth Justice*, *18*(2), 111–130. https://doi.org/10.1177/1473225418779850

Díez-Ripollés, J. L. (2011). La dimensión inclusión/exclusión social como guía de la política criminal comparada. *Revista Electrónica de Ciencia Penal y Criminología*, *13*, 12. http://criminet.ugr.es/recpc/13/recpc13-12.pdf

Dünkel, F. (2014). Juvenile Justice Systems in Europe – Reform Developments Between Justice, Welfare and 'New Punitiveness'. *Kriminologijos Studijos*, *1*. https://doi.org/10.15388/CrimLithuan.2014.1.3676

Dünkel, F. (2015). Juvenile Justice and Crime Policy in Europe. In F. E. Zimring, M. Langer, & D. S. Tanenhaus (Eds.), *Juvenile Justice in Global Perspective* (pp. 9–61). New York University Press.

Tonry, M., & Chambers, C. (2011). Juvenile Justice Cross-Nationally Considered. In *The Oxford Handbook of Juvenile Crime and Juvenile Justice*. https://doi.org/10.1093/oxfordhb/9780195385106.013.0034

UN Committee on the Rights of the Child in General Comment No. 10 (2007). on Children's Rights in Juvenile Justice (cap. IV, No. 32). www.iom.int/sites/g/files/tmzbdl486/files/jahia/webdav/shared/shared/mainsite/policy_and_research/un/63/es/A_63_41_ES.pdf (Consulted 21/03/2022)

Zimring, F. E., & Langer, M. (2015). One Theme or Many? The Search for a Deep Structure in Global Juvenile Justice. In F. E. Zimring, M. Langer, & D. S. Tanenhaus (Eds.), *Juvenile Justice in Global Perspective* (pp. 383–412). New York University Press.

15 Overview of the RIMES application

Insights for comparative criminal policy

Elisa García-España and Anabel Cerezo

1 Introduction

Comparative criminal policy is currently one of the most promising and ambitious areas of research in penal law and criminology. Academic interest in this subject has significantly increased in recent decades, with comparative criminal studies centred on national penalty systems (Newburn & Jones, 2022). Certain investigations revealed the phenomenon labelled as punitive populism (Bottoms, 1995; Pratt, 2007), highlighting a punitive shift towards a continuous rise in the frequency and duration of incarceration in numerous countries. The study of comparative criminal policy via imprisonment (McAra, 2011) has led to an enhanced comprehension of the relation between criminal policy and punishment by several scholars (among others, Lacey et al., 2018). Nonetheless, other scholars suggest comparing alternative forms of penalties (Newburn, 2020) or investigating procedural measures (Hamilton, 2014) to broaden the research scope. In this regard, Newburn and Jones (2022) suggest conducting a comparative analysis of police action as an important part of the national penal system, as the police are the gateway to the criminal justice system and, consequently, to punitivism. These authors argue that to achieve a thorough comprehension of criminal policy and effective comparisons between penal systems, it is necessary to include policing activities in the analysis. Although broadening the scope of penality analysis is intriguing, the research conducted employs "punitive populism" as the criterion for analysis.

Díez-Ripollés (2011, 2013) presents a novel proposal contributing to this field of comparative criminal policy, with a theoretical model based on the social exclusion capacity of national criminal justice systems. Unlike the strong current trend of comparing different penal control systems according to their degree of punitive severity, this proposal takes a different theoretical approach. The former criterion, advanced by Garland (2001), stemmed from an analysis of socio-political factors which, associated with late modern society, led to the consolidation of a new model of criminal policy in the United States and the United Kingdom, and features a generalised hardening of the penal system. The idea implicit in Garland's work is that other countries' criminal strategies

DOI: 10.4324/9781032661766-18

would become increasingly homogeneous and in line with this model of punitive severity (also Christie, 2000; Wacquant, 1999).

According to Díez-Ripollés, such criterion for the analysis of comparative criminal policy has some theoretical and methodological shortcomings. This author argues that, from a theoretical point of view, focusing only on punishment moderation has limited potential as it does not take into account the penal system's objectives. Criticism of this model is similar to that of guaranteeism, in the sense that, although it is essential to guarantee the freedoms and rights inherent to the rule of law, it fails to identify or structure an alternative criminal policy that is compatible with these values or develop an adequate crime prevention strategy (Lahti, 2000; Díez-Ripollés, 2004).

On the other hand, in terms of methodological approach, the analysis of punitive severity focuses almost exclusively on a single indicator, that of the incarceration rate per 100,000 inhabitants, which has certain limitations to assess many other aspects of criminal policy models. Beyond the virtues of such indicator – such as the reliability of data sources and the availability of international time series (Cavadino & Dignan, 2006; Tonry, 2007) – criminological and penal policy doctrine has repeatedly stressed its inadequacy. The fact of relying only on imprisonment rates overlooks other indicators that have a significant capacity to assess the severity of the punishment, like the number of criminal proceedings or the accumulation of penalties (Hinds, 2005 [2000]; Tonry, 2007; Nelken, 2005, 2010; Tamarit Sumalla, 2007; Lappi-Seppälä, 2007, 2008; Roché, 2007; Newburn, 2007; Larrauri Pijoan, 2009).

The theoretical model of Díez-Ripollés aims to overcome the shortcomings of the punitive moderation approach through the criterion of social exclusion. He argues that a socially exclusionary approach essentially aspires to neutralise the groups to which criminal justice is applied, which means ensuring that suspects, defendants, offenders or ex-offenders, after their contact with penal institutions, are in individual and social conditions that make it more difficult for them to break the law or avoid being captured.

This theoretical proposal (developed in Chapters 2 and 3) is further specified by a methodological design (Chapter 4) that aims to overcome the limitations of the indicator focused on incarceration rates, despite the fact that such data are easily accessible (Lappi-Seppälä, 2008). Considering that international comparison is the main objective of this theoretical framework, we believe that the best tool to achieve this is to design an instrument to measure the social exclusion caused by criminal policy. As explained in Chapter 4, this instrument has been created through a rigorous methodology and has been validated by almost 100 international experts from 18 different countries. It consists of 39 items (28 rules and 11 practices) grouped into 9 thematic pools or areas that characterise national criminal justice systems. These pools include: 1) Control of Public Spaces (gated communities, video-surveillance, restriction of access to public spaces); 2) Legal Safeguards (undermining of due process safeguards, hindering or restriction of legal remedies); 3) Sentencing and Sanctions Systems (judicial discretion, aggravated provisions for recidivists, extensive use of prison, community sanctions, electronic monitoring); 4) Harshest Penalties (death penalty, life imprisonment, long-term prison sentences); 5) Prison Rules (living conditions in prison, respect for prisoners' rights, release on parole); 6) Preventive Intervention (pre-trial detention, indefinite post-sentence internment); 7) Legal and Social Status of Offenders and Ex-Offenders (disenfranchisement, deprivation of further civil rights, accessibility to social resources); 8) Police and Criminal Records (extension and accessibility of records, whereabouts of former convicts); and 9) Youth Criminal Justice (age thresholds, treatment differentiated from adults).

This instrument, called RIMES, has already been applied in seven jurisdictions: California, England and Wales, Germany, Italy, New York, Poland and Spain. The results of its implementation have been described in previous chapters, on the basis of the nine thematic pools that make up the instrument.

In this chapter we shall provide the results of the application of RIMES as regards the level of social exclusion caused by the different criminal justice systems in European and American jurisdictions, as well as comparisons among them. By doing so, we fulfil the objectives set by the RIMES and AP-RIMES projects: to operationalise the theoretical model of Díez-Ripollés (2011, 2013) through the design and implementation of an instrument that allows to compare criminal policies from the perspective of the social exclusion caused by penal systems on suspects, defendants, offenders and ex-offenders.

Therefore, we position each jurisdiction on a continuum ranging from the least to the most socially exclusionary criminal justice system. In this regard, here we address the following aspects: 1) number of items expressing social exclusion in each jurisdiction; 2) percentage of practices and rules that were responded in the affirmative in each jurisdiction; 3) comparison among jurisdictions on the basis of the instrument's pools; 4) position of the pools within each jurisdiction; and 5) position of jurisdictions on the continuum of socially exclusionary criminal justice systems.

We believe that the results of applying RIMES will help to design national criminal justice policies that are less socially exclusionary. Finally, as other criminologists have pointed out (Brandariz García, 2023; Cid Moliné, 2023; Hamilton, 2023), we present the contribution of the RIMES instrument for the international comparison of penal systems.

2 Number and distribution of items responded with "yes" or "no" by jurisdiction

Before we begin the analysis of items responded in the affirmative or negative in each jurisdiction, we need to assess the discrimination capacity of the RIMES instrument. The items – taken as a whole or one by one – are discriminatory in the sense that they are usually not answered with a "yes" or a "no" in all jurisdictions, as can be seen in Table 15.1. In a comparison among countries, we find that the Anglo-Saxon territories (California, New York and England and Wales) have a higher number of items responded in the affirmative, i.e., it appears that these are the jurisdictions with the greatest social exclusion caused by the criminal justice system.

In all three Anglo-Saxon territories, the percentage of affirmative responses exceeds 50 per cent of the total number of items included in the RIMES instrument. By contrast, in Spain only 23 per cent of the total number of items

Table 15.1 Results obtained by pools and items in each jurisdiction

	*Items**	*Germany*	*California*	*Italy*	*New York*	*Poland*	*England & Wales*	*Spain*
Pool 1	1	NO	YES	YES	YES	NO	YES	NO
	2	NO	YES	NO	YES	NO	YES	NO
	3	YES	NO	YES	YES	NO	YES	NO
	11	YES	YES	YES	YES	NO	YES	YES
Pool 2	21	NO	NO	NO	NO	NO	NO	NO
	22	NO	NO	NO	NO	NO	NO	NO
	24	YES	NO	NO	NO	NO	NO	NO
	25	YES	YES	YES	YES	NO	YES	NO
Pool 3	33	NO	NO	NO	NO	NO	NO	NO
	35	NO	YES	NO	NO	YES	NO	NO
	36	NO	YES	NO	NO	NO	YES	NO
	37	NO	YES	NO	YES	YES	YES	YES
	38	YES	YES	YES	YES	YES	YES	YES
Pool 4	42	NO	YES	NO	NO	NO	NO	NO
	43	NO	YES	YES	YES	NO	YES	NO
	46	NO	YES	YES	YES	YES	YES	YES
	50	NO	NO	YES	NO	YES	NO	NO
Pool 5	55	NO	NO	NO	YES	NO	NO	NO
	62	NO	YES	NO	YES	NO	NO	NO
	64	NO	YES	NO	YES	NO	YES	NO
	68	YES	YES	YES	YES	YES	YES	NO
Pool 6	74	YES	YES	NO	YES	YES	NO	NO
	79	YES	YES	YES	YES	YES	YES	YES
	81	YES	YES		NO	YES	YES	NO
	82	NO	NO	NO	NO	NO	NO	NO
Pool 7	86	NO	NO	NO	NO	YES	NO	NO
	88	YES	YES	NO	YES	YES	YES	YES
	91	YES	NO	NO	YES	YES	YES	NO
	92	NO	NO	NO	YES	NO	YES	NO
	93	NO	NO	NO	NO	NO	NO	NO
Pool 8	99	YES	YES	NO	YES	YES	YES	YES
	100	NO	YES	NO	YES	YES	NO	NO
	101	NO	YES	NO	YES	YES	NO	NO
	107	YES	YES	YES	YES	NO	YES	YES
Pool 9	113	NO	YES	YES	YES	NO	YES	NO
	117	YES	YES	YES	YES	YES	YES	NO
	120	YES	YES	YES	YES	NO	YES	NO
	121	NO	YES	NO	YES	NO	NO	YES
	126	YES	YES	NO	YES	NO	YES	NO

Source: * The items in bold are punitive practices, while the others are rules. Own elaboration.

were answered with a "yes", while the remaining 77 per cent obtained a "no". Therefore, the criminal justice system of the latter jurisdiction causes the least social exclusion of all those analysed (see Table 15.2).

In Table 15.2, there are jurisdictions with the same number of items responded in the affirmative, like, for example, Germany and Poland (with 16 items, representing 41 per cent of the total items), or California and New York (with 27 items responded with "yes", representing 69.2 per cent of the total items). However, we shall see that, despite having the same number of items answered in the affirmative, the position of each jurisdiction on the continuum is different, due to the weighting given to each item. So, even if several jurisdictions got the same number of items with a positive response, these cases are not always the same to the extent that some items, due to the weighting accorded by experts, have a greater exclusionary capacity than others. Therefore, the position of the jurisdictions become more nuanced, as can be seen below (Table 15.3).

It is also interesting to analyse which of those items responded in the affirmative are punitive rules or practices, in the seven jurisdictions under study. In most cases, the rules causing social exclusion are more frequent than the practices, as shown below, in Figure 15.1. However, Spain stands out as the

Table 15.2 Absolute and relative results of items responded in the affirmative by jurisdiction

Jurisdiction	*Number of items responded in the affirmative*	*Percentage of items responded in the affirmative*
Spain	9	23.1%
Italy	14	35.9%
Germany	16	41.0%
Poland	16	41.0%
England & Wales	23	59.0%
New York	27	69.2%
California	27	69.2%

Source: Own elaboration

Table 15.3 Number and weight of items answered with "yes" by pool and jurisdiction

	Pool 1	*Pool 2*	*Pool 3*	*Pool 4*	*Pool 5*	*Pool 6*	*Pool 7*	*Pool 8*	*Pool 9*
Germany	2 (50%)	2 (50%)	1 (20%)	0 (0%)	1 (25%)	3 (75%)	2 (40%)	2 (50%)	3 (60%)
California	3 (75%)	1 (25%)	4 (80%)	3 (75%)	3 (75%)	3 (75%)	1 (20%)	4 (100%)	5 (100%)
Spain	1 (25%)	0 (0%)	2 (40%)	1 (25%)	0 (0%)	1 (25%)	1 (20%)	2 (50%)	1 (20%)
England & Wales	4 (100%)	1 (25%)	3 (60%)	2 (50%)	2 (50%)	2 (50%)	3 (60%)	2 (50%)	4 (80%)
Italy	3 (75%)	1 (25%)	1 (20%)	3 (75%)	1 (25%)	1 (25%)	0 (0%)	1 (25%)	3 (60%)
New York	4 (100%)	1 (25%)	2 (40%)	2 (50%)	4 (100%)	2 (50%)	3 (60%)	4 (100%)	5 (100%)
Poland	0 (0%)	0 (0%)	3 (60%)	2 (50%)	1 (25%)	3 (75%)	3 (60%)	3 (75%)	1 (20%)

Source: Own elaboration

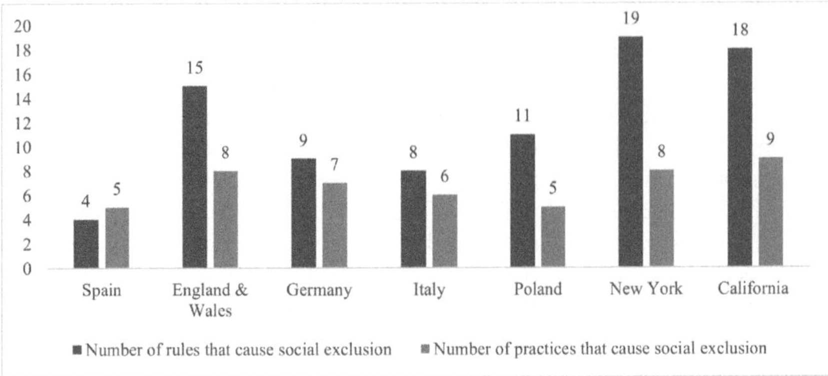

Figure 15.1 Distribution of rules and practices responded in the affirmative, by jurisdiction

only jurisdiction where this ratio is reversed, insofar as the number of punitive practices with a positive response (5) is higher than the number of rules that were answered with a "yes" (4).

3 Comparison of jurisdictions by thematic pools

If we take a closer look at the data shown in Table 15.3, we can affirm that the results by pool, taken both as a whole and individually, are discriminatory. This means that certain areas of the criminal justice system cause little or much social exclusion in all the jurisdictions analysed. This is also a test of the discrimination capacity of the RIMES instrument.

Now, if we compare the results for each jurisdiction by pool, we can see that there are some pools where all the jurisdictions have responded affirmatively to at least one item. This is the case for pools number 3 (Sentencing and Sanctions Systems), 6 (Preventive Intervention), 8 (Police and Criminal Records) and 9 (Youth Criminal Justice), while some jurisdictions do not score in the other pools, i.e., none of the items of the pool were responded positively. This is the case of Germany in pool 4 (Harshest Penalties), Spain in pools 2 (Legal Safeguards) and 5 (Prison Rules), Italy in pools 7 (Legal and Social Status of Offenders and Ex-Offenders), and Poland in pools 1 (Control of Public Spaces) and 2 (Legal Safeguards).

Conversely, as can also be seen in Table 15.3, there are jurisdictions where all items in a pool are responded in the affirmative. These is the case of California in pools 8 (Police and Criminal Records) and 9 (Youth Criminal Justice); England in pool 1 (Control of Public Spaces); and New York in pools 1 (Control of Public Spaces), 8 (Police and Criminal Records) and 9 (Youth Criminal Justice). Furthermore, according to Table 15.3, all pools show – to a greater or lesser extent – varying results across jurisdictions, which is also testimony to the instrument's capacity to discriminate in each of the thematic areas.

The results by pool have been discussed in depth in previous chapters. We will therefore summarise here the position of the seven jurisdictions in each of the nine pools that make up the RIMES instrument.

3.1 Control of public spaces (pool 1)

In this pool, consisting of items 1 (arrest for repeated begging on the street), 2 (arrest for loitering), 3 (discriminatory police restrictions on specific individuals accessing certain public spaces) and 11 (discriminatory police stops), high scores are predominant. The state of New York and England and Wales are the most exclusionary jurisdictions, as they are the only cases where all four items of this pool are fulfilled, and thus they obtain the maximum score of 10. California and Italy are close behind, with three of the four items in the pool being met, scoring 7.45 and 7.59 respectively. At the opposite end of the scale is Poland, where no items are fulfilled (score: 0), and Spain, where only one item is responded in the affirmative (score: 2.49). All this is shown below in Figure 15.2.

The prohibition of begging (item 1) and loitering (item 2) appear to be more widespread in Anglo-Saxon jurisdictions, although this is not exclusive to that context as it also occurs in Italy. Apart from that, it is not easy to classify the jurisdictions' responses to the rule regarding discriminatory police restrictions on some people in certain public places (item 3), as it occurs in European jurisdictions – such as Germany and Italy – but not in California. Discriminatory police practices (item 11) are found in almost all the geographical areas analysed, except in Poland where it was not possible to confirm it, so it is the most widespread socially exclusionary behaviour (see Figure 15.1). Finally, we should note that, except for item 11, there is no homogeneous attitude among the different jurisdictions regarding the rules and practices included in this pool.

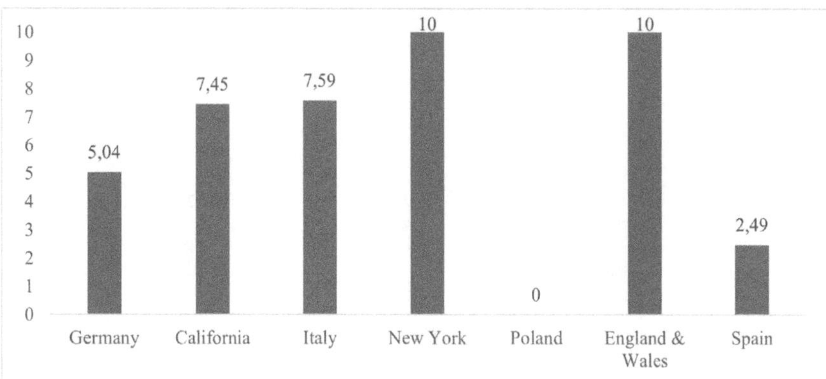

Figure 15.2 Weight of pool 1 in each of the analysed jurisdictions

3.2 Legal safeguards (pool 2)

In contrast to the previous pool, the jurisdictions analysed generate little social exclusion in terms of legal safeguards, judging by the items studied here: rules 21 (absence of a public defender's office), 22 (payment of court fees for appellate review) and 24 (police detention time exceeding 5 days), and practice 25 (high percentage of mentally ill inmates serving sentences in regular prisons). Within these low levels, Germany is the jurisdiction whose criminal justice system has the highest capacity to cause social exclusion, with a score of 4.86, while Spain and Poland both score 0 in this pool, and the other jurisdictions are grouped around a score of 2.5 (see Figure 15.3).

At the time of analysing this pool's items, we should note that all jurisdictions recognise the right to free legal aid for those who cannot afford it (item 21), as well as the right to appeal without prior payment of fees (item 22). However, only in Germany does the regular duration of police detention exceed five days (item 24). The most notorious differences among jurisdictions are in the number of mentally ill inmates serving prison sentences (item 25). This item is met in all jurisdictions, except Spain and Poland.

3.3 Sentencing and sanctions systems (pool 3)

This sentencing and sanctions systems pool consists of five items. The rules are items 33 (no alternatives to imprisonment or suspended sentences), 35 (no alternatives to imprisonment for less serious offences) and 36 (imprisonment as the only alternative to non-payment of fines). The punitive practices are items 37 (imprisonment rate above 120 inmates per 100,000 inhabitants) and 38 (three quarters of inmates serve their sentences in closed prisons).

Figure 15.3 Weight of pool 2 in each of the analysed jurisdictions

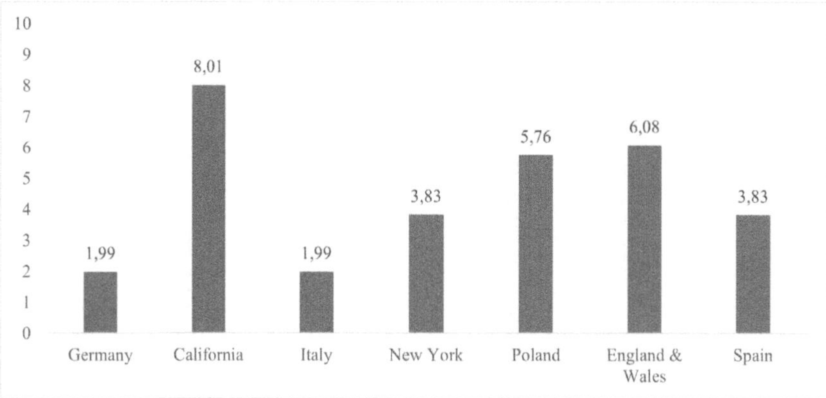

Figure 15.4 Weight of pool 3 in each of the analysed jurisdictions

In this pool, on the one hand, California stands out as the most exclusionary jurisdiction, with four positive responses out of the five items in the pool (score: 8.01). On the other hand, Germany and Italy only respond positively to one item (score: 1.99). The other jurisdictions are in-between, with England & Wales and Poland scoring around 6, and Spain and New York scoring 3.83. All this is shown below, in Figure 15.4.

Practice 38 (on the number of inmates serving their sentences in closed prisons) is fulfilled in all the jurisdictions analysed (see Figure 15.1), while rule 33 (on the inexistence of the possibility of suspended prison sentences) is not met in any of them. Item 37 (concerning the prison population per 100,000 inhabitants) is fulfilled in most of the jurisdictions, except Germany and Italy, while items 35 (absence of penalties other than prison for less serious offences) and item 36 (imprisonment as the only alternative to non-payment of fines) are met in only a couple of jurisdictions, like California. To sum it up, in this pool the burden of greater social exclusion falls on practices, as the two indicators in this pool (items 37 and 38) are responded in the affirmative by all or a clear majority of the jurisdictions analysed.

3.4 *Harshest penalties (pool 4)*

Overall, the values in this pool are moderate. It includes three rules: item 42 (death penalty), item 43 (life imprisonment) and item 46 (more than 20 years served for life sentence review), and one punitive practice, item 50 (more than 25 years served on life imprisonment). As discussed in the chapter regarding this pool (see Chapter 9, above), item 46 replaced item 52.

Here California is clearly the most exclusionary jurisdiction (score: 7.52), closely followed by Italy (score: 7.46). Then there is New York, England & Wales and Poland, with scores close to 5. Spain's results are lower (score: 2.35), but it should be noted that item 50 could not yet be responded. Germany does not answer any of these items in the affirmative.

Figure 15.5 Weight of pool 4 in each of the analysed jurisdictions

Death penalty (item 42) is only in force in California, while life imprisonment is more frequent. When the latter penalty is unreviewable (item 43) this is fulfilled in all countries except Germany, Spain and Poland. Life imprisonment is reviewable when at least 20 years have been served (item 46) in all jurisdictions, except Germany. In Italy and Poland, those sentenced to life imprisonment do not regularly serve more than 25 years (item 50), which is the case in all other countries except Spain, where this information is not yet available.

3.5 Prison rules (pool 5)

According to the results of applying the RIMES instrument, there is clearly an exclusionary tendency in criminal policy concerning prison matters in Anglo-Saxon jurisdictions, where New York stands out with a score of 10, followed by

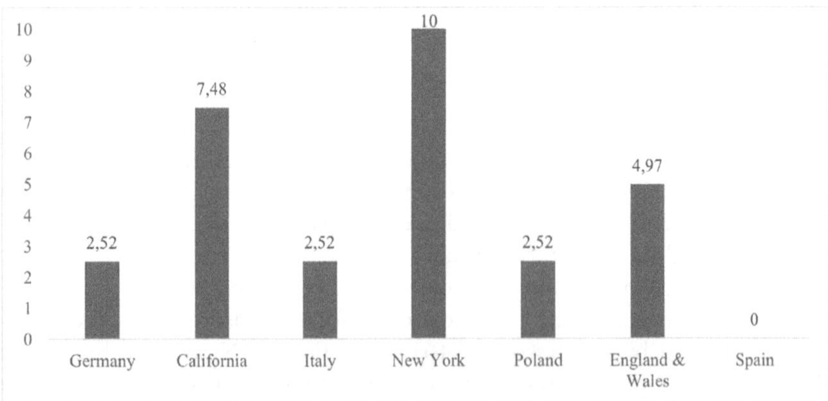

Figure 15.6 Weight of pool 5 in each of the analysed jurisdictions

California (score: 7.48) and England and Wales (score: 4.97). Exclusionary values are quite moderate in Germany, Poland and Italy (all with a score of 2.52). Spain is the only jurisdiction which has responded to all items in the negative.

It is worth underlining that the affirmative response to practice 68 is the one which determines that Germany, Poland and Italy are equally exclusionary. Item 68 is also the most exclusionary indicator in the whole pool, largely due to the restrictions and prohibitions of intimate or sexual visits.

As for the rules in the pool (item 55 on the lack of a specific prison regime for juveniles, item 62 on the lack of statutory provisions for legal aid for prison matters and item 64 on the payment of fees by inmates for the review of judicial decisions), these items cause Anglo-Saxon jurisdictions to score highest on social exclusion. Indeed, in all three Anglo-Saxon jurisdictions inmates must pay fees to claim review of court decisions (item 64), California and New York have no legal assistance for prison matters (item 62) and only in England and Wales there is no specific prison regime for juveniles (item 55).

3.6 Preventive intervention (pool 6)

The values in this pool are in the moderate-high level in almost all cases. Here the highest scores are obtained by Germany, California and Poland, with similar values in all three jurisdictions (7.58). Then, New York, Italy and England and Wales which score above 5. Spain is the lowest scoring jurisdiction (2.68), as shown below, in Figure 15.7.

Preventive intervention shows significant differences among the various jurisdictions. In Germany, California and Poland inmates, after serving their sentence, may be confined for an indeterminate period in a closed facility according to their dangerousness (rule 74), and in practice, inmates spend an average of more than five years serving this measure (item 81). New York allows

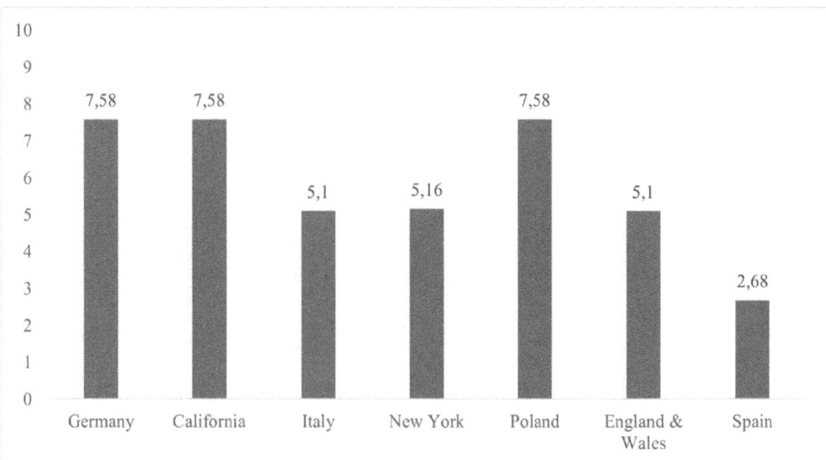

Figure 15.7 Weight of pool 6 in each of the analysed jurisdictions

indefinite post-sentence detention, but the overall length of security intervention is not excessive. On the contrary, England and Wales does not allow indefinite post-conviction detention, which was abolished in 2012. However, as this abolition is not applied retroactively, in practice 64 per cent of prisoners who have served their sentence are confined indefinitely and are therefore serving a post-conviction preventive sentence of more than five years on average.

In the case of measuring pre-trial detention (item 79) there are no differences among the jurisdictions studied so far. All have regulations allowing pre-trial detention for more than three years, but in none of them do remand detainees exceed 30 per cent of the total prison population (item 82).

3.7 Legal and social status of offenders and ex-offenders (pool 7)

The values in this pool are moderate. New York and England and Wales stand out, both with a score of 5.94, and Poland, with a score of 5.87. All these jurisdictions responded in the affirmative to three of the five items analysed. Germany has the next highest value (3.88), while California and Spain score low, although not as low as Italy, where no items are fulfilled. All this can be seen below, in Figure 15.8.

Deportation of foreign convicted persons, even if they have been sentenced to minor penalties, is a common rule for foreign residents in both regular and irregular situation, except for Italy, where this only applies to non-residents (item 88). The rule prohibiting the exercise of certain jobs, even those unrelated to the offence committed or affecting public order, also has a significant presence (item 91). Apart from that, ex-offenders are not deprived of access to social benefits (item 93) in any jurisdiction and, if the prison sentences for which they have been convicted are not very long, few jurisdictions deprive them of access to social housing, as referred to in item 99 (New York, England and Wales), or of the right to vote, as explained in item 93 (Poland).

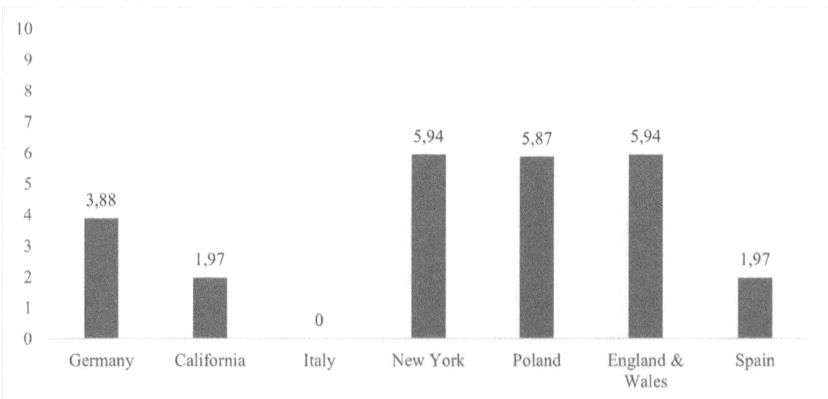

Figure 15.8 Weight of pool 7 in each of the analysed jurisdictions

3.8. Police and criminal records (pool 8)

The values in this pool are generally high or moderate. The most exclusionary jurisdictions are California and New York, where all the items analysed are met and receive a score of 10. Poland also has a significant score of 7.37. The least exclusionary is Italy, even though item 107 is fulfilled there (score: 2.63). The other jurisdictions (Germany, England & Wales, and Spain) have a moderate score of 5.1.

The rules in this pool focus on the ease of access to other people's criminal records, either by a private employer as regards the job applicant (item 99), by anyone with no need to give a reason (item 100), or by anyone through the Internet (item 101). Practice 107 concerns the disclosure of ex-offenders' personal data and pictures by the media.

The possibility of any person requesting criminal records without providing a reason, either from the official register (item 100) or via the Internet (item 101), only happens in the jurisdictions of California, New York and Poland. In contrast, the possibility for private employers to request criminal records from job applicants (item 99) or the fact that the media publish personal data or pictures of ex-offenders (item 107) are frequent in all jurisdictions, except Italy and Poland, respectively.

3.9 Youth criminal justice (pool 9)

In this pool high values are predominant, with Anglo-Saxon jurisdictions at the top of the ranking. New York and California (score: 10) are the jurisdictions with the highest capacity to generate social exclusion in this thematic area, followed by England and Wales (score: 8.18). Germany and Italy (both with a score of 6.12) continue to show significant values. Poland (score: 2.16)

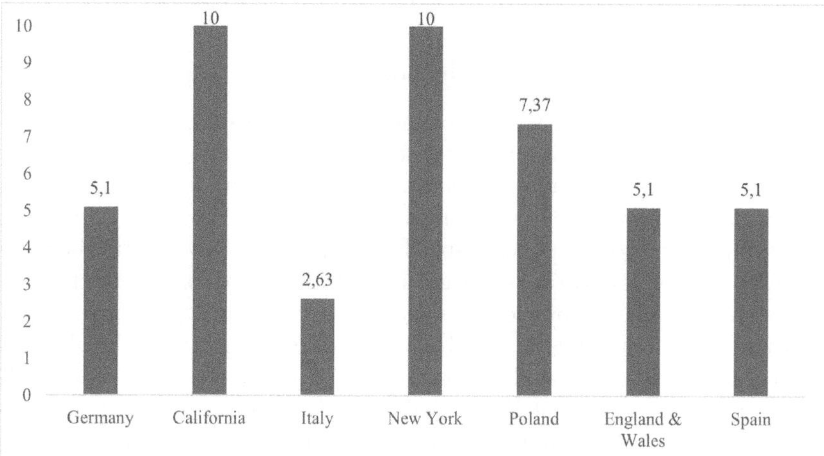

Figure 15.9 Weight of pool 8 in each of the analysed jurisdictions

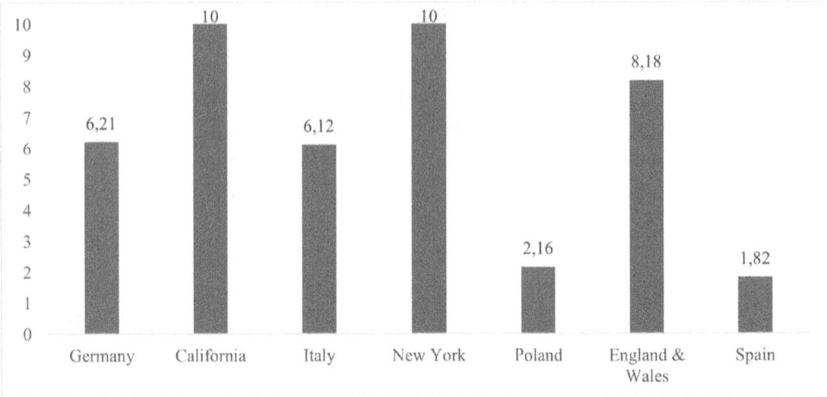

Figure 15.10 Weight of pool 9 in each of the analysed jurisdictions

and Spain (score: 1.82) score low, with an affirmative response to practice 121 (on the frequency with which custodial sentences are applied to minors).

The indicator of this pool most widespread in all jurisdictions, except Spain, is item 117 (on the provision of custodial sentences of over 10 years for juveniles). It is followed by item 120 (on juveniles' criminal records that keep their legal effects after reaching the age of majority), which is fulfilled in all jurisdictions, except Spain and Poland. Custodial sentence as the most frequent sanction for juveniles (item 121) is met in the jurisdictions of California and New York, along with Spain. The Anglo-Saxon jurisdictions stand out in rule 113 (on the possibility of applying youth justice to minors of 12 years old or younger), and in practice 126 (on deportation of foreign juvenile offenders). All three jurisdictions (California, New York, and England & Wales) score on both items. So do Italy (on the rule) and Germany (on the practice).

4 Analysis of each jurisdiction by pool

Now we shall analyse the scores obtained by each jurisdiction in each of the pools. Once again, we have verified that the RIMES instrument has the capacity to discriminate, as it has allowed us to distinguish among jurisdictions, in this third and final dimension. In the following figures (15.11 to 15.17), the points correspond to the position of each specific jurisdiction with respect to the pools. These points are placed on an imaginary vertical line, according to the score (from 0 to 10) obtained by each jurisdiction in every pool. A red horizontal line marks the threshold value (5), which is half of the scoring that can be obtained.

We can clearly see that the scores obtained in the various pools by the jurisdictions of continental Europe (Poland, Italy, Spain and Germany) are generally below the threshold line, with a few exceptions. But the situation is quite the opposite in the Anglo-Saxon jurisdictions (California, New York and England and Wales).

4.1 *Spain*

As far as Spain is concerned, there are two pools that score 0 for social exclusion: pool 2 (legal safeguards) and pool 5 (prison rules), as no item was responded in the affirmative there. Only pool 8 (police and criminal records) is slightly above red horizontal line. Among those below this threshold, pool 3 (sentencing and sanctions systems) stands out, with a score of 3.83. Besides, in this pool only the practices cause social exclusion, which is a difference as regards the other pools. The remaining pools scored low, between 2.68 and 1.82, as shown in Figure 15.11.

In Spain, there are certain areas that do not entail social exclusion; specifically, those referring to legal safeguards (pool 2) and prison rules (pool 8). The latter aspect is not surprising, as the Spanish prison rules are highly valued internationally for their progressive nature. Likewise, it is necessary to highlight the need for Spanish criminal policy to reflect on the practices related to the sentencing and sanctions systems (pool 3). Thus, although Spain does not score in any of the rules in this pool, it does score in both practices, which means that it has an incarceration rate of over 120 inmates per 100,000 inhabitants (item 37) and that most prisoners serve their sentences in closed facilities (item 38). It is interesting to note that, despite having a high prison population rate and most of this population serving sentences in closed institutions, its prison rules (pool 5) do not seem affected insofar as Spain does not score on any of the items that cause social exclusion in this area. Finally, Spain

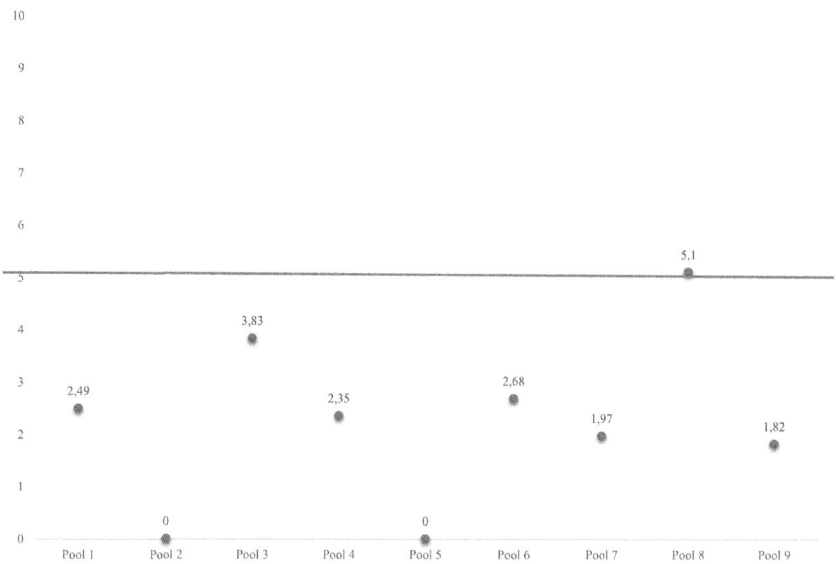

Figure 15.11 Weight of the pools in Spain*

Source: *Values range from the least (0) to the most (10) social exclusion

scores in rule 99 (the possibility for private employers to request information on criminal records from job applicants) and in practice 107 (the media regularly disclose personal data or pictures of ex-offenders).

4.2 Italy

In Italy, pool 7 (social and legal status of offenders and ex-offenders) scores 0 for social exclusion, as no items have been answered with a "yes". There are, however, four pools where it gets more than half of the scoring that can be obtained, although in one case – pool 6 (preventive intervention) – only slightly (score: 5.1). Such pools are: pool 1 (control of public spaces) with a score of 7.59, pool 4 (harshest penalties) with a score of 7.46, and pool 9 (youth criminal justice) with a score of 6.12. The remaining pools get low scores, between 2.63 and 1.99. All this is shown in Figure 15.12.

Italy scores above 5 in more pools than, for example, Spain, which is the previously analysed jurisdiction. These are pools 1 (control of public spaces), 4 (harshest penalties) and 9 (youth criminal justice), and also pool 6 (preventive intervention), by a very small margin. In the latter case, item 81 could not be responded as it was impossible to find out whether the average duration of preventive intervention exceeds five years (for an explanation on the methodological difficulties to find this data, see above).

If we look at the items of each pool responded in the affirmative, Italy has the capacity to cause social exclusion in the area of pool 1 (control of public spaces) because a person can be arrested for repeated street begging (item 1),

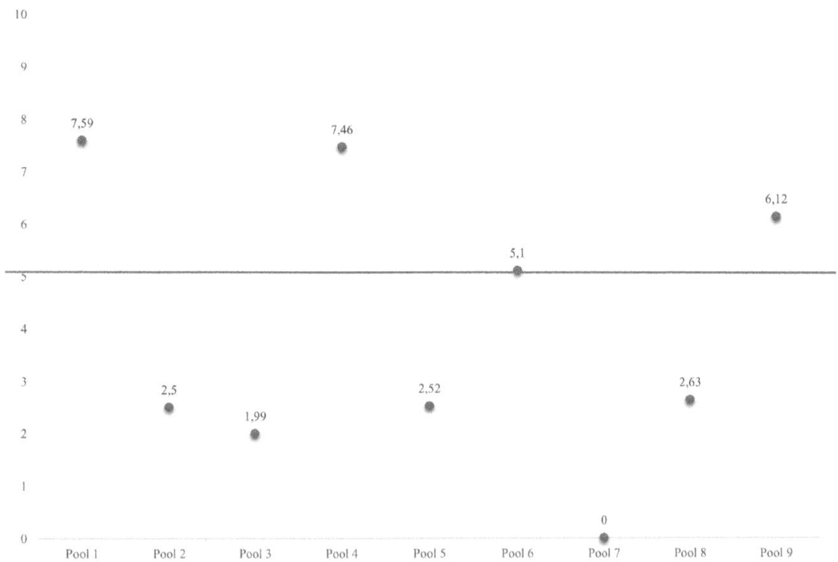

Figure 15.12 Weight of the pools in Italy*

Source: * Values range from the least (0) to the most (10) social exclusion

because the police can restrict access of certain people to public spaces (item 3) and because they frequently carry out stops of certain groups of citizens in the street (item 11). With respect to pool 4, it also has a high capacity to cause social exclusion, because except for the death penalty, it scores positively on all other items, namely: it has a non-reviewable life imprisonment sentence (item 43), when life sentence review is allowed, it is only permitted after 20 years of serving imprisonment (item 46), and those sentenced to life imprisonment often serve more than 25 years (item 50). Finally, Italy lacks exclusionary capacity in the social and legal status of offenders and ex-offenders.

4.3 Poland

Poland scores 0 for social exclusion in pool 1 (control of public spaces) and pool 2 (legal safeguards), as no items are fulfilled there. However, this jurisdiction scores above 5 (the threshold marked with a red line) in four thematic areas. The scoring is clearly above in pool 6 (preventive intervention) with a score of 7.58, and pool 8 (criminal and police records) with a score of 7.37. This is also the case, albeit to a lesser extent, with pool 7 (legal and social status of offenders and ex-offenders) with a score of 5.87, and pool 3 (sentencing and sanctions systems) with a score of 5.76. In addition, pool 4 (harshest penalties) with a score of 4.82, is close to the red line limit. Finally, pool 5 (prison rules) with a score of 2.52, and pool 9 (youth criminal justice) with a score of 2.19, do not exceed the threshold of 5, together with the first two mentioned.

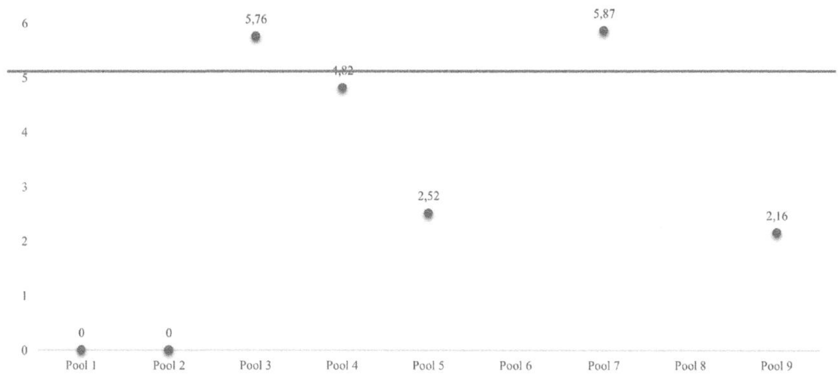

Figure 15.13 Weight of the pools in Poland*

Source: * Values range from the least (0) to the most (10) social exclusion

As in the Italian case, Poland scores high as regards social exclusion in several areas of penal policy. However, unlike Italy, in Poland the areas of criminal policy with the greatest capacity to cause social exclusion are the sentencing and sanctions systems (pool 3), preventive intervention (pool 6), police and criminal records (pool 8), and the legal and social status of offenders and ex-offenders (pool 7). These pools can be grouped into two main groups that feature the Polish criminal policy: on the one hand, the system of penalties (pools 3 and 4) and, on the other hand, penal interventions based on the belief in the persistent dangerousness of the offender (pools 6, 7 and 8). Furthermore, it does not score in control of public spaces (pool 1) or in legal safeguards (pool 2), and gets a very low score in prison rules (pool 5), where only the practice concerning family and intimate visits taking place at intervals of over one month (item 68) is fulfilled. Finally, in pool 9 (youth criminal justice) only item 117 is met, on the possibility of sentencing minors to more than 10 years of internment. Perhaps those results explain the moderate level of social exclusion obtained through the implementation of the RIMES instrument.

4.4 Germany

Germany does not fulfil any items in pool 4 (harshest penalties), but maintains four pools above the threshold of 5, although only two of them clearly exceed it. The latter are pool 6 (preventive intervention) with a score of 7.58, and pool 9 (youth criminal justice) with a score of 6.21. Also in the top half of the results Figure 15.14 are pool 8 (police and criminal records) with a score of 5.1, and pool 1 (control of public spaces) with a score of 5.04. Pool

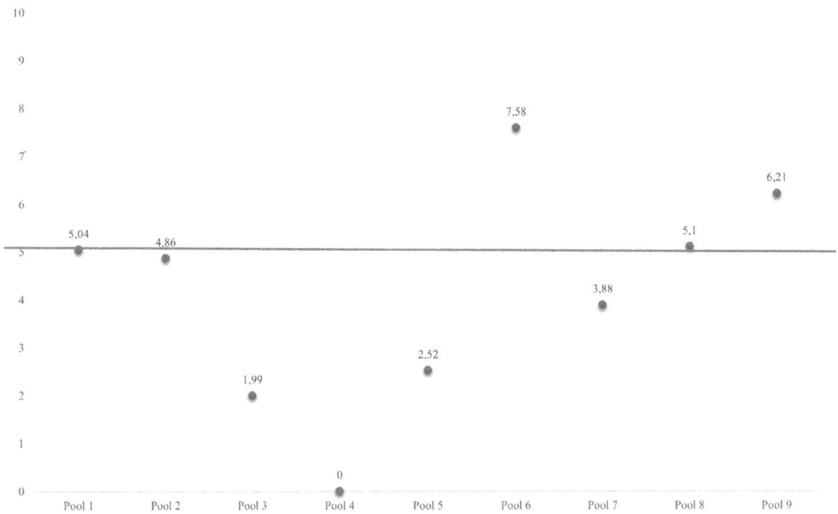

Figure 15.14 Weight of the pools in Germany*

Source: * Values range from the least (0) to the most (10) social exclusion

2 (legal safeguards) is slightly below the red line limit, with a score of 4.86. The remaining three pools are in the lower half of the Figure 15.14, in a broad scoring range, from 3.88 for pool 7 (legal and social status of offenders and ex-offenders), to 1.99 for pool 3 (sentencing and sanctions systems). It is, together with Spain, one of the two jurisdictions with the greatest homogeneity of scores across pools.

Germany also has a quite large number of practices that were responded in the affirmative. Overall, this jurisdiction offers a picture of moderate intensity with respect to social exclusion as measured by the RIMES instrument, while showing its best non-exclusionary performance in the areas of the sentencing system and in the enforcement of prison sentences.

4.5 England and Wales

Unlike the preceding jurisdictions, in England and Wales there are items from all the pools causing social exclusion. Five pools exceed the threshold of 5, most notably pool 1 (control of public spaces) which scores the highest (10), but also pool 9 (youth criminal justice) with a score of 8.18. Two more are clearly above that limit: pool 3 (sentencing and sanctions systems) with a score of 6.08, and pool 7 (legal and social status of offenders and ex-offenders) with a score of 5.94. Pools 6 (preventive intervention) and 8 (police and criminal records) both scored 5.1. Then two more pools are very close to the red line

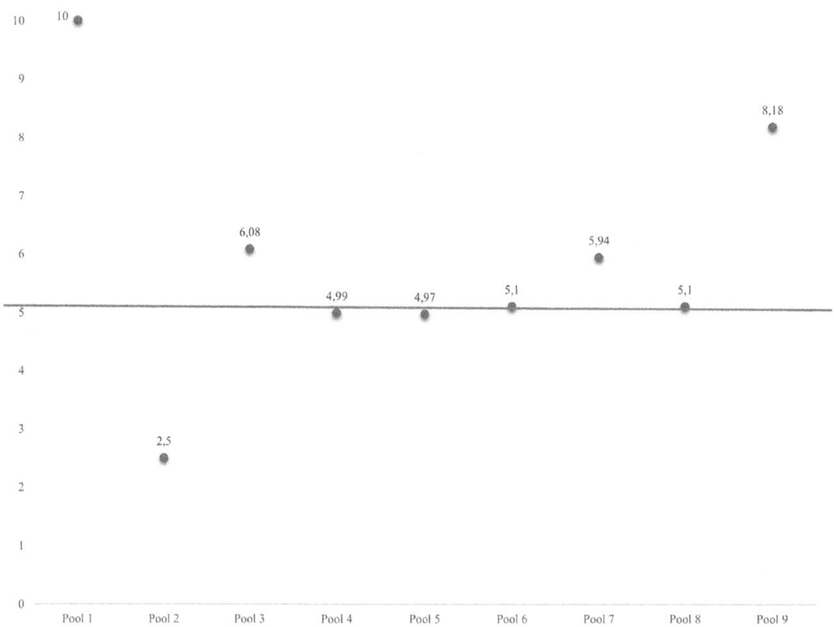

Figure 15.15 Weight of the pools in England and Wales*

Source: * Values range from the least (0) to the most (10) social exclusion

threshold: pool 4 (harshest penalties) with a score of 4.99, and pool 7 (legal and social status of offenders and ex-offenders) with a score of 4.97. And there is only one thematic area, pool 2 (legal safeguards), which is clearly at a low value (2.5). This case shows the transition from the lowest values of continental European jurisdictions to the highest values of Anglo-Saxon ones.

England & Wales have moderately high values for social exclusion as measured by the RIMES instrument, and it is difficult to establish a distinctive pattern across the different pools, apart from the low score in pool 2 (legal safeguards). This jurisdiction only scores in this pool in practice 25 (concerning the number of mentally ill inmates serving time in regular prisons).

4.6 California

California scores high in all thematic areas, except in pool 2 (legal safeguards) with a score of 2.5, and pool 7 (legal and social status of offenders and ex-offenders) with a score of 1.97. All the other pools obtain scores above the threshold of 5, with four of them ranging from 7.45 for public space control (pool 1) to 7.58 for preventive intervention (pool 6). There is also pool 3 (sentencing and sanctions systems) with a score of 8.01 and, with the highest scores, pool 8 (police and criminal records) and pool 9 (youth criminal justice) both with 10.

The jurisdiction of this US state appears to be a highly exclusionary. Despite this general consideration, some pools that have a deep impact on individual

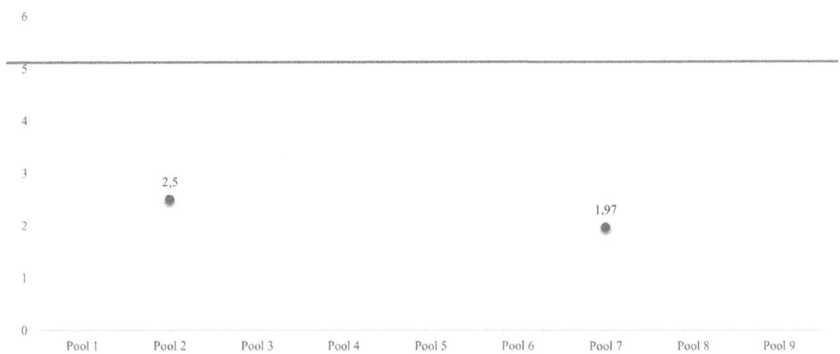

Figure 15.16 Weight of the pools in California*

Source: * Values range from the least (0) to the most (10) social exclusion

rights, such as pool 2 (legal safeguards) and pool 7 (legal and social status of offenders and ex-offenders), obtained remarkably low scores.

4.7 New York

Finally, New York scores the highest (10) in no less than four areas: pool 1 (public space control), pool 5 (prison rules), pool 8 (police and criminal records) and pool 9 (youth criminal justice). In the latter two pools it shares the top score with California and in pool 1, with England and Wales. It only has two pools where it is clearly below 5: pool 2 (legal safeguards) with a score of 2.5 and pool 3 (sentencing and sanctions systems) with a score of 3.83. The remaining three pools either exceed the bottom half of the ranking, such as pool 6 (preventive intervention) with a score of 5.16 and pool 7 (legal and social status of offenders and ex-offenders) with a score of 5.94, or come very close, such as pool 4 (harshest penalties) with a score of 4.99.

Thus, New York becomes the most exclusionary jurisdiction of all those studied so far. However, this position is mainly due to the fact that it obtained the maximum score in four pools, i.e., all the rules and practices included in those pools cause social exclusion in this jurisdiction. In short, its tough reaction to convicted offenders, the harshness of its youth criminal justice and its rigorous control of public spaces, largely explain the high values obtained for social exclusion, according to the RIMES instrument.

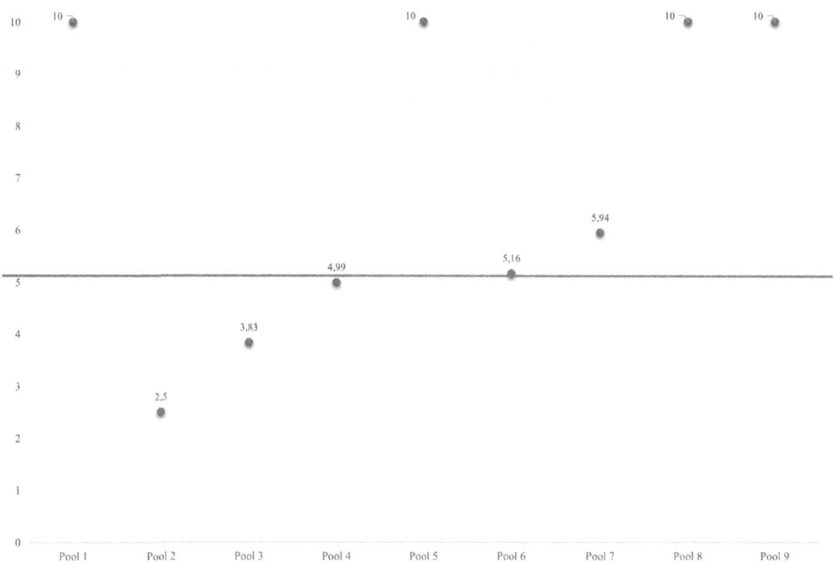

Figure 15.17 Weight of the pools in New York*

Source: * Values range from the least (0) to the most (10) social exclusion

5 Position of jurisdictions on the continuum, from the least to the most socially exclusionary

As shown in Figure 15.18, the continental European jurisdictions (Germany, Spain, Italy and Poland) are closer to the extreme of less social exclusion, while the US states (California and New York) are closer to the extreme of more social exclusion. England and Wales are in an intermediate position, although somewhat nearer to the position of the US states.

None of the jurisdictions analysed are sufficiently exclusionary or non-exclusionary to be at the extremes of the scale. The highest scoring jurisdictions still have three points left to reach the extreme end of the scale of highest social exclusion, and the lowest scoring jurisdiction has just over two points left to reach the extreme end of the scale of lowest social exclusion. This is, in principle, an acceptable result, which should be compared with the results obtained by the new jurisdictions to which the RIMES instrument is applied in the future.

Moreover, RIMES has shown striking differences between the jurisdictions studied, which means that the main objective of the comparison instrument has been achieved. As mentioned above, we can affirm that the US states under study are clearly more socially exclusionary than any of the European nations analysed. Furthermore, the Anglo-Saxon jurisdictions – which include England and Wales along with the two US states – are obviously more socially exclusionary than the continental European jurisdictions under study.

It is also worth noting that most of the continental European jurisdictions analysed score very closely, except for Spain. We should also highlight that the two European Mediterranean jurisdictions show the lowest values for social exclusion, although Italy is not too far behind the two Central European jurisdictions. Finally, Spain distances itself from the rest of the continental European jurisdictions by the low levels of social exclusion shown in its criminal policy.

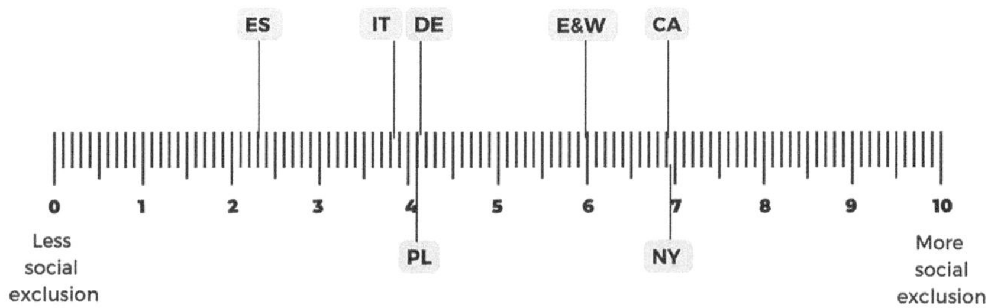

Figure 15.18 Position of the analysed jurisdictions on the continuum, from the least to the most socially exclusionary

6 Discussion

We believe that this first application of RIMES to seven relevant jurisdictions has accredited the instrument's capacity to establish differences in the levels of social exclusion caused by various national criminal justice systems on the four target groups of our study. From our point of view, the instrument has also shown its discriminatory capacity. RIMES does not tend to place the different national penal systems analysed at one of the two extremes of the continuum, but rather distributes them along the scale.

Indeed, the ability of the RIMES instrument to apply its measurement to several thematic areas that are sufficiently representative of the way in which criminal justice systems operate means that the results provided by it do not match those obtained by focusing on items of only one pool. For example, pool 3 (sentencing and sanctions systems) contains some of the items most frequently used to establish the punitive rigour of different jurisdictions, which is the usual criterion for comparing criminal policy. There are substantial differences when comparing the results obtained by the different jurisdictions in pools 3 and 4 – which measure punitiveness to a large extent – with the results obtained by these same jurisdictions on the global RIMES scale.

Thus, if we take, for example, the average values obtained in both pools with those in the final scale for all jurisdictions, we can see that there are two jurisdictions (New York and Germany) that have notably lower values in pools 3 and 4, on average, than in the final scale of the instrument. Specifically, New York goes from a score of 4.41 in both pools to 6.98 in the final score, moving from fifth to first place on a scale of highest to lowest social exclusion. Even more striking is the case of Germany, which scores 0.99 on the average of pools 3 and 4, while scoring 4.13 on the overall RIMES scale, and moves from seventh last to fourth on the scale of the most to the least social exclusion.

In terms of discriminatory capacity, it is true that we have detected two pools that do not really discriminate. We refer to pools 2 and 6. Thus, we need to delve into the discriminatory capacity of those items that have been responded in the negative in all the jurisdictions. To achieve this, we would need to analyse in detail the differences of each jurisdiction in order to find nuances that would allow to refine the criminal policy comparisons as regards the social exclusion effects of criminal interventions on suspects, defendants, offenders and ex-offenders.

And it is true that five items of social exclusion could not be found in any of the jurisdictions analysed. These are items 21 (the criminal justice system lacks a public defender's office), 22 (requirement of fees for appeals), 33 (lack of provisional release or suspended prison sentences), 82 (more than 30 per cent of the prison population is in pre-trial detention) and 93 (suspension of passive suffrage for ex-convicts). Conversely, there are two items which were found in all jurisdictions: items 38 (three quarters of prisoners are held in closed prisons) and 79 (pre-trial detention exceeds three years).

We believe that these facts do not question the discriminatory nature of these items, as RIMES has been applied to only seven jurisdictions so far. Objections to any or some of these items will have to wait until the instrument has been applied to a larger number of jurisdictions, as is already envisaged. We hope to confirm this trend when other jurisdictions are added to the scale.

Cid Moliné (2023) has pointed out that a very relevant part of the items of RIMES refer only to tertiary prevention, i.e., to the response to people who have committed offences, in order to try to prevent their recidivism. We object to this argument, as although it is true that most of the items used refer to tertiary prevention, there are others that focus on secondary prevention, i.e., aimed at suspects committing offences, such as all those items included in pools 1 and 8.

7 Conclusions

The application of RIMES to the jurisdiction of many Western developed countries intended to compare their national penal policies from the social exclusion perspective, which is particularly illustrative of the performance of their criminal justice systems. Thanks to the creation, validation and implementation of this instrument, we have been able to draw a continuum – with a scale from the least to the most social exclusion – positioning the diverse criminal policies. This helps to identify the extent to which exclusionary intervention techniques are expanding in the Western and developed world, and to group these results in nine relevant areas or pools of penal justice system.

These are the conclusions that can be drawn from the results of applying the RIMES instrument:

Firstly, it has been proved that there are significant differences among criminal policies in the different jurisdictions under study, as already pointed out. A final general assessment allows us to reiterate that the two US states analysed – California and New York – are the ones that seem to have the most socially exclusionary criminal policy for those groups of citizens that come into contact with criminal law. As to the European jurisdictions analysed, England and Wales stands out for its exclusionary criminal policy, as shown by the RIMES instrument, although clearly below the mentioned US states. The socially exclusionary effects of the penal justice systems in Poland and Germany are very similar, but clearly less so than England and Wales. They are followed by Italy, and then Spain, which have proved to be the jurisdictions with the least exclusionary criminal systems of all those analysed so far.

This identifies two criminal policy models, with clearly differentiated strategies: the first, composed of the Anglo-Saxon criminal justice systems, which have scored above 5 on the social exclusion scale; and the second, composed of the continental European jurisdictions, all of which are positioned in the lower half of the continuum. We will have to wait for the implementation of RIMES in a larger number of jurisdictions to verify this trend and to identify further lines of distinction.

The results obtained can be further refined by grouping the different pools of the RIMES instrument according to the main areas of criminal justice system. Thus, we can set up the following groups:

1 A group dealing with central aspects of criminal law, composed of pools 2 (legal safeguards), 3 (sentencing and sanctions systems), 4 (harshest penalties) and 5 (prison rules). In this group, US jurisdictions get the highest scores in all pools as regards social exclusion, except in pool 2, where Germany is at the top. In pool 4, Italy scores near the top. In contrast, only continental European jurisdictions, with the repeated presence of Spain and Germany, get the lowest scores in these pools.
2 Another group of pools deals with penal interventions, especially those related to the dangerousness of the prosecuted or convicted offender. This includes pools 6 (preventive intervention), 7 (social and legal status of offenders and ex-offenders) and 8 (police and criminal records). In this group it is again the US jurisdictions that get the highest scores, but this time with the repeated presence of Poland, together with Germany and England and Wales. On the other hand, Italy and Spain obtain, once again, the lowest scores.
3 And a final group, referred to interventions at the margins of criminal law, which would include pools 1 (control of public spaces) and 9 (youth criminal justice). Again, the two US jurisdictions (California and New York), together with England and Wales, obtain the highest scores, while two continental European jurisdictions (Poland and Spain) get the lowest.

We can therefore conclude that, given the design of the RIMES instrument around 9 pools and 39 items, we have provided incomparably richer and more useful information on the reality of national criminal justice systems than any other currently available tool.

To conclude, this investigation assumed that knowledge of penal policy requires rigorous methodological instruments to evaluate and propose correct and effective criminal policies. For that purpose, it is necessary to choose a criterion to analyse contemporary criminal policies that can obtain significant, complete and consistent results. In this research we have chosen the aspect of social exclusion that criminal justice systems can cause on groups particularly affected by punitive intervention. This promising analytical criterion, proposed by Díez-Ripollés, had to be made operational with an instrument that would deploy all its explanatory and critical potential. On the basis of the results presented throughout this book, we believe that this objective is successfully achieved with the RIMES instrument. In short, this tool provides highly relevant information for legal practitioners and political agents with a view to designing and promoting criminal policies that are less socially exclusionary on the groups most affected by criminal intervention. This is the ultimate goal that inspired the creation of RIMES and its application in more jurisdictions. We are convinced that a less socially exclusionary penal policy is a powerful way to control crime more effectively, and to do so within the values of a social and democratic state governed by the rule of law.

References

Bottoms, A. E. (1995). The Philosophy and Politics of Sentencing and Punishment, in C. Clarkson and R. Morgan, eds., *The Politics of Sentencing Reform*. Oxford University Press.

Brandariz García, J. A. (2023). El legado académico de José Luis Díez-Ripollés: una aproximación al proyecto RIMES, in Muñoz, J., García, O., Cerezo, A.I., García-España, E., eds., *Estudios político-criminales, jurídico-penales y criminológicos. Libro homenaje al Profesor José Luis Díez-Ripollés*. Tirant lo Blanch.

Cavadino, M., Dignan, J. (2006). *Penal Systems. A Comparative Approach*. Sage Publications.

Cid Moliné, J. (2023). Inclusión/exclusión tras pasar por el sistema penal español. In Muñoz, J., García, O., Cerezo, A.I., García-España, E., eds., *Estudios político-criminales, jurídico-penales y criminológicos. Libro homenaje al Profesor José Luis Díez-Ripollés*. Tirant lo Blanch.

Christie, N. (2000). *Crime Control as Industry*, 2nd edn. Oxford University Press.

Díez-Ripollés, J.L. (2004). El nuevo modelo penal de la seguridad ciudadana. *Revista electrónica de ciencia penal y criminología*. http://criminet.ugr.es/recpc

Díez-Ripollés, J.L. (2011). La dimensión inclusión/exclusión social como guía de la política criminal comparada. *Revista Electrónica de Ciencia Penal y Criminología*, *13*, 12. http://criminet.ugr.es/recpc/13/recpc13-12.pdf

Díez-Ripollés, J.L. (2013). Social Inclusion and Comparative Criminal Justice Policy. *Journal of Scandinavian Studies in Criminology and Crime Prevention*, 14, 62–78.

Garland, D. (2001). *The Culture of Control. Crime and Social Order in Contemporary Society*. University of Chicago Press.

Hamilton, C. (2014). Reconceptualising Penality: Towards a Multidimensional Measure of Punitiveness. *British Journal of Criminology*, 54, 321–343.

Hamilton, C. (2023). Deconstructing Penality: A Long Way from Liege, in Muñoz, J., García, O., Cerezo, A.I., García-España, E., eds., *Estudios politico-criminales, jurídico-penales y criminológicos. Libro homenaje al Profesor José Luis Díez-Ripollés*. Tirant lo Blanch.

Hinds, L. (2005 [2000]). Crime Control in Western Countries, in Pratt, J., Brown, D., Brown, M., Hallsworth, S., Morrison, W., eds. *The New Punitiveness: Trends, Theories and Perspectives*. Willan Publishing.

Lacey, N., Soskice, D., Hope, D. (2018). Understanding the Determinants of Penal Policy: Crime, Culture and Comparative Political Economy, *Annual Review of Criminology*, 1, 195–217.

Lappi-Seppälä, T. (2007). Penal Policy in Scandinavia, in Tonry, M., ed., *Crime, Punishment and Politics in Comparative Perspective. Crime and Justice*. n. 36. University of Chicago Press.

Lappi-Seppälä, T. (2008). Trust, Welfare, and Political Culture: Explaining Differences in National Penal Policies, in Tonry, M., ed., *Crime and Justice. A Review of Research*. n. 37. University of Chicago Press.

Larrauri Pijoan, E. (2009). La economía política del castigo. Revista electrónica de ciencia penal y criminología. http://criminet.ugr.es/recpc 11: 06.

Lahti, R. (2000). Towards a Rational and Humane Criminal Policy. Trends in Scandinavian Penal Thinking. *Journal of Scandinavian Studies in Criminology and Crime Prevention*, 1(2), 141–155. https://doi.org/10.1080/140438500300076135

McAra, L. (2011). Global Politics and Local Culture: A Response to Nicola Lacey. *Punishment and Society*, 13, 96–104.

Nelken, D. (2005). When Is a Society Non-Punitive? The Italian Case, in Pratt, J., Brown, D., Brown, M., Hallsworth, S., Morrison, W., eds. *The New Punitiveness: Trends, Theories and Perspectives.* Willan Publishing.

Nelken, D. (2010). *Comparative Criminal Justice.* Sage Publications.

Newburn, T. (2007). 'Tough on Crime': Penal Policy in England and Wales, in Tonry, M., ed., *Crime, Punishment and Politics in Comparative Perspective. Crime and Justice.* n. 36. University of Chicago Press.

Newburn, T. (2020). Contemporary Conceptual and Analytical Challenges in Comparative Penality, in Daems, T., Pleysier, S., eds., *Criminology and Democratic Politics.* Routledge.

Newburn, T. & Jones, T. (2022). Policing, Punishment and Comparative Penalty. *The British Journal of Criminology*, *62*, 1196–1212.

Pratt, J. (2007). *Penal Populism.* Routledge.

Roché, S. (2007). Criminal Justice Policy in France: Illusions of Severity, in Tonry, M., ed., *Crime, Punishment and Politics in Comparative Perspective. Crime and Justice.* n. 36. University of Chicago Press.

Tamarit Sumalla. (2007). Sistema de sanciones y política criminal. Un estudio de derecho comparado europeo. *Revista electrónica de ciencia penal y criminología.* http://criminet.ugr.es/recpc/

Tonry, M. ed. (2007). *Crime, Punishment and Politics in Comparative Perspective. Crime and Justice.* n. 36. University of Chicago Press.

Wacquant, L. (1999). How Penal Common Sense Comes to Europeans: Notes on the Transatlantic Diffusion of the Neoliberal Doxa, *European Societies*, 1, 319–352.

Appendix
RIMES instrument

Pools	*Rules*	*Practices*
1. Control of public spaces	1. Any person may be arrested for repeated street begging 2. An individual may be arrested for loitering 3. At its discretion, the police may enforce restrictions on specific individuals to access some public spaces (parks, squares, streets . . .)	11. Discriminatory street police interventions (stop and search, arrests, frisks/body searches . . .) targeting specific groups occur regularly
2. Legal safeguards	21. The criminal justice system lacks indigent defense services 22. Payment of court fees is legally required from the defendant in order to get access to appellate review 24. The regular term for police detention established by the law exceeds 5 days	25. A significant number of mentally ill inmates serve their sentences in regular correctional facilities
3. Sentencing and sanctions systems	33. In the case of prison sentences, neither probation as an alternative to sentencing nor suspended sentences are envisaged in the law 35. The law lacks provisions for penalties other than prison (community service, fines, house arrest . . .) in case of less serious felonies 36. Default imprisonment is the sole alternative to non-payment of a fine	37. The incarceration rate is higher than 120 inmates per 100,000 inhabitants 38. At least three quarters of the inmates are serving their sentences in closed prisons
4. Harshest penalties	42. Death penalty is legally available 43. Life imprisonment without release is legally available 46. A minimum of 20 years served is required before claiming release from life imprisonment	50. Those sentenced to life imprisonment regularly serve more than 25 years

Pools	*Rules*	*Practices*
5. Prison rules	55. The system lacks a specific prison regime for young adults 62. The law lacks statutory provisions regulating inmates' legal assistance for penitentiary matters 64. The law requires payment of fees by the inmate before claiming judicial review of penitentiary decisions	68. Family and intimate visits take place at intervals of over one month
6. Preventive intervention	74. Preventive detention may last for an unlimited period of time	81. The average length of preventive detention exceeds 5 years
	79. The maximum statutory term for pretrial detention exceeds 3 years	82. Over 30% of the prison population is in pre-trial detention
7. Legal and social status of offenders and ex-offenders	86. Those sentenced to up 3 years of imprisonment for any criminal offence may be deprived of the right to vote for over 4 years after serving their sentences 88. Legally resident foreigners may be deported if they receive a custodial sentence up to one year or a non-custodial sentence 91. Those sentenced to up to 3 years of imprisonment are prohibited from doing certain jobs not connected with their offences or with law enforcement for a period of more than 5 years after their sentence has been completed 92. Those sentenced to up to 3 years of imprisonment for any criminal offence are not eligible for public housing for a certain period after having served their sentences 93. Nationals sentenced to imprisonment for any criminal offence are not eligible for welfare benefits for a certain period after having served their sentences	
8. Police and criminal records	99. Private employers which are not related to private security companies or to those working with children or vulnerable adults are entitled to request information about criminal records to potential employees. 100. Anyone may request information about other people's criminal records without needing to argue grounds established by law	107. The media regularly disclose the full names, current addresses or pictures of ex-felons

(*Continued*)

(Continued)

Pools	*Rules*	*Practices*
	101. The criminal records of any citizen are legally accessible through internet	
9. Youth criminal justice	113. Youth justice applies to children who are 12 years old or younger	121. Custodial sanction is one of the three most common sanctions applied to minors
	117. Youth justice provides custodial sanctions of over 10 years	126. Alien minors are deported because of an offence
	120. Minors' criminal records keep legal effects after reaching the age of majority	

Index

Note: Page numbers in *italics* indicate a figure and page numbers in **bold** indicate a table on the corresponding page. Page numbers followed by "n" with numbers refer to notes.